The A.I. Sports Book

ANDREW W. PEARSON

Intelligencia Limited
www.intelligencia.co

Intelligencia Limited also publishes its books in a variety of electronic formats. Some content that appears in print may not be available in electronic books. For more information about Intelligentsia's products, visit our website at www.intelligencia.co.

First published by Intelligencia

CONTENTS

ACKNOWLEDGMENT

鄭慧琪: you know who you are

ANDREW W. PEARSON

PREFACE

My first book on the subject of the use of analytics by sports betting companies was *The Predictive Sports Book*. I decided to write a second book on the subject more focused on A.I., machine learning, and deep learning because this technology shows great promise for companies in an industry so reliant on the customer experience. Since my first book on the subject was published in 2018, there have been substantial developments in business intelligence, customer intelligence, data integration, and the analytics field and AI has almost sucked up all the oxygen in the analytics space, almost to a troubling degree because there are profound limitations to AI that many champions of it are underestimating. Artificial Intelligence or "AI" as it's known is everywhere and, throughout this book, I explain how AI can be used in a multitude technology areas.

Before this book, I had written four other books in this *Predictive* series as well as one focused on AI—*The A.I. Marketer*. Since I have several sports books as clients, I thought the subject matter might prove interesting to research and write about. I subscribe to Samuel Johnson's dictum that, "What is written without effort is in general read without pleasure" and, in that vein, I have tirelessly worked to keep up with the latest technological developments that I describe herein. I try to keep my points as concise as possible, but these concepts can be complicated so bare with me when things get deep and involving. Or...skip ahead.

Subjects such as AI, real-time stream processing, data lakes, customer loyalty, attribution analysis, psychometrics, web morphing, and the IoT are going to radically change the business landscape over the next decade. They are subjects that drastically evolve by the month, so keeping up with them is imperative if companies want to have positive ROI outcomes from their technology investments.

Parts of this book have been written on the Macau-Taipa bus, the Macau-Hong Kong ferry, 30,000 feet above both the Pacific and the Dark Continent of Africa, on the Guangzhou-Macau high-speed rail line, in a French café on Jeju island off Korea's south coast, in a charming tea room in Siem Reap, Cambodia, within a taxi stuck in the smog-choked streets of Manila, as well as on Hong Kong's MTR, to say nothing of all the hotel and motel rooms I've been scribing in; planes, trains, automobiles, tuk tuks, *and* ferries, too.

If you find this book instructive, please keep up to date with my latest work on social media, a list of sites I can be found on are on my author page at the end of this book.

INTRODUCTION

Gambling—the wagering of something valuable on an event of an uncertain outcome with the primary intent of winning additional money or material goods—is nothing new. It has been with us since ancient times. Greek mythology tells the story of Poseidon, Zeus, and Hades rolling the dice to divide the world between themselves. For the record, Poseidon won the sea, Zeus the heavens, and Hades the underworld, supposedly. Thankfully, the land was left to the rest of us and we've been gambling on it ever since.

The history of gambling shadows human history, going back centuries, even millennia. For example, Sauer[1] quotes a contemporary description of crowds en route to the Circus Maximus in Ancient Rome as "already in a fury of anxiety about their bets"; and historians such as Munting[2] document a close association between gambling and sports such as cricket and baseball in eighteenth- and nineteenth-century Britain and America respectively.

One could even say that a direct gambling line stretches from the gladiators of Rome, who fought and died in the Eternal City's midday sun, to today's gladiators who fight in the mud-filled trenches of modern day coliseums like, well, USC's Los Angeles Coliseum. In that Coliseum, during every USC home game, a galea and manica-wearing gladiator corrals the crowd in chants that probably differ little in vitriol or volume from the cries of the barbaric hordes of Rome, who were betting their hard-earned aureuses—gold coins—on life and death. Literally.

In the modern era, one of man's greatest accomplishments—Neil Armstrong's walk on the moon—was actually the first time a bookmaker took a bet on a non-sports related event.[3] As Todd Dewey explains in his *Las Vegas Review-Journal* article *Bookmaker William Hill lost bets when US landed on moon in 1969*[4], "When Neil Armstrong set foot on the moon 50 years ago, the historic achievement won one small bet for a man from England and was one giant loss for British bookmaker William Hill."

"Inspired by President John F. Kennedy's 1962 'We choose to go to the moon' speech, David Threlfall of Lancashire, England, asked William Hill in 1964 for odds on a man landing on the moon by the end of the decade," explains Dewey.[4]

"Offered 1,000-1 odds, Threlfall, who was 20 at the time, wagered 10 pounds (the equivalent of $170 in today's money) 'for any man, woman or child, from any nation on Earth, being on the moon, or any other planet, star or heavenly body of comparable distance from Earth, before January 1971," notes Dewey.[4]

"After Apollo 11 landed on the moon and Armstrong uttered the famous phrase

1

'The Eagle has landed,' a William Hill representative handed Threlfall a check on live TV for 10,010 pounds—debunking conspiracy theories that the moon landing didn't happen," claims Dewey.[4]

The moon bet was reportedly Threlfall's first wager.[4] He celebrated the win with a holiday in the Bahamas and a brand new Jaguar sports car. Sadly, he didn't get around to enjoying his windfall for long, as he was killed in a car accident in November 1970.[4] Perhaps a reminder from the gambling gods that shooting for the moon can also have its downside.

Recognizing the enormous potential for positive press coverage for the company, William Hill had given Threlfall exceptionally generous odds.[4] "Only months before his bet, a NASA-commissioned risk assessment had forecast the chance of a moon landing by 1970 at 1-in-20," says Dewey.[4]

Today, William Hill's non-sports offerings have probably multiplied by a thousand-fold. According to Dewey, "William Hill UK currently offers 50-1 odds that man walks on Mars before the end of 2030 and 1,000-1 odds that intelligent alien life is confirmed to exist before the end of 2020."[4] Many would call these sucker bets, but every now and then a sucker bet pays off (just ask the people who won Leicester to win the Premier League at 5,000-1) and it's bets like these that keeps the gambling world turning.

As David Forrest explains in his article *Sport and Gambling* in the *Handbook on the Economics of Sport*[5], the world "now appears to be in a phase of secularly increasing legal toleration of all manner of gaming activities." Over the past two decades, gambling has exploded as a worldwide phenomenon; sports books in Asia offer bets on worldwide soccer leagues, U.S. and European basketball leagues, F1, and all kinds of Australian sports. Sports books like Betfair make markets in over 30 different sports, including esports, as well as politics, and even offer an exchange where gamblers can lay off bets at prices he or she dictates.

"In America," Forrest notes, "the first state lottery game did not appear until 1964 and only Nevada permitted casinos prior to 1976. But the 'lotto mania' of the 1980s and 1990s, and the growth of Indian and riverboat casinos in the 1990s, gave a large majority of Americans access to these gambling media by the turn of the century." This liberalization wasn't good for sports like horse and dog racing and jai alai, which enjoyed monopoly-like control of the gambling environment because they were the only legal betting opportunities available to the public.[5]

Sports betting has, however, "flourished in most of the world in the new liberal environment for gambling, further boosted by new opportunities to place internet bets with offshore bookmakers," adds Forrest.[5] Jurisdictions such as Singapore and Hong Kong introduced soccer wagering to curb the flow of bettors' funds to offshore centres and, potentially, illegal sectors.[5]

On 14th May 2018, the U.S. supreme court struck down the *Professional and Amateur Sports Protection Act*, a 1992 law that barred state-authorized sports gambling with some exceptions.[6] That 1992 law made "Nevada the only state where a person could wager on the results of a single game."[6] According to *The Guardian*, "The court's decision came in a case from New Jersey, which has fought for years to legalize gambling on sports at casinos and racetracks in the state."[6] New Jersey was not alone, more than a dozen states had supported them, arguing "that Congress exceeded its authority when it passed the *1992 Professional and Amateur Sports Protection Act*, barring states from authorizing sports betting. New Jersey said the constitution allows Congress to pass laws barring wagering on sports, but Congress can't require states to keep sports gambling prohibitions in place."[6]

"All four major US professional sports leagues, the NCAA and the federal government had urged the court to uphold the federal law. In court, the NBA, NFL, NHL and Major League Baseball had argued that New Jersey's gambling expansion would hurt the integrity of their games," says *The Guardian*.[6] To show the hypocrisy of their positions, "Outside court, however, leaders of all but the NFL have shown varying degrees of openness to legalized sports gambling."[6]

This was a perfect example of the authorities trying to prohibit behavior that was going to occur in one way or another, it's just human nature to want to put down a wager on an event, whether its legal or illegal usually matters little to the punter. "The American Gaming Association estimates that Americans illegally wager about $150bn on sports each year," claims *The Guardian*.[6]

In his *Fortune* article *Inside the Battle for the Future of Sports Betting*[7], Rey Mashayekhi writes that, "Buoyed by the commercial possibilities, the likes of the NBA, MLB, NHL, and Major League Soccer have each struck official partnerships with MGM Resorts, while the NFL announced its own deal with Caesars Entertainment." However, Rey claims that, "these commercial agreements represent only a piece of the larger sports betting puzzle for the leagues. Ask them, and they'll tell you that much more significant is the opportunity to use gambling as a vehicle to draw in, engage and interact with millions of sports fans across the country."[7]

"We always saw, and we still see it, as a fan engagement opportunity," Keith Wachtel, the NHL's chief revenue officer, told *Fortune*.[7] "That's the holy grail of sports betting; it's not the short-term [gambling] revenue," Wachtel added.[7] The billions of dollars in potential revenue from legalized sports betting directly counters Wachtel's argument, however.

"Simply put, more betting on sports means more eyeballs watching and paying attention to those sports, and that equals more money flowing into the leagues' coffers," says Mashayekhi.[7] "According to an October study commissioned by the American Gaming Association (AGA), legal sports betting could result in an additional $4.2 billion in annual revenues for the four major North American sports leagues (NFL, NBA, MLB and NHL)—with the majority of that influx resulting from increased fan engagement with the product, rather than revenue coming directly from the gaming industry," adds Mashayekhi.[7]

"I think [the leagues] absolutely view this as something that's going to increase fan viewership and engagement," said Scott Butera, MGM's president of interactive gaming, who is spearheading the company's sports betting strategy.[7] "They see this as a way of letting fans have some skin in the game, and more reasons to watch a game now."[7] This is something the European sports leagues have known for decades and this is clearly a case of it's better to be late than never.

In 2018, "the NBA, MLB, and PGA Tour teamed up on a lobbying effort targeting state legislatures across the U.S. The three pro sports organizations share ideas that they believe should govern sports betting and stand in contrast to the NFL and NHL, which have taken a more lax approach toward the regulatory environment."[7]

"Some of the leagues' positions are in line with casino industry groups like the AGA, including an embrace of mobile betting and support for cooperation between the leagues and bookmakers on detecting irregular betting patterns that could signal 'integrity issues' with certain games and contests," says Mashayekhi.[7]

"Other proposals have been flatly shot down by the gaming industry. Perhaps no stance has been less popular than the notion of an 'integrity fee,' which would see the leagues get a cut of the revenue from each bet placed on one of their contests," explains Mashayekhi.[7] "While the NBA, MLB, and PGA Tour initially floated the idea of a 1% fee, they've since revised their stance to 0.25% of every bet. Nothing screams integrity more than trying to strongarm an 'integrity fee' out of unwilling sports betting operators. What a wonderfully misnamed emolument demand.

Understandably, the "position garners little sympathy from the gaming industry, which cites its own low-margin business model in ruling out the leagues getting any cut of betting revenues," says Mashayekhi[7]; rightfully so. "Sara Slane, the AGA's senior vice president of public affairs, says that the originally proposed 1% integrity fee on each bet would amount to bookmakers effectively sacrificing up to 20% of their profits—given how bookmakers pay out 95 cents in winnings for every every $1 that is bet, according to Slane."[7]

Slane also shoots down the notion of a more limited 0.25% fee on bets.[7] "At the end of the day, this is a low-margin business," she says.[7] Slane adds that, "Taking that money off the top hurts our ability to compete with illegal operators."[7]

So far, it appears that the sports betting lobby is winning on this issue, says

Mashayekhi.[7] "While integrity fees have been included in several proposed pieces of sports betting legislation across the country (such as a bill introduced in Connecticut last month), they've yet to make it into law anywhere," he adds.[7]

Mashayekhi notes that there are also "other issues that relate to in-play betting—a massive and ever-growing piece of the sports betting market that's enabled by the vast amount of data collected by the leagues and sports data partners like Sportradar and Genius Sports."[7]

"On the first count, the NBA, MLB, and PGA Tour want bookmakers to be required to pay for their official, league-sanctioned data streams. They claim this is important to provide the most accurate, up-to-date betting data for wagers, and also to protect the proprietary data collection operations that they've spent millions of dollars to establish," says Mashayekhi.[7]

"We capture data from every single [golf] shot at a PGA Tour event—on a Thursday and Friday, that's 10,000-plus shots a day," according to David Miller, a vice president and assistant general counsel for the PGA Tour.[7] "We don't think it's fair, in a regulated market, for someone to be able to use a tracking tool or web-scraping device and turn around the data we collected to bookmakers for a fraction of the cost."[7]

"Additionally, as part of their efforts to protect the integrity of their games, the leagues want to see restrictions on certain kinds of wagers," explains Mashayekhi.[7] "We want to make sure that, as we get into more granular bets, we don't encounter integrity issues," says Seeley.[7] "It's very difficult for an individual to fix a nine-inning baseball game. It's a lot easier to fix the next at-bat; a batter is in complete control of when he strikes out."[7] Although these are problems that can definitely arise, it's not like spot betting hasn't been available in cricket for years now. The European sports betting companies have enough belief in the integrity of the game to accept wagers on all kinds of spot bets and the US leagues should recognize this as a solvable problem that fits within their current league management system.

"Miller says the PGA Tour agrees with that stance when it comes to 'negative bets,' such as 'a bet that [a golfer will] miss a putt or drive it less than 300 yards'—and particularly 'at the lower levels of our sport,' where the winnings are smaller and players are potentially more prone to manipulation," says Mashayekhi.[7]

"Unsurprisingly," notes Mashayekhi, "the casino lobby is at odds with both a mandate on where bookmakers can buy their data from and what kinds of bets they can take."[7] Slane says such a mandate "enables [the leagues] to have a monopoly over data rights,"[7] while restricting the types of wagers that operators can offer would simply "drive [bettors] to offshore, illegal [gambling] websites" to find certain bets.[7]

Slanes "adds that the gaming industry has 'just as much invested' in ensuring that the integrity of the contests it takes bets on are not comprised."[7] "When we're paying out to winners who have insider info, that hurts us just as much," she notes.[7] "If there's something suspicious happening, it's bad for the leagues but it's also bad for us."[7]

Carsten Koerl, the founder and CEO of Sportradar, tells *Fortune* that while it's "very understandable that [the leagues] want to protect the sport," the idea that they can dictate where gambling operators can obtain their data from "is not going to work in a free market."[7] "Having provided betting data to sports books around the world over the past two decades, Sportradar now has similar partnerships with most of the major American sports leagues," says Mashayekhi.[7]

"Crucially, the company also helps leagues and authorities monitor potential integrity issues, such as betting irregularities that may indicate a contest is fixed in some way," says Mashayekhi.[7] "I understand the leagues have an interest, but betting operators have the same interest that the sport stays clean and nobody is using these small side bets to influence it," says Koerl.[7]

Koerl adds that the debate over the use of official data "is not very positive, because it will slow down the process" of getting sports betting up and running in many states.[7] "I would like to see that [the leagues and gambling operators] are both lobbying in the same direction."[7]

"Like the integrity fee issue, the leagues' efforts to mandate the use of official data and restrict certain types of bets have yet to gain much traction at the state level," claims Mashayekhi.[7] That bill represents the first piece of federal legislation governing the legal sports betting industry in the U.S.[7] "While the gaming industry appears to be against such legislation—Slane said it would add another level of bureaucracy "for gaming operators already heavily regulated at the state level—the idea is met with virtually unanimous approval among leagues, data providers, mobile betting operators, and other industry participants," says Mashayekhi.[7]

Whatever comes of the integrity fee, sports betting has clearly arrived in places like New Jersey and in Washington. As Mashayekhi explains[7]:

> *"At Prudential Center in Newark, N.J., fans attending a New Jersey Devils game can visit the William Hill Sports Lounge, buy a drink, and survey several screens that list the most up-to-date betting odds for any number of sporting events. While there are no betting windows available to take wagers in person— New Jersey law still restricts where you can establish a brick-and-mortar betting operation—all one has to do is flip open bookmaker William Hill's mobile sports betting app (or any other sports betting app, if they like) and place a wager with*

the tap of a finger."

"We've made it a priority to make sure that when our fans come to the games, they are getting a unique and connective experience, and we saw sports gambling as additive to that," says Hugh Weber, the president of Harris Blitzer Sports & Entertainment (HBSE), the company that owns both the Devils and the Prudential Center (as well as the NBA's Philadelphia 76ers and the English Premier League's Crystal Palace F.C.).[7] As Weber explains, patrons don't have to visit the lounge if they want to place a bet, they can simply "place bets from their seats in the arena."[7]

Ted Leonsis, the owner of both the NHL's Washington Capitals and the NBA's Washington Wizards, "recently announced that he will open a physical on-site sports book at the arena his teams share in downtown Washington, D.C., after the District's city council voted to legalize sports betting in February."[7] The Sacramento Kings have also "offered fans predictive gaming platforms on the team's official app."[7] Major League Soccer, a nascent league that has perhaps the most to gain from sports betting as a fan engagement tool, is "developing a free-to-play game" with new partner MGM, according to MLS deputy commissioner Gary Stevenson.[7]

"Despite opposition from state gaming lobbies across the country, most people in the sports betting industry agree that mobile sports betting is the way of the future, if not the present," says Mashayekhi.[7] "While some gaming operators have expressed reservations about whether mobile betting will drive traffic to their casinos, the consensus is that it's necessary should the legal market wish to capture the bulk of the illegal, black market's share," concludes Mashayekhi.[7]

Statista reports that the online gambling market rose from US $20.51 billion in 2009 to US $47.77 billion in 2017 and is expected to top US $59.79 in 2020.[8] This book could be a timely addition to the sports betting oeuvre, just in time for the all-out land—or, more accurately, people—grab these worldwide sports books are attempting now that these wealthy American punters have joined in the sports betting party. Legalization will, undoubtedly, usher in a new day of internet gambling, which will, hopefully, reroute some of the money that is currently being funneled into the coffers of illegal gambling syndicates into legal sports books and punting companies. This might help mitigate match fixing, which is undoubtedly being funded by several of these illegal gambling syndicates.

The *A.I. Sports Book* is a book for the sports book executive who wants to utilize analytics in ways that will not only increase the client experience, but also exploit data produced through their operation in ways that make it predictive, optimized and, most of all, increases ROI. This book is not a book for gamblers looking to beat a sports book, it is not about those kinds of analytics. It's a book for sports betting executives who want to provide a world-class customer experience to their punters.

According to IBM[9], 2.5 quintillion bytes of data are created each day. That is 10 to the power of 18 and this number is growing exponentially each year; 90% of the world's data was created over the past two years and data creation is certainly not going to slow down any time soon. This data—which has been dubbed "Big Data"—comes from everywhere; our daily financial transactions; our personal online shopping history; our social media uploads; our mobile downloads, even, in some cases, sensor data coming off machines and people.

The social nature of sharing personal content with family, friends and associates may be the driver behind this growth and it is a growth that several studies[10][11] suggest will soon outpace revenue generated by commercial media, such as music downloads, video clips, and games. This is the kind of growth that a sports book ignores at its own peril, but when a sports book delves into this Big Data world, it needs to ensure that what it is opening up is a treasure chest of information and not a Pandora's Box full of pain.

The Age of A.I.

Today, it can safely be said, we are living in the age of AI. Everywhere you look, companies are touting their most recent AI, machine learning (ML), and deep learning breakthroughs, even when they are far short of anything that could be dubbed "breakthroughs." "AI" has probably superseded "Blockchain", "Crypto", and/or "ICO" as the buzzword of the day. Indeed, one of the best ways to raise VC funding is to stick 'AI' or 'ML' at the front of your prospectus and ".ai" at the end of your website. Separating AI fact from fiction is one of the main goals of this book; the other is to help sports book marketing executives understand AI so that they can utilize this groundbreaking technology in ways that are simple and complex and, hopefully, rather ingenious. Most importantly, in ways that will be recognized by their customers.

In the article *Sports Trading and AI: Taking the human out of sports betting*[12], *Gambling Insider* argues that, "Online platforms enable gamblers to bet whenever and wherever they want, reducing the need for the traditional bookmaking shop. However, it has proven to be a double-edged sword, with the increasing number of available betting markets growing beyond the capacity of human odds makers to efficiently manage them."[12]

In the *Gambling Insider* article, Tom Daniel, Head of Risk and Player Analytics for sportsbook provider Kambi, details how the industry has evolved from a place where a single trader prices up to ten markets manually to today, where that single trader might manage the output for scores of events offering hundreds of markets.[12]

This second technical revolution in sports betting, which many consider is still in its infancy includes the "increasing use of artificial intelligence and machine learning in odds making."[12] "Designed to increase the accuracy of odds calculation, efficiency and output, AI sports trading represents the next digital frontier in sports betting," *Gambling Insider* notes.[12]

"The basic theory is that greater automation leads a drive towards greater efficiency", *Gambling Insider* argues.[12] However, Christopher Langeland, Managing Director of BettingCloud argues: "In reality it will take some time and considerable skill to set up AI/automated systems to do a lot of the jobs that have traditionally been done by humans, so the most valuable people in a bookmaking organisation will become the analysts/programmers who set up this automation."[12]

Major tech companies have embraced AI and machine learning as if it was one of the most important discoveries ever invented; Google, whose CEO compares it to the discovery of fire and electricity, is now an "AI-first" company; Amazon's entire business is shaped by AI, from its customer personalization, to its warehousing, robotics and logistics capabilities, to its voice-activated smart speakers; IBM has Watson; Facebook has AI and ML algorithms that test out which of its AI and ML ideas are most effective and should be rolled-out company-wide; Adobe, a big player in the multi-channel marketing space, runs much of its Experience Cloud marketing platform through its Sensei AI product; even the analytics powerhouse SAS has recently announced[13] that it will spend US $1B over the next three years on AI software and initiatives. Even some of the smaller vendors we are partnered with at Intelligencia have embraced AI for fear of missing out on this burgeoning market.

In its report *Sizing the prize. What's the real value of AI for your business and how you can capitalise*[14], PWC believes that, "AI could contribute up to $15.7 trillion to the global economy in 2030, more than the current output of China and India combined. Of this, $6.6 trillion is likely to come from increased productivity and $9.1 trillion is likely to come from consumption-side effects."

Because AI is still in its infancy, PWC believes that there are opportunities for emerging markets to leapfrog more developed counterparts with AI.[14] Although this is a possibility, the inherent requirements of AI–a highly educated workforce, strong backing from higher learning institutes, a strong legal and regulatory framework, and access to huge sources of data—might limit emerging market successes. However, this shouldn't make companies in the industrial world too comfy. PWC's claim that, "within your business sector, one of today's start-ups or a business that hasn't even been founded yet could be the market leader in ten years' time"[14] probably holds true. AI threatens on both the micro and macro front, which is rare in a technology.

According to PWC's analysis, "global GDP will be up to 14% higher in 2030 as a result of the accelerating development and take-up of AI–the equivalent of an additional $15.7 trillion."[14] For PWC, the economic impact of AI will be driven by[14]:

1. Productivity gains from businesses automating processes (including use of robots and autonomous vehicles).
2. Productivity gains from businesses augmenting their existing labour force with AI technologies (assisted and augmented intelligence).
3. Increased consumer demand resulting from the availability of personalised and/or higher-quality AI-enhanced products and services.[14]

As behavioral economist Susan Menke explains in her paper *Humanizing Loyalty*[15], "Decision fatigue and cognitive fatigue are the opposite of flow and seamlessness. We are making too many decisions that tax our cognitive bank account. We dole it out on important things and not on things that are already operating well." In her paper, Menke touches upon the concept of psychological scripts—the idea that the mind doesn't have to focus on many day-to-day activities as they can be handled without much thought.[15] The more seamless a company can make the interaction process, the more likely a customer will continue to do business with it.[15] Tom Fishburne, the founder of Marketoonist, says "the best marketing doesn't feel like marketing," and his words are a good motto for today's digital marketer. AI can help make marketing so personalized and wanted that customers actually enjoy and respond to it positively. The seamlessness of the marketing is paramount.

We live in an instant gratification world and the companies that are likely to thrive in this new environment will be the ones who can both keep up with the requirements of their discerning and demanding customers and predict what these customers will be wanting throughout their customer journeys. Today, companies need every advantage they can get so that they provide better service than their competitors.

Being able to accurately predict not only who a marketer's best leads and prospects are, as well as how and when it is best to engage them is nice but understanding how their acceptance of these marketing offers will affect the overall bottom line is what the *A.I. Sports Book* is all about.

This ability will not only empower marketers and salespeople in the coming seasons to be radically more productive and profitable than they are today, but also give multiple corporate departments visibility on their micro and macro needs. Used properly, predictive analytics and AI can transform the science of sales forecasting from a dart-throwing exercise to a precision instrument.

The concept of sales and marketing automation has already produced some of the highest-flying successes in high-tech. Companies like Salesforce.com have been wildly successful in automating the sales process for salespeople and sales managers. Big software vendors like SAP, Microsoft, and Oracle are vying for supremacy, while smaller players like Pegasystems, SugarCRM, Netsuite, and Sage are offering interesting products at highly affordable prices.

In their article *10 Principles of Modern Marketing*[16], Ann Lewnes and Kevin Lane Keller argue that, "Technology has changed everything. Fundamentally, it allows for new ways to create customer experiences, new mediums to connect with customers and other constituents, and trillions of data points to understand customer behavior and the impact of marketing programs and activities. Yet, with all that progress, we are still only at the tip of the iceberg in terms of the profound impact technology will have on the future of marketing."

In their *AI: Your behind-the-scenes marketing companion*[17], the Adobe Sensei Team claims that, "The battle to win customer hearts and minds is no longer simply about your product. It's about the experience. Because that's what keeps customers coming back. To compete on experience, you need to understand what customers want now while anticipating what they'll do next. And because your customers have lots of choices, you don't have a lot of time to get it right."

"But many times, the knowledge you need to personalize interactions and compel customers to act is locked up in huge amounts of data," says the Adobe Sensei Team.[17] "This means someone has to sift through it all to recognize patterns, trends, and profiles, so you can quickly act on insights. The problem is, it's too much data for humans to sort through alone. That's where artificial intelligence and machine learning come in," the team says.[17]

"Customers will always expect a human touch in their interactions," warns the Adobe Sensei Team.[17] "These new technologies won't replace marketing jobs, but they will change them," the team claims.[17] Brands should think of AI and machine learning as their behind-the-scenes marketing assistant who helps unlock insights in volumes of data, develops a deeper understanding of what customers want, a forecasting tool that predicts trends, as well as monitors unusual activity, such as spikes or drops in sales—all while giving brands more time to make decisions that matter.[17]

"To fully realize the potential of technology," Lewnes and Keller argue that, "it takes transformation across people, processes, *and* technology. Only by recognizing all three forces will modern marketers reap the full benefits that technology can have on marketing transformation."[16]

"To thrive in this new era, it is imperative that marketers embrace developments in technology and test and adopt new advancements that fit their business—whether AI, or voice, or augmented reality—before they lose a competitive edge," claim Lewnes and Keller.[16] "At the same time, mastering technology is not the only criterion for success in the modern marketing era—the right people and processes must also be put in place to properly develop, manage, and nurture the benefits of that technology," they add.[16]

"In terms of people, today's marketers must possess many traits. They must be curious, flexible, agile, and nimble. They must be willing to be change agents, always looking around the corner and helping to scale transformation as champions for change," say Lewnes and Keller.[16] The status quo no longer works—continuous development of new skills for all marketers is critical.[16]

Today's marketing organization needs people with diverse skill sets and expertise in key areas.[16] "Managers should ensure their marketing teams include members who bring creative and analytical capabilities, as well as individuals who can play newly evolved roles on a team—whether that's someone skilled in web development, data analytics, e-commerce, or new media," argue Lewnes and Keller.[16] Marketing organization almost have an impossible job as "many of these jobs didn't exist four or five years ago, and even if they did, they have changed dramatically in recent years."[16]

Furthermore, while these new, specialized jobs have emerged, marketers must keep in mind the broadening marketing ecosystem.[16] "The dynamic cross-channel nature of marketing today requires that campaigns be integrated and connected across every channel," say Lewnes and Keller.[16]

"Processes must also change for technology organizations. Today, the customer-decision process is becoming more complex and varied. As the customer journey becomes increasingly nonlinear, the organization must change to reflect that," warn Lewnes and Keller.[16] "In a more complex marketplace, internal organizational lines need to be redrawn. Silos must be broken down and cross-functional relationships established so that marketing works seamlessly across other groups in the organization such as IT, finance, sales, and product management," say Lewnes and Keller.[16]

"Marketing can benefit from the output of these other groups and also contribute to the groups' effectiveness and success at the same time," claim Lewnes and Keller.[16] "For example, to improve the reliability of financial forecasting, marketing can share early-warning lead indicators that have been shown to affect bottom-of-the-funnel behaviors and ultimately revenue (for example, the number of customer visits to company-controlled websites)."[16] The marketing department can show its growing worth and value by demonstrating "its impact on the business, validating the ROI of every dollar to peer groups in the organization and becoming a strategic driver of the business."[16]

All these changes, however, require that technology organizations adapt to this new marketing and technological environment. Lewnes and Keller argue that marketers "must learn to be agile, take risks, fail fast, and apply lessons. They must also learn how to get the most out of a data-rich world by testing, optimizing, and activating."[16]

Lewnes and Keller claim "experience is the new brand."[16] They are right, experience will be one of the big differentiators for companies going forward.[16]

"With traditional marketing, the customer-decision and company-selling process was comparatively simple with customers entering into a company's sales and marketing funnel and making various choices along the way to becoming loyal, repeat customers," say Lewnes and Keller.[16] Today, every "customer touch point online and offline—as wide-ranging as a tweet, product download, in-store purchase, the company's social purpose, its executives' behavior, and the corporate culture—can shape experiences that define a brand for customers," warn Lewnes and Keller.[16]

"Marketers operate at the intersection of many of these customer experiences and are uniquely positioned to help steer the future directions for brands," claim Lewnes and Keller.[16] "In doing so, marketers of technology products cannot just worship the product alone and be transactional in their customer interactions. They must create full-on, immersive experiences for customers that build strong ties to the company and the brand as a whole. Experiences are the new competitive battlefield and a means to create powerful differentiation from competitors," argue Lewnes and Keller.[16]

"With technology products, seamless product installation and operation, in particular, is absolutely critical," say Lewnes and Keller.[16] "If customers cannot successfully use a company's products, there will be no value realization, and they will eventually switch to products from other companies that they can more easily access and use," warn Lewnes and Keller.[16] "Beyond designing products that are as easy to use as possible, technology companies must have a wide range of support and services for customers to help them with product installation and use, employing ample training resources as well as informative forums, social channels, and websites," conclude Lewnes and Keller.[16]

A new acronym that is making the software rounds these days is CXM—Customer Experience Management—and it helps businesses collect and process real-time data from across an organization. A CXM platform activates content based on customer profiles, allowing personalized experiences to be delivered in real time. This is the future of both AI and brand marketing.

So why choose to go down the complex AI road? Well, in the article *Artificial intelligence Unlocks the True Power of Analytics[18]*, Adobe explains the vast difference between doing things in a rules-based analytics way and an AI-powered way, including:

- Provide warnings whenever a company activity falls outside the norm. The difference:
  - **Rules-based analytics:** You set a threshold for activity (e.g., "200–275 orders per hour") and then manually investigate whether each alert is important.

- o **AI-powered analytics:** The AI analytics tool automatically determines that the event is worthy of an alert, then fires it off unaided.
- Conduct a root cause analysis and recommend action. The difference:
  - o **Rules-based analytics:** You manually investigate why an event may have happened and consider possible actions.
  - o **AI-powered analytics:** Your tool automatically evaluates what factors contributed to the event and suggests a cause and an action.
- Evaluate campaign effectiveness:
  - o **Rules-based analytics:** The business manually sets rules and weights to attribute the value of each touch that led to a conversion.
  - o **AI-powered analytics:** The AI analytics tool automatically weights and reports the factors that led to each successful outcome and attributes credit to each campaign element or step accordingly.
- Identify customers who are at risk of defecting:
  - o **Rules-based analytics:** You manually study reports on groups of customers that have defected and try to see patterns.
  - o **AI-powered analytics:** Your tool automatically Identifies which segments are at greatest risk of defection.
- Select segments that will be the most responsive to upcoming campaigns:
  - o **Rules-based analytics:** You manually consider and hypothesize about the attributes of customers that might prove to be predictive of their response.
  - o **AI-powered analytics:** Your tool automatically creates segments based on attributes that currently drive the desired response.
- Find your best customers:
  - o **Rules-based analytics:** You manually analyze segments in order to understand what makes high-quality customers different.
  - o **AI-powered analytics:** Your tool automatically identifies statistically significant attributes that high-performing customers have in common and creates segments with these customers for you to take action on.

Beyond the reasons listed above, I will discuss how AI can be used in website morphing, customer and media recommendations, purchase prediction, demand forecasting, programmatic advertising, social listening, and much, much more.

In chapter two, I lay the foundation of how a sports book can utilize both AI and

ML, while in the final chapter I detail specific examples of how these technologies can be utilized on several different fronts. Certainly, many sports book are already using these technologies for things like odds making, customer segmentation, market and marketing forecasting, recommendation engines, and in target marketing, but they can also be used to weed out problem or addicted gamblers, as well as increase employee productivity.

The A.I. Sports Book is a sports book that takes into account all kinds of data that can be created at a sports book, including both online and its physical branches, if it has any. Data created by its employees, vendors, patrons, and customers (we'll consider these the people who haven't signed up for a player card yet and aren't, therefore, as trackable as patrons who are in the sports book's database) are also quantified and optimized.

The A.I. Sports Book utilizes all of the data associated with a sports books' many departments in order to make better business decisions for the company as a whole. *The A.I. Sports Book* is viewed holistically and the proverbial butterfly's wing that flaps somewhere inside the brand can set off a chain of events that either helps or hurts the company's bottom line, potentially months down the line; captured and analyzed the data will be, so that surprises and negative impacts can be mitigated, if not reversed.

Descriptive analytics, diagnostic analytics, predictive analytics, prescriptive analytics and the newest field of analytics—edge analytics—are exploited throughout *The A.I. Sports Book* to try to reach as real-time an IT environment as possible. The data I will be focusing on throughout this book will be culled from the following sources:

- Operational systems.
- Gaming data from commercial or other in-house gaming systems.
- Customer Relationship Management (CRM) software.
- Transaction data from Point-of-Sales (POS) systems.
- Clickstreams from the sports book's website.
- Call center systems.
- Surveillance and security systems, including facial recognition datasets.
- Geo-location data from in-house Wi-Fi systems.
- Social media data from WeChat, Facebook, Weibo, Twitter, Jiepang, Instagram, YouTube, Twitch, and other mobile and social media apps.
- Patron management systems.
- Social media listening hubs.
- Google analytics and web tracking information.
- HR and ERP systems.

All of this information can be fed into a data lake or an Enterprise Data Warehouse (EDW), where it can be utilized by a multitude of departments, including call center/customer service, marketing, social media marketing, patron management, affiliate marketing, all the way up to the top executive branches, including individuals in the C-level suite.

In recent years, businesses in general and sports books in particular have come to the realization that data warehouses, while perfectly able to handle the BI and analytics needs of yesterday, don't always work in today's complex IT environments, which contain structured, unstructured, and semi-structured data.

Normal relational databases worked fine when business users were restricted to proprietary databases and the scope of work was confined to canned reports and modest dashboards that included limited drill down functionality. Today, however, with the inclusion of so much unstructured data coming from mobile, social, web logs, etc., and semi-structured data originating from a multitude of sources, limitations abound. Standard data warehouses require built-in, understandable schemas, but unstructured data, by definition, doesn't have a definable schema that is accessible and understandable in every case. Data lakes have been a response to these—and other—limitations.

James Dixon, "Chief Geek" at Pentaho, is credited with coining the phrase "Data Lake" and Dixon posited that each specialized data mart in a data warehouse could be likened to a bottle of water.[19] The data was ready for use in a small, identifiable container. In contrast, a data "lake" was a massive, intermingled repository of all data in its rawest form.

A data lake is a hub or a repository of all the data that a sports book has access to, where the data is ingested and stored in as close to the rawest form as possible, without enforcing any restrictive schema on it. This provides an unlimited window into the data for anyone to run ad-hoc queries and perform cross-source navigation and analysis on the fly. Successful data lake implementations respond to queries in real-time and provide users an easy and uniform access interface to the disparate sources of data. Data lakes retain all data, support all data types and all users, as well as adapt easily to change, while providing faster insights.

Today's IT environment is nothing like the IT environment of even three years ago. Real-time data management capabilities have brought a whole new level of data available to customer intelligence, customer interaction, patron management and social media systems.

One of the biggest challenges for IT departments today is scalability. With a Hadoop back-ended data lake, sports books can dynamically scale up or down, according to their storage needs. Over the past few years, the cost of storage has plummeted and virtual servers can be spun up very quickly, as well as quite inexpensively (relative to the outright purchase of hardware). With this instant access to data, a whole new world of real-time interactions can flourish and I will detail how a sports book can set up a real-time stream processing environment in chapter five.

The concept of "Edge Analytics"—i.e., the processing of analytics at the point or very close to the point of data collection—exponentially increases the ability to use predictive analytics where it can be utilized best—at the point of interaction between the business and the consumer. In short, edge analytics brings analytics to the data rather than vice-versa, which, understandably, can reduce cost and increase its usage as the data is analyzed close to where it can best be utilized. This also reduces latency, which could be the difference between useful and useless analytics.

Today, the analytics space is more crowded than ever before; standard ETL-solution providers are adding analytics to their multitude of offerings. Many new players in the Master Data Management (MDM) field have BI platforms that combine integration, preparation, analytics and visualization capabilities with governance and security features. Such standard analytics processes as column dependencies, clustering, decision trees, and a recommendation engine are all included in many of these new software packages.

Instead of forcing clients to frustratingly purchase module on top of module on top of module, new software companies are creating packages that contain many pre-built analytical functions. Open source products like R, Python, and the WEKA collection in Pentaho can easily be added to many of these software solutions as well, thereby reducing the need for expensive analytics layers.

The fact that many of these analytical packages are open source is a further advantage because, since they are free to download and use, they have a robust user base and consultants are sometimes easier to find than analysts with highly developed SAS, SAP PAL or H2O skills, for example.

Before going any further, I believe one of the first questions that needs to be answered here is, "What exactly is analytics?" The standard answer is that there are four types of analytics and they are:

- Descriptive analytics—What happened?
- Diagnostic analytics—Why did it happen?
- Predictive analytics—What will happen?
- Prescriptive analytics—How can we make it happen again?

For a sports book, descriptive analytics could include pattern discovery methods such as customer segmentation, i.e., culling through a patron database to understand a patron's preferred game of choice.

Simple cluster segmentation models could divide customers into their preferred betting sport of choice. This information could be given to the marketing department to create lists of Champions League football bettors so that when the Champions League games roll around, these people could be marketed to with specific offers that should entice them to gamble further.

Market basket analysis, which utilizes association rules, would also be considered a descriptive analytics procedure. Sports books could use market basket analysis to bundle and offer promotions as well as gain insight into its customer's gaming habits. Detailed patron shopping and purchasing behavior could also be used to develop future products. I will go into full detail on all of this topic in chapter two.

In her article *How Much ROI Can Data Analytics Deliver?*[20], Annie Eissler points out that, according to Nucleus Research "analytics and business intelligence solutions deliver, on average, $13.01 for every dollar spent" and leading companies have been achieving double-digit return on investment (ROI) from their analytics investments for several years now."[20] In chapter two, I will delve deeper into how sports book can utilize analytics to both reduce costs and, by delivering personalized marketing, increase customer satisfaction.

In his article *Will 'Analytics on The Edge' Be The Future Of Big Data?*[21], Bernard Marr ponders the question: "Rather than designing centralized systems where all the data is sent back to your data warehouse in a raw state, where it has to be cleaned and analyzed before being of any value, why not do everything at the 'edge' of the system?"

Marr uses the example of a massive scale CCTV security system that is capturing real-time video feeds from tens of thousands of cameras.[21] "It's likely that 99.9% of the footage captured by the cameras will be of no use for the job it's supposed to be doing—e.g. detecting intruders. Hours and hours of still footage is likely to be captured for every second of useful video. So what's the point of all of that data being streamed in real-time across your network, generating expense as well as possible compliance burdens?"[21]

The solution to this problem, Marr argues is for the images themselves to be analyzed within the cameras at the moment the video is captured.[21] Anything deemed out-of-the-ordinary will trigger alerts, while everything considered to be unimportant will either be discarded or marked as low priority, thereby freeing up centralized resources to work on data of actual value.[21]

For a sports book, the CCTV security systems could be set up to alert a brand manager that a VIP player steps in a store, or it could also catch when a problem gambler is attempting to make a bet.

Using edge analytics and real-time stream processing engines, sports book could "analyze point-of-sales data as it is captured, and enable cross selling or up-selling on-the-fly, while reducing bandwidth overheads of sending all sales data to a centralized analytics server in real time."[21]

Edge analytics, of course, goes hand-in-hand with the Internet of Things—"the network of physical objects that contain embedded technology to communicate and sense or interact with their internal states or the external environment."[22]

In his seminal 2009 article for the *RFID Journal, That 'Internet o Things' Thing*[23], Kevin Ashton made the following assessment:

> *Today computers—and, therefore, the Internet—are almost wholly dependent on human beings for information. Nearly all of the roughly 50 petabytes (a petabyte is 1,024 terabytes) of data available on the Internet were first captured and created by human beings—by typing, pressing a record button, taking a digital picture, or scanning a bar code. Conventional diagrams of the Internet include servers and routers and so on, but leave out the most numerous and important routers of all—people. The problem is, people have limited time, attention and accuracy—all of which means they are not very good at capturing data about things in the real world. And that's a big deal. We're physical, and so is our environment. Our economy, society and survival aren't based on ideas or information— they're based on things. You can't eat bits, burn them to stay warm or put them in your gas tank. Ideas and information are important, but things matter much more. Yet today's information technology is so dependent on data originated by people that our computers know more about ideas than things. If we had computers that knew everything there was to know about things—using data they gathered without any help from us—we would be able to track and count everything, and greatly reduce waste, loss and cost. We would know when things needed replacing, repairing or recalling, and whether they were fresh or past their best. The Internet of Things has the potential to change the world, just as the Internet did. Maybe even more so.*

The term "Big Data" has become a way-too-common and enormously prevalent term and it is being bandied about a lot in the world of IT these days because it has become a kind of catch-all for analytics, IoT, social media, etc., etc. Although not a comprehensive list, Big Data analytics techniques can include association, classification, cluster analysis, crowdsourcing, data fusion, data mining, machine learning (ML), modeling, network analysis, optimization, predictive, regression, rule learning, special analysis, text analytics, time series analysis, amongst many, many others. Which techniques should a sports book use? Well, that all depends on what type of data is being analyzed, the technology available to it, the skills of the business users, and the business problems it is trying to solve.

In chapter two, I break down how these analytical techniques would work in the concept of the customer journey, and I will specifically explain in what circumstances decision trees, time series, discriminant analysis, *K-means clustering,* and *K-Nearest Neighbor* processes, amongst others, should be utilized.

None of these techniques, however, will amount to anything if the underlying data environment isn't robust and cleansed properly; "junk in, junk out", as most analysts warn. The quality and quantity of the data gathered will be directly proportional to the accuracy of the predictive model. Enormous attention must be paid to ensure the data is prepped and cleansed, otherwise nothing of value will be achieved, no matter how fast and/or robust your analytics software might be able to crunch the underlying numbers.

IoT technology costs are coming down, broadband's price has dropped, while its availability has increased, and there is a proliferation of devices with Wi-Fi capabilities and censors built into them. Smart phone penetration is also exploding. All of these individual technological advances were good for the IoT environment, together, however, they have created a perfect storm for it.[24] With less than 0.1% of all the devices that could be connected to the Internet currently connected[24], there is tremendous growth potential here and those who embrace it now should have the first mover advantage that could prove enormously valuable in terms of ROI over the long term.

Combining IoT data together with other structured and unstructured data isn't easy, though. Previous attempts at broad-based data integration has forced users to build data sets around common predetermined schema, or a unifying data model, but this becomes impossible when unstructured and semi-structured data are included in the mix. This is where data lakes come in.

Unlike the monolithic view of a single enterprise-wide data model, the data lake relaxes standardization and defers modeling, resulting in a nearly unlimited potential for operational insight and data discovery. As data volumes, data variety, and metadata richness grows, so, too, do the benefits.

Today, data is coming from everywhere, from business mainframes, from corporate databases, from log files, cloud services, APIs, RSS feed, as well as from social media feeds; most of this information does contain meaning, if one knows what and where to look for it. A data lake makes it easier to read and understand that data, at least that's the theory that is being tested out by several forward-thinking companies right now. Using and understanding all of this data is going to be the challenge, however.

For this book, I will consider CRM as a two-part process that allows a sports book to track and organize its current and prospective customers, as well as to manage the endpoints of customer relationships through its marketing promotions. When done right, CRM systems enable data to be converted into information that provides insight into customer behavior and, from these insights, some form of behavioral influencing can occur.

Although widely recognized as an important element of most business' customer experience platform, there is no universally accepted definition of CRM. In his paper *Accelerating customer relationships: Using CRM and relationship technology*[25], R. Swift defines CRM as an "enterprise approach to understanding and influencing meaningful communications in order to improve customer acquisition, customer retention, customer loyalty, and customer profitability." J. Kincaid adds that CRM is "the strategic use of information, processes, technology and people to manage the customer's relationship with your company (Marketing, Sales, Services, and Support) across the whole customer lifecycle."[26]

In their paper *Customer Relationship Management: Emerging Practice, Process*[27]*, and Discipline*, Parvatiyar and Sheth claim CRM is: "a comprehensive strategy and process of acquiring, retaining, and partnering with selective customers to create superior value for the company and the customer. It involved the integration of marketing, sales, customer service, and the supply chain functions of the organization to achieve greater efficiencies and effectiveness in delivering customer value."

In their comprehensive article on the subject, *Application of Data Mining Techniques in Customer Relationship Management: a Literature Review and Classification*[28], Ngai et al. argue that these varying definitions emphasize the importance of "viewing CRM as a comprehensive process of acquiring and retaining customers, with the help of business intelligence, to maximize the customer value to the organization."

In this book, we will consider CRM as a two-part process that allows a sports book to track and organize its current and prospective customers, as well as to manage the endpoints of customer relationships through its marketing promotions. When done right, CRM systems enable data to be converted into information that provides insight into customer behavior.

The process of segmenting a market is deceptively simple; seven basic steps describe the entire process, including segmentation, targeting, and positioning. In practice, however, the task can be very laborious since it involves poring over loads of data, and it requires a great deal of skill in analysis, interpretation and some personal judgment.

Today, personalized web pages can be rendered during a web page load and elements of the page can take into account past purchase history, clickstream information, as well as a whole host of other details. In chapter two, I will delve into the how and why of these systems in detail.

Data coming from mobile and social media sources like WeChat, Weibo, Facebook, YouTube, Twitter, YouKu, etc., tend to be highly unstructured, while data coming from CSVs, XML and JSON feeds are considered semi-structured.

NoSQL databases are also considered semi-structured, while text within documents, logs, survey results, and e-mails also fall into the unstructured category. Structured data coming in from the plethora of sports betting source systems, undoubtedly, can feed into a data lake, where it can be merged with unstructured data and then utilized in ways that are almost impossible for a normal relational DW to handle.

Highly structured patron data could be combined with unstructured data coming in from social media to reveal deep customer insights. If a patron tweets about an upcoming premiere league match, why shouldn't the sports betting's marketing department be alerted? This could help with real-time marketing.

Setting up JSON feeds for Twitter user accounts is a very simple process and many other social media companies offer APIs that allow access to customer accounts. These are two-way systems as well, and the sports book's marketing department could include social media as a channel to connect with customers and potential customers. These and other social media marketing campaign ideas will be discussed further in chapters three and four.

How does a sports book get a player's WeChat, RenRen, Facebook, Twitter, Weibo, YouTube, or even Twitch account? Easy, just make the patron an offer he or she can't refuse and, in most cases, that offer probably wouldn't have to be much more than a coupon for free play.

With quick and easy accessibility to a sports book's data, customer conversion rates can be improved, revenue can be increased, and customer churn can be predicted and, hopefully, mitigated as much as possible. Customer acquisition costs can also be lowered. By utilizing the complex web of customer data coming in from several different channels—mobile, social media, customer loyalty programs, transaction data, e-commerce weblogs, sensors, amongst others—a sports book can also work more productively.

As Kai Wähner explains in his article *Real-Time Stream Processing as Game Changer in a Big Data World with Hadoop and Data Warehouse*[29], "Stream processing is required when data has to be processed fast and/or continuously, i.e. reactions have to be computed and initiated in real time." Wähner continues[29]:

> *"'Streaming processing' is the ideal platform to process data streams or sensor data (usually a high ratio of event throughput versus numbers of queries), whereas "complex event processing" (CEP) utilizes event-by-event processing and aggregation (e.g. on potentially out-of-order events from a variety of sources—often with large numbers of rules or business logic). CEP engines are optimized to process discreet 'business events' for example, to compare out-of-order or out-of-stream events, applying decisions and reactions to event patterns, and so on. For this reason multiple types of event processing have evolved, described as queries, rules and procedural approaches (to event pattern detection)."*

Stream processing acts on real-time streaming data feeds, using "continuous queries" (i.e., SQL-type queries that operate over time and buffer windows).[29] With its ability to continuously calculate mathematical or statistical analytics on the fly within the stream, streaming analytics is an essential part of stream processing.[29] "Stream processing solutions are designed to handle high volume in real time with a scalable, highly available and fault tolerant architecture," adds Wähner.[29]

"In contrast to the traditional database model where data is first stored and indexed and then subsequently processed by queries, stream processing takes the inbound data while it is in flight, as it streams through the server," explains Wähner.[29] Stream processing can also connect to an external data source, thereby adding a whole new dimension to analytical processes. Think data from social media, geo-location, facial recognition, shelf sensor data, RFID inputs, or a whole host of other data streams.

In chapter five, I detail several different stream processing engines currently available, with each one's pros and cons. I also lay out the required components of a stream processing system. Since these are highly complex systems, there are only a few market-ready products available, and a lot of custom coding is required to implement them.[29] However, products like Apache Storm, Apache Spark, IBM InfoSphere Streams, Hitachi's Streaming Data Platform, TIBCO StreamBase, and Apache Samza are all interesting platforms to explore and I will go into detail about them in chapter five.

Table 1 shows the general use cases for AI broken down by industry. This is a generalized list and many of these use cases can be utilized by industries other than the ones specified.

GENERAL USE CASE	INDUSTRY
Sound	
Voice recognition	UX/UI, Automotive, Security, IoT
Voice search	Handset maker, Telecoms
Sentiment analysis	CRM for most industries
Flaw detection	Automotive, Aviation
Fraud detection	Finance, Credit cards
Time Series	
Log analysis/Risk detection	Data centers, Security, Finance
Enterprise resource planning	Manufacturing, Auto, Supply Chain
Predictive analytics using sensor data	IoT, Smart home, Hardware

GENERAL USE CASE	INDUSTRY
	manufacturing
Business and Economic analytics	Finance, Accounting, Government
Recommendation engine	E-Commerce, Media, Social Networks
Text	
Sentiment analysis	CRM, Social Media, Reputation mgmt.
Augmented search, Theme detection	Finance
Threat detection	Social Media, Government
Fraud detection	Insurance, Finance
Image	
Facial recognition	Multiple industries
Image search	Social Media
Machine vision	Automotive, Aviation
Photo clustering	Telecom, Handset makers
Video	
Motion detection	Gaming, UX, UI
Real-time threat detection	Security, Airports

Table 1: A.I. use cases
Source: deeplearning4j.org

AI can also play a huge role in automation in a multitude of industries, including the sports betting industry. Currently, there is an interesting philosophical problem rearing its ugly head around automation, something perfectly captured in Kevin Roose's *NY Times* article *The Hidden Automation Agenda of the Davos Elite*.[30] Roose reports that, at Davos 2019, there were "panel discussions about building 'human-centered A.I.' for the 'Fourth Industrial Revolution'—Davos speak for the corporate adoption of machine learning and other advanced technology—and talk about the need to provide a safety net for people who lose their jobs as a result of automation."[30]

What's interesting about the article is Roose's explanation that, whereas the corporate CEOs who attended Davos were publicly fretting about the potential job loses an automation revolution will unquestionably bring, behind the scenes executive were racing to automate as fast as they could, with little concern for the impending cuts to their work force.[30] Automation was seen as just another way for businesses to get a leg up on their competition, the worker be damned.[30] This attitude speaks of how integral AI will be to future IT ROI endeavors and, although many will fail in their AI and ML journey, it won't be for wont of trying.

"All over the world, executives are spending billions of dollars to transform their businesses into lean, digitized, highly automated operations. They crave the fat profit margins automation can deliver, and they see A.I. as a golden ticket to savings, perhaps by letting them whittle departments with thousands of workers down to just a few dozen," says Roose.[30]

"People are looking to achieve very big numbers," said Mohit Joshi, the president of Infosys, a technology and consulting firm that helps other businesses automate their operations.[30] "Earlier they had incremental, 5 to 10 percent goals in reducing their work force. Now they're saying, 'Why can't we do it with 1 percent of the people we have?'"[30]

Some experts claim that AI will create more jobs than it destroys, and that job losses caused by automation won't be catastrophic, but rather automation will help workers become more productive and will free them from repetitive work, giving them more time for creative tasks over routine ones, notes Roose.[30]

Much of this discussion is going on behind closed doors as political unrest in the West makes automation a taboo subject right now.[30] "That's the great dichotomy," says Ben Pring, the director of Center for the Future of Work at Cognizant, a technology services firm, "On the one hand, Pring says, these profit-minded executives want to automate as much as possible, on the other hand, they fear a backlash in civic society."[30]

However, if you want to hear how American leaders talk about automation in private, you need only listen to what their counterparts in Asia say, claims Roose.[30] Terry Gou, the chairman of the Taiwanese electronics manufacturer Foxconn, says the company plans to replace 80 percent of its workforce with robots in the next five to 10 years.[31] Richard Liu, the founder and CEO of Chinese e-commerce company JD.com, hopes to one day have a completely automated company—100% operated by AI and robots—and it has invested $4.5 billion to build an AI center in Guangdong, China, to implement such a scenario.[32]

Automation doesn't just have to be about robots and factories, however, but can remove the day-to-day drudgery work. As I will explain later in the book, there are AI tools out there that can automate away the repetitive processes like cataloging images or video and let human do what humans do best—create.

Google Duplex has shown that AI bots can do things like make reservations at hair salons and restaurants and this is one of the deep learning futures. Sports books need to develop voice and speech understanding technology or they risk being left behind by their competition. Voice, in particular, is a technology waiting for mass use. We communicate through voice as much as any other sense and the companies that win the battle in voice will win the battle for the 21st Century consumer, I believe.

In a March 2017 note to clients[33], RBC Capital argued that Amazon's voice assistant Alexa "could bring the U.S. e-commerce giant $10 billion of revenues by 2020 and be a 'mega-hit.'" According to Arjun Kharpal, "The investment bank has dubbed the technology 'voice-activated internet (VAI)' and said it represents a 'material opportunity' for both Amazon and Google, which has its own technology called Google Assistant."[33]

RBC breaks down the numbers as follows[33]:

- Alexa device sales, which could reach $60 million by 2020.
- Voice driven shopping sales, which could reach $400 per customer by 2020.
- Platform revenues: If Amazon reaches over 100 million installed Alexa devices then it could create an app store and tap into "platform revenue."
- Amazon Web Services (AWS) tailwind.[33]

RBC Capital notes that, "As the number of skills rises, Amazon will create a marketplace that will allow them to charge companies to appear more prominently in its app store."[33] Paid skills on Alexa could be lucrative and Amazon could collect revenue share payments accordingly.

Of course, Amazon is not alone in the voice activated internet (VAI) market.[33] Google has its own voice assistant built into Android smartphones and its own smart speaker called Google Home.[33] According to Kharpal, "RBC was surprised by the popularity of Google Home since it was only launched in October 2016 in the U.S."[33] Apple and Microsoft are also highly involved here. Siri hasn't been the success Apple hoped it would be but they still see it as an integral part of their VAI future.

"Awareness of Google Home among 1,748 Amazon customers surveyed by RBC was 60 percent. Whereas when RBC did a similar survey in September 2015, just shortly after the Echo had launched widely in the U.S., only 33 percent of respondents had heard of Alexa. Google however still only has around 80 Actions, which are like Alexa's skills, which total above 10,000," explains Kharpal.[33]

All-in-all, the *A.I. Sports Book* doesn't have to concern itself with who might win the VAI battle as any of these platforms can bring considerable eyeballs to the table. However, any money spent to reach these eyeballs should produce a healthy ROI. The app market that Amazon could build atop Alexa could also be a hidden opportunity for creative marketers.

One of the major use cases for AI is sentiment analysis, which uses natural language processing (NLP) to gain insight into how a business is seen on social media. According to skymind.ai[34]:

> "Natural language refers to language that is spoken and

written by people, and natural language processing (NLP) attempts to extract information from the spoken and written word using algorithms. NLP encompasses active and a [sic] passive modes: natural language generation (NLG), or the ability to formulate phrases that humans might emit, and natural language understanding (NLU), or the ability to build a comprehension of a phrase, what the words in the phrase refer to, and its intent. In a conversational system, NLU and NLG alternate, as algorithms parse and comprehend a natural-language statement and formulate a satisfactory response to it."

Another important area for AI is text analytics. In his article *Text Analytics: How to Analyse and Mine Words and Natural Language in Businesses*[35], Bernard Marr states that, "Text analytics, also known as text mining, is a process of extracting value from large quantities of unstructured text data." Marr explains that, "While the text itself is structured to make sense to a human being (i.e., A company report split into sensible sections) it is unstructured from an analytics perspective because it doesn't fit neatly into a relational database or rows and columns of a spreadsheet. Traditionally, the only structured part of text was the name of the document, the date it was created and who created it."[35]

"Access to huge text data sets and improved technical capability means text can be analysed to extract high-quality information above and beyond what the document actually says," Marr argues.[35] "Text can be assessed for commercially relevant patterns such as an increase or decrease in positive feedback from customers, or new insights that could lead to product tweaks, etc."[35] This means text analytics can help us discover things we didn't already know but, perhaps more importantly, had no way of previously knowing.[35] These could be incredibly important insights for a business both about itself and, potentially, about its competitors.[35]

Marr says that, "Text analytics is particularly useful for information retrieval, pattern recognition, tagging and annotation, information extraction, sentiment assessment and predictive analytics."[35] It could both reveal what customers think about a company's products or services, or highlight the most common issues that instigate customer complaints.[35]

China and Chinese apps like WeChat don't have the problem that every America and European app has—the need for privacy—which allows them to collect all kinds of data on their users. Because the Chinese government places the onus of censorship on the social media companies, these companies need to collect as much information as they can to ensure compliance, even to the point of not allowing messages about particular people and/or topic across their platforms for fear of government reprisals.

Human beings are, first and foremost, creatures of habit and, if a business can understand these habits on both a micro and macro level, it can not only predict what its customers are going to want, but also what they will do, so a business can, potentially, shape that behavior. Smart businesses can utilize all this behavior in a predictive way and optimize multiple parts of their operations, including labor management.

Marketing has always been about influencing people's behavior and what could be different here is *The A.I. Sports Book's* ability to understand how one customer's actions will affect the company's entire operation. With this insight extrapolated over a million customers over 365 days of the year, the brand can take the most appropriate—and optimized—action to reap the highest profit.

In his article *How Real-time Marketing Technology Can Transform Your Business*[36], Dan Woods makes an amusing comparison of the differing environments that today's marketers face compared to what their 1980s counterparts did:

> *"Technology has changed marketing and market research into something less like golf and more like a multi-player first-person-shooter game. Crouched behind a hut, the stealthy marketers, dressed in business-casual camouflage, assess their weapons for sending outbound messages. Email campaigns, events, blogging, tweeting, PR, ebooks, white papers, apps, banner ads, Google Ad Words, social media outreach, search engine optimization. The brave marketers rise up and blast away, using weapons not to kill consumers but to attract them to their sites, to their offers, to their communities. If the weapons work, you get incoming traffic."*[36]

Real-time stream processing is an integral part of this rapidly changing marketing environment and if sports books don't join the real-time marketing world, they will certainly be left behind, I have no doubt.

Successful mobile advertising requires three things—reach, purity and analytics; reach can be fostered by accessing accounts through multiple platforms like blogs, geofencing applications, OTT services, mobile apps, QR codes, push and pull services, RSS feeds, search, social media sites, and video-casting, amongst others.[37] "Purity" refers to the message and its cleanliness; if the data is unstructured and untrustworthy it is, basically, useless and data governance is paramount for real-time advertising to work properly.[37] The third ingredient, analytics, "involves matching users' interests—implicit and explicit, context, preferences, network and handset conditions—to ads and promotions in real time."[37]

Knowing what might interest a consumer is only half the battle to making the sale and this is where customer analytics comes in. Customer analytics has evolved from simply reporting customer behavior to segmenting a customer based on his or her profitability, to predicting that profitability, to improving those predictions (because of the inclusion of new data), to *actually manipulating customer behavior* with target-specific promotional offers and context-aware marketing campaigns. These are the channels that real-time thrives in and this is where a sports book can gain a powerful competitive advantage.

Think about how much more powerful a marketing offer would be if it was sent to a customer as they were settling into a seat at an AFL game if they had shown a past propensity to bet while attending a game, especially if it was for a particular type of bet that the customer often made; personalization at its finest.

Composing the marketing message, however, is probably the easiest part of the process. In its *Delivering New Levels of Personalization In Consumer Engagement*[38], Forrester Research found that survey participants believed that personalization had the potential to increase traffic, raise customer conversion rates, and increase average order value. Surveyed marketers felt that personalization capabilities could improve a variety of business metrics, including customer retention (75%), lifetime customer value (75%), and customer conversion rates (71%).[38]

Today, "Personalization" is becoming the optimum word in a radically different business environment and even though this personalization comes at a price—privacy—it is a price most consumers seem more than willing to pay if a recognized value is received in return. For the sports book, "personalization" requires an investment in software analytics, but sports books should recognize that this price must be paid because highly sophisticated consumers will soon need an exceptional betting experience to keep them from switching to a competitor. This kind of personalization also gives the sports book powerful information to build optimization models that can reduce cost and increase productivity down the line.

These survey participants see email, call centers, corporate websites, mobile websites and physical locations (such as stadiums, sporting venues and hospitality sites) as today's key customer interaction channels, but any future marketing efforts to reach them should be "focused on mobile websites, applications, and social media channels."[38] Sport book operators should keep these channels in mind while devising their customer experience (CX) campaigns.

Understanding customer-specified preferences is imperative for personalization; "80% of marketing executives currently use them in some or all interaction channels. In addition, 68% of marketers personalize current customer interactions based on past customer interaction history. Other commonly used personalization methods used by nearly 60% of firms in some or all of their interaction channels are based on the time of day or day of the week of customer interactions."[38] *Forrester Research* states that the difficulties of personalization include[38]:

1. Continuously optimizing campaigns in response to a customer's most recent interactions.
2. Optimizing content or offers for each person by matching identities to available products, promotions, messages, etc.
3. Creating a single repository containing structured and unstructured data about a consumer.
4. Delivering content or offers to a customer's chosen channel in real time for purposes of conversion.
5. Analyzing all available data in real time to create a comprehensive, contextually sensitive consumer profile.

The executives pooled by *Forrester Research* expected there to be a "huge rise in personalization using consumer's emotional state, social media sentiment, and context"[38] as well. "Only 29% of respondents claim today to use inferences about the consumer's emotional state in some or all channels. But 53% expect to do this in two to three years' time."[38] Forester's report goes on to add, "Only 52% of marketers currently use sentiments that consumers express in social media to personalize interactions today, but fully 79% expect to do this in two to three years. In addition, only 54% capitalize on the consumer's current contextual behavior, but 77% expect to do so in two to three years' time."[38]

Today, mobile apps, mobile commerce, mobile chat, and mobile gaming have revolutionized the way people do business, seek entertainment, and gamble. Mobile commerce has evolved into what has become known as "omni-commerce", a seamless approach to selling that puts the shopper's experience front and center, giving that shopper access to what he or she wants through these multiple channels.

Mobile marketing via Bluetooth, OTT, SMS, MMS, CSC and/or QR codes has become some of the most effective marketing around, while social media has turned the normal customer channels—and even the idea of marketing—on its head. By accessing the web through a wireless connection, mobile users can surf the Internet as seamlessly as if they were using a PC at home. At the touch of a button, photos and videos can be uploaded seconds after they are taken, then shared with the most intimate of friends or the most distant of peoples. Live streaming channels allow cheap video streams that can be viewed almost anywhere on the planet as well. People in the crowd at a soccer match can, literally, live stream a football match to their friends and followers via Facebook Live, Periscope, YouTube, or Twitch, while adding his or her own personality to the commentary.

The mobile platform is so robust and it holds so much promise that if a marketing executive had been asked to dream up the perfect device to connect to, market to, and sell its company's products and/or services to its customers and potential customers, he or she could hardly have come up with something more superior to it. One of mobile's best features is its ability to cross-pollinate the marketing message through several mediums, which include social media—and I will expound upon this throughout the book.

In its paper *5 E-Commerce Marketing Prediction For the Next 5 Years*[39], the B2C marketing cloud company Emarsys argues that, "Smart marketers need real-time insights into mobile marketing performance in order to understand how end users are (or aren't) engaging with their mobile marketing programs or applications."

Emarsys adds that[39]:

> *"We will move from a world focused on designing for mobile as a secondary approach, to designing for mobile first. E-commerce organizations will finally fully alter the online shopping experience from responsive to completely mobile experiences. This mobile-only approach will be different, as it won't just be a smaller design but will also include more responsive websites and shopping experiences. The mobile-only experience will lead to fully tailored shopping experiences primarily designed for engagement on a mobile device."*

Emarsys goes on to say that: "Within the next five years, consumers will be able to swipe right, up, and down to make their selections, all via their mobile devices. And when the consumer is ready to complete the transaction? Easy. It just takes one click; the purchase is complete, and the items arrive at the consumer's house."[39]

The stakes couldn't be any higher. In its paper, Emarsys concludes that, "In an effort to remain competitive and innovative in today's digital and always-connected world, marketers should continually be piloting and testing mobile strategies with a small subset of their users or target audience."[39] However, "If a brand slows mobile innovation, or pauses testing and optimization for mobile devices, the brand is risking the loyalty of current users as well as jeopardizing new user acquisition," warns Emarsys.[39]

Much more than a wireless transmitter optimized for voice input and output, a mobile phone, a tablet, or a phablet is an always-on, anytime, anywhere marketing and sales tool that follows a mobile user throughout his or her digital day.[37] It is also an entertainment, CRM, and social networking tool, which makes it, potentially, the most powerful device in the history of marketing and customer relations.[37] The mobile device is, literally, a marketing tool that can—and usually is—personalized by its owner, and it is within reach of that owner almost every hour of every single day—once again a marketer's dream.[37]

Push technology even puts the power of communication into the hands of the marketer, allowing sports books to both initiate contact with an opted-in customer and then sending him or her a wide variety of products and content. Most large sports books now have mobile apps in which they can connect to their patrons. As long as a customer is opted into a CRM system, a sports book can foster a two-way dialogue with that customer and this dialogue can grow more sophisticated over time as more is learned about the customer's wants, desires, habits, and needs.

Push technology has moved from clumsy blanket SMS blasts to the sophisticated use of mobile apps that allow customers to interact with their personal patron points balance information.

I didn't want this book to only focus on developments in the United States, as I believe some of the most interesting things happening right now in the betting industry occurs in Asia. I had thought this before I moved to Macau in 2011 and my suspicions were confirmed after I made a few trips into China during the ensuing years.

One of the most important elements of social media is its inter-connectedness. An upload to YouTube can go viral through Twitter, Facebook, LinkedIn, WeChat, WhatsApp, Youku, as well as a whole host of other social media and mobile media platforms instantly.

Within seconds, something uploaded onto a social media website in the US can end up on a mobile application in China or Japan or Korea, or almost anywhere else in the world that has mobile or Wi-Fi access. We are truly living in an interconnected world and this interconnectedness is creating a whole host of ways to market a product, a service, or even a sports book. Of course, Macau and Hong Kong sports books cannot market their gambling offerings inside China, but there is no restriction on marketing sports book product to a Chinese audience outside the Mainland.

Social media will also be explored in depth throughout this book. It is quite ironic that, in one sense, engaging in social media can be one of the most anti-social behaviors one can do; sitting alone in a room, typing away on a computer was once the realm of solitary computer geeks, but it has now become an activity that most people engage in almost every single day. Perhaps this is because human beings are, first and foremost, social beings and we crave a connectedness that social media offers, even if it is a virtual connection. The use of social media on mobile has expanded its reach exponentially as well, making it the perfect place to market sports betting products and services.

It should be of no surprise that one of the greatest inventions of the twentieth century—the internet—would became the watering hole of the twenty-first century; a place where human beings can quickly gather to socialize and connect with friends, family members, and acquaintances in a way that was almost inconceivable only 20 years ago. Smart sports betting marketers can tap into this interconnectedness to get their marketing message out far and wide.

Almost a decade ago, "most consumers logged onto the Internet to access e-mail, search the web, and do some online shopping. Company web sites functioned as vehicles for corporate communication, product promotion, customer service, and, in some cases, e-commerce. Relatively few people were members of online communities"[40] and "Liking" something had no social context at all. How times have changed.

"Today, more than 1.5 billion people around the globe have an account on a social networking site, and almost one in five online hours is spent on social networks—increasingly via mobile devices."[40] In little more than a decade, social technology has become a cultural, social, political and economic phenomenon.[40] Most importantly, "hundreds of millions of people have adopted new behaviors using social media—conducting social activities on the Internet, creating and joining virtual communities, organizing political activities"[40], even, as with the case of Egypt's "Twitter Revolution", toppling corrupt governments.

In his article *Understanding social media in China*[40], C.I. Chui argues that the secret to social media's growth is right there in its name—"Social"—as in the fundamental human behavior of seeking "identity and 'connectedness' through affiliations with other individuals and groups that share their characteristics, interests, or beliefs."[40] For Chui, "Social media taps into well known, basic sociological patterns and behaviors, sharing information with members of the family or community, telling stories, comparing experiences and social status with others, embracing stories by people with whom we desire to build relations, forming groups, and defining relationships to others."[40]

Social technologies allow individuals to interact with large groups of people at almost any location in the world, at any time of the day, at marginal, if not no cost at all.[40] With advantages like these, it is not surprising that social media has become so widespread that almost one-in-four people worldwide uses it. It is actually surprising that the figure is so low, although with mobile technology rolling out in some of the most remote locations on earth, that figure is sure to climb rapidly over the next few years.

Businesses are also quickly recognizing the power of social media. In his article *The social economy: Unlocking the value and productivity through social technologies*, M.M. Chui argues that, "Thousands of companies have found that social technologies can generate rich new forms of consumer insights—at lower cost and faster than conventional methods."[41] In addition to this, businesses can watch what "consumers do and say to one another on social platforms, which provide unfiltered feedback and behavioral data (i.e., do people who "like" this movie also "like" this brand of vodka?)."[40] This can be a treasure trove of company competitive analysis and I believe sports books would profit from spending more on these types of social media listening efforts.

Social technologies also "have enormous potential to raise the productivity of knowledge workers,"[41] a very significant development in a world where knowledge workers are becoming highly sought-after assets. "Social technologies promise to extend the capabilities of such high-skill workers (who are increasingly in short supply) by streamlining communication and collaboration, lowering barriers between functional silos, and even redrawing the boundaries of the enterprise to bring in additional knowledge and expertise in 'extended networked enterprises.'"[41] Gambling can be seen as a sin industry and therefore not a coveted industry to work it. Raising the productivity of skilled workers within this industry would be a very welcomed benefit.

In this book, I will use Chui et al.'s definition of "social technologies" as the "products and services that enable social interactions in the digital realm, and thus allow people to connect and interact virtually."[41] These include:

> "A message to be communicated (a tweet or a blog), adding content to what is already online, or adding information about content ('liking' a piece of content). Content creation also includes performing an action that an individual knows will be automatically shared (e.g., listening to a piece of music when you know your music choice will be displayed to others). Social technologies allow anyone within a group to access and consume content or information. They include technologies that also have been described as 'social media,' 'Web 2.0' and 'Collaboration tools'."[41]

In their book *Marketing Communications: Integrating Offline and Online with Social Media*[42], P.R. Smith and Ze Zook show just how powerful social media marketing can be. Smith and Zook looked at the target audiences for three different types of marketing platforms—broadcast network, telephone and email network, and social media.[42]

According to Smith and Zook, "Broadcast network is based on a 'one to many' model (e.g., old TV advertising)."[42] It is the Sarnoff network (after David Sarnoff, the broadcasting legend).[42] A hypothetical Sarnoff network with 20 viewers has a score of 20.[42] The network score is simply the number of nodes (i.e., audience members)" and this equates to a paltry sum of twenty individuals.[42]

The telephone and email network is based on the Metcalf model (named after Bob Metcalf, one of the inventors of the internet) and this is a "many to each other" model.[42] This model allows everyone in the group to connect with everyone else.[42] Because any member of the group can contact anyone else in the group, the total number of potential contacts is 20 squared, or 400.[42] Obviously, this is a much more powerful communication model than the Sarnoff model as the network score is the node number to the power of 2, which is 400.[42]

A good number, but it still pales in comparison to the social network model.

Named after David Reed (who noticed that people in social situations usually belong to more than just one network), the social network model is a "many belong to numerous networks" model.[42] "The possible value of a Reed network is two to the power of the number of nodes on the network," explain Smith and Zook.[42] If you take the same group of 20 people in a social situation, a "Reed network generates a score of 2 to the power of the node"[42], which generates a network score of over one million people; obviously, this is a number exponentially higher than the number of people reached by the Sarnoff and Metcalf models. This is the power of social media and it cannot be underestimated. When coupled with mobile, that number can be even greater and, just as importantly, the reach can be lightning fast.

In China, users spend more than 40 percent of their time online on social media websites, a figure that is expected to continue its rapid rise over the next few years.[40] "This appetite for all things social has spawned a dizzying array of companies, many with tools that are more advanced than those in the West: for example, Chinese users were able to embed multimedia content in social media more than 18 months before Twitter users could do so in the United States."[40]

There is an old adage in social media marketing that says, "Content is king" and, with social media, that adage has never been more true. Those destined to succeed in the social media sphere won't be the ones with the most content; they will be the ones with the best and most searchable content, especially amongst sports books, which should see social media as a great channel to find and connect with its audience.

This content will drive eyeballs unlike any other form of marketing in the history of advertising. To succeed in this new environment, sports books should think of themselves first and foremost as creators and syndicators of content.[43] But "If content is king, then 'conversion is queen,'" argues John Munsel, CEO of Bizzuka, and he has an important point there; social media is about converting customers, driving eyeballs, and building channels to reach them.

For sports books, the content they can create is content around the games they take bets on. There are countless sporting events to market to sports bettors. Social media can also contain memes, status updates, images as well as user generated content. The idea is to get a reaction from the fans and followers; engagement is key, selling is not.

Chapter three delves into the world of social media, including a breakdown of Kaplan and Haelein's six types of social media.[44] In their influential article *Users of the world, unite! The challenge and opportunities of Social Media*[44], Kaplan and Haenlein show how all social media websites can be broken down into one of six different types; collaborative projects; blogs and micro-blogs; content communities; social networking sites; virtual game worlds; and virtual social worlds.[44] Anyone devising a sports book's social media marketing plan should find this chapter particularly helpful in understanding how to use each separate channel and platform, both singularly and combined together.

Besides being an interesting place to market to companies, one of the six types of social media--virtual game worlds—actually offers betting opportunities. Esports, which exist in virtual game worlds, has exploded, becoming a massive industry that has drawn sponsorship money in the tens of millions of dollars. Betting on esports is now available on most large sports books and skins betting, i.e., betting on in-game items, became so prevalent that it caused serious problems for game publishers the Steam marketplace.

As per Wikipedia[45], "Valve added random skin rewards as part of an update to *Counter-Strike: Global Offensive* in 2013, believing that players would use these to trade with other players and bolster both the player community and its Steam marketplace." However, a "number of websites were created to bypass monetary restrictions Valve set on the Steam marketplace to aid in high-value trading and allowing users to receive cash value for skins."[45] Some sites let players gamble on the results of professional matches or in games of chance with these skins[45], which "in 2016 was estimated to handle around $5 billion of the virtual goods."[45] "These sites, as well as Valve, quickly came under scrutiny because of legal and ethical questions relating to gambling on sporting matches, underage gambling, undisclosed promotion, and outcome rigging.[45] As Wikipedia explains, "Evidence of such unethical practices was discovered in June 2016, and led to two formal lawsuits filed against these sites and Valve in the following month."[45]

This is the world we now live in, people, even underage kids, are gambling on virtual items to win real money on games in virtual environments. A gambling market of $5 billion appeared almost overnight and shut down a year later, but this story alone reveals the extraordinary betting market available to sports books that chose to offer odds on esports.

In chapter five, Hadoop and data lakes take center stage. A Hadoop database is the cornerstone of any data lake and, throughout this chapter, I will explain how to design an HDFS schema, what to consider regarding data ingestion, compression, and extraction. Hadoop can get very complicated, very quickly, so any company wishing to implement a Hadoop database should understand all of the components it is made of; from A(vro) to Z(ookeeper) and everything in-between.

I will also explain the current stream processing and machine learning (ML) solutions available in the market so that a sports book can build a powerful EDW that ingests social media data and then fires off a marketing coupon to the right person at the right time, at the right price, to be used at the right location, at just the right time, at a set ROI. A worthy goal, if ever there was one.

Fraud can wreak havoc on a sports book's bottom line and every sports book must be extremely vigilant to ensure that there is no fraud or match fixing in the games they offer odds on. Real-time stream processing can help with both cases as I discuss in the match-fixing section in chapter six. In this chapter, I attempt to create a holistic view of how the sports book of the future—*the A.I. Sports Book*—would operate. I have added some real-world examples of how a sports book's IT department would build a data lake or a real-time streaming system that could surface information from facial recognition cameras, POS systems, geo-locating devices, and online behavior. This data would quickly become actionable intelligence once it is put into the hands of front-line staff.

I will also reveal ways to increase website traffic. I will also offer some suggestions on how sports books can build up customer profiles by tracking IP addresses, then associating those with browser footprints, device IDs, social IDs, email addresses, and, ultimately, with onsite or instore transactions. Creating a holistic views of one's customer reveals the true value of that customer and once a true value has been created, marketing offers can be better tailored to the individual, which usually means they are more likely to be used.

My hope is this book can be a blueprint for a sports book to step into the Big Data/predictive analytics/Hadoop/Data Lake world, so that it can both understand its customers on a truly intimate level and also shape the experiences of those customers so that a healthy ROI can be extracted.

Every sports book must ask the question: "When will we reach the point of diminishing returns?", and "Where does the incremental cost of improved performance equal or exceed the incremental value created?" Having a data driven organization is imperative in today's world of demanding customers, who expect highly sophisticated technology to be available to them 24 hours a day.

In this second addition, I have added a full section on the deep learning technologies available in the market. I, along with the Googles, Facebooks, Amazons, etc., of the world, see this as the next important step in the evolution of AI and Machine Learning. Many of these solutions have been open sourced by their creators and a large and active community is growing up around them. TensorFlow and Caffe2 are the two most popular platforms and I will detail why a sports book might choose one over the other, as well as explain most of the other available options.

I started this introduction with an allusion of Big Data being either a useful treasure trove or a Pandora's Box full of pain and it can certainly be either one, but going down the Big Data and AI road requires a commitment that is all encompassing and difficult to implement. State of the art technology is required and that always means the potential for severe bumps in the road along the way. However, it is a road that must be traversed as today's consumer have become highly sophisticated and they demand a level of personalization for their continuing patronage; if a company's marketing efforts aren't personal enough, these consumers will find another company that will provide the level of service they insist upon.

Throughout the book, I will try to avoid what has become known as "wishcasting", a useful term that the field of meteorology has recently given us. As Rob Tracinski explains in his article *How Not to Predict the Future*[46], "It started with the observation that weathermen disproportionately predict sunny weather on the 4th of July and snow on Christmas Day. Their forecasts are influenced not just by the evidence, but by what they (or their audience) want to hear." The writer of any book that delves into current and future technology will, obviously, be susceptible to wishcasting, but I will try to temper my enthusiasm and add a dash of skepticism to all written here.

I will also try to avoid "Zeerust"—"The particular kind of datedness which afflicts things that were originally designed to look futuristic."[47] Taken from *The Meaning of Liff* by Douglas Adams, *TV Tropes* explains it this way: "datedness behind zeerusty designs lies in the attempt of the past designers to get an advantage over the technology of their time, only to find out that more mundane designs are actually far more efficient if advanced engineering and craftsmanship are used on them."[47]

Although the focus of this book is the sports betting industry, some examples I provide are for industries other than gaming. Many of the business use cases I discuss won't be from the sports betting industry because there are no use cases, but explanations of how they are being used in the retail, property management, and advertising industries will still be relevant to a sports betting executive, I believe.

Throughout this book, I will offer my honest assessment of the technology I discuss, trying to be as agnostic and objective as possible. Personally, I prefer not to go down rabbit holes of technology that, while proving quite colorful, exciting and interesting, really lead to nowhere, so I will try to point out paths that I think advisable to both take, as well as those not to take, always keeping a firm eye on the prize – the sports book's financial bottom line. In French, "ROI" (or "Roi", more precisely) literally means "King" and in this book, ROI is king; every piece of technology I discuss will be looked at through the principal lens of ROI.

---

1 Sauer, R. (1998), 'The economics of wagering markets', Journal of Economic Literature, 36, 2021–64.
2 Munting, R. (1996), An Economic and Social History of Gambling, Manchester: Manchester University Press.
3 The Daily Telegraph. (2019). Bet was giant step for bookmakers. 20 July 2019.

4 Dewey, Todd. (2019). Las Vegas Review-Journal. Bookmaker William Hill lost bets when US landed on moon in 1969. 17 July 2019. https://www.reviewjournal.com/sports/betting/bookmaker-william-hill-lost-bets-when-us-landed-on-moon-in-1969-1784771/ (Accessed 25 July 2019).

5 Forrest, David. (2006). Handbook on the Economics of Sport. The Economics of Sport. P. 40 – 48. Edward Elgar Publishing Limited. 2006. http://www.ahmetguvener.com/wp-content/uploads/Handbook-on-the-Economics-of-Sport.pdf#page=59

6 The Guardian. (2018). Sports betting set to become legal across US after supreme court decision. Guardian.com. 14 May 2018. https://www.theguardian.com/law/2018/may/14/sports-betting-gambling-legal-supreme-court-decision (Accessed 26 July 2019).

7 Mashayekhi, Rey. (2019). Fortune. Inside the Battle for the Future of Sports Betting. April 10, 2019. https://fortune.com/longform/sports-betting-battle/ (Accessed 26 July 2019).

8 http:www.statista.com/statistics/270757/revenue-sports-betting-companies/ (Accessed 16 January 2018).

9 http://www-01.ibm.com/software/data/bigdata/ (accessed: December 6, 2016)

10 Anderson, C. (2004). Wired. The Long Tail, pp. 171-177.

11 Berman, S. J. (2007). Executive Brief: Navigating the media divide: Innovating and enabling new business models. IBM Institute for Business Value.

12 Gambling Insider. (2018). Sports trading and AI: Taking the human out of sports betting. 5 January 2018. https://www.gamblinginsider.com/in-depth/4729/sports-trading-and-ai-taking-the-human-out-of-sports-betting (Accessed 16 January 2018).

13 SAS. (2019). SAS announces $1 Billion investment in Artificial Intelligence (AI). March 17, 2019. https://www.sas.com/en_us/news/press-releases/2019/march/artificial-intelligence-investment.html (Accessed 28 March 2019).

14 PWC. (2017). Sizing the prize. What's the real value of AI for your business and how you can capitalise. https://www.pwc.com/gx/en/issues/analytics/assets/pwc-ai-analysis-sizing-the-prize-report.pdf (Accessed 19 February 2019).

15 Humanizing Loyalty A road map to establishing genuine emotional loyalty at scale. Olson1to1.com. https://go.lcf.com/rs/072-WJX-782/images/Humanizing%20Loyalty%20-%20Olson%201to1.pdf (Accessed 6 August 2018).

16 Lewnes, Ann and Keller, Kevin Lane. (2019). MIT Sloan Management Review. 10 Principles of Modern Marketing. April 3, 2019. https://sloanreview.mit.edu/article/10-principles-of-modern-marketing/ (Accessed 5 April 2019).

17 Adobe Sensei Team. Adobe. AI: Your behind-the-scenes marketing companion. https://www.adobe.com/insights/sensei-ai-for-marketers.html (Accessed 7 April 2019).

18 Adobe. Artificial intelligence Unlocks the True Power of Analytics. https://www.adobe.com/au/insights/ai-unlocks-the-true-power-of-analytics.html (Accessed 14 January 2019).

19 https://en.wikipedia.org/wiki/Data_lake (Accessed 26 July 2019).

20 Eissler, Annie. 25 April 2017. How Much ROI Can Data Analytics Deliver? MITS Blog. https://www.mits.com/blog/how-much-roi-can-data-analytics-deliver (accessed 22 August 2017)

21 Marr, Bernard. August 23, 2016. Will 'Analytics On The Edge' Be the Future of Big Data? Online: http://www.forbes.com/sites/bernardmarr/2016/08/23/will-analytics-on-the-edge-be-the-future-of-big-data/#124af7ea2b09

22 Gartner. (2013, December 12). Gartner Says the Internet of Things Installed Base Will Grow to 26 Billion Units By 2020. Retrieved from Gartner.com: http://www.gartner.com/newsroom/id/2636073

23 Ashton, K. (2009, June 22). That 'Internet of Things' Thing. Retrieved from RFID Journal: http://www.rfidjournal.com/articles/view?4986

24 Morgan, J. (2014, May 13). A Simple Explanation of 'the Internet of Things'. Retrieved from Forbes.com: http://www.forbes.com/sites/jacobmorgan/2014/05/13/simple-explanation-internet-things-that-anyone-can-understand/

25 Swift, R. (2001). Accelerating customer relationships: Using CRM and relationship technologies. Upper Saddle River: Prentice Hall.

26 Kincaid, J. (2003). *Customer relationship management: Getting it right.* Upper Saddle River, NJ: Prentice Hall.

27 Parvatiyar, A. &. Sheth, JN (2001). Customer relationship management: Emerging practice, process, and discipline. *Journal of Economic & Social Research, 3*, 1 - 34.

28 Ngai, N. X. (2009). Application of data mining techniques in customer relationship management: a literature review and classification. *Expert systems with applications*, 2592-2602.

29 Wähner, Kai (2014, September 10). Real-Time Stream Processing as Game Changer in a Big Data World with Hadoop and Data Warehouse. InfoQ. https://www.infoq.com/articles/stream-processing-hadoop/

30 Roose, Kevin. (2019). NY Times. The Hidden Automation Agenda of the Davos Elite. January 25, 2019. https://www.nytimes.com/2019/01/25/technology/automation-davos-world-economic-forum.html (Accessed 27 January 2019).

31 Tang, Ziyi, and Lahiri, Tripti. (2018). Quartz. Here's how the plan to replace the humans who make iPhones with bots is going. June 22, 2018. https://qz.com/1312079/iphone-maker-foxconn-is-churning-out-foxbots-to-replace-its-human-workers/ (Accessed 27 January 2019).

32 Bird, Jon. (2018). Forbes. Chilling or Thrilling? JD.com Founder Envisions a '100%' Robot Workforce. April 27, 2018. https://www.forbes.com/sites/jonbird1/2018/04/27/chilling-or-thrilling-jd-coms-robotic-retail-future/#520fb59f7fcf (Accessed 27 January 2019).

33 Kharpal, Arjun. (2017). CNBC. Amazon's Alexa voice assistant could be a 10 billion 'mega hit' by 2020: Research. https://www.cnbc.com/2017/03/10/amazon-alexa-voice-assistan-could-be-a-10-billion-mega-hit-by-2020-research.html (Accessed 12 January 2019).

34 Skymind. A beginning's guide to natural language processing. https://skymind.ai/wiki/natural-language-processing-nlp (Accessed 2 January 2019).

35 Marr, Bernard. Bernardmarr.com. Text Analytics: How to Analyse and Mine Words And Natural Language in Businesses. https://bernardmarr.com/default.asp?contentID=1754 (Accessed 8 January 2018).

36 Woods, D. (2011, May 6). How Real-time Marketing Technology Can Transform Your Business. Retrieved from Forbes.com: http://www.forbes.com/sites/ciocentral/2011/05/06/how-real-time-marketing-technology-can-transform-your-business/

37 Sharma, C. H. (2008). Mobile Advertising: Supercharge Your Brand in the Exploding Wireless Market. John Wiley & Sons, Inc.

38 Forrester Research. (2013, November). Delivering New Levels Of Personalization In Consumer Engagement. Retrieved from sap.com: https://www.sap.com/bin/sapcom/he_il/downloadasset.2013-11-nov-21-22.delivering-new-levels-of-personalization-in-consumer-engagement-pdf.html

39 Emarsys. 5 E-Commerce Marketing Predictions for the Next 5 Years. https://www.emarsys.com/en/resources/whitepapers/5-e-commerce-marketing-predictions-for-the-next-5-years/

40 Chiu, C. I. (2012, April). Understanding social media in China. Retrieved from www.mckinsey.com: http://www.mckinsey.com/insights/marketing_sales/understanding_social_media_in_china

41 Chui, Michael, Manyika, James, Bughin, Jaques, Dobbs, Richard, Roxburgh, Charles, Sarrazin, Hugo, Sands, Geoffrey, Westergren. (2012). The social economy: Unlocking value and productivity through social technologies. McKinsey Global Institute.

42 Smith, P. Z. (2011). Marketing Communications: Integrating Offline and Online with Social Media; Third Edition. Kogan Page.

43 Black, L. M. (2012, November 11). 7 social media marketing tips for artists and galleries. Retrieved from Mashable: http://mashable.com/2012/11/10/social-media-marketing-tips-artists-galleries/

44 Kaplan, A. H. (2010). Users of the world unite! The challenges and opportunities of social media. Business Horizons, Vol. 53, Issue 1.

45 https://en.wikipedia.org/wiki/Skin_gambling (Accessed 24 January 2018).

46 Tracinski, Rob. October 13, 2016. How Not to Predict the Future. Real Clear Future. http://www.realclearfuture.com/articles/2016/10/13/how_not_to_predict_the_future_111945.html

47 http://tvtropes.org/pmwiki/pmwiki.php/Main/Zeerust

CHAPTER ONE

Customer Intelligence

"Personalization is table stakes for today's retailers, who are increasingly competing to be relevant in the hearts and minds of shoppers."

~Giselle Abramovich, Adobe

Overview

Today, "Personalization"—the process of utilizing geo-location, mobile app, Wi-Fi, and OTT technology to tailor messages or experiences to an individual interacting with them—is becoming the optimum word in a radically new customer intelligence environment. Even though this personalization comes at a hefty cost—privacy—it is a price most consumers seem more than willing to pay if a recognized value is received in return.

For a sports book marketer, "personalization" requires an investment in analytical software, but sports book should recognize that this price must be paid because highly sophisticated consumers will soon need an exceptional customer shopping experience to keep them from visiting a competitor (who will, undoubtedly, offer such services). This kind of personalization also gives the sports book powerful information to build optimization models that can reduce cost and increase productivity.

In his article *The Loyalty Effect*, Fred Reichheld cites some CRM research that found a 5% lift in customer retention raised a company's profits by 25% to 95%.[48] *In ROI on CRM: a customer-journey approach*[49], Ang and Buttle argue that, "This is due to the high cost of acquisition, plus the fact that in the early years, customers are often unprofitable. It is only in the latter years when the volumes purchased increase that the customers become profitable." Ang and Buttle add that, "This leads to the idea that a customer should not be viewed from a single transaction, but as a lifetime income stream."[48]

Ang and Buttle also describe the CRM initiatives of the Royal Bank of Canada (RBC), which won the first international award for CRM excellence in large corporations.[48] Started in 1995, RBC's Vice President for CRM claims "we no longer view CRM as a program. [It] is our core strategy."[48] "Revenue growth is running at 10-15% p.a., and profit growth at 25%."[48] The VP adds: "We absolutely conclude the CRM is paying us back in spades. It enabled us to grow both top of the house revenue line and at the same time achieve huge cost savings."[48] The facts don't lie: "RBC's retention of customers is exceptionally high in an industry where some 22% of commercial customers change banks every five years."[50]

Accenture[51], a consultancy active in the CRM space, "found that a 10% improvement in 21 CRM capabilities boosted profits (pre-tax) by as much as $40-$50 million in a $1 billion company."[51] They concluded "that this could be improved even further to $120-150 million if further improvements were made to CRM capability."[51]

A few industry examples from *Information Week's In-memory Databases, IBM, Microsoft, Oracle, and SAP Are Fighting to Become Your In-memory Technology Providers. Do You Really Need the Speed?*[52] might shed some light on why speed is such an important differentiator when it comes to real-time marketing and customer interactions. These include[52]:

- Online gaming company Bwin.party uses in-memory capabilities to handle 150,000 bets per second. This compares to their normal system rate of 12,000 bets per second.
- For retail services company Edgenet, "in-memory technology has brought near-real-time insight into product availability for customers of AutoZone, Home Depot, and Lowe's. That translates into fewer wasted trips and higher customer satisfaction"[52]
- ConAgra, an $18 billion-a-year consumer packaged goods company, "must quickly respond to the fluctuating costs of 4,000 raw materials that go into more than 20,000 products, from Swiss Miss cocoa to Chef Boyardee pasta"[52] and an in-memory system assists them in material forecasting, planning, and pricing.
- ConAgra also taps its in-memory solution to make company promotions more relevant by using faster analysis, which allows ConAgra and its retail customers to command higher prices in an industry notorious for razor-thin profit margins.
- Maple Leaf Foods, a $5 billion-a-year Canadian supplier of meats, baked goods, and packaged foods, finds that profit-and-loss reports which "used to take 15 to 18 minutes on conventional databases now take 15 to 18 seconds on their in-memory platform."[52]
- Temenos, a banking software provider that uses IBM's in-memory-based BLU Acceleration for DB2 system, reports that queries that used to take 30 seconds now take one-third of a second thanks to BLU's columnar compression and in-memory analysis.

Bwin.party's example reveals this technology is giving them a huge improvement from their older technology and it might be good enough to give them a big competitive advantage over their rivals; not only are more bets being taken, but more customers are being made happy. In-play betting has become a huge revenue generator for sports books and speeding up the time it takes to close bets means more money flows into the company's coffers and, in some cases, better odds can be offered to bettors, which could mean the sports book attracts more bettors; it is a virtuous cycle that will certainly help CRM ROI.

For Temenos, that difference in speed means that mobile customers will be able to quickly retrieve all of their banking transactions on their mobile devices, rather than just their last five, which could mean the difference between handling customer issues on a mobile device rather than in a company store.[52] According to *Information Week*, "Online or mobile interaction costs the bank 10 to 20 cents to support versus $5 or more for a branch visit," therefore the cost savings are substantial.[52] A sports book could see similar customer service savings.

Not all of these examples might seem easily relatable to the sports betting industry, but they could be as the potential to market to a patron when he or she is primed to accept a company's advertising is advantageous for both parties involved. Sports book marketers don't have to waste time advertising to consumers when they aren't primed to accept the advertisements, yet do market to consumers when and where they might want to use said advertisements.

At the 2018 CES show, some of the biggest software and hardware manufacturers around, including Google, LG, and Samsung displayed their latest products that included AI, in many cases as part of the interface between product and user. In the retail industry, AI has been used to drive mobile sales and social commerce, to promote products, to create personalized recommendations, as well as understand sentiment analysis and this technology should be directly translatable to the sports betting industry.[53]

To get ahead in this highly competitive sports betting industry, sports books are recognizing the importance of personalization when it comes to customer interactions. Most sports book today have customer loyalty programs that are a part of a CRM and/or a SCRM initiative, which provides its customers with an intimate experience that will make them want to return to the sports book again and again and again.

Currently, however, there is an big disconnect between what companies think they are delivering in terms of personalization and what consumers are actually experiencing. In his article *Study finds marketers are prioritizing personalization... but are further behind then they realize*[54], Andrew Jones says that, "Although two-thirds of the marketers surveyed rate their personalization efforts as 'very good' or 'excellent,' just 31 percent of consumers reported that companies are consistently delivering personalized experiences."[54]

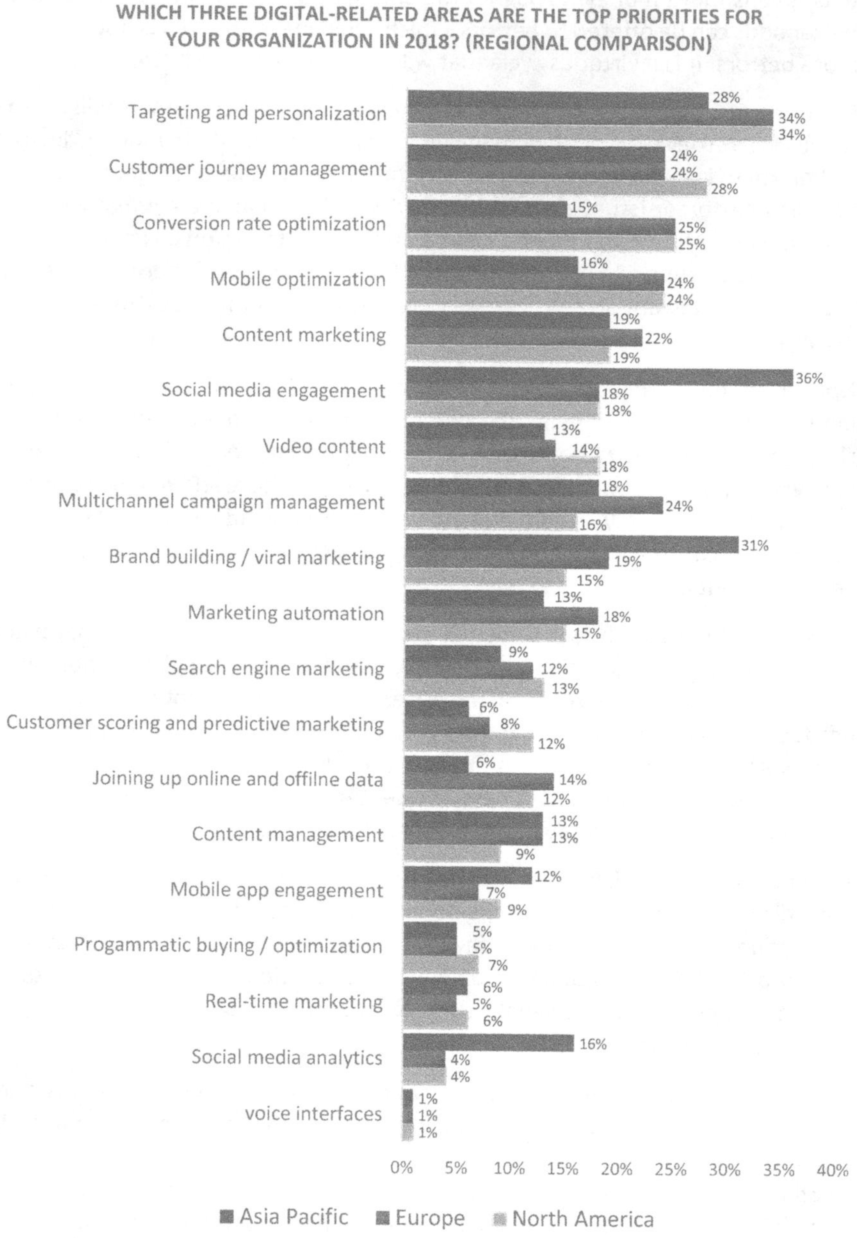

WHICH THREE DIGITAL-RELATED AREAS ARE THE TOP PRIORITIES FOR YOUR ORGANIZATION IN 2018? (REGIONAL COMPARISON)

Priority	Asia Pacific	Europe	North America
Targeting and personalization	28%	34%	34%
Customer journey management	24%	24%	28%
Conversion rate optimization	15%	25%	25%
Mobile optimization	16%	24%	24%
Content marketing	19%	22%	19%
Social media engagement	36%	18%	18%
Video content	13%	14%	18%
Multichannel campaign management	18%	24%	16%
Brand building / viral marketing	31%	19%	15%
Marketing automation	13%	18%	15%
Search engine marketing	9%	12%	13%
Customer scoring and predictive marketing	6%	8%	12%
Joining up online and offilne data	6%	14%	12%
Content management	13%	13%	9%
Mobile app engagement	12%	7%	9%
Progammatic buying / optimization	5%	5%	7%
Real-time marketing	6%	5%	6%
Social media analytics	16%	4%	4%
voice interfaces	1%	1%	1%

■ Asia Pacific ■ Europe ■ North America

Figure 1: Organizations top priorities in 2018?
Source: Adobe 2018 Digital Trends in Retail[55]

Figure 1 "compares the top digital-related 2018 priorities for retailers across regions, with *targeting and personalization* leading the way in both North America and Europe. While not explicitly mentioned, the theme of data again looms large for retailers seeking to personalize and target effectively."[55]

"Aside from this disparity, the report finds that personalization strategies today are immature. It shows that 91 percent of the marketers surveyed are prioritizing personalization over the coming year, yet many still rely on basic segmentation strategies," Jones notes.[54] This isn't that surprising as many companies are struggling with the ability to not just capture the information necessary for personalization, but also creating data warehouses that can silo the data properly, then deliver it to highly complex analytical programs that can make sense of all that data. It's like finding a needle in a haystack for each and every customer in a massive database; a herculean task, no doubt.[54]

It is obvious that creating a consolidated customer view is a necessary component of personalization, but, unfortunately, "most marketers today are working with customer data that is decentralized, spread across the organization in multiple databases that are updated in batch processes. To find success, marketers must prioritize consolidating data into a single database," states Jones.[54]

In its *2018 Digital Trends in Retail*[55], Adobe revealed that "the most exciting prospect through the lens of the retailer is delivering personalized experiences in real time, cited by 37% of retail respondents compared to 36% for client-side respondents in other sectors."[55] This is an interesting survey to keep in mind as retailers are often on the cutting edge of technology. Once they start receiving personalization marketing from the retailer they buy from, customers will expect similar service from just about every other business they deal with from that moment on.

Adobe's *2018 Digital Trends in Retail* reveals that "retailers in Asia are much more focused on social media engagement and brand-building/viral marketing that their counterparts in the West, suggesting that the social and viral marketing opportunity is disproportionally higher in Asia where social uptake has not hit the same kind of plateau as it has in Western markets."[55]

One big cultural difference between the Asian and North American markets is the impact of messaging apps.[55] "Prompted by the launch of brand-friendly Official Accounts on WeChat in 2013, the potential of messaging apps in retail has been embraced more quickly by brands and consumers in China than in the United States, where conversational commerce has been relatively slow to get off the ground."[55]

As Adobe's *2018 Digital Trends in Retail* discovered, "Retailers recognize that the quality of the customer experience will increasingly depend on being able to serve up the most relevant content and messaging at the right moment, with companies embracing predictive analytics to help them anticipate the most effective way of converting prospects into customers, and then meeting their needs on an ongoing basis."[55]

Adobe's *2018 Digital Trends in Retail* reveals that, "The appeal of real-time personalization suggests a focus on providing the most engaging and relevant experiences, a trend that cuts across numerous digital marketing techniques, including analytics, marketing automation, programmatic ad buying and dynamic content."[55]

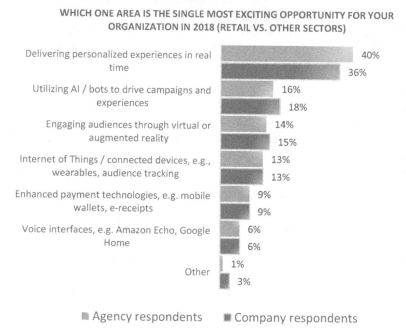

WHICH ONE AREA IS THE SINGLE MOST EXCITING OPPORTUNITY FOR YOUR ORGANIZATION IN 2018 (RETAIL VS. OTHER SECTORS)

Figure 2: Most Exciting Prospects in Three Years' Time?
Source: Adobe 2018 Digital Trends in Retail

"While a range of potential game-changing technological trends in Figure 2 will undoubtedly have a powerful impact, from the Internet of Things and connected devices, to voice interfaces and augmented reality, retailers are predominantly focused on creating a relevant, timely and engaging experience to each of their users, to maximize sales and efficiency."[55]

AI is an example of an emerging technology that can itself help to make the experience more relevant and personalized.[55] "AI-powered machine learning can increasingly help retailers comb through vast quantities of data to provide the best possible content and recommendations to consumers as they progress through the shipping journey from awareness and discovery to conversion."[55]

According to Michael Klein in his article *Machine Learning and AI: If Only My Computer Had a Brain Wired for Business*[56], "AI helps retailers by serving as an adaptive, automated interface for customer interaction. Similar to a human interaction, this interface can work with customers to resolve issues, route deeper concerns to the right people, and offer personalized recommendations." "This is because AI can act on real-time insights supplied from databases that house a user's browsing history, past purchases, and demographics," explains Klein.[56] "Understanding this data opens opportunities for more personalized targeting, and AI can adapt automated approaches in real time to turn shoppers into buyers," says Klein.[56] This is going to be a big deal as, according to Tractica[57], global revenue resulting from AI technologies just in the retail sector alone is expected to top $36.8 billion by 2025.

One thing that was surprising to the researchers was the lack of interest in voice technology, with only 6% of respondents pointing to voice interfaces as the most exciting opportunity.[55] "The popularity of voice assistants offered by the likes of Amazon, Google, Microsoft and Apple give retail brands the chance to increase their presence, including in homes and cars, provided that they can find the right kind of utility to consumers at the right time."[55]

In her 2019 article *8 Things to Expect from CES, Consumer Tech's Big Shindig*[58], Lauren Goode points out that, "There are now over 20,000 smart devices compatible with Alexa, and over 10,000 that work with Google Assistant. CES 2019 will undoubtedly be a noisy cacophony of voice-controlled devices, ranging from refrigerators to sound systems to smart lights in the home, to wearables and cars outside of the home." Goode rightfully claims that "if you add another voice assistant to an existing product, you can call it 'new.'"[58] Snark aside, this is the wave of the future, people are getting very comfortable talking and giving instructions to devices. Goode concludes the article by pointing out a common problem: "The question around voice technology, though, isn't so much whether it will have a presence; the question is whether it will grow more seamless and less awkward this year."[58]

Bright Local, an SEO platform used by thousands of businesses, produced an interesting study[59] on the potential of voice search, which found:

- 58% of consumers have used voice search to find local business information in the last 12 months.
- 46% of voice search users look for a local business on a daily basis.
- What consumers want most: to be able to use voice search to make reservations, to hear business prices, and to find out which products businesses have.
- 27% visit the website of a local business after making a voice search.

- 25% of consumers say they haven't yet tried local voice search but would consider it.
- 76% of smart speaker users perform local searches at least weekly—with 53% searching using these devices every day.
- Consumers are most likely to perform voice searches to find further information on local businesses they already know about.
- Voice searchers are most likely to look for restaurants, grocery stores, and food delivery.
- Just 18% of consumers have used smart speakers for local voice searches.

One of the most important stats about voice is the fact that voice searches on Google are now 30 times more likely than text searches to be action queries.[60]

One of the key demographic findings of the *2018 Adobe Digital Insights (ADI) State of Digital Advertising* report was that Millennials and Gen Zers differ from Generation X, Baby Boomers, and older generations in that, "social channels are where these generations see the most relevant content in their lives."[55] According to Taylor Schreiner, "social advertising is clearly a key part of a paid/owned/earned media strategy, especially if your audience is under 40."[55] This is a fact that businesses should keep in mind going forward as Millennials and Gen Zers are now reaching an age when they will have disposable income, as well as the desire to spend it.

It should be obvious that creating a consolidated customer view is a necessary component of personalization, but, unfortunately, "most marketers today are working with customer data that is decentralized, spread across the organization in multiple databases that are updated in batch processes. To find success, marketers must prioritize consolidating data into a single database," states Jones.[54]

Psychographics—the study and classification of people according to their attitudes, aspirations, and other psychological criteria, especially in market research—is a minor mention in this study, but, as data about people and their behaviors becomes more abundant, this will become an important area to discover customer intelligence. The Cambridge Analytica-Facebook scandal is only now starting to reveal how powerful this kind of information is and, in chapter four, I delve further into this fascinating subject.

Another important step to bringing personalization efforts up to a user's expectation level will be by using behavioral data. "In order to create these types of customer experiences, marketers must strategically collect and utilize customer data, including real-time signals of intent, which are typically not captured today," argues Jones.[54] Figure 3 lists the identity-related data sources that can be used for personalization and it is a considerable amount of data that must be culled through, siloed, and understood for personalization marketing to work properly and effectively.

Identity-related data sources used for personalization

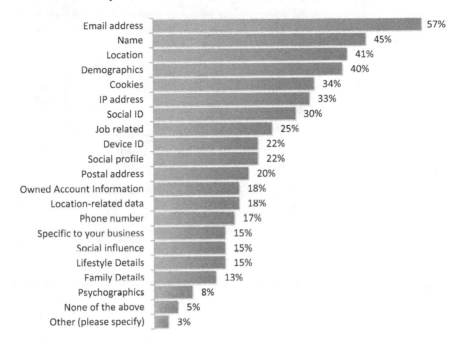

Email address	57%
Name	45%
Location	41%
Demographics	40%
Cookies	34%
IP address	33%
Social ID	30%
Job related	25%
Device ID	22%
Social profile	22%
Postal address	20%
Owned Account Information	18%
Location-related data	18%
Phone number	17%
Specific to your business	15%
Social influence	15%
Lifestyle Details	15%
Family Details	13%
Psychographics	8%
None of the above	5%
Other (please specify)	3%

Figure 3: Identity-related data sources used for personalization
Source: VB Insights[61]

Figure 4 shows the current data types that a typical travel company might be collecting and utilizing. With customer attitudes towards personalized content being shaped by recommendation engines on platforms like Amazon, Pandora, and Netflix, consumers are becoming more and more used to receiving what they want, when they want it, and on whatever channel they want it on.[54] Sports books must keep this in mind when developing personalization programs. The consumer has become highly sophisticated and he or she expects the level of sophistication received on platforms like Amazon to filter over to all his or her other company communications; don't waste a customer's time with non-matching offers or he or she will bet with a competitor.

In her article *3 AI-driven strategies for retailers in 2019[62]*, Giselle Abramovich claims that, "Personalization is table stakes for today's retailers, who are increasingly competing to be relevant in the hearts and minds of shoppers." This is a great analogy as personalization will soon be the base level upon which customers will accept marketing from the companies they choose to buy from.

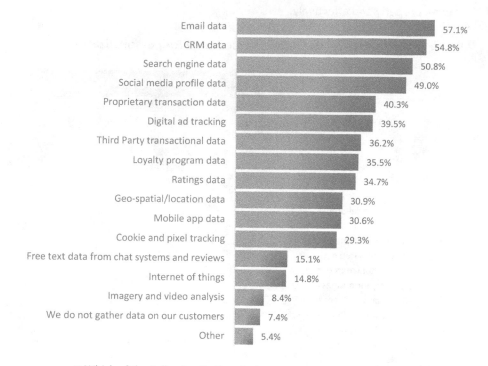

Email data	57.1%
CRM data	54.8%
Search engine data	50.8%
Social media profile data	49.0%
Proprietary transaction data	40.3%
Digital ad tracking	39.5%
Third Party transactional data	36.2%
Loyalty program data	35.5%
Ratings data	34.7%
Geo-spatial/location data	30.9%
Mobile app data	30.6%
Cookie and pixel tracking	29.3%
Free text data from chat systems and reviews	15.1%
Internet of things	14.8%
Imagery and video analysis	8.4%
We do not gather data on our customers	7.4%
Other	5.4%

■ Which of the Following Do You Gather to Generate Insight into Your Customers?

Figure 4: State of Data in Travel Survey, 2017
Source: eyefortravel.com[63]

VB Insights claims that, "Although we may think of the sales process as 'top-down,' most companies implement personalization with a bottom-up approach. That is, most companies begin their personalization efforts based on 'known' prospects or customers. The channels where personalization is being employed reinforce this finding."[61]

According to VB Insights, "Email is the dominant channel for personalized content, yet is often limited to field insertion (e.g. "Dear "). Most personalization efforts are also based on transaction history and limited demographic data, meaning personalization is not done to a high degree in most cases."[61] Figure 5 breaks down the different digital channels that brands can utilize to connect with their customers.

With customer attitudes towards personalized content being shaped by recommendation engines like Amazon, Pandora, and Netflix, consumers are becoming more used to receiving what they want, when they want it, and on whatever channel they want it on.[54] Sports books must keep this in mind when developing personalization programs. The consumer has become highly sophisticated and he or she expects the level of sophistication received on platforms like Amazon, Netflix, and Pandora to filter over to all their other business communications; don't waste his or her time with non-matching offers or he or she will go down the street to a competitor's property.

Digital channels in which personalized messages/experiences are delivered

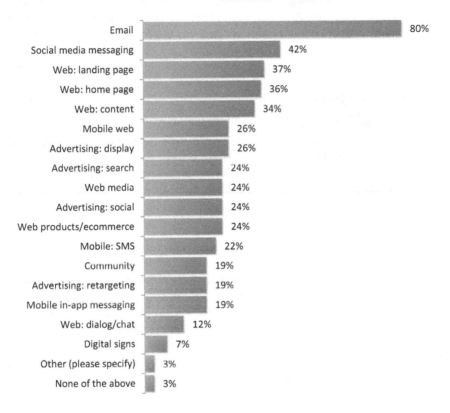

Email	80%
Social media messaging	42%
Web: landing page	37%
Web: home page	36%
Web: content	34%
Mobile web	26%
Advertising: display	26%
Advertising: search	24%
Web media	24%
Advertising: social	24%
Web products/ecommerce	24%
Mobile: SMS	22%
Community	19%
Advertising: retargeting	19%
Mobile in-app messaging	19%
Web: dialog/chat	12%
Digital signs	7%
Other (please specify)	3%
None of the above	3%

Figure 5: Digital Channels for personalized messages/experiences
Source: VB Insights[61]

In its article *Creating the Ultimate Single Customer View[64]*, the Adobe Experience Cloud team argues that, real-time access to data enables an "organization to trigger personalized messages and outreach in the moment of highest impact. What's more, leveraging a variety of signals emerging from the buying process, marketers can engage with a customer when it's both most relevant for her, and when she's most likely to convert—maximizing the value on both sides."

Of course, not all campaign management systems are alike or have the functionality that helps businesses deliver experiences at the moment of highest impact.[64] Systems that have lags in data access due to third-party partnerships and integrations are especially susceptible to problems as they are forced to do double duty—first, they have to remind customers how they felt earlier and, second, they have to encourage shoppers to act based on those earlier experiences and emotions; this is far from ideal.[64]

Composing the marketing message, however, is probably the easiest part of the process. In its *Delivering New Levels of Personalization in Consumer Engagement*[65], *Forrester Research* found that survey participants believed that personalization had the potential to increase traffic, raise customer conversion rates, and increase average order value. Surveyed marketers felt that personalization capabilities could improve a variety of business metrics, including customer retention (75%), lifetime customer value (75%), and customer conversion rates (71%).[38]

Understanding customer-specified preferences is imperative for personalization; "80% of marketing executives currently use them in some or all interaction channels."[38] "In addition, 68% of marketers personalize current customer interactions based on past customer interaction history. Other commonly used personalization methods used by nearly 60% of firms in some or all of their interaction channels are based on the time of day or day of the week of customer interactions."[38]

The executives pooled by *Forrester Research* expected there to be a "huge rise in personalization using consumer's emotional state, social media sentiment, and context"[38] as well. "Only 29% of respondents claim today to use inferences about the consumer's emotional state in some or all channels. But 53% expect to do this in two to three years' time."[38] *Forrester's* report goes on to add, "Only 52% of marketers currently use sentiments that consumers express in social media to personalize interactions today, but fully 79% expect to do this in two to three years. In addition, only 54% capitalize on the consumer's current contextual behavior, but 77% expect to do so in two to three years."[38]

Today, mobile apps, mobile commerce, mobile chat, and mobile gaming have revolutionized the way people do business, seek entertainment, and gamble. Mobile commerce has now evolved into what has become known as "omni-commerce", a seamless approach to selling that puts the shopper's experience front and center, giving that shopper access to what he or she wants through these multiple channels.

In its *Creating the Single Customer View with Adobe Campaign*[66], the Adobe Experience Cloud team recommends businesses "Rely on sales-centric campaign management tools and you'll be hard-pressed to create these single views, let alone construct meaningful mosaics that adapt and evolve in real time. And if you can't capture the granular details surrounding customer interactions—if you can't understand the data you do have—it's virtually impossible to deliver personalized experiences at scale and build a loyal customer base."

Currently, however, there is a big disconnect between what companies think they are delivering in terms of personalization and what consumers are really experiencing. In his article *Study finds marketers are prioritizing personalization...but are further behind then they realize[67]*, Andrew Jones states that, "Although two-thirds of the marketers surveyed rate their personalization efforts as 'very good' or 'excellent,' just 31 percent of consumers reported that companies are consistently delivering personalized experiences."[54]

"Aside from this disparity, the report finds that personalization strategies today are immature. It shows that 91 percent of the marketers surveyed are prioritizing personalization over the coming year, yet many still rely on basic segmentation strategies," Jones notes.[54] This isn't that surprising as many companies are struggling with the ability to not just capture the information necessary for personalization, but also creating DWs that can silo the data appropriately, then deliver it to highly complex analytical programs that can make sense of all that data. It is like finding a needle in a haystack for each and every customer in a massive database; a herculean task, no doubt.[54]

"Personalization is critical to any cross-channel strategy—and at the heart of any personalization strategy is the ability to segment," argues the Adobe Experience Cloud team.[66] Unsurprisingly, "Tapping into more complex segmentation strategies helps organizations deliver better, more meaningful cross-channel experiences."[66] AI and machine learning brings a whole new level of depth and detail to customer segmentation modeling. "Being able to easily create control vs. test groups based on nuanced criteria helps arrive at the insight necessary to design optimal experiences for different sets of customers," argues the Adobe Experience Cloud team.[66] "Applying the same nuanced criteria to the delivery of those experiences is how that insight is transformed into personalization at scale," they contend.[66] Adobe argues that the numbers don't lie—segmented and targeted emails generate 58 percent of all revenue.[66] That's total revenue, not lift, which is a highly impressive number.

"Without advanced filtering it's virtually impossible to extract detailed data and uncover the nuances behind the numbers. Beyond that, though, creating and managing lists also becomes a challenge," warns Adobe.[66] "Want to target customers based on their preferred device? If filtering isn't native to your campaign management system, that simple task is going to be time-consuming and costly at best. Personalization becomes a trade-off between quality and speed," says Adobe.[66]

"Businesses should also focus on solutions that utilize artificial intelligence (AI) in a tangible and effective way," argues Adobe.[66] At best, "AI can take the grunt work of data stitching, data cleaning, and anomaly detection off your plate, freeing you up for more meaningful marketing work—gaining a better understanding of customer wants and needs, for example, then spending time designing perfectly personalized experiences," recommends Adobe.[66]

Abby Parasnis, Adobe's chief technology officer argues that Adobe Sensei "gives marketers and analysts new visibility into which segments are most important to their businesses, and allows them to target overlapping or adjacent segments, making it possible to acquire customers much more efficiently."[66]

"By having an integrated customer profile that combines online and offline data, marketers can more easily provide truly meaningful customer experiences that reinforce the brand message across all channels," says Bruce Swan, senior product manager for Adobe Campaign.[66] "The results include increased engagement as well as a higher likelihood for conversion, long-term loyalty, and brand advocacy," adds Swan.[66]

A unified or single customer view can help marketers "harvest the insights they need to develop targeted marketing campaigns—that, in turn, drives customer loyalty, purchases, and conversions."[66] It is a virtuous cycle that feeds upon itself, as long as the customer continues to see the value in loyalty. "Data-driven marketing also speeds time-to-market, and reduces overall campaign costs," the Adobe team believes.[66]

Ultimately, Adobe concludes that, "it comes down to one key consideration: your customers deserve to be treated like individuals—and you need to deliver. You need to collect cross-channel insights that can be pulled together into a cohesive single view. You need to have the capabilities to adjust that view in real time, as your consumers pivot—and even change course. And you need both the powerful insights and powerful technology to drive consistent, cohesive, and meaningful cross-channel journeys for every customer."[66]

The *A.I. Sports Book* can personalize the customer experience in the following ways:

- Customer Service:
    o Geo-locating a customer when he or she signs onto a business' customer Wi-Fi system.
    o Video analytics with facial recognition technology to spot and/or confirm a customer's true identity.
    o Social media customer service can cut down on normal customer service expenses, as well as connect with customers on the channels that they prefer, i.e., Facebook, WhatsApp, WeChat, or Instagram.
    o Chatbots can automate customer service requests, as well as disseminate info seamlessly.
- E-Commerce

- Clickstream analysis could allow personalized offers to be sent to a potentially returning customer when he or she is browsing the company's website or making a purchase.
- Customer Management:
  - The ecommerce department can get more accurate attribution analysis—so that the sports book can understand which advertising is associated with which user, making the advertising more quantifiable and, therefore, much more actionable.
  - CRM systems can add social media as a channel feeding targeted messages to only those customers who are most likely to respond to them.
  - The amount of promotions available and channels through which to market through increases exponentially as campaign lift can be assessed in terms of hours, rather than in terms of days or weeks.
  - Customer acquisition is accelerated because business users throughout the company can quickly derive answers to the following questions:
    - Which combinations of campaigns accelerate conversion?
    - What behavior signals churn?
    - Do web search key words influence deal size?
    - Which product features do users struggle with?
    - Which product features drive product adoption and renewal?
    - What drives customers to use costly sales channels?
  - Customer interaction data can be rapidly turned into business opportunities.
  - Powerful recommendation engines can ingest data from a multitude of sources and then be made available to frontline staff, who can react in near real-time.
- Point-of-Sale:
  - Brands can better target merchandise, sales, and promotions and help redesign store layouts and product placement to improve the customer experience.

In her article *The 5 Biggest Marketing Trends for 2019*[68], Giselle Abramovich quotes Stacy Martinet, VP of marketing strategy and communications at Adobe, saying, "Companies that want to provide truly transformative customer experiences need customer data that is real-time, intelligent, and predictive." Martinet adds that, "In 2019 we'll see enterprises focused on building a seamless flow of connected customer data—behavioral, transactional, financial, operational, and more—to get a true end-to-end view of their customers for immediate actionability."[68]

Giselle Abramovich believes marketers have long been talking about personalization marketing, but they are still at a very basic level of personalization.[68] "To truly unlock the value of personalization, companies must first create a unified view of their customers," believes Anudit Vikram, SVP of audience solutions at Dun & Bradstreet.[68]

Jason Heller, partner and global lead, digital marketing operations at McKinsey agrees, claiming, "The single view of the customer is the single most important asset that a modern marketer can have, and it's the core of their personalization efforts."[68] "It also becomes the core of their next-generation marketing ROI capability, as well," he adds.[68]

One of the keys to personalization at scale is internal structure.[68] Heller "expects companies in 2019 will work on building agile marketing execution models in which cross-functional teams can experiment, leveraging the data and technology stack to capture value."[68]

"Privacy, of course, will play a big role in an organization's personalization strategy," says Abramovich.[68] "New laws such as GDPR—plus California's privacy law, which comes into effect in January 2020—means marketers must be focused on ensuring ethical data collection practices and earning consumers' trust," argues Martinet.[68]

"When choosing partners to work with, brands need to look for products and services that protect the data that is entrusted to them and are designed with privacy in mind," says Martinet.[68] "Privacy is about respecting your customers and giving them control over how their data is being used. Be transparent and help them understand the value proposition," adds Martinet.[68]

Abramovich believes that, in 2019, many organizations will have what McKinsey refers to as a "consent management" function, which includes "having an ethical view of how the organization manages customers' data, protects that data, and establishes governance around how that data is utilized."[68]

"I think this is an absolute obligation that we have regardless of whether the regulations exist or not because eventually they will exist," says Heller.[68] "So starting to operate that way today will only set you up for more success in the future."[68]

In terms of privacy, as reported in CB Insights *What's Next in AI? Artificial Intelligence Trends*[69], Google's federated learning approach aims to add a layer of privacy by utilizing a person's mobile messaging while also keeping it private. "In a nutshell, your data stays on your phone. It is not sent to or stored in a central cloud server. A cloud server sends the most updated version of an algorithm—called the 'global state of the algorithm—to a random selection of user devices.'"[69]

THE A.I. SPORTS BOOK

"Your phone makes improvements and updates to the model based on your localized data. Only this update (and updates from other users) are sent back to the cloud to improve the "global state" and the process repeats itself," explains CB Insights.[69] Real world examples include Firefox's use of federated learning to "rank suggestions that appear when a user starts typing into the URL bar." Google Ventures-backed AI startup OWKIN is using the approach to protect sensitive patient drug discovery data.[69] "The model allows different cancer treatment centers to collaborate without patients' data ever leaving the premises," claims CB Insights.[69]

Data has been called the new oil and although it is an interesting metaphor data companies like Facebook, Google, Apple, Netflix, and Amazon need to be careful not to go down the dark road that the oil industry has traversed to become one of the least liked industries in the world. Many people view oil companies as destructors of nature and the data companies need to take the privacy needs of their customers and potential customers seriously or they, too, will be viewed in a similarly dark light.

According to Adobe's *Indelible content, incredible experiences*[70], "Marketers want to surface the right content precisely when and where customers need it. But to be efficient, you want to create once and deliver everywhere, with content automatically adjusting to fit connected experiences on any channel. Machine learning lets you do that—finding better ways to optimize layout and copy wherever they're used." For example, "Adobe's smart summarisation can take your product manager's blog post about gourmet hot dogs and trim the redundant content for a news clip or email."

Personal Shopping

Personalization, of course, helps personal shopping in a multitude of ways. In its article *Retailers: Adopt Artificial Intelligence Now for Personalized and Relevant Experiences*[71], the Adobe Retail Team's reports how "ASOS.com, a British online fashion and beauty store, uses AI to uncover and solve issues specific to online retailers, like helping customers find the right size, thereby minimizing returns." "By analyzing which items customers keep, in which sizes, versus the items and sizes that get returned most often, ASOS is able to use machine learning to recommend appropriate sizes for individual customers regardless of the brand or fit of specific items of clothing," explains the Adobe Retail Team.[71] The result: returns of ill-fitting clothing are minimized, while the customer experience is improved, and there is an overall cost reduction for ASOS.[71]

AI is completely revolutionizing the retail industry as we know it.[71] "From personalized customer experiences across digital touch points to improved product management, this powerful area of computing is helping retailers up their relevance, efficiency, and, ultimately, their bottom line," claims the Adobe

Retail Team.[71]

"When we look across the retail industry, there is, surprisingly, quite a broad use of AI already," says Vish Ganapathy, managing director and global retail technology lead at Accenture.[71] "A lot of that has got to do with the fact that more and more technology vendors are injecting AI into everything that they do within their applications."[71]

According to Ganapathy, "AI's ability to absorb and sort through a lot of unstructured data and use that information to gain more relevance among customers is a big boon for retailers."[71] "When I say personalization, I mean it to be a deeper level of relevance," Ganapathy explains.[71] "If you simply put my name on an email, that's personalized, but if your email has an offer for wine and I'm a beer drinker, it's not very relevant."[71]

Nikki Baird, vice president of retail innovation at Aptos, claims that, "the majority of investment in AI today by retailers revolves around personalization of product recommendations and the next offer to give."[71] Personalized product creation is the next level of AI, she predicts, with some retailers already venturing into that space already.[71]

Jeff Barrett, CEO of Barrett Digital, predicts that our phones will soon become the main delivery mechanism for any relevant retail experience we have.[71] "Retailers will start putting retail pop-ups in the locations where they see there's a lot more traffic," Barrett adds.[71] "Experiences will become more fluid about what physical retail looks like, meaning that it will adapt to where people want to be."[71]

"There are some interesting developments around how to onboard new products much more quickly," Accenture's Ganapathy said.[71] "Image recognition, character recognition, etc., can very quickly predefine product attributes and allow a retailer to onboard new products into the business very quickly. This makes a big difference."[71]

AI can also be used for better inventory management and more accurate product and advertising attribution, which should help merchants reduce costs.[71] For example, Walmart uses AI to adjust inventory levels based on real time information.[71] If rain is forecasted for the next week, "Walmart will shift its inventory to highlight the items that were most sought after the last time it rained for a while. At the same time, merchandise that is less likely to sell when it rains based on the company's data is taken off the shelves."[71]

Chatbots are probably "the most common AI-powered customer service application today."[71] "To date, bots have predominantly been used to provide search and discovery and product recommendations," says Abramovich.[71]

Sephora, which has two Facebook chatbots, is leading the way.[71] The first chatbot—*Sephora Reservation Assistant*—books appointments for makeovers.[71]

The bot has seen "an 11% higher conversion rate versus any other channel for doing so."[71]

The second bot—*Color Match for Sephora Virtual Artist*—is a shade-matching bot that "can scan the face of a celebrity and provide a list of the closest-matching lipsticks."[71]

As Ann Lewnes, EVP & CMO of Adobe says in the *Executives Are Eyeing These 2019 Consumer Trends*[72]:

> "While digital has blazed forward in recent years, leaving many to question the lasting significance of traditional offline vehicles, the pendulum is swinging back toward a midpoint where both online and offline channels play complimentary roles in the customer experience. Consumers continue to demand well-designed, personalized digital experiences at every turn, but they equally crave the on-demand satisfaction of a great in-store experience or the inexplicable power of community that exists at a live event. Creativity will never go out of style. It's at the core of every great experience. Marketers who can deliver the ideal blend of online and offline experiences with creativity at the center will win the hearts and minds of customers for years to come."

Sports books should build customer analytics capabilities that help it win, serve, and retain increasingly empowered customers. Basic customer analytics can help a brand's marketing team understand a customer's stated and unstated needs and buying motivations to design appropriate offers and experiences.

Customer analytics have evolved in six core dimensions: strategy, organization, data, technology, analytics and measurement, and process. In terms of analytics, sports books should start with segmentation to build a comprehensive view of their customers. Segmentation provides multiple payoffs across the customer life cycle, from acquisition through retention. Segmentation might start with simple attributes such as bets, or even geography, but it should evolve over time to characteristics such as lifetime value. Table 2 shows the other types of analytics that should be used during a customer life-cycle.

Many of these models require complex data integration / data virtualization, CRM, social, and analytics systems working in harmony with each other.

Life-cycle stage	Business objective	Analytical method
Discover	Profile customers	Segmentation
	Evaluate prospects	Lead scoring
	Reach the right prospects	Customer lookalike targeting
Explore	Analyze customers' responses	Offer/contact optimization
	Optimize marketing mix	Marketing mix modeling
	Delivering contextually relevant content	Customer location analysis
	Test marketing inputs	A/B and multivariate testing
Buy	Predict future events	Propensity models
	Expand wallet share	Cross-sell/upsell
	Target accurately	In-market timing models
Use	Drive deeper product use	Product and recommendation analysis
	Understand use	Customer device use analysis
	Understand customer satisfaction	Customer satisfaction analysis
Ask	Learn about drivers of engagement	Engagement analysis
	Improve customer service	Customer device use analyss
	Identify customer pain points	Voice of the customer analysis
Engage	Manage defection of customers	Churn models
	Personalize marketing efforts	Next-best-action models
	Maximize customer value	Lifetime value models
	Increase depth of relationship	Loyalty models
	Optimize customer interactions	Customer journey analysis
	Understand customer relationships	Social network analysis

Table 2: Analytics Across the Customer Life-Cycle
Source: Forrester's How Analytics Drives Customer Life-Cycle Management[73]

Website Morphing

It is all well and good to offer personalized service to customers face-to-face, but what happens when a customer visits a brand's website for the first time, or even the hundredth time? Today, personalized web pages can be rendered during the web page load and elements of the page can take into account past purchase history, clickstream behavior, as well as a whole host of other data points. For a marketer, their website is really their customer center.

In her article *The Art and Science Behind Every "Add to Cart"*[74], Christie Chew argues that, "Neuroscience and the way people make decisions impact what compels people to click and buy. Together, these considerations and best practices can work together to drive customers to take action."

Guliz Sicotte, head of product design and content for Magento, says to prompt a customer purchase, brands must create online experiences that focus on four principal characteristics—they must be personalized, reflective, transparent, and use pleasing aesthetics.[74]

Morphing is one of the ways a brand can hyper-personalize the customer shopping experience. So, what exactly is morphing? In their article *Website Morphing*[75], Hauser et al. state that, "'Morphing' involves automatically matching the basic 'look and feel' of a website, not just the content, to cognitive styles." Hauser et al. use Bayesian updating to "infer cognitive styles from clickstream data."[75] Then they "balance exploration (learning how morphing affects purchase probabilities) with exploitation (maximizing short-term sales) by solving a dynamic program (partially observable Markov decision process)."[75]

In a world of deep personalization, website design becomes a major profit driver.[75] As Hauser et al. see it, "Websites that match the preferences and information needs of visitors are efficient; those that do not forego potential profit and may be driven from the market."[75] The authors believe that "retailers might serve their customers better and sell more products and services if their websites matched the cognitive styles of their visitors."[75] I'd argue it is not just retailers who would profit from this, most B-2-C companies would.

Keeping with the themes of simplicity and seamlessness, Hauser et al. do not believe personal self-selection—the process in which a customer is given many options and allowed to select how to navigate and interact with the site—is viable.[75] "As the customer's options grow, this strategy leads to sites that are complex, confusing, and difficult to use," they argue.[75] The second option, which requires "visitors to complete a set of cognitive style tasks and then select a website from a predetermined set of websites"[75] is just as problematic. Website visitors probably won't see value in taking the time to answer these questions and there is always the problem of self-bias hindering any potential results.[75]

Hauser et al. propose another approach: "'morphing' the website automatically by matching website characteristics to customers' cognitive styles."[75] A cognitive style is "a person's preferred way of gathering, processing, and evaluating information."[76] It can be identified as "individual differences in how we perceive, think, solve problems, learn and relate to others."[77] "A person's cognitive style is fixed early on in life and is thought to be deeply pervasive [and is] a relatively fixed aspect of learning performance."[78]

The "goal is to morph the website's basic structure (site backbone) and other functional characteristics in real time."[75] "Website morphing complements self-selected branching (as in http://www.Dell.com), recommendations (as in http://www.Amazon.com), factorial experiments (Google's Website Optimizer), or customized content.[79] [80]"[75]

For Hauser et al., cognitive styles dimensions "might include impulsive (makes decisions quickly) versus deliberative (explores options in depth before making a decision), visual (prefers images) versus verbal (prefers text and numbers), or analytic (wants all details) versus holistic (just the bottom line)."[75] For example, "a website might morph by changing the ratio of graphs and pictures to text, by reducing a display to just a few options (broadband service plans), or by carefully selecting the amount of information presented about each plan. A website might also morph by adding or deleting functional characteristics such as column headings, links, tools, persona, and dialogue boxes."[75] There are, literally, hundreds of thousands or even millions of ways a website can morph to better serve its customers.

Because of its real-time nature, website morphing is not easy. It presents at least the following four technical challenges[75]:

1. The customer acquisition problem, i.e., the website must morph based on relatively few clicks of a first-time visitor; otherwise, the customer sees little benefit.
2. Even knowing a customer's cognitive style is not enough, the website must learn which characteristics are best for which customers (in terms of sales or profit).
3. To be practical, a system needs prior distributions on parameters.
4. Implementation requires a real-time working system, which is one of the most complex systems to set up, run, and maintain.

For their website morphing, Hauser et al. used[75]:

> "a Bayesian learning system to address the rapid assessment of cognitive styles and a dynamic program to optimally manage the tension between exploitation (serving the morph most likely to be best for a customer) and exploration (serving alternative morphs to learn which morph is best). Uncertainty in customer styles implies a partially observable Markov

decision process (POMDP), which we address with fast heuristics that are close to optimal. Surveys, using both conjoint analysis and experimentation, provide priors and 'prime' the Bayesian and dynamic programming engines. We demonstrate feasibility and potential profit increases with an experimental website developed for the BT Group to sell broadband service in Great Britain."

Hauser et al. expect different morphs to appeal differentially depending on the visitors' cognitive style.[75] "For example, impulsive visitors might prefer less-detailed information, whereas deliberative visitors might prefer more information. Similarly, the more focused of the two morphs might appeal to visitors who are holistic, while the ability to compare many plans in a table might appeal to analytic visitors."[75] If preferences match behavior, then, by matching a website's characteristics to a customer's cognitive style, the morphing website should be able to sell more effectively, thereby producing greater profits for the brand.

Hauser et al. applied a "Bayesian updating and dynamic programming to an experimental BT Group (formerly British Telecom) website using data from 835 priming respondents."[75] The challenge was to infer the cognitive-segment to which each visitor belonged, "while simultaneously learning how to maximize profit by assigning morphs to cognitive-style segments."[75]

Web visitors cognitive style segments are inferred from their clickstreams.[75] This was possible "because each visitor's click is a decision point that reveals the visitor's cognitive-style preferences."[75] Hauser et al. believe that with enough observed clicks, they could have been able to identify a visitor's cognitive-style segment quite conclusively.[75] However, in any real application, the number of clicks observed before morphing would be quite small, yielding at best a noisy indicator of segment membership.[75]

Hauser et al. observed about ten clicks, inferred probabilities for the visitor's cognitive-style segment, then morphed the website based on their inference of the visitor's segment.[75] "The visitor continued until he or she purchased a BT broadband service or left the website without purchasing."[75]

In most cases, cognitive styles are measured with methods that "include direct classification, neuro-fuzzy logic, decision trees, multilayer perceptrons, Bayesian networks, and judgment."[75] Hauser et al. acknowledge that, while most authors match the learning or search environment based on judgment by an expert pedagogue or based on predefined distance measures, they inferred cognitive styles from a relatively small set of clicks, then automatically balanced exploration and exploitation to select the most appropriate morph.[75]

To set a baseline cognitive style standard Hauser et al. used "a professional market research company (Applied Marketing Science, Inc.) and a respected

British online panel (Research Now)."[75] They invited "current and potential broadband users to complete an online questionnaire that combined BT's experimental website with a series of preference and cognitive style questions."[75]

835 respondents completed the questionnaire, which contained the following sequential sections[75]:

- Identify whether respondent was in the target market.
- Identify which of 16 broadband providers they might be considering, along with purchase-intention probabilities.
- Eight randomly-assigned potential morphs of the BT website. Each respondent was encouraged to spend at least five minutes on BT's experimental website.
- Post-visit response consideration and purchase-intention probabilities.
- Identify their preferences between eight pairs of websites, with a choice-based conjoint analysis-like exercise. These data augment clickstream data when estimating.
- A cognitive style measure.

Hauser et al. expected "these scales to identify whether the respondent was analytic or holistic, impulsive or deliberative, visual or verbal, and a leader or a follower."[75] "The analytic versus holistic dimension is widely studied in psychology and viewed as being a major differentiator of how individuals organize and process information,"[75] including by Riding and Rayner[81], Allinson and Hayes[82], Kirton[83], and Riding and Cheema.[84] According to Hauser et al., "Researchers in both psychology and marketing suggest that cognitive styles can be further differentiated as either impulsive or deliberative.[85][86]"[75]

In summary, Hauser et al. identified the following four empirical constructs to measure respondents' cognitive styles[75]:

- Leader versus follower.
- Analytic/visual versus holistic/verbal.
- Impulsive versus deliberative.
- (Active) reader versus (passive) listener.

In conclusion, Hauser et al. "used segments of cognitive styles rather than continuously defined cognitive styles because the dynamic program requires finitely many 'arms.'"[75] Websites were morphed once per visit, in part, because Hauser et al. observed a single subscription decision per customer.[75]

In her article *The Art and Science Behind Every "Add to Cart"*, Christie Chew notes that the central question driving most purchases is, "What's in it for me?"[74] "Customers should feel that products are relevant to their intentions," adds Guliz.[74] "This sense of relevance can be traced back to what Carmen Simon, Ph.D., cognitive neuroscientist at Memzy, describes as habitual decision-making—habits are conscious at first but eventually become subconscious," adds Guliz.[74]

"Link your techniques, content, value proposition, or whatever you're offering, to something that feels familiar to the customer's brain," says Simon.[74] This increases a person's comfort level, which makes them more likely to take a favorable action for your brand because what you're asking them will feel easy.[74]

Guliz concurs: "In the end, customers are faced with a barrage of e-commerce opportunities. Expedite the shopping experience and increase conversions by identifying products that 'people like me' have purchased. Once I can vet a product based on people who closely match my profile, I am that much closer to feeling comfortable in making the purchase."[74]

"It's also essential that each step in your e-commerce experience reflects intention," says Chew.[74] "For example, the category page should include curiosity-triggering components," adds Guliz.[74] "If you're displaying an array of products online, make it easy to determine the sentiment around each, without customers needing to invest time to dive into each."[74] "From here, be sure to show customers the most important details and features relevant to them and their purchase experience," recommends Chew.[74]

"This process can help create a series of clicks that drive those customers closer to making a purchase," says Chew.[74] "Don't pitch immediately. Don't make people think too hard. Work toward a series of smaller, more habitual 'yeses,'" advises Simon.[74] "This creates more momentum and a pattern of 'yes,' which can make a customer more comfortable with a bigger, riskier purchase decision," she says.[74]

For example, if you're promoting high-end travel, query users about their overall travel experience, rather than asking them outright if they are booking travel for a vacation or business.[74] These kinds of questions will likely elicit positive responses, whereas direct questions can often be off-putting.[74]

Posing questions about a customer's travel habits and preferences can lead potential customers to the critical "yes"—and they might at least consider booking a luxury vacation.[74] By that point, Chew argues, "they've been habituated toward a positive response and will be more open to bigger considerations—and bigger purchases."[74]

According to Carmen, "the brain makes decisions in a reflexive, habitual, and/or goal-oriented way."[74] "The mistake some businesses make is asking people to tap into their goals too quickly, at the expense of tapping into reflexes and habits first," believes Chew.[74] She recommends brands, "Create opportunities for the buyer to take small steps first, toward a larger goal or purchase."[74]

Transparency is essential to ensure positive customer experiences that will drive customers toward a purchase.[74] "It's important to bring high visibility to the critical decision-making factors like return policies and shipping times, by writing them in clear, simple ways," Guliz says.[74] "If an array of products is displayed, make it easy to determine the sentiment around these products without needing to invest time to dive into each product offering."[74]

"This type of layout will play well to a customer's need to feel like they're in control of their environment," says Chew.[74] Guliz adds that brand should ensure users can "easily navigate to different aspects of the product page."[74] "Take them to reviews when they click on star ratings. Let them filter product reviews

"Retailers are making people think way too much," Simon says.[74] "If you start with something that feels familiar and habitual, you'll have an easier time when it comes to persuasion. Show customers something that doesn't require a lot of cognitive energy to process."[74]

"Humans are innately emotional—we react to everything from people to environments to colors and sounds, based on our existing and real-time experiences. This insight can help e-commerce brands better structure their retail experiences," argues Guliz.[74] "The right aesthetics are major elements of trustworthiness in your store," explains Guliz.[74] "Lots of detailed photos of key features is crucial to a good experience."[74] In chapter three, I explain the psychology of personalization and detail 15 types of psychological effects that, when used correctly, can motivate consumers to buy.

Simon adds that "there are a series of innate behaviors in which you already know what to do next. In the buying process, that includes your reflex toward something beautiful."[74]

Marcia Flicker, Ph.D., associate professor at Fordham University's Gabelli School of Business, argues that, "Creating this aesthetic experience requires having the right visuals."[74] E-commerce brands need bigger and more detailed photos, especially apparel brands.[74] "It can be hard for customers to buy apparel online because they want to try it on, feel the fabric," says Flicker.[74] "Retailers need to reproduce that experience of being able to see the actual item. Customers need to see large images from a variety of angles—or even video."[74]

"This aesthetics-focused notion can, then, be woven into an e-commerce brand's UX design to help pave a customer's path to purchase," says Guliz.[74] "When you design an interface, you're more likely to have people use it if it's aesthetically appealing," Simon says.[74] "Principles like proximity, balance, unity, and contrast are important to this notion of aesthetics."[74]

"Understanding why customers buy and designing experiences to match their patterns is just the beginning. Going forward, brands will continue to fine-tune these strategies, layering in more future-forward technologies," predicts Guliz.[74] "Augmented reality could be a game-changer, especially for retailers," says Flicker.[74] "Think about using AR to overlay dress styles on online models that look just like you. This enables you to envision the real-life equivalent without actually being in store, and that has value."[74]

However, Guliz concludes that, "even with the most cutting-edge understanding of what makes us tick—and click—and stunning aesthetics and powerful UX design, none of it matters if the experience doesn't fill a need in the customer's purchase path."[74] Experience is both the fallback and the reason for purchases.

Affective Computing

In his article *We Know How You Feel*[87], Raffi Khatchadourian profiles Rana el Kaliouby, co-founder and CEO of Affectiva, a startup that specializes in AI systems that sense and understand human emotions. Affectiva develops "cutting-edge AI technologies that apply machine learning, deep learning, and data science to bring new levels of emotional intelligence to AI."[88] It has been ranked by the business press as one of the United States' fastest-growing startups.[87] Affectiva is the most visible among a host of competing startups that are building emotionally responsive machines.[87] Its competitors include Emotient, Realeyes, and Sension.[87]

Khatchadourian explains that, "Our faces are organs of emotional communication; by some estimates, we transmit more data with our expressions than with what we say, and a few pioneers dedicated to decoding this information have made tremendous progress."[87] Arguably, The most successful of these pioneers is Rana el Kaliouby.[87]

"Since the nineteen-nineties a small number of researchers have been working to give computers the capacity to read our feelings and react, in ways that have come to seem startlingly human," explains Khatchadourian.[87] Researchers "have trained computers to identify deep patterns in vocal pitch, rhythm, and intensity; their software can scan a conversation between a woman and a child and determine if the woman is a mother, whether she is looking the child in the eye, whether she is angry or frustrated or joyful."[87] "Other machines can measure sentiment by assessing the arrangement of our words, or by reading our gestures. Still others can do so from facial expressions," says Khatchadourian.[87]

In his book *Architects of Intelligence*[88], Martin Ford interviews the CEO of Affectiva, Rana el Kaliouby, and she explains her work in the following way:

> "If you think about a lot of people who are building these devices, right now, they're focused on the cognitive intelligence aspect of these devices, and they're not paying much attention to the emotional intelligence. But if you look at humans, it's not just your IQ that matters in how successful you are in your professional and personal life; it's often really about your emotional and social intelligence. Are you able to understand

the mental states of people around you? Are you able to adapt your behavior to take that into consideration and then motivate them to change their behavior, or persuade them to take action?" All of these situations, where we are asking people to take action, we all need to be emotionally intelligent to get to that point. I think that this is equally true for technology that is going to be interfacing with you on a day-to-day basis and potentially asking you to do things."

Kaliouby's thesis "is that this kind of interface between humans and machines is going to become ubiquitous, that it will just be ingrained in the future human-machine interfaces, whether it's our car, our phone or smart devices at our home or in the office."[88] She sees a world where, "We will just be coexisting and collaborating with these new devices, and new kinds of interfaces."[88] "I think that, ten years down the line, we won't remember what it was like when we couldn't just frown at our device, and our device would say, 'Oh, you didn't like that, did you?'" says Kaliouby.[87]

Afectiva's signature software, Affdex, tracks four emotional "classifiers"—happy, confused, surprised, and disgusted.[87] "The software scans for a face; if there are multiple faces, it isolates each one. It then identifies the face's main region—mouth, nose, eyes, eyebrows—and it ascribes points to each, rendering the features in simple geometries," explains Khatchadourian.[87]

"Affdex also scans for the shifting texture of skin—the distribution of wrinkles around an eye, or the furrow of a brow—and combines that information with the deformable points to build detailed models of the face as it reacts," says Khatchadourian.[87] The algorithm identifies an emotional expression by comparing it with countless others that it has previously analyzed. "If you smile, for example, it recognizes that you are smiling in real time," Kaliouby says.[87]

Like every company working in the emotional intelligence field, "Affectiva relies on the work of Paul Ekman, a research psychologist who, beginning in the sixties, built a convincing body of evidence that there are at least six universal human emotions, expressed by everyone's face identically, regardless of gender, age, or cultural upbringing."[87] Classifying human expressions into combinations of forty-six individual movements called "action units", Ekman compiled the Facial Action Coding System, or FACS—a five-hundred-page taxonomy of facial movements.[87] FACS "has been in use for decades by academics and professionals, from computer animators to police officers interested in the subtleties of deception."[87]

Although widely used, Ekman and FACS has its critics, "among them social scientists who argue that context plays a far greater role in reading emotions than his theory allows."[87] However, context-blind computers appear to support Ekman's conclusions.[87] "By scanning facial action units, computers can now outperform most people in distinguishing social smiles from those triggered by spontaneous joy, and in differentiating between faked pain and genuine pain," says Khatchadourian.[87] "Operating with unflagging attention, they can register expressions so fleeting that they are unknown even to the person making them," notes Khatchadourian.[87]

"The human face is a moving landscape of tremendous nuance and complexity. It is a marvel of computation that people so often effortlessly interpret expressions, regardless of the particularities of the face they are looking at, the setting, the light, or the angle," notes Khatchadourian.[87] He adds that, "A programmer trying to teach a computer to do the same thing must contend with nearly infinite contingencies. The process requires machine learning, in which computers find patterns in large tranches of data, and then use those patterns to interpret new data."[87]

In March, 2011, Kaliouby and her team were invited to demonstrate an early version of their technology to executives from Millward Brown, a global market-research company.[87] "Kaliouby was frank about the system's limitations—the software still was having trouble distinguishing a smile from a grimace—but the executives were impressed," reports Khatchadourian.[87] Ad testing relies heavily on subjective surveys, which can be easily tainted by human bias.[87] Spontaneous, even unconscious, sentiment is what really interests marketers and Kaliouby's technology promised that, along with better results.[87]

"A year earlier, Millward Brown had formed a neuroscience unit, which attempted to bring EEG technology into the work, and it had hired experts in Ekman's system to study video of interviews," explains Khatchadourian.[87] However, these ideas had proved impossible to scale up.[87] The Millward Brown executives proposed a test to Kaliouby: "if Affdex could successfully measure people's emotional responses to four ads that they had already studied, Millward Brown would become a client, and also an investor."[87]

Millward Brown chose the Dove TV commercial "Onslaught," which begins with an image of a young girl, then "shifts to her perspective as she is bombarded by a montage of video clips—a lifetime of female stereotypes compressed into thirty-two seconds—before the ad ends with the girl, all innocence, and the tagline 'Talk to your daughter before the beauty industry does.'"[87] Although the ad was critically acclaimed, surveys revealed that many people considered it emotionally difficult to watch.[87] In its study, Affdex scanned more than a hundred respondents watching the ad, and discovered more complicated responses. Although respondents were uncomfortable during the ad, at the moment of resolution this discomfort vanished.[87] "The software was telling us something we were potentially not seeing," Graham Page, a Millward Brown executive, explained.[87] Recognizing the power of Affectiva's technology, Millward Brown's parent company, WPP, invested $4.5 million in the company.[87] Affdex was soon being used to test thousands of ads per year.[87]

Kaliouby claims that her company has analyzed more than two million videos, of respondents from over eighty countries.[87] "This is data we have never had before," says Kaliouby.[87] When Affectiva began, she had trained the software on just a few hundred expressions, but, once she started working with Millward Brown, hundreds of thousands of people on six continents began turning on web cams to watch ads for testing, and all their emotional responses—natural reactions, in relatively uncontrolled settings—flowed back to Kaliouby's team.[87]

Affdex can now read the nuances of smiles better than most people can. As the company's database of emotional reactions grows, the software is getting better at reading other expressions, including furrowed eyebrows. "A brow furrow is a very important indicator of confusion or concentration, and it can be a negative facial expression," explains Kaliouby.[87]

Today, Kaliouby says companies pay millions of dollars to create funny and emotionally compelling ads, but the advertisers and the brands have no idea if they are striking the right emotional chord with their audience.[88] The only way to find out, before emotional response technology existed, was to ask people.[88] So, if you are the person watching the ad, you'd get a survey with some basic questions, but the answers wouldn't be very reliable because it is biased believes Kaliouby.[88]

With Affdex, however, Kaliouby explains that, "as you're watching the ad, with your consent it will analyze on a moment-by-moment basis all your facial expressions and aggregate that over the thousands of people who watched that same ad."[88] The result: "an unbiased, objective set of data around how people respond emotionally to the advertising."[88] Affectiva can "then correlate that data with things like customer purchase intent, or even actual sales data and virality."[88]

"People are pretty good at monitoring the mental states of the people around them," says Kaliouby.[88] "We know that about 55% of the signals we use are in facial expression and your gestures, while about 38% of the signal we respond to is from tone of voice. So how fast someone is speaking, the pitch, and how much energy is in the voice. Only 7% of the signal is in the text and the actual choice of words that someone uses!"[88]

A multi-billion-dollar industry that tracks people's sentiments about this product or that service has been built within just a couple of years ago, which is amazing when you think that all of these tweets, likes and posts only account for about 7% of how humans communicate overall.[88] "What I like to think about what we're doing here, is trying to capture the other 93% of non-verbal communication," contends Kaliouby.[88]

According to Kaliouby, Affectiva looks "at the tone of voice and the occurrence of speech events, such as how many times you say 'um' or how many times you laughed. All of these speech events are independent of the actual words that we're saying."[88] Affectiva combines "these things and takes what we call a multimodal approach, where different modalities are combined, to truly understand a person's cognitive, social or emotional state," explains Kaliouby.[88]

"If you take facial expressions or even the tone of a person's voice, the underlying expressions are universal," says Khatchadourian.[88] A smile is a smile no matter where in the world it breaks across a face. "However, we are seeing this additional layer of cultural display norms, or rules, that depict when people portray their emotions, or how often, or how intensely they show their emotion," says Khatchadourian.[88] "We see examples of people amplifying their emotions, dampening their emotions, or even masking their emotions altogether."[88] Masking often occurs in Asian markets, where Asian populations are less likely to show negative emotions.[88] In Asia, there is an increased incidence of what's known as a "social smile", or a "politeness smile."[88] These are not expressions of joy, but rather expressions that say, "I acknowledge you," and, in that sense, they are very social signals.[88]

Affdex is sold "as a tool that can make reliable inferences about people's emotions—a tap into the unconscious,"[87] if you will. Clients like CBS use it to tests new TV shows.[87] Affectiva is also working with Oovoo, an instant messaging service, to integrate the technology into video calls.[87] "People are doing more and more videoconferencing, but all this data is not captured in an analytic way," says Kallouby.[87] "Capturing analytics, it turns out, means using the software—say, during a business negotiation—to determine what the person on the other end of the call is not telling you," writes Khatchadourian. "The technology will say, 'O.K., Mr. Whatever is showing signs of engagement—or he just smirked, and that means he was not persuaded,'" says Kaliouby.[87]

Kaliouby believes Affectiva's technology has the potential to monetize what she calls an 'Emotion Economy'. [87] "Tech gurus have for some time been predicting the Internet of Things, the wiring together of all our devices to create 'ambient intelligence'—an unseen fog of digital knowingness," explains Khatchadourian.[87] Emotion could be a part of this IoT.[87] Kaliouby predicts that, in the coming years, mobile devices will contain an "emotion chip," which constantly runs in the background, the way geolocation currently works on phones now.[87] "Every time you pick up your phone, it gets an emotion pulse, if you like, on how you're feeling," Kaliouby says.[87] "In our research, we found that people check their phones ten to twelve times an hour—and so that gives this many data points of the person's experience," she explains.[87]

The free economy is, in fact, an economy of the bartered self, but attention can never be limitless.[87] Thales Teixeira, a business professor who collaborated with Kaliouby on her technology, explains that, "There are three major fungible resources that we as individuals have. The first is money, the second is time, and the third is attention. Attention is the least explored."[87] Teixeira calculated the value of attention, and found that, like the dollar, its price fluctuates.[87]

Using Super Bowl ads as a rough indicator of the high end of the market, Teixeira "determined that in 2010 the price of an American's attention was six cents per minute. By 2014, the rate had increased by twenty per cent—more than double inflation."[87] The jump was attributed to the fact that attention, at least, the kind worth selling, is becoming increasingly scarce as people spend their free time distracted by a growing array of devices and services.[87] "What people in the industry are saying is 'I need to get people's attention in a shorter period of time,' so they are trying to focus on capturing the intensity of it," explains Teixeira.[87] "People who are emotional are much more engaged. And because emotions are 'memory markers' they remember more. So the idea now is shifting to: how do we get people who are feeling these emotions?" says Teixeira.[87]

Affectiva filed a patent for "a system that could dynamically price advertising depending on how people responded to it."[87] However, they soon discovered that they were not alone; more than a hundred similar patents for emotion-sensing technology existed, many of them, unsurprisingly, also focused on advertising.[87] Companies like AOL, Hitachi, eBay, IBM, Yahoo!, and Motorola are also developing technology in this space.[87] Sony had filed several patents; "its researchers anticipated games that build emotional maps of players, combining data from sensors and from social media to create 'almost dangerous kinds of interactivity,'" notes Khatchadourian.[87] There are "patents for emotion-sensing vending machines, and for A.T.M.s that would understand if users were 'in a relaxed mood,' and receptive to advertising," claims Khatchadourian.[87]

Incredibly, Verizon had drafted a plan for "a media console packed with sensors, including a thermographic camera (to measure body temperature), an infrared laser (to gauge depth), and a multi-array microphone. By scanning a room, the system could determine the occupants' age, gender, weight, height, skin color, hair length, facial features, mannerisms, what language they spoke, and whether they had an accent."[87]

According to Khatchadourian, "the console could identify pets, furniture, paintings, even a bag of chips."[87] It could track "ambient actions," such as "eating, exercising, reading, sleeping, cuddling, cleaning, playing a musical instrument."[87] It could even probe other devices, learning what a person might be browsing on the web, or writing in an e-mail.[87] The console could scan for affect, tracking moments of laughter or the raised voice of an argument.[87] All of this data tracking would then shape the console's choice of TV ads.[87] "A marital fight might prompt an ad for a counsellor. Signs of stress might prompt ads for aromatherapy candles. Upbeat humming might prompt ads 'configured to target happy people,'" which is a pretty scary idea.[87] Verizon's plan was for the system to then broadcast the ads on every device in the room.[87]

Although Verizon's system seems very Big Botheresque, it was not an anomaly, explains Khatchadourian.[87] Microsoft's Xbox One system already contains many of these features, including "a high-definition camera that can monitor players at thirty frames per second."[87] "Using a technology called Time of Flight, it can track the movement of individual photons, picking up minute alterations in a viewer's skin color to measure blood flow, then calculate changes in heart rate."[87] "The software can monitor six people simultaneously, in visible or infrared light, charting their gaze and their basic emotional states, using technology similar to Affectiva's."[87] As Khatchadourian sees it, "the system has tremendous potential for making digital games more immersive."[87] Microsoft isn't stopping at game development either, they envision TV ads that target a viewer's emotions, and program priced according to how many people are watching in the room.[87] Google, Comcast, and Intel are charting a similar path.[87]

Wearables like Nike's *FuelBand* and particularly Fitbit collect a tremendous amount of health data on a person.[87] Apple's Health app, a fitness app pre-installed on new iPhones "can track weight, respiratory rate, sleep, even blood-oxygen saturation."[87] This information could be used to build emotional profiles, says Khatchadourian.[87] Researchers at Dartmouth have already "demonstrated that smartphones can be configured to detect stress, loneliness, depression, and productivity, and to predict G.P.A.s."[87]

For Affectiva, there is now plenty of interest in its Affdex solution.[87] The company has conducted research for Facebook, experimenting with video ads.[87] Samsung has licensed it and a company in San Francisco wants to give its digital nurses the ability to read faces.[87] A Belfast entrepreneur is interested in its use at night clubs.[87] A state initiative in Dubai, the *Happiness Index*, wants to measure social contentment.[87] "Dubai is known to have one of the world's tightest CCTV networks, so the infrastructure to acquire video footage to be analyzed by Affdex already exists," says Kaliouby.[87]

All-in-all, Affective could be showing us the future of customer engagement. Although somewhat Big Brotheresque, all of this data collection is incredibly seamless, which means it will probably be popping up in all kinds of technology in the coming years. For that reason alone, it is important for sports books to keep an eye on this potentially revolutionary technology.

Customer Relationship Management

CRM is a strategy used to learn more about a customer's needs and behaviors in order to develop a stronger relationship with him or her, thereby creating a value exchange on both sides.

As Lovelock and Wirtz state in *Services Marketing, People, Technology, Strategy*[89], "from a customer perspective, well-implemented CRM systems can offer a unified customer interface that delivers customization and personalization." Lovelock and Wirtz argue that at each transaction point, such relevant patron data as a customer's personal preferences, as well as his or her overall past history transactions are available to the clerk serving the customer, giving them valuable information about how to interact with that person.[89] This is not an easy thing to do, however, especially when unstructured data like social media feeds are added to the mix. However, in this day and age, this level of customer service is a necessity as consumers expect personalized service like this from the companies with whom they choose to interact.

According to Lovelock and Wirtz, most CRM solutions contain the following stages[89]:

- Data collection: the system captures customer contact details, such as demographics, purchasing history, service preferences, etc.
- Data Analysis: data captured is analyzed and categorized into a unique set of criteria. This information is then used to tier the customer base and tailor service delivery accordingly.
- Sales force automation: sales leads, cross-sell, and up-sell opportunities can be effectively identified and processed, and the entire cycle from lead generation to close of sales and after-sales service can be tracked and facilitated through the CRM system.
- Marketing automation: the mining of customer data can help a company achieve one-to-one marketing to each one of its customers. Loyalty and retention programs can reduce costs, which can result in an increase of marketing expenditure ROI. By analyzing campaign responses, CRM systems can easily assess a marketing campaign's quantifiable success rate.
- Call center automation: with customer information available right at their fingertips, call center staff can improve customer service levels because they will be able to immediately identify a customer's tier level, as well as compare and contrast him or her against similar customers so that only promotions that are likely to be accepted are offered.

Most sports books will have plenty of data collection, data analysis, sales force automation, marketing automation, and call center automation software to help them in their CRM endeavors, but it is not easy getting all of these complicated systems and processes working together to provide a level of personalized service that wows a customer.

Beyond simple CRM (which, I guess, is never really *that* simple), Social CRM (SCRM) adds a whole new level of sophistication to the mix. SCRM is the use of "social media services, techniques and technology to enable organizations to engage with customers."[90] In his article *Time to Put a Stake in the Ground on Social CRM*[91], Paul Greenberg states that:

> *"Social CRM is a philosophy and a business strategy, supported by a technology platform, business rules, workflow, processes*

and social characteristics, designed to engage and react accordingly in a collaborative conversation in order to promote mutually beneficial value in a trusted and transparent business environment. It's the company's response to the customer's ownership of the conversation."

One aspect of "Social CRM" is "Social Media Monitoring," the process by which companies monitor sites like Facebook, Twitter, LinkedIn, Weibo, YouTube, Instagram, and others for relevant brand and anti-brand comments and mentions. Social media monitoring tools allow for continuous and strong customer engagement.

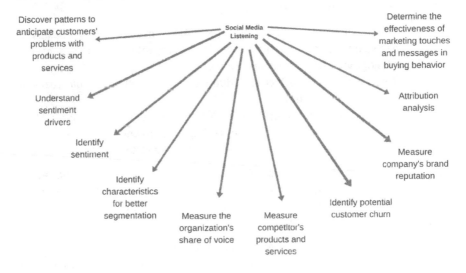

Figure 6: Social Media Listening objectives
Source: www.intelligencia.co

When it comes to social media and implementing it into a sports book, the one constant question should be is, "How does this affect my ROI?" For many businesses, there is the sense that social media is an ethereal, unquantifiable thing, but this shouldn't be the case. As Figure 6 shows, social media listening can be used in a multitude of ways, like anticipating customer problems, understanding and identifying sentiment, measuring a company's share of voice, as well as keeping track of a company's brand. All of these are important in their own right and, together, they can give a sports book deep detail into a marketing campaign's performance and assist quantifying attribution analysis, which can help with planning and implementing future marketing campaigns.

A good example of how a company can test whether a social media solution would work for it is to consider the experience of a telecommunication company that proactively adopted social media recently, as mentioned in R.E. Divol's article *Demystifying social media*.[92] "The company had launched Twitter-based customer service capabilities, several promotional campaigns built around social contests, a fan page with discounts and tech tips, and an active response program to engage with people speaking with the brand."[92]

In social-media terms, the investment was not insignificant, and the company's senior executives wanted quantifiable ROI, not anecdotal evidence that the strategy was paying off.[92] "As a starting point, to ensure that the company was doing a quality job designing and executing its social presence, it benchmarked its efforts against approaches used by other companies known to be successful in social media."[92] According to Divol, "the telecommunication company advanced the following hypotheses[92]:

- "If all of these social-media activities improve general service perceptions about the brand, that improvement should be reflected in a higher volume of positive online posts.
- If social sharing is effective, added clicks and traffic should result in higher search placements.
- If both of these assumption hold true, social-media activity should help drive sales—ideally, at a rate even higher than the company achieves with its average gross rating point (GRP) of advertising expenditures."[92]

The company tested its options. "At various times, it spent less money on conventional advertising, especially as social-media activity ramped up, and it modeled the rising positive sentiment and higher search positions just as it would using traditional metrics."[92]

The results were quite conclusive: "social-media activity not only boosted sales but also had higher ROIs than traditional marketing did. Thus, while the company took a risk by shifting emphasis toward social-media efforts before it had data confirming that this was the correct course, the bet paid off."[92] Just as importantly, the company had now created an analytic baseline that gave the company confidence to continue exploring a growing role for social media.[92] It is very easy to quantify search rankings and it is pretty obvious that if a sports book ranks higher in Google search, it should garner more business.

CRM is an integral part of what businesses hope will be a value exchange on both sides of the customer-company equation, one that will, hopefully, create loyal customers who become apostles for the business. Lovelock and Wirtz created the "Wheel of Loyalty" as an organizing structure to help businesses build customer loyalty and it is highly relevant to the gaming industry.[89] The first of its three sequential steps include building a foundation for loyalty, including "targeting the right portfolio of customer segments, attracting the right customers, tiering the service, and delivering high levels of satisfaction."[89]

The second step—creating loyalty bonds that either deepen the relationship through cross-selling and bundling or adding value to the customer through loyalty rewards and higher level bonds—can be achieved by the sports books gaining a fuller understanding of the patron.[89] It is important to understand as much about the patron as possible, his wants, desires and needs, all the way down to his preferred choice of game, his preferred time to gamble, his preferred amount of spend, and any other preference he might want to share with the sports book.

The third factor—identify and reduce the factors that result in "churn"—is also extremely important to a sports book's bottom line.[89] Engagement is paramount here and mobile apps and social media are great channels to keep customers interested.

Sports books should also feel compelled to reward their customers through Facebook, Twitter, WeChat, and Weibo, or any number of social network, blogging, and/or micro-blogging services. The beauty of using these channels is the ability of the customer to share these awards or stories of these awards with friends and family; the Reed Network[42] will work its magic from there. It wouldn't be that hard to get patrons to share their social media accounts, either, as a sports book can ask patrons for their social media accounts at sign up through methods likes social bridging. Social media is now often a preferred contact channel and it does make connecting with users in a real-time way exceptionally easy.

Customer satisfaction is the foundation of true customer loyalty, while customer dissatisfaction is one of the main reasons why customers leave.[89] This may sound obvious, but its importance cannot be stressed enough.

According to Jones and Sasser, "the satisfaction-loyalty relationship can be divided into three main zones: Defection, indifference, and affection. The *zone of defection* occurs at low satisfaction levels. Customers will switch unless switching costs are high or there are no viable or convenient alternatives."[93] This, obviously, isn't the case with a sports book, where switching often constitutes little more than browsing to a competing sports book's website (that is also probably willing to give a switching user a sign-up bonus for his or her future patronage). With the vast echo chamber of social media against them, losing only one disgruntled patron could be the least of the sports book's problems.

Jones and Sasser warn that, "Extremely dissatisfied customers can turn into 'terrorists,' providing an abundance of negative feedback about the service provider."[93] Through social media channels, negative feedback can reverberate around the world within seconds. Today, more than ever, sports books must spot dissatisfied customers and approach them before they do irreparable harm to the company's image and reputation and social media is one of the best channels in which to engage them. Like the proverbial canary in the coal mine, the *A.I. Sports Book* will have systems set in place that can warn the business about these customers before they become figurative terrorists.

Sports books need to empower their patrons to post on Facebook or WeChat or Weibo or Twitter or comment about their sports book experiences and, hopefully, turn them into apostles. In Jones and Sasser's *zone of affection*, satisfaction levels are high and "customers may have such high attitudinal loyalty that they don't look for alternative service."[93] It is within this group that "Apostles"—members who praise the firm in public—reside and this is the group that is responsible for improved future business performance.[94] *The A.I. Sports Book* will not only be able to spot these apostles, but also understand them on such a unique and personal level that their loyalty and patronage will almost be guaranteed.

As Darrell Rigby explains in Bain & Company's *Management Tools 2015 An Executive's Guide*[95], CRM "is a process companies use to understand their customer groups and respond quickly—and at times, instantly—to shifting customer desires. CRM technology allows firms to collect and manage large amounts of customer data and then carry out strategies based on that information."[95]

Sports book operators can utilize CRM to:

- Create databases of customers segmented into buckets that allow more effective marketing.
- Generate more accurate sales leads.
- Gather market research on customers.
- Rapidly coordinate information between the sales and marketing staff and front-facing hosts and reps, thereby increasing the customer experience.
- Enable reps to see and understand the financial impact of different product configurations before they set prices.
- Accurately gauge the return on individual promotional programs and the effect of integrated marketing activities, and redirect spending accordingly.
- Accumulate data on customer preferences and problems for product and service designers.
- Increase sales by systematically identifying, managing, and automating sales leads.
- Improve customer retention by uncovering the reason(s) for customer churn.
- Design proactive customer service programs.

Today, CRM is evolving into what has been dubbed "Customer Centric Relationship Management" (CCRM), a style of CRM that focuses on customer preferences above all else. CCRM attempts to understand the client in a deep, behavioral way, and it engages customers in individual, interactive relationships through tailored marketing and one-to-one customer service. This personalization can help a sports book retain customers, build brand loyalty, provide customers not only with the information that they really want, but also with the rewards that they actually might use. Today's technology allows sports books to not only surface the information that they need to know about their customers, but it can also provide front-facing employees with offers that these clients will actually like and, therefore, probably use.

In their comprehensive article on the subject, *Application of Data Mining Techniques in Customer Relationship Management: a Literature Review and Classification*[28], Ngai et al. state that CRM "comprises a set of processes and enabling systems supporting a business strategy to build long term, profitable relationships with specific customers."

In Bain & Company's *Management Tools 2015 An Executive's Guide*[95], Darrell K. Rigby claims, CRM requires managers to:

1. "Start by defining strategic 'pain points' in the customer relationship cycle. These are problems that have a large impact on customer satisfaction and loyalty, where solutions would lead to superior financial rewards and competitive advantage.
2. Evaluate whether—and what kind of—CRM data can fix those pain points. Calculate the value that such information would bring the company.
3. Select the appropriate technology platform, and calculate the cost of implementing it and training employees to use it.
4. Assess whether the benefits of the CRM information outweigh the expenses involved.
5. Design incentive programs to ensure that personnel are encouraged to participate in the CRM program. Many companies have discovered that realigning the organization away from product groups and toward a customer-centered structure improves the success of CRM.
6. Measure CRM progress and impact. Aggressively monitor participation of key personnel in the CRM program. In addition, put measurement systems in place to track the improvement in customer profitability with the use of CRM. Once the data is collected, share the information widely with employees to encourage further participation in the program."[95]

Once a sports book implements a CRM program, data segmentation can begin. According to Wikipedia, market segmentation "is the process of dividing a broad consumer or business market, normally consisting of existing and potential customers, into sub-groups of consumers (known as *segments*) based on some type of shared characteristics."[96]

In dividing or segmenting markets, sports books can look for shared characteristics, such as similar games played, common spend, similar lifestyles choices, or even similar demographic profiles. Market segmentation tries to identify *high yield segments*—i.e., those segments that are likely to be the most profitable or that have outsized growth potential—so that these can be selected for special attention (i.e., become target markets).

Rigby states that customer segmentation "is the subdivision of a market into discrete customer groups that share similar characteristics. Customer Segmentation can be a powerful means to identify unmet customer needs. Companies that identify underserved segments can then outperform the competition by developing uniquely appealing products and services."[95] Rigby adds that customer segmentation is most effective when a company can discover its most profitable segments and then tailor offerings to them, thereby providing the customer with a distinct competitive advantage.[95]

As Rigby explains, "Customer Segmentation requires managers to[95]:

- "Divide the market into meaningful and measurable segments according to customers' needs, their past behaviors or their demographic profiles.
- Determine the profit potential of each segment by analyzing the revenue and cost impacts of serving each segment.
- Target segments according to their profit potential and the company's ability to serve them in a proprietary way.
- Invest resources to tailor product, service, marketing and distribution programs to match the needs of each target segment.
- Measure performance of each segment and adjust the segmentation approach over time as market conditions change decision making throughout the organization."[95]

For a sports book, the pain points might be things like customer loyalty and the marketing department should be asking things like, "Why does it cost so much money to retain customers?" "Can we not find cheaper but more meaningful offers that show understanding of the customer?" Also, "How can we drive customer loyalty to such a degree that our customers rave about us on social media?"

Beside the above methods, customer segmentation can be used to:

- Prioritize new product development efforts.
- Develop customized marketing programs.
- Choose specific product features.
- Establish appropriate service options.
- Design an optimal distribution strategy.
- Determine appropriate product pricing.

Market segmentation assumes that different market segments require different marketing programs—that is, different offers, prices, promotion, distribution or some combination of marketing variables. Market segmentation is not only designed to identify the most profitable segments, but also to develop profiles of key segments in order to better understand their needs and purchase motivations. Insights from segmentation analysis are subsequently used to support marketing strategy development and planning.

Many marketers use the S-T-P approach; Segmentation→ Targeting → Positioning to provide the framework for marketing planning objectives. That is, a market is segmented, one or more segments are selected for targeting, and products or services are positioned in a way that resonates with the selected target market or markets. With real-time technology, segmentation can reach a whole new customer experience level.

The process of segmenting the market is deceptively simple. Seven basic steps describe the entire process, including segmentation, targeting and positioning. In practice, however, the task can be very laborious since it involves poring over loads of data, and it requires a great deal of skill in analysis, interpretation and some judgment. Although a great deal of analysis needs to be undertaken, and many decisions need to be made, marketers tend to use the so-called S-T-P process as a broad framework for simplifying the process outlined here:

- Segmentation:
    - Identify market (also known as the universe) to be segmented.
    - Identify, select and apply base or bases to be used in the segmentation.
    - Develop segment profiles.
- Targeting:
    - Evaluate each segment's attractiveness.
    - Select segment or segments to be targeted.
- Positioning:
    - Identify optimal positioning for each segment.
    - Develop the marketing program for each segment.

Markets can be broken down into the following segments:

- Geographic segment.
- Demographic segment.
- Psychographic segment.
- Behavioral segment.
- Purchase/usage occasion.
- Generational segment.
- Cultural segmentation.

For the sports betting industry, customers can also be further segmented into the following areas:

- Game preference

- Day of week
- Time of day
- Length of session
- Size of stake
- Most and least profitable customers

Although customer segmentation is a common business practice, it has received the following criticisms:

- That it fails to identify sufficiently meaningful clusters.
- That it is no better than mass marketing at building brands.
- That in competitive markets, segments rarely exhibit major differences in the way they use brands.
- Geographic/demographic segmentation is overly descriptive and lacks sufficient insights into the motivations necessary to drive communications strategy.
- Difficulties with market dynamics, notably the instability of segments over time and structural change that leads to segment creep and membership migration as individuals move from one segment to another.

Market segmentation has many critics, but, in spite of its limitations, it remains one of the most enduring concepts in marketing and it continues to be widely used in practice.

As Wikipedia explains[96], there are no formulas for evaluating the attractiveness of market segments and a good deal of judgment must be exercised. Nevertheless, a number of considerations can be used to evaluate market segments for attractiveness, including:

- Segment Size and Growth:
  - How large is the market?
  - Is the market segment substantial enough to be profitable?
  - Segment size can be measured in number of customers, but superior measures are likely to include sales value or volume.
  - Is the market segment growing or contracting?
  - What are the indications that growth will be sustained in the long term? Is any observed growth sustainable?
  - Is the segment stable over time?

- Segment Structural Attractiveness:
  o To what extent are competitors targeting this market segment?
  o Can we carve out a viable position to differentiate from any competitors?
  o How responsive are members of the market segment to the marketing program?
  o Is this market segment reachable and accessible?
- Company Objectives and Resources:
  o Is this market segment aligned with our company's operating philosophy?
  o Do we have the resources necessary to enter this market segment?
  o Do we have prior experience with this market segment or similar market segments?
  o Do we have the skills and/or know-how to enter this market segment successfully?

Caesars is one gaming company that has been able to use social media to measure marketing data quite successfully. In his article *At Caesars, Digital Marketing Is No Crap Shoot*[97], Al Urbanski explains that[97]:

> "While social media networks like Facebook provide metrics that measure activity within its platform, integrating that data to enable visibility across a brand's entire marketing organization is difficult. Caesars, however, unites information from customers coming through social channels across business units, program teams, time zones, and languages. A content-building component allows Caesars' marketers to listen in and respond in real time."

No matter where the customer interaction originates, engagement is a key factor in moving those interactions from the top of the sales funnel to an eventual purchase.[97] "It doesn't matter where customers come in or leave or reenter," says Chris Kahle, Caesars Web Analytics Manager, "if they come to your social page and click your button, or if they go into your content or email and click on that, it's all the same app and you've got them."[97] Caesars IDs a cookie and if the prospects come back around on paid search three days later, Caesars tracks them.[97] "We can track them on every website, even if they came in on a Las Vegas site and then jump markets to Atlantic City," adds Kahle.[97]

Caesars also tracks activity in real time, while responding to customer cues.[97] Unsurprisingly, different types of customers are more responsive to different interactions from Caesars. Aside from dividing customers into categories such as "Frequent Independent Traveler"—or FITs and Total Rewards members, the Caesars team uses tracking data to further segment customers by property or market as well as to determine how each of their various segments respond to content.[97]

Using this data, Caesars evaluates campaigns in regard to KPIs, such as number of nights booked, and adjusts them on the fly to ramp up conversion rates.[97] "What's really dramatic about this is that you can determine what is engaging individuals and target them with it," says Adobe's Langie.[97] "The high-roller segment, for example. They might respond to a very different Web design than the casual visitor and Caesars tailors the page view to who is visiting. Think of the website as a canvas. You can paint a still life of a fruit for one person and something different for another. The canvas is dynamic."[97]

"The speed and the manner with which the chosen website designs and digital marketing tactics are implemented across the Caesars network may well be the most transforming development of the company's new data culture," adds Kahle.[97] And this was no easy task as the Caesars landscape extends over 60 websites for its various properties and services as well as 40 Facebook pages.

"Prior to implementing a data-centric approach to the decision-making process, it could take as long as two weeks to furnish the field with actionable data. They now get it done in a matter of hours," adds Kahle.[97] In 2013, Caesars' implemented Adobe's Digital Marketing Suite, which "includes real-time tracking and segmentation of digital site visitors, analysis of social media's role in purchasing, and content testing by segment or individual visitor."[97]

"The people at the individual properties who are managing the content of the websites are not all technically sophisticated, but Adobe system provides them with built-in capabilities," says Kahle.[97] "Say one of our properties wants to track social. Before, they'd have to spend a lot of time manually adding tracking codes. With Adobe, tracking codes are integrated," Kahle adds.[97]

In this day and age, it is all about one-to-one marketing. "There's a competitive advantage to using customer data to track and customize marketing appeals for targets of one as opposed to solely focusing on the general masses. High rollers frequently drop tens of thousands of dollars at gaming tables, and they are the segment being lured to brand new, luxury casinos in Macau, Singapore, and South Korea."[97]

"Right now we can assign a percentage value to social media if a booking doesn't result right away," Kahle says.[97] "But with social we're going to be experimenting with a longer funnel, maybe a two-week time frame."[97] "Values are ascribed to social media for being the site of initial contact with a new customer, for instance, or for numbers of positive reviews by current customers."[97]

Currently, Caesars can't measure the total value of a reservation booked online and also can't determine how much an online booker spends at the tables during his or her stay.[97] This is important information when it comes to truly understanding a patron. Caesars would also like to know if, for example, "customers left the Caesars' casino in Las Vegas and went to dinner at Gordon Ramsay's restaurant at the Paris Las Vegas, so they could offer them a free dinner at the restaurant to close the deal on a future booking."[97]

"Eventually we're going to set a time frame that will never expire [on the sales funnel]," Kahle says.[97] "But for now we've built a sales allocation model that goes beyond the last click, and that's OK. Most organizations using multiple marketing channels are still stuck on that last click."[97]

The latest developments in CRM technology is adding AI to the process. As explained in the *MIT Technology Review* article *Transform Customer Experience by Harnessing the Power of AI in CRM*[98];

> *"Unlike traditional customer-facing platforms that deliver a fragmented view of the buyer, an intelligent platform presents a single aggregated view of customer data. The built-in intelligence layer helps businesses spot trends, anticipate needs, and respond more proactively. With that complete picture, for example, a business knows exactly when the customer last purchased a product, what that product was, whether he or she had a problem, and, if so, exactly how it was resolved."*

MIT Technology Review goes on to add that, "the wide range of machine-learning (ML) models learns from what is collected to unearth and match patterns, as well as act on correlations that would otherwise remain hidden."[98] Using a consumer shopping experience an as example, the *MIT Technology Review* article explains that "AI models embedded within the CRM system's personalization engine take into account the catalog that any given shopper sees and the context on how the merchant is engaging with that shopper, and then ranks every product for that buyer in terms of relevance from search results, making the most targeted and personalized results ever."[98] This can be done at scale, with a constant refining of shopper recommendations based on the ML, explains the *MIT Technology Review*.[98]

"The data for such recommendations include both historic and real-time click-stream data from multiple sources."[98] *MIT Technology Review* warns that, "What is challenging is that the algorithms used to create predictions are as heterogeneous as the sources of data used. To deliver predictive recommendations with the highest accuracy, a range of different algorithms is applied."[98] "In selecting the right algorithm, the champion-challenger model is used, meaning that every time an algorithm yields accuracy, it is automatically set to default over other models within the platform," the article states.[98] "That way, the path to personalization is very short," the article notes. "The end result of such accurate recommendations is that both customer conversions and the overall potential value of the merchant's inventory goes up," the article concludes.[98]

Beyond product recommendations, the article states that, "other powerful capabilities that enhance CRM for both employee and customer experiences include the algorithms for speech recognition, sentiment analysis, intent, content summarization through natural language processing, and question answering based on tables of data."[98]

"Predicting customer's future behaviors and needs often turns on the ability to parse their emotions, more than just their past purchases, and creating a shared bond," claims the *MIT Technology Review* article.[98] The article describes a CRM system that online retailer Fanatics utilizes to ensure that it understands its customers in the best possible way, through his or her emotional team bond, because, as Fanatics puts it, "sports merchandise is an emotional business."[98]

"We want to deliver the most relevant merchandise to you, at the right time, for your team," explains Jonathan Wilbur, the company's director of CRM.[98] "If you're a Yankees fan, we want to make sure we're never showing you anything Boston Red Sox," Wilbur adds.[98]

"The company's ability to engage with customers around the biggest sporting events in near real time is unmatched," claims the *MIT Technology Review*.[98] Fanatics carries merchandise for more than 1,000 professional and college teams, including from the NFL, MLB, NBA, NHL, NASCAR, and football leagues from around the world.[98] "The company is event-driven, engaging fans around everything from the World Series to football star Peyton Manning's retirement announcement," explains the *MIT Technology Review*.[98] "Multiply a thousand teams by an endless stream of sports news events, and you've got billions of e-mails going to fans each year."[98]

"In 2015, we sent about 3.5 billion messages," says Wilbur.[98] "When a team wins the Super Bowl, we can have 350 products live with a press of a button three seconds after the game," Wilbur adds.[98] Wilbur's team "built scripts that searched customer data to display fans' favorite teams, pulled in real-time scores and stats from vendor feeds, and personalized branding using partner IDs."[98]

"The resulting campaigns were customized according to multi-tier segments. Fanatics was able to deliver merchandise relevant to fans and their teams at just the right time," explains the *MIT Technology Review*.[98] "Carolina Panther fans didn't get e-mails about "Super Bowl Champs" T-shirts after their team lost the big game, but Denver Broncos fans had offers in their inboxes within minutes after the final whistle."[98]

"Fanatics is even building automatically triggered rules-driven campaigns based on dynamic information," notes the *MIT Technology Review*.[98] "Any time a baseball player hits three homes runs in a game, we'll send an e-mail featuring his jersey. Set it and forget it," Wilbur adds.[98] Although hitting three home runs in a game is a rare event, Fanatics needs to be careful not to overdo it. Fans will, of course, want to celebrate if such an occurrence happened, but businesses should be careful not to hit their customers too often. In terms of marketing, even if it is contextually aware and hyper-personalized, there can be too much of a good thing.

Sports books should emulate what Fanatics is doing because gambling is often just another form of support people make to the teams they love. As any Arsenal fan will tell you, one of their biggest rivals is Tottenham and a customer who shows a propensity to like Arsenal might find bets for a team playing against Tottenham a particularly interesting proposition, especially if they are in a heated Premier League title race.

Companies like Adobe, IBM, Oracle, Microsoft, SAP, Pega Systems, Salesforce.com, and SugarCRM all have products that not only include contact management systems that integrate emails, documents, jobs and faxes, but also integrate with mobile and social media accounts as well, so the market doesn't lack product, but this will be a case where one side doesn't fit all. A deep understanding of the sports book's current systems and pain points should be explored before any solution is chosen and implemented.

Loyalty is so important to a sports book because, as repeated studies have shown, customers become more profitable over time. In their study *Zero Defections: Quality Comes to Service*[99], Reichheld and Sasser demonstrated that a customer's profitability increases as his or her loyalty increases. In this study, the authors found that it usually took more than a year to recoup any customer acquisition costs, but then profits increased as customers remained with the service or firm. Reichheld and Sasser believe there are four factors for this growth and, in order of their importance, they are[99]:

1. Profit derived from increased purchases: as a customer ages, he or she will probably become more affluent, therefore will have more money to spend for company products/services.
2. Profit from reduced operating costs: As customers become more experienced, they should make fewer demands on the business, perhaps taking advantage of available self-service options.
3. Profit from referrals to other customers.
4. Profit from price premiums: long-term customers are more likely to pay regular prices for services rather than being tempted into using a businesses' lower profit products and/or services.

As previously mentioned, customer satisfaction is the foundation of true customer loyalty, while customer dissatisfaction is the key factor that drives customers away.[89] This may sound obvious, but its importance cannot be overstated. The number one thing that creates loyalty in *anybody* (that includes your customers) is the social construct of reciprocity—the social norm that's been evaluated and debated since the days of Aristotle. Many scholars believe it to be one of the single most defining aspects of social interaction that keeps society whole. Reciprocity doesn't have to be a bar of gold, like some casinos in

Macau like to offer their high rollers, it could simply be an acknowledgement of poor customer service along with the promise to do better in the future.

Social media can help amplify the "relationship" in "Customer Relationship Management", thereby enabling organizations to connect and engage consumers in a unique way, as well as personalize and monetize customer relationships on a sustained basis, which should increase profitability.[175] "Social media also provides a path to richer customer analysis, using technologies capable of funneling and consolidating customer insights."[175] Insights derived from this analysis can help companies to "dynamically calibrate, anticipate, and offer products and services that meet perpetually shifting consumer demands in a hyper-competitive marketplace."[175]

Specifically for a sports book, it would be advantageous to link a patron's account with his or her social media accounts so that the sports book could get a heads-up on what a patron might be saying about them on social media.

In his article *Customer Analytics in the Age of Social Media*[100] for TDWI, David Stodder reports that the importance of customer analytics is in the boardroom; "overwhelmingly, respondents cited giving executive management customer and market insight (71%) as the most important business benefit that their organization seeks to achieve from implementing customer analytics."[100] "This percentage rises to 81% when survey results are filtered to see only the responses from those who indicated 'strong acceptance' of data-driven customer analytics over gut feel."[100]The second highest benefit cited, at 62%, was "the ability to react more quickly to changing market conditions, which speaks to the need for customer data insights to help decision makers address competitive pressures from rapid product or service commoditization."[100]

With the commoditization of products and services, customer loyalty can be elusive; innovation must be constant and it should help to reveal why an organization might be losing its customer base.[100] "Information insights from analytics can help organizations align product and service development with strategic business objectives for customer loyalty."[100] These insights can also help an organization be selective about how they deploy their marketing campaigns and customer-touch processes so that they emphasize features in new products and services that are important to each specific customer.[100]

Customer analytics can also provide answers to questions like[100]:

- When in the life cycle are customers most likely to churn?
- What types of products or services would prevent them from churning?
- When should customers be offered complimentary items?
- When is it too costly to try to keep certain customers?

Businesses can realize significant ROI from investing in customer analytics as it can improve the marketing department's efficiency, effectiveness[100], and reach.

However, customer analytics ROI is a difficult thing to fully quantify. Better customer knowledge equates to more optimized marketing spend because a business can focus its resources on those campaigns that have the highest predicted chances of success for particular segments, as well as cutting off or avoiding those that have the least.[100]

"By using analytics to eliminate mismatches of campaigns targeting the wrong customers or using the wrong messages and offers, marketing functions can reduce wasteful spending and increase gains relative to costs."[100] Customer segmentation allows organizations to move "away from one-size-fits-all, brand-level-only marketing and toward the 'market of one': that is, personalized, one-to-one marketing."[100]

Reaching a customization and customer service level that makes a customer feel as though he or she is a preferred customer is not easy, scaling that up so that an entire database of customers feel that they are unique and receiving outstanding customer service is even more challenging, but, in this day and age of hyper-personalization, it is almost a necessity if a company wants to provide good and engaging customer service.

TDWI Research[100] examined the importance of accomplishing various objectives for gaining positive ROI from customer analytics (see Figure 7). "Using customer analytics to target cross-sell and up-sell opportunities was the objective cited by the biggest percentage of respondents (54%)."[100] This objective is about gaining more value from existing customers understanding their purchasing habits and trying to get them to buy more products more often.[100]

"Some organizations (18%) are implementing an advanced technique called 'uplift modeling' (also called incremental or true-lift modeling), which enables marketers to use data mining to measure the impact and influence of marketing actions on customers."[100] Insights such as these allow marketers to develop new kinds of predictive models to determine the best prospects for up-sell and cross-sell offerings.[100] "As firms scale up to execute large numbers of campaigns across multiple channels, the efficiency gained from predictive modeling can be critical to marketing spending optimization," argues Stodder.[100]

Analytics can improve marketing performance by quantifying a customer's lifetime value as well as customer worth at the many different stages in the customer's life cycle.[100] Armed with this kind of information, managers can align their deployment of resources to achieve the highest value, as well as avoid the costs and inefficiencies of marketing to the wrong people at the wrong time.[100]

Organizations have long used demographics such as gender, household size, education, occupation, and income to segment customers, but data mining techniques let organizations segment much larger customer populations and, perhaps, more importantly, determine whether to apply new characteristics that refine segmentation to fit the specific attributes of the organization's products and services.[100] AI can increase these demographic, education, occupation, and incomes variants exponentially, as well as add behavioral ones as well.

In your organization, which of the following marketing objectives are most important to achieve for customer analytics to deliver a return on investment? (Please select all that apply.)

Target cross-sell and up-sell opportunities	54%
Improve customer segmentation	49%
Predict retention, attrition, and churn rates	47%
Determine lifetime customer value	42%
Increase portfolio penetration per customer	39%
Optimize marketing across multiple channels	37%
Impact other business functions (sales, service, support)	35%
Forecast buying habits and lifestyle preferences	32%
Measure types of loyalty for campaign targeting	26%
Prioritize marketing e-mail messages	23%
Implement uplift, incremental, or true-lift modeling	18%
Increase speed of multivariate testing analysis	14%

Figure 7: Which Are the Most Important Business Objectives When It Comes to Customer Analytics?
Source: TDWI Research[100], Based on 1,625 responses from 432 respondents; almost four responses per respondent, on average.

"Customer analytics using data mining tools improves the speed of segmentation analysis over manual and spreadsheet efforts that are often used in less mature organizations."[100] Speed is a vital ingredient for marketing initiatives that are time sensitive, particularly for those companies that need to provide real-time cross-sell and up-sell offers to customers clicking through web pages.

With social media added to the mix, as well as clickstreams, and other behavioral data, the volume and variety of data is exploding, but that can be a godsend for sports books that want to increase personalization.[100] "Social networking sites such as Facebook, Twitter, LinkedIn, and MySpace have files containing petabytes of data, often in vast Hadoop clusters."[100] Weibo and WeChat add hundreds of millions of users into the mix and, with it, petabytes of data as well.

Text analytics can be used to increase the speed, depth, and consistency of unstructured content analysis far greater than what can be done manually.[100] "More advanced analytics can look for correlations between satisfaction ratings, commented sentiments, and other records, such as first-call-resolution metrics."[100]

"To analyze data generated by social media networking services such as Twitter, Facebook, Weibo, and LinkedIn, many organizations are implementing Hadoop and NoSQL technologies, which do not force a schema on the source data prior to storage, as traditional BI and data warehousing systems do."[100] Because of this, the discovery analytics processes can run against the raw data.[100] "Customer analytics tools need to be able to consume data from sources such as Hadoop clusters and then integrate the insights into overall customer profiles," advises Stodder.[100]

The data sources can be varied for these technologies and methods; "they include transaction data, clickstreams, satisfaction surveys, loyalty card membership data, credit card purchases, voter registration, location data, and a host of [other] demographic data types."[100]

In its *Retail Analytics: Game Changer for Customer Loyalty*[101], Cognizant argues that in the retail industry, "predictive models can be used to analyze past performance to assess the likelihood that a customer will exhibit a specific behavior in order to improve marketing effectiveness." This can help with "predicting customer reactions to a given product and can be leveraged to improve basket size, increase the value of the basket and switch the customer to a better and more profitable offering."[177] Predictive models can also help tailor pricing strategies that take into account both the need for competitive pricing and the company's financial bottom line.[177]

Predictive analytics and data mining are used to discover which variables out of possibly hundreds are most influential in determining customer loyalty within certain segments.[100] "Advanced analytics generally involves statistical, quantitative, or mathematical analysis and centers on developing, testing, training, scoring, and monitoring predictive models."[100]

Models can be created that will uncover patterns, affinities, anomalies, and other useful insights for marketing campaigns and for determining cross-sell and up-sell opportunities.[100] "The tools and techniques are also used for developing and deploying behavioral scoring models for marketing, deciding whether to adjust customers' credit limits for purchases, and a variety of highly time-sensitive analytic processes," notes Stodder.[100]

"As more online customer behavior is recorded in Web logs and tracked through cookies and other observation devices, sizeable amounts of information are becoming available to organizations that seek a more accurate view of a customer's path to purchase," says Stodder.[100] Attribution analysis is, first and foremost, a big-data problem, given the quantity and variety of data available from today's multiple platforms.[100]

Businesses that are performing attribution analysis will frequently employ Hadoop and/or MapReduce, with analytic software solutions such as R, SAS's eMiner, SAP's InfiniteInsights, Python, and IBM's SPSS, amongst others.[100] This allows a business to run sophisticated algorithms against detailed data to find the correct path to purchase. This analysis can then be integrated with analysis from other data types and sources, including those which might have been generated by some offline customer activity.[100]

Attribution analysis can reveal such things as what kinds of campaigns most influence customer behavior.[100] "The analysis can help organizations determine where to allocate marketing resources to gain the highest level of success, as well as how to more accurately assign the percentage of credit due to specific marketing and advertising processes," Stodder concludes.[100]

On August 13, 2014, Facebook announced a major step forward in the area of attribution analysis. In his article *Facebook Now Tells Whether Mobile Ads Lead to Desktop Purchases*[102], T. Peterson says that Facebook "would start telling advertisers on what device people saw an ad and on what device they took an action, such as buying a product or signing up for a test drive, as a result of seeing that ad. That means Facebook will be able to credit mobile ads that lead to desktop sales and desktop ads that result in mobile purchases."

Peterson notes that, "Advertisers can already track conversions through Facebook on desktop and on mobile, but to date Facebook hasn't broken out conversions by device type for advertisers to see. For example, advertisers have been able to see if their desktop and mobile ads lead to conversions, but they didn't know on which device type those conversions were taking place."[102]

However, Facebook's new cross-device conversion measurement only works for advertisers who place specific Facebook trackers on their websites and mobile apps.[102] "Without sharing users' personal information with the advertiser, those trackers can see that a Facebook user is checking out the advertisers' site or app and whether they've converted in the advertiser-specified fashion."[102] If the person does convert, "Facebook's trackers can trace back to see if that person has seen an ad from that advertiser on Facebook, which may have directly or indirectly led to the conversion."[102] Of course, nothing is 100% certain when it comes to attribution analysis, but this is a big step in the right direction.

With many of the following analytical marketing models, businesses should keep in mind that it is important to create control groups to measure the true effects of their models and marketing campaigns. Control groups are typical components in marketing analysis and are fundamental to statistical studies.[103]

In his article *Control Group Marketing—With or Without CRM Software Systems*[179], Rick Cook states that, "The basic idea of a control group is simple. Select a random (or nearly random) sample from your campaign's marketing list and exclude them from promotion. Then measure the control group's activity and compare it to the activity of the group targeted via a campaign. The difference between the control and campaign group gives you a pretty good notion of how effective—and profitable—the campaign is.

"The theory is that a certain fraction of the customers in the campaign are going to purchase from you anyway during the campaign period. The control group lets you filter out that effect, as well as the effects of other channels which may be influencing behavior, such as display advertising, and shows you how much the campaign has affected customer behavior," explains Cook.[179]

Although control groups should be used to test out the effects of marketing campaigns, few companies include them in their marketing processes.[179] "Marketing control groups become even more effective when combined with the customer analytics found in most marketing automation or customer relationship management systems," notes Cook.[179]

Cook argues that, "With a CRM system and a control group you can also detect the halo effect of your campaign. These are purchases and other actions which are influenced by the campaign but don't come in through the normal campaign channels."[179] For example, a customer could be so inspired by one particular campaign that he or she picks up the phone and orders products directly from the company instead of going through the call-to-action channel.[179] "Another example is the customer who doesn't use the promotional coupon you included in your marketing campaign but who purchases the product anyway."[179] Cook notes that brands "can assume that customers in the test group who respond in unconventional methods are still influenced by the campaign and so should be counted as part of the campaign effect."[179] "Because CRM software lets you track all points of customer contact, and not just the direct response to the campaign, it can capture these halo customers," concludes Cook.[179]

The size of the control group is usually 10 percent of the size of the campaign or test group.[179] Ideally you want the control group to be a truly random sample from the company's campaign list, but this is difficult to attain in practice as complete randomness is hard to achieve.[179] "Many companies select their control group by a simpler process, such as selecting every 10th name on the list to make up the control group," but there are other more scientific ways to choose the participants, which could and should be utilized.[179]

Customer Lifecycle

Today, we can safely say that the mass marketing experience is over. According to *Gartner*, there are five stages of customer experience maturity—initial, developing, defined, managed and optimizing. The goal here is to improve the customer experience through a systematic process to improve customer satisfaction, loyalty and advocacy.

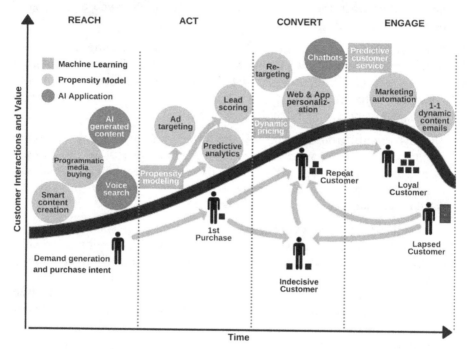

Figure 8: A.I. for marketers across the customer lifecycle
Source: Huguesrey[104]

In its *15 Applications of Artificial Intelligence in Marketing*[104], Huguesrey maps out the most effective AI technologies for marketing across the customer lifecycle. "All the techniques are 'AI' in the sense that they involve computer intelligence, but we've broken them down into 3 different types of technology—Machine Learning Techniques, Applied Propensity Models, and AI Applications," says Huguesrey.[104] The steps are broken down into the customer lifecycle RACE framework (See Figure 8), which contains four separate groups—Reach, Act, Convert, and Engage.[104]

"Each different application has major implications for marketers, but the applications have different roles to play across the customer journey. Some are better for attracting customers, whilst others are useful for conversion or re-engaging past customers," says Huguesrey.[104]

According to Huguesrey, reach "involves using techniques such as content marketing, SEO and other 'earned media' to bring visitors to your site and start them on the buyer's journey."[104] "AI & applied propensity models can be used at this stage to attract more visitors and provide those that do reach your site with a more engaging experience."[104]

AI-generated content can be a good place to start. "AI can't write a political opinion column or a blog post on industry-specific best practice advice, but there are certain areas where AI generated content can be useful and help draw visitors to your site," says Huguesrey.[104] AI content writing programs like Wordsmith can pick elements from a dataset and structure a "human sounding" article.[104]

"AI writers are useful for reporting on regular, data-focused events. Examples include quarterly earnings reports, sports matches, and market data," says Huguesrey.[104] If you operate in a niche such as financial services or sports, then "AI generated content could form a useful component of your content marketing strategy."[104] AI-powered content curation allows brands to better engage visitors and customers on their site by showing them relevant content.[104] Huguesrey sees it as "a great technique for subscription businesses, where the more someone uses the service, more data the machine learning algorithm has to use and the better the recommendations of content become."[104] The systems becomes somewhat of a self-fulfilling prophecy, like it has become for companies like Netflix, Pandora, and Amazon.

In the coming years, voice search is expected to change the future of SEO and brands need to keep up.[104] Huguesrey believes "A brand that nails voice search can leverage big gains in organic traffic with high purchase intent thanks to increased voice search traffic due to AI driven virtual personal assistants."[104]

Programmatic media buying—the algorithmic purchase and sale of advertisements in real time—"can use propensity models generated by machine learning algorithms to more effectively target ads at the most relevant customers."[104] AI can ensure programmatic ads don't appear on questionable websites and/or remove them from a list of sites that the advertiser doesn't want them to appear on.[104]

In her article *Programmatic Advertising 101: How it Works*[105], Sara Vicioso states that, "programmatic advertising is the automated process of buying and selling ad inventory through an exchange, connecting advertisers to publishers." This process uses artificial intelligence technologies "and real-time bidding for inventory across mobile, display, video and social channels—even making its way into television."[105]

Vicioso adds that, "Artificial intelligence technologies have algorithms that analyze a visitor's behavior allowing for real time campaign optimizations towards an audience more likely to convert. Programmatic companies have the ability to gather this audience data to then target more precisely, whether it's from 1st party (their own) or from a 3rd party data provider."[105]

Programmatic media buying includes the use of demand-side platforms (DSPs), supply-side platforms (SSPs) and data management platforms (DMPs).[105] DSPs facilitate the process of buying ad inventory on the open market, as well as provide the ability to reach a brand's target audience due to the integration of DMPs.[105] "DMPs collect and analyze a substantial amount of cookie data to then allow the marketer to make more informed decisions of whom their target audience may be," says Vicioso.[105]

"On the publisher side of things, publishers manage their unsold ad inventory through an SSP,"[105] which reports such clickstream activity as how long a visitor was on a specific site or how many pages were viewed per visit.[105] Vicioso explains that, "SSPs will ultimately be in charge of picking the winning bid and will serve the winning banner ad on the publisher's site."[105]

As Allie Shaw notes in her article *AI could save television advertising with advanced personalization*[106], "In short, AI programs draw from data pools to make decisions about where and when to buy or sell ad space according to demographic and cost-versus-benefit information." "Essentially, your TV can learn about your habits in the way your web browser already does, allowing advertisers to present you with ads based on that information—so you'll see fewer repetitive ads that you don't care about. This means you and your neighbors may all be watching the premiere of *The Walking Dead* but seeing different ads based on your unique interests," explains Shaw.[106]

"Thanks to programmatic TV advertising, advertisers can know how many people have viewed their ads, where these viewers are located, and what their viewing history looks like—with information updating by the minute," says Shaw.[106] "They're also able to get more accurate data about an ad's cost per impression (CPM, or the cost for each 1,000 people who see the ad), allowing for more relevant and cost-efficient targeting," she explains.[106]

The second step of the RACE framework is "Act". Brands must draw visitors in and make them aware of the company's product and/or services. Machine learning algorithms can build propensity models that can predict the likelihood of a given customer to convert, the price at which a customer is likely to convert, and/or what customers are most likely to turn into repeat customers.[104]

"Propensity models generated by machine learning can be trained to score leads based on certain criteria so that your sales team can establish how 'hot' a given lead is, and if they are worth devoting time to," explains Huguesrey.[104] "This can be particularly important in B2B businesses with consultative sales processes, where each sale takes a considerable amount of time on the part of the sales team," says Huguesrey.[104]

The machine learning algorithms can run through vast amounts of historical data to establish which ads perform best on which people and at what stage in the buying process.[104] Using this data, ads can be served to them with the most effective content at the most effective time.[104] By using machine learning to constantly optimize thousands of variables, businesses can achieve more effective ad placement and content than traditional methods.[104] However, humans will still be needed for the creative parts.[104]

The third step of the RACE framework—"Content"—is one of the most important steps and it includes dynamic pricing, re-targeting, web and app personalization, and chatbots.[104]

All marketers know that sales are one of the most effective ways of moving product, but they can also hurt the financial bottom line.[104] Sales are so effective because they get people to buy a product that they might not have previously considered because they couldn't justify the cost of the purchase. But sales also mean people who would have paid the higher price pay less than they would have. The trick is to understand the threshold between buying and not buying the product and this is where dynamic pricing comes in.

By targeting special offers only at those who are likely to need them in order to convert, brands can ensure they don't give offers to people who have the propensity to pay full price.[104] "Machine learning can build a propensity model of which traits show a customer is likely to need an offer to convert, and which are likely to convert without the need for an offer," says Huguesrey.[104] This means companies can increase sales, while also maximizing their profit margins.[104]

By using a propensity model to predict a customer's stage in the buying cycle, sports books can serve the customer, either through an app or on a web page, with the most relevant and timely content.[104] "If someone is still new to a site, content that informs them and keeps them interested will be most effective, whilst if they have visited many times and are clearly interested in the product then more in-depth content about a product's benefits will perform better," recommends Huguesrey.[104]

Another way to convert customers is with chatbots that mimic human intelligence by interpreting a consumer's queries and potentially complete an order for them.[104] Chatbots are relatively easy to build and Facebook is simplifying the process of developing chatbots for brands.[104] Facebook "wants to make its Messenger app the go-to place for people to have conversations with brand's virtual ambassadors."[104] Facebook has created the wit.ai bot engine, which allows brands to train bots with sample conversations and have these bots continually learn from customer interactions.[104]

"Much like with ad targeting, machine learning can be used to establish what content is most likely to bring customers back to the site based on historical data," says Huguesrey.[104] By building an accurate prediction model of what content works best to win back different customer types, machine learning can help optimize a brand's retargeting ads to make them as effective as possible.[104]

The final step of the RACE framework is "Engage". As previously mentioned, it is far easier to sell to an existing customer than it is to attract new ones, therefore keeping current customers happy is paramount.[104] "This is particularly true in subscription-based business, where a high churn rate can be extremely costly," argues Huguesrey.[104] "Predictive analytics can be used to work out which customers are most likely to unsubscribe from a service, by assessing what features are most common in customers who do unsubscribe," says Huguesrey.[104] "It's then possible to reach out to these customers with offers, prompts or assistance to prevent them from churning," recommends Huguesrey.[104]

Marketing automation techniques usually involve a series of business rules, which, once triggered, initiate or continue interactions with a given customer.[104] However, these rules can be quite arbitrary.[104] "Machine learning can run through billions of points of customer data and establish when are the most effective times to make contact, what words in subject lines are most effective and much more," says Huguesrey.[104] "These insights can then be applied to boost the effectiveness of your marketing automation efforts," he adds.[104]

"In a similar fashion to marketing automation, applying insights generated from machine learning can create extremely effective 1:1 dynamic emails," says Huguesrey.[104] Propensity models can "establish a subscribers propensity to buy certain categories, sizes and colors through their previous behavior and displays the most relevant products in newsletters."[104] The product stock, deals, pricing specifically individualized for each customer would all be correct at the time the customer opens the offer email.[104]

For most businesses, customer information housed in an EDW would include things like transactional data, customer and CRM data, mobile, social, and location data, as well as information from web logs that track its user's web behavior, and online advertising bid management systems. EDWs should also give a business the ability to do analytics on the fly, which could help the customer's experience in a multitude of ways.

Today, most big companies which have large customer databases have loyalty programs that are part of a CRM and/or an SCRM initiative. These companies should provide their customers with an intimate experience that will make them want to return to again and again and again.

Obviously, creating a consolidated customer view is a necessary component of personalization. Another important step of bringing personalization efforts up to a user's expectation level will be using behavioral data in the process. In order to create these types of customer experiences, businesses need to strategically collect and utilize customer data, including real-time signals of intent, which aren't always captured today. They are not easy to capture, either.

Today, I think we can safely say the mass marketing experience is over. According to *Gartner*, there are five stages of customer experience maturity—initial, developing, defined, managed and optimizing. The goal for the sports book is to improve the customer experience through a systematic process to improve customer satisfaction, loyalty, and advocacy.

For sports betting companies, information housed in an EDW would include things like transactional data, patron and customer relationship management (CRM) data, mobile, social, and location data, as well as information from web logs that track its user's web behavior, and online advertising bid management systems. A sports book should have the ability to do analytics on the fly, which could help the customer's experience in a multitude of ways.

Attribution analysis can also help a sports book understand a person's preferences; someone who responds to an offer that contains images of their team players or a sports book is revealing information that is helpful in future marketing campaigns.

Today, most major sports betting companies have customer loyalty programs that are a part of a CRM and/or a SCRM initiative to provide their customers with an intimate experience that will make them want to return to the sports book again and again and again.

Obviously, creating a consolidated customer view is a necessary component of personalization. Another important step of bringing personalization efforts up to a user's expectation level will be using behavioral data. In order to create these types of customer experiences, sports betting companies should strategically collect and utilize customer data, including real-time signals of intent, which are typically not captured today.

In their article *Knowing What to Sell, When, and to Whom*[107], authors V. Kumar, R. Venkatesan, and W. Reinartz showed how, by simply understanding and tweaking behavioral patterns, they could increase the hit rate for offers and promotions to consumers, which then had an immediate impact on revenue.

By applying statistical models based on the work of Nobel prize-winning economist Daniel McFadden, researchers accurately predicted not only a specific person's purchasing habits, but also the specific time of the purchase to an accuracy of 80%.[107]

Obviously, the potential to market to an individual when he or she is primed to accept the advertising is advantageous for both parties involved. By utilizing data from past campaigns and measures generated by a predictive modeling process, sports books can track actual campaign responses versus expected campaign responses, which can often prove wildly divergent. Additionally, sports betting companies can generate upper and lower "control" limits that can be used to automatically alert campaign managers when a campaign is over or underperforming, letting them focus on campaigns that specifically require attention.

One of the benefits of automating campaigns is that offers based on either stated or inferred preferences of patrons can be developed. Analysis can identify which customers may or may not be more responsive to an offer centered around a particular team or bet type. The result: more individualized offers are sent out to the sport book's patrons and, because these offers tap into a customer's wants, desires, needs *and* expectations, they are more likely to be used; more offers used mean more successful campaigns, which means more money coming into the Sports book's coffers.

With predictive analytics, sports book can even predict which low-tier and mid-tier customers are likely to become the next high rollers. In so doing, the sports book can afford to be more generous in its offers as it will know that there is a high likelihood that these customers will appreciate the personalized attention and therefore become long term—and, hopefully, highly profitable—patrons.

Once the patron leaves the sports book's website, the marketing cycle begins anew. RFM models can project the time at which a patron is likely to return and social media should be checked for any comments, likes or uploads, left by a customer, something that should already be occurring.

A campaign management solution can enable the sports book to develop and manage personalised customer communications strategies and the delivery of offers. It will also allow users to rapidly create, modify and manage multi-channel, multi-wave marketing campaigns that integrate easily with any fulfilment channel, automatically producing outbound (contact) and inbound (response) communication history. Users can define target segments, prioritise selection rules, prioritise offers across multiple campaigns and channels, select communication channels, schedule and execute campaigns, and perform advanced analyses to predict and evaluate the success of customer communications.

With customer attitudes towards personalized content being shaped by recommendation engines like Amazon, Pandora, and Netflix, consumers are becoming more used to receiving what they want, when they want it, and on whatever channel they prefer it on. Sports books must keep this in mind when developing personalization programs. The consumer has become highly sophisticated and he or she expects the level of sophistication received on platforms like Amazon, Netflix, Roku, Google, and Pandora to filter over to all his or her other company communications; companies shouldn't waste their time with non-matching offers or the customer will probably go down the street to a competitor's casino.

The customer journey starts the moment a potential customer browses to a sports book's webpage or notices an advertisement for a bet on television, or on the Internet, or in print. With a few browser clickstrokes, a sports book's ecommerce department can create a click path analysis that reveals customer interactions on the sport book's website. Descriptive analytical functionalities can then provide a deeper understanding of the customer journey. Column dependencies (standard in most of today's Data Integration software tools) can visually display the strength of a relationship between attributes within any dataset. This helps users better understand the characteristics of their data and is often used to help target further analytics.

A recommendation engine can help predict a person's interest based on historical data from many users. This is useful in increasing client engagement, recommending more relevant choices and increasing customer satisfaction. For example, recommendations can predict interest in the sports book's games and services.

Rapid advancements in facial-recognition technology have reached the point where a single face can be compared against 36 million others in about one second.[108] A system made by Hitachi Kokusai Electric and reported by DigInfo TV shown at a security trade show recently was able to achieve this blazing speed by not wasting time on image processing. Using edge analytics, it takes visual data directly from the camera to compare the face in real time.[108] The software also groups faces with similar features, so it is able to narrow down the field of choices very quickly. The usefulness to the sports book's security enforcement is pretty obvious, but it can be used by multiple departments; facial recognition technology can be set up to send alerts to hosts, store clerks or managers, or just about anyone needing it.

Once a face has been recognized, alerts can be sent to a sports book's personnel through a mobile app or an SMS message. A screen can display the patron's name, or a photo just taken from the video feed. Betting preferences, and other details, like a customer's average daily Theo or ADT, can also be surfaced onto a mobile device.

Predictive modeling is only useful if it is deployed *and* it creates an action. Taking advantage of the more powerful, statistically based segmentation methods, customers can be segmented not only by dollar values, but also on all known information, which can include behavioral information gleaned from resort activities, as well as the patron's simple demographic information. This more detailed segmentation allows for more targeted and customer-focused marketing campaigns. Models can be evaluated and reports generated on multiple statistical measures, such as neural networks, decision trees, genetic algorithms, the nearest neighbor method, rule induction, and lift and gains charts. Once built, scores can be generated in a variety of ways to facilitate quick and easy implementation. The projects themselves can be re-used and shared to facilitate faster model development and knowledge transfer.

In his paper *Predictive Analytics*[109], Wayne Eckerson advises creating predictive models by using the following six steps:

1. Define the business objectives and desired outcomes for the project and then translate them into predictive analytic objectives and tasks.
2. Explore and analyze the source data to determine the most appropriate data and model building approach and then scope the effort.
3. Prepare the data by selecting, extracting, and transforming the data, which will be the basis for the models.
4. Build the models, as well as test and validate them.
5. Deploy the models by applying them to the business decisions and processes.
6. Manage and update the models accordingly.

By utilizing data from past campaigns and measures generated by the predictive modeling process, a sports book can track actual campaign responses versus expected campaign responses, which can often prove wildly divergent. Additionally, a sports book can generate upper and lower "control" limits that can be used to automatically alert campaign managers when a campaign is over or underperforming, letting them focus on campaigns that specifically require attention.

By understanding what type of patron is on its website, why they are there, and what they like to do while they are there, a sports book can individualize its marketing campaigns so that they can be more effective, thereby increasing the sports book's ROI.

All of a patron's captured information can now become part of the Master Marketing Profile that will be the basis for future marketing efforts. Combining the daily, weekly and monthly Master Marketing Profiles will also allow the sports book to develop insightful macro views of its data, views that could help with labor management and vendor needs.

The *Sports Book Engagement and Loyalty Platform* (see Figure 9) shows how a sports book would engage its customers in a loyalty platform that utilizes social media as an important part of the process. The *Sports Book Engagement and Loyalty Platform* can be implemented in a multitude of ways. In the *Listening* part, sports books should define and look out for triggers such as photos, hashtags, keywords, likes, video views, etc., etc. This runs the gamut, from staying on top of keywords and hashtags on Twitter, Facebook, Instagram, and a whole host of other potential image-related social sites.

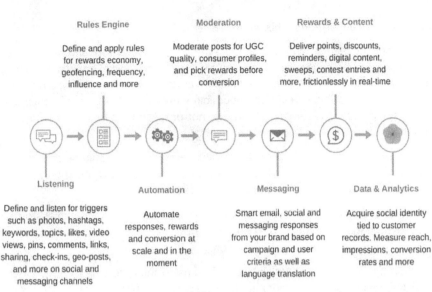

Figure 9: Sports Book Engagement and Loyalty Platform
Source: chirpify.com

Check-ins and geo-posts from sites like Foursquare, WeChat, Instagram, Facebook, WhatsApp, YouTube, as well as a whole host of other social networks can help sports books connect with a nearby audience. Sports betting operators should also be listening to comment boards or short-term blogging sites like Tumblr or social news aggregation sites like Reddit for comments about their products and services.

The *Rules Engine* step is pretty straightforward; sports books are already creating considerable business rules for their establishments and these should be extended to the company's defined rewards program, their reward's economy, and the marketing of the program.

Rewards programs are difficult to implement and costly to maintain because there are so many moving parts; each reward point and free offer has to be correlated against the department that offered it, the right budget it should be assigned to and every reward point has a monetary value that has to be enumerated properly. Building a rules engines can simplify the marketing process by defining who gets what, when he or she gets it, and through which channel it gets delivered on. With mobile and social being added to the customer channel mix, things are going to get exponentially more complex very quickly, so building a rules engine that lays things out in a highly definable way is imperative.

Once the rules engine is in place, automation has to kick in. With sports books now handling databases filled with millions of customers, it would be impossible to market to customers without considerable automation going on behind the scenes. Segmenting customers and building campaigns that market to thousands of individuals would be impossible without it.

Understanding the ROI of each marketing campaign is imperative and, with today's real-time personalization capabilities, sports books can quickly understand who is accepting their marketing and how much revenue it is driving. Adding a real-time element to the process would be impossible without strict rules set in place and powerful marketing automation tools that not only send out marketing offers but also quantify them once they are utilized.

In terms of marketing and customer service, Facebook bots could be created and automated to answer standard customer service questions and this should lighten the load on a sports book's customer service department.

Moderating boards and UGC posts are a great channel to connect with customers and/or potential customers. They are also good places to pick up both customer service issues and competitor information.

As Chirpify sees it: "Moderation allows brands to increase social efficiency and effectiveness by uniting automated listening triggers while giving moderators the ability to manually review posts and user content for fit before determining their qualification for a reward. This helps brands better personalize the reward based on the user while making sure that the reward is one that the customer appreciates and/or makes them feel special."[110]

Rewards and marketing content can deliver points, discounts, reminders, as well as contest entries in real-time, but reaching today's audiences can be tricky.

Marriott won the *Chief Marketer's* 2017 Gold for Best Loyalty Marketing for the development of a loyalty engagement platform that uses rewards points as social currently to incentivize engagement on Twitter, Facebook and Instagram.[111] In the *Chief Marketer* write up about the award, the magazine noted that, "The platform was designed as a reciprocal ecosystem where members are empowered to engage via social media and advocate on behalf of the program. The platform engages guests one-to-one at scale with personalized content and instant rewards, enabling members to engage with the loyalty program even when they aren't on property."[111]

"By connecting their social media accounts with the platform, members can earn points by engaging with a variety of triggers throughout the year. The platform is integrated directly with Marriott Rewards' member database, allowing the program to recognize and reward members the moment they post," *Chief Marketer* notes.[111]

According to *Chief Marketer*, engagement was huge. "When it came time to amplify the launch of Marriott Rewards' Reward-a-Friend enrollment program, connected members helped spread the word with a simple retweet. The campaign generated 7.4M earned media impressions in four days."[111]

"Connected members generated more than 65 million positive earned media impressions in 2016 on behalf of Marriott Rewards. More than 84 million Rewards points were awarded in response to 326,000 social media engagements, equivalent to earning roughly 11,000 free nights."[111] This kind of engagement comes at a cost, obviously (the free rooms), but the enormous amount of engagement is worth the cost because it is word-of-mouth marketing and it allows verifiable visibility on the engagement. The ROI shouldn't be hard to quantify.

Data & Marketing

The history of the methodical use of data in marketing begins in 1910, with the work of Charles Coolidge Parlin for the Curtis Publishing Company in Boston.[112] As Wedel & Kannan explain in their article *Marketing Analytics for Data-Rich Environments*[113], "Parlin gathered information on markets to guide advertising and other business practices, prompting several major U.S. companies to establish commercial research departments."[113] Questionnaire survey research, which Gallup popularized in the 1820s with its opinion polling, became increasingly common in the 1920s.[114] At about the same time, "concepts from psychology were being brought into marketing to foster greater understanding of the consumer," explain Wedel and Kannan.[113]

Starch's attention, interest, desire, action (AIDA) model[115] is an example of this. Starch is widely considered to be one of the pioneers of marketing and consumer research. This is also the era in which eye-tracking technology debuted, including the ability to collect data that followed the movements of the eye.[116] Interestingly, it is a technology that is making a strong comeback almost a century later.

"In 1923, A.C. Nielsen founded one of the first market research companies. Nielsen started by measuring product sales in stores, and in the 1930s and 1950s, he began assessing radio and television audiences."[113] Today, Nielsen is a household name in the United States and it dominates TV ratings in the US and several other countries. It is also moving into social media measurement today.

Beginning in the late 1970s, geo-demographic data was collected from government databases and credit agencies by the market research firm Claritas.[113] "The introduction of the Universal Product Code and IBM's computerized point-of-sale scanning devices in food retailing in 1972 marked the first automated capture of data by retailers."[113]

Companies like Nielsen "quickly recognized the promise of using point-of-sale scanner data for research purposes and replaced bimonthly store audits with more granular scanner data," notes Wedel and Kannan.[113] Shortly after the start of the data collection process, individual customers could be traced through their loyalty cards use, which led to the emergence of scanner panel data.[117]

The introduction of IBM's personal computer in 1981 enabled the collection of customer data on a massive scale.[113] Personal computers allowed marketers to store data on current and potential customers[113], contributing to the emergence of database marketing, which was pioneered by Robert and Kate Kestenbaum and Robert Shaw.[118]

"In 1990, CRM software emerged, for which earlier work on sales force automation at Siebel Systems paved the way."[113] Personal computers simplified survey research through personal and telephone interviewing.[113]

In 1995, after more than two decades of development at the Defense Advanced Research Projects Agency and several American universities, the internet was born, and this meant large volumes of marketing data were suddenly accessible.[113]

Clickstream data extracted from server logs allowed businesses to track page views and website clicks using cookies.[113] Click-through data revealed the true effectiveness of online advertising.[113] "The Internet stimulated the development of CRM systems by firms such as Oracle, and in 1999 Salesforce was the first company to deliver CRM systems through cloud computing," state Wedel and Kannan.[113]

Founded in 1998, Google championed keyword search and the capture of search data.[113] Google emerged from the highly competitive 1990s search environment, beating out the likes of Alta Vista, Yahoo!, Infoseek, and Lycos.

The launch of Facebook in 2004 opened up an era of social network data and it quickly eclipsed MySpace as the dominant social network.[113] The arrival of UGC, including pictures, online product reviews, blogs, and videos, resulted in an explosion in the volume and variety of data.[113] Big data then added the velocity.

"With the advent of YouTube in 2005, vast amounts of data in the form of user-uploaded text and video became the raw material for behavioral targeting," explain Wedel and Kannan.[113] Twitter, with its much simpler 140-character messages, appeared in 2006. While the social network, blogging, and micro-blogging scene solidified in the early 2000s, another important step for marketing measurement appeared in 2007 when Apple introduced the iPhone. With its global positioning system (GPS) capabilities, the first iPhone meant one could capture consumer location data at an unprecedented rate.[113]

Early Analytics

The initiative of the Ford Foundation and the Harvard Institute of *Basic Mathematics for Applications in Business in late 1950s and early 1960s* is widely credited for providing the catalyst that introduced analytics into marketing.[119] By then, statistical methods, such as analysis of variance, had been utilized in marketing research for more than a decade[120], but the development of statistical and econometric models tailored to specific marketing problems only took off "when marketing was recognized as a field of decision making through the Ford/Harvard initiative."[121]

The development of Bayesian decision theory at the Harvard Institute[122] also played a key role, demonstrated by its successful application to, among other things, pricing decisions.[123] Academic research in marketing then started focusing more on the development of statistical models and predictive analytics.[113]

New product diffusion models[124] involved applications of differential equations from epidemiology. Stochastic models of buyer behavior[125] were "rooted in statistics and involved distributional assumptions on measures of consumers' purchase behavior," argue Wedel and Kannan.[113]

The application of decision calculus[126] [127] to optimize spending on advertising and the sales force became popular after its introduction to marketing by John Little in his *Models and Managers: The Concept of a Decision Calculus*.[128] Nakanishi and Cooper introduced market share and demand models for store-level scanner data in 1974, which were derived from econometric models of demand.[129]

According to Wedel and Kannan, multidimensional scaling and unfolding techniques, founded in psychometrics[130], also became an active area of research.[113] "These techniques paved the way for market structure and product positioning research by deriving spatial maps from proximity and preference judgments and choice," argue Wedel and Kannan.[113]

Conjoint analysis[131] and, later, conjoint choice analysis[132] are unique contributions that evolved from work in psychometrics by Luce on the quantification of psychological attributes.[133] Also, "The nested logit model that captures hierarchical consumer decision making, i.e., understanding the factors that influence the way a consumer shops, was introduced in marketing[134], and it recognized that models of multiple aspects of consumer behavior (e.g., incidence, choice, timing, quantity) could be integrated[135] into the marketing mix. This proved to be a powerful insight for models of recency, frequency, and monetary metrics[136], which is the method for analyzing customer value by looking at how recently someone has purchased an item, how often they purchase, and how much they spend.

Time-series methods[137] can help sports books forecast sales, project yields and workloads, analyze budgets, as well as enable researchers to test whether marketing instruments result in permanent or transient changes in sales.

In their paper *A Probabilistic Choice Model for Market Segmentation and Elasticity Structure*[138], Kamakura and Russell state that heterogeneity in the behaviors of individual consumers becomes a core premise on which marketing strategy should be based, and the mixture choice model is the first to enable managers to identify response-based consumer segments from scanner data.[138] Wedel and DeSarbo expound upon this, arguing that the model should be generalized to accommodate a wide range of models of consumer behavior.[139] Rossi, McCulloch and Allenby conclude that consumer heterogeneity was represented in a continuous fashion in hierarchical Bayes models.[140]

Although scholars have hotly debated which of these two approaches best represents heterogeneity, research has revealed that the two different approaches each match specific types of marketing problems, with few differences between them.[141] Today, it can safely be stated that the Bayesian approach is one of the most dominant modeling approaches in marketing, offering a powerful framework to develop integrated models of consumer behavior.[142] Bayesian models have been successfully applied to advertisement eye tracking[143], e-mail marketing[144], web browsing[145], social networks[146], and paid search advertising.[147]

According to Wedel and Kannan[113], Data-driven analytics in marketing has progressed from its inception around 1900 up to the introduction of the World Wide Web in 1995 through approximately three stages:

1. "The description of observable market conditions through simple statistical approaches.
2. "The development of models to provide insights and diagnostics using theories from economics and psychology.
3. "The evaluation of marketing policies, in which their effects are predicted and marketing decision making is supported using statistical, econometric, and OR approaches."[113]

In many cases, throughout the history of marketing analytics, once new sources of data get introduced, methods to analyze them are immediately developed (Figure 10 contains an outline of the history of data and analytical methods). "Many of the methods developed by marketing academics since the 1960s have now found their way into practice and support decision making in areas such as CRM, marketing mix, and personalization and have increased the financial performance of the firms deploying them," note Wedel and Kannan.[113]

"Since 2000, the automated capture of online clickstream, messaging, word-of-mouth (WOM), transaction, and location data has greatly reduced the variable cost of data collection and has resulted in unprecedented volumes of data that provide insights on consumer behavior at exceptional levels of depth and granularity," explain Wedel and Kannan.[113]

Although academics have risen to the challenge of developing diagnostic and predictive models for the variety and velocity of data we've seen over the last decade, these developments are admittedly still in their infancy.[113]

On the one hand, descriptive metrics displayed on dashboards are popular in practice.[113] Perhaps because of "constraints on computing power, a need for rapid real-time insights, a lack of trained analysts, and/or the presence of organizational barriers to implementing advanced analytics."[113] In particular, unstructured data in the form of blogs, reviews, and tweets offer opportunities for deep insights into the economics and psychology of consumer behavior, which could usher in the second stage in digital marketing analytics once appropriate models are developed and applied," argue Wedel and Kannan.[113]

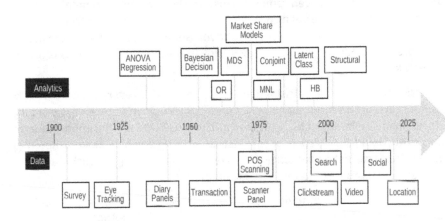

Notes: ANOVA = analysis of variance; MDS = multidimensional scaling; POS = point of sale; MNL = multinomial logit model; HB = hierarchical Bayes.
This timeline summarizes the availability of new marketing data and the development of the major classes of marketing models. As new types of data become available, new models to analyze them followed.

Figure 10: Timeline of Marketing Data and Analytics
Source: *Marketing Analytics for Data-Rich Environments*[113]

On the other hand, machine learning methods have become popular in practice, but have been infrequently researched in marketing academia. "It is reasonable to expect that the third step in the evolution of analytics in the digital economy— the development of models to generate diagnostic insights and support real-time decisions from big data—is imminent," contend Wedel and Kannan.[113]

Mobile Marketing

If an advertising executive had set about to create the perfect marketing and advertising tool, she could hardly have created something more superior to the mobile phone. Not only is the mobile phone within reach of its owner almost every single hour of every single day but, because it can connect to a marketer in a highly personalized way with the simple touch of a button, it has the potential to become not only more effective than television or radio advertising but, just as importantly, more analyzable. It is also an extremely powerful marketing outbound tool as the owner can become a word-of-mouth marketing tool on steroids.

As the authors of *Mobile Advertising*[37] point out that, "With respect to targeting, no other medium can provide the accurate and rich user profile, psychographic, social engagement and demographic data available from mobile. No other medium has the viral capability that mobile possesses—within seconds following a simple click, a unit of advertisement can spread like wildfire."

No other media comes even remotely close to the data measurement capacity that mobile offers either, which begins with exposure to the advertisement, followed by the persuasive effect of the advertisement and, finally, to the actual purchase of a product.[37] Just about every link in the marketer's chain is touched by mobile.

In 1996, the Internet advertising landscape changed forever when Procter & Gamble convinced Yahoo! that it would only pay for ads on a cost-per-click basis, rather than for banner ads.[37] Procter & Gamble realized the importance of gaining truthful user metrics for Internet advertising and this move ushered in the world of Internet analytics; eyeballs were no longer the goal, click-thrus that showed actual product interest became paramount.

As Sharma et al. state in their book *Mobile Advertising*[37], the time is right for mobile because "the heavy lifting of measurements and metrics; of banner ad standards; of search keyword auctions; of advertising cost models and the new, digital ad networks that support them have been built. The groundwork for digital advertising in mobile is largely in place." However, because there are so many players involved, the mobile advertising value chain is incredibly complicated.[37]

As the authors point out in *Mobile Advertising*, "the mobile value chain comprises advertisers, agencies, solution providers and enablers, content publishers, operators and consumers. Phone manufacturers or original equipment manufacturers (OEMs) are enablers in this value chain rather than active participants."[37] The bottleneck in the chain arises because, even though there are only a limited number of mobile operators, the number of vendors in the value chain is exceedingly high.[37] Although this book was written almost a decade ago, the complexity of the environment still remains and it is something that must be kept in mind when developing mobile marketing campaigns.

In their article *The Typological Classification of the Participants' Subjectivity to Plan the Policy and Strategy for the Smart Mobile Market*[148], Kim et al. argue that the core technologies of cloud computing can greatly enhance mobile marketing efforts. Without cloud computing, it would be impossible to successfully produce targeting context-aware ads, real-time LBS ads, interactive-rich media ads, mobile semantic webs or in-app ads, advanced banner ads or incentive-based coupon ads, AR or QR codes, social network ads, and n-screen ads.[148] It would be especially difficult integrating and converging multifunctional mash-up ads involving a mix of the aforementioned.[148] "Smart mobile advertising products continuously derive combined services where two or more advertising techniques integrate and interlock due to innovative hardware or software technologies."[148]

Mobile advertising has the potential to give sports books the best bang for their marketing buck, but a mobile marketing campaign should not simply be viewed as an extension of a company's internet marketing brought to the mobile phone. In *Mobile Advertising*, the authors state that the three basic types of mobile advertising are[37]:

- Broad-based brand advertising: broad-based campaigns that take advantage of user filtering and targeting. These can include subsidized premium content, sponsorships, video pre-rolls or intromercials, post-roll video, on-demand mobile media and contextual or behavioral advertising.
- Interactive, direct response campaigns: these are opt-in campaigns in which the mobile user usually exchanges some personal information for some type of content. TXT short codes, mobile subscription portals, and user registration campaigns are all examples of this type of campaign.
- Highly targeted search advertising: mobile's ability to inform advertiser of the user's basic age, sex, and address information is far better than any other form of advertising around. These campaigns include content targeted search advertising and paid placement or paid inclusion search.

Although there were hints that a marketing revolution was underway at the beginning of the 21st Century, few people would have predicted the radical changes that have transformed the industry today. In their article *Interactivitys Unanticipated Consequences for Marketers and Marketing[149]*, Deighton and Kornfeld argue that:

> "Mass communication technology empowered marketers with marketer-to-consumer tools such as radio, television and database-driven direct marketing. The digital innovations of the last decade made it effortless, indeed second nature, for audiences to talk back and talk to each other. They gave us peer-to-peer tools like Napster, eBay, Tivo, MySpace, YouTube, Facebook, Craigslist and blogs, and information search tools like Google and Wikipedia. Mobile platforms have given us ubiquitous connectivity, context-aware search, and the ability to tag and annotate physical spaces with digital information that can be retrieved by others. In sum, new traffic lanes were being built, not for the convenience of marketers, but for consumers."

Successful marketing is about reaching a consumer with an interesting offer when he or she is primed to accept it. Knowing what might interest the consumer is half the battle to making the sale and this is where customer analytics comes in.

Customer analytics have evolved from simply reporting customer behavior to segmenting customers based on their profitability, to predicting that profitability, to improving those predictions (because of the inclusion of new data), to *actually manipulating customer behavior* with target-specific promotional offers and marketing campaigns.

Data must be gathered from disparate sources and seamlessly integrated into a data warehouse that can then cleanse it and make it ready for consumption.[150] Trends that surface from the data mining process can help in monetization, as well as in future advertising and service planning.[37] As the authors state in *Mobile Advertising*[37]:

> *"The analytical system must have the capability to digest all the user data, summarize it, and update the master user profile. This functionality is essential to provide the rich user segmentation that is at the heart of recommendations, campaign and offer management, and advertisements. The segmentation engine can cluster users into affinities and different groups based on geographic, demographic or socio-economic, psychographic, and behavioral characteristics."*

Of course, with all of this data collection comes justified privacy concerns and the most important aspect of mobile marketing is ensuring the consumer has control of the advertising.[37] Without this, it is doubtful mobile marketing will reach its true potential.[37] If mobile advertisers do allow users to configure and control the ads depending on where they are, what mood they are in, who they are with, and what their current needs and desires happen to be, mobile marketing could prove to be one of the most successful forms of advertising available to sports book marketers.[37]

The potential to market to an individual when she is primed to accept the advertising is advantageous for both parties involved. Marketers don't waste time advertising to consumers when they aren't primed to accept the advertisements, but do market to consumers when and where they might want to use the advertisements.

One of the key criteria of mobile marketing is that a consumer must opt-in to the service. Mobile marketing is primarily a "pull" media model, meaning a consumer must sign up for the service rather than the traditional "push" media model, which gives the consumer no choice in whether they want to be advertised to or not.

Sports book mobile marketers must spend money to get users to sign up, but, if they do, the potential market for mobile marketing is huge. It is also a market that is rapidly evolving and its advantages include:

- Ubiquity: mobile devices and their users are everywhere.
- Effective: over 90% of received text messages are read by the recipient.
- Powerful two-way dialogue: an instantaneous link between the business and its customer is generated.
- Economical: compared to other marketing channels, mobile marketing is incredibly cheap per marketed individual.
- Spam-free: in the U.S. (but not in many other parts of the world) it is illegal to send a text message to someone who hasn't opted-in to a marketing campaign.

In her book, *The Mobile Marketing Handbook*[151], Kim Dushinski lists eight types of advertising campaigns that a mobile marketer can engage in:

1. Voice: this includes text-to-call messages in which users are sent a link that, when clicked upon, initiates a phone call to the company sending out the message. These days, Apple's SIRI, Microsoft's Tellme and Google's Now are adding a whole new dimension to voice.
2. Text messaging: this used to be the "now" marketing tool of mobile, and it is still one of the most important tools available. Text messaging includes both SMS and Common Short Codes (CSC), which are abbreviated phone numbers. Text messages are sent to mobile users, the content of which are limited only by SMS character limitations and the marketer's overall imagination.
3. Mobile web: most smart phones have the ability to connect to the web and many of them have graphic capabilities that rival computer screens.
4. Mobile search: as previously discussed, a mobile user can search company listings through his or her mobile phone, just as he or she can find this information on the Internet.
5. Mobile advertising: placing banner ads and text ads on mobile websites can build brand awareness.
6. Mobile publicity: presenting a company's executives as experts in his or her field can be useful to members of the media who need instant information for fast approaching deadlines.
7. Social networking: done right, this can help marketers tap into word-of-mouth campaigns, which will, hopefully, have their marketing messages lighting up social media websites.
8. Proximity marketing: Bluetooth and geofencing campaigns that invite users to accept a multimedia message can deliver unique and location-specific marketing messages.

To these eight, I would add another two—OTT and mobile apps marketing—and

I will break each of these campaigns down throughout the rest of this book.

Digital Interactive Marketing: The Five Paradigms

In their article *Interactivity's Unanticpated Consequences for Marketers and Marketing*[149], Deighton and Kornfeld state that in today's new media environment, there are five emerging marketing paradigms that are responses to the decrease of marketing's power relative to the consumer. Digital interactive marketing has little use for words such as "viewer" and "listener".[149] Even the label "consumer" is of limited value because today's interactions with a person will include encounters that have nothing to do with consuming or being part of a "target market."[149] Deighton and Kornfeld see this new digital interactive marketing breaking down into five different paradigms[149], as per Table 3.

Interactive marketing paradigm	How people use interactive technology	How firms interpose themselves to pursue marketing goals	Resulting digital media markets
Thought tracing	People search the web for information and browse for entertainment.	Firms infer states of mind from search terms and Web page content and serve relevant advertising.	A market in search terms develops.
Activity tracing	People integrate always-on computing into everyday life.	Firms exploit information on proximity and pertinence to intrude.	A market in access and identity develops.
Property exchanges	People participate in anonymous exchanges of goods and services.	Firms compete with these exchanges, rather than participating with them.	A market in service and reputation and reliability develops.
Social exchanges	People build identities within virtual communities.	Firms sponsor or co-opt communities.	A market in community develops, competing on functionality and status.
Cultural exchanges	People observe and participate in cultural production and exchange.	Firms offer cultural products or sponsor their production.	Firms compete in buzz markets.

Table 3: Digital Interactive Marketing: Five Paradigms
Source: Journal of Interactive Marketing[149], 23 pg. 4-10

Today, when a user searches for information or entertainment on sites like Google, she leaves a trail (also known as a "clickstream") that reveals what is on her mind.[149] This information, which Deighton and Kornfeld refer to as "thought tracing", may be "available to marketers in exactly the sense that it is available to marketers through Google, as a clue to our thoughts, goals and feelings."[149]

Mobile and social media alter the marketing landscape because the ubiquitous nature of computing makes it an "always on" proposition; both the thought *and* the activity are being traced.[149] "The argument is that when a person is always connected to the Internet, the person is always in the market, always available to be communicated with, and always an audience" contend Deighton and Kornfeld.[149]

Of course, most people don't like to be marketed to continuously throughout the day so technology that allows people to filter out messages that don't interest them needs to be developed.[149] However, customized marketing messages will be allowed to get through. Just as television demands its audience sit through commercials in order to enjoy free programming, Deighton and Kornfeld contend that, "we will enjoy ubiquitous computer connectivity for the price of voluntary exposure to context-specific persuasion efforts."[149]

If businesses want to succeed in this new marketing environment they must become an ally to the marketed individual, someone who is actually sought out as a person with cultural capital.[149] "Property exchanges", "social exchanges" and "cultural exchanges" are all paradigms that are "built on peer-to-peer interactivity motivated by the desire to exchange, to share information, or to express one's self" state Deighton and Kornfeld.[149]

Arguably, internet property exchanges were introduced on a mass scale by Napster, which was the first company to allow users to share and exchange files in an anonymous way.[149] Unsurprisingly, Napster ran into trouble with copyright holders and quickly left the content exchange business, but sites such as eBay, Flicker and YouTube allow users to share and even sell their property over the Internet. This is a trend that is not going away any time soon.

While the property exchange deals in things, the social exchange deals in identities and reputations.[149] In general, social networking sites let a person present a face to the world, "including information about whereabouts and action and a 'wall' on which friends can post short, often time-sensitive notes, allows people to exchange digital gifts, provides a marketplace for buying and selling, and allows posting of photographs and video clips."[149]

These sites allow for contextually relevant advertising because friends can share information amongst each other and some of this information can include a marketer's message. Since this messaging is coming from a trusted source, the message is considered much more trustworthy and enticing and, therefore, much more likely to be acted upon. For example, "a recent Nielsen analysis of 79 campaigns on Facebook over six months showed that, on average, social ads— those that are served to users who have friends that are fans of or have interacted with the advertised brand and prominently call the relationship out— generate a 55 percent greater lift in ad recall than non-social ads."[152]

Proximity Marketing

Proximity marketing "is the localized wireless distribution of advertising content associated with a particular place. Transmissions can be received by individuals in that location who wish to receive them and have the necessary equipment to do so," explains Wikipedia.org.[153] There are four main systems used for proximity marketing; Bluetooth-based systems; NFC-based systems; GSM-based systems (via SMS); and iBeacon-based systems.

Considered the "killer-app" for mobile commerce, the commercial viability for proximity marketing or "location-aware advertising" (LAA) is enormous. In location-aware advertising, a cellular subscriber receives an advertising message based on his or her location, so a shopper wandering through a mall could set his or her mobile phone to accept all available mobile offers or just offers from a specific store.

In their article *Foundations of SMS Commerce Success: Lessons from SMS Messaging and Co-opetition*[154], Xu et al. argue that LAA allows advertisers to deliver highly customized promotions, coupons and offers to an individual, specifically taking into account their geographical location, as well as the time of day of the offer. LAA also allows advertisers to reach their customers when they are primed to make a purchase.

iBeacon is the trademark for an indoor proximity marketing system that Apple calls, "A new class of low-powered, low-cost transmitters that can notify nearby iOS 7 devices of their presence. The technology enables an iOS device or other hardware to send push notifications to iOS devices in close proximity. Devices running the Android operating system can receive iBeacon advertisements but cannot emit iBeacon advertisements."[155]

According to Wikipedia, the iBeacon system uses "Bluetooth low energy Proximity sensing to transmit a universally unique identifier picked up by a compatible app or operating system that can be turned into a physical location or trigger an action on the device such as a check-in on social media or a push notification."[155]

In her article *Your iPhone is Now a Homing Beacon (But It's Ridiculously Easy to Turn it Off)*[156], Kashmir Hill warns that this technology opens the door to more aggressive monitoring, tracking and communication from people with apps on their phone, which will vary from convenient to invasive. In those lengthy terms of service and privacy (that few people read), app makers can slip in tracking permission warns Hill.[156] "Hypothetically, a retailer with its app on your phone could tell iBeacon to turn the app on when you're in or near the store, send information about your being there to a database and then pop up some advertising," Hill warns.[156] This is true for sports book as well.

"At this point, every party that wants to communicate with you needs its app on your phone. Inevitably, some monster advertising network will develop a one-stop-iBeacon-shop app that will allow it to act as the conduit for lots of different people to ping your phone," Hill claims.[156] But that day is probably still a ways away.

Currently, as Shane Paul Neil explains in his article *Is iBeacon Marketing Finally Taking Off?*[157], "McDonald's has seen an increase in sales from a test run using the iBeacons, and Virgin Atlantic is among the first to use them as thermostats to supply cold passengers with blankets. iBeacons also have the potential to enhance B2B marketing with its ability to target users' smartphones at trade shows or other events."

However, as Shane Paul Neil warns, the delay in implementing beacon technology probably has to do with one of the following four possible reasons[157]:

1. Installing, managing, and maintaining beacons can be a struggle.
2. Beacon signals are often obstructed by physical objects.
3. Beacon marketing requires user opt-in.
4. Consumers aren't sold on the benefits of beacons.

In his *Washington Post* article *How iBeacons could change the world forever*[158], Matt McFarland sees a world where iBeacon technology can do the following:

1. Send a coupon to a consumer because they have entered a particular area.
2. React when a user walks into his or her home, turning on lights or televisions.
3. Provide tours of museums.
4. Automatically send concert or sporting events tickets to a phone that approaches an arena's turnstiles.
5. Win something for visiting a car dealership or a retail outlet.
6. Be warned when someone's car of bike is no longer in his or her garage.

These and many other examples can be created for proximity marketing and even though each upcoming year is claimed to be the "Year of iBeacons technology", betting against Apple is usually not a smart thing and one of these years that moniker will, undoubtedly, come true. For sports book, a geofence could be a football of basketball stadium and offers could be sent to fans as kick-off or tip-off nears.

Geofencing Applications

Today, most smart phones have geofencing capabilities, which tap into GPS or RFID technology to define geographical boundaries. Basically, geofencing programs allow an administrator to set up triggers—usually SMS push notifications or email alerts—so when a device crosses a "geofence" and enters or exits a set area, a user is notified. Applications such as Facebook, Foursquare and China's WeChat and Jiepang use geofencing to locate users, as well as help them find their friends and/or check into places.

As TechTarget explains, geofencing has many uses, including[159]:

- Mobile Device Management—When a host's tablet PC leaves the business' property an administrator receives a notification so the device can be disabled.
- Fleet management—When a truck driver breaks from his route, the dispatcher receives an alert.
- Human resource management—An employee smart card will send an alert to security if an employee attempts to enter an unauthorized area.
- Compliance management—Network logs record geofence crossings to document the proper use of devices and their compliance with established rules.
- Marketing—A business can trigger a text message to an opted-in customer when the customer enters a defined geographical area.
- Asset management—An RFID tag on a pallet can send an alert if the pallet is removed from the warehouse without authorization.

SERVICES	EXAMPLES	ACCURACY NEEDS	APPLICATION ENVIRONMENT
EMERGENCY SERVICES	Emergency calls	Medium to High	Indoor/Outdoor
	Automotive Assistance	Medium	Outdoor
NAVIGATION SERVICES	Traffic Management	High	Outdoor
	Indoor Routing	Medium	Outdoor
	Group Management	Lot to Medium	Indoor
INFORMATION SERVICES	Travel Services	Medium to High	Outdoor
	Mobile Yellow Pages	Medium	Outdoor
	Infotainment Services	Medium to High	Outdoor
MARKETING SERVICES	Banners, Alerts, Advertisements	Medium to High	Outdoor
TRACKING SERVICES	People Tracking	High	Indoor/Outdoor
	Vehicle Tracking	Low	Outdoor
	Personnel Tracking	Medium	Outdoor
	Product Tracking	High	Indoor
BILLING SERVICES	Location-sensitive billing	Low to Medium	Indoor/Outdoor

Table 4: Taxonomy of mobile location services
Source: Durlacher Research

With geofencing applications, "users can also offer peer reviews of locations, which add a layer of user-generated content. In exchange for loyalty, more and more businesses—from local retailers to larger organizations like Bravo TV, Starbucks and The History Channel—are offering coupons, discounts, free goods and marketing materials."[160]

As users continue to enter personal details as well as update and check-in to their locations, geofencing applications like Foursquare can "collect a historical view of consumer habits and preferences and, over time, possibly recommend a much larger variety of targeted marketing materials in real time—as a consumer walks into a store to look for a specific item or service."[160]

In their paper *On the Potential Use of Mobile Positioning Technologies in Indoor Environments*[161], Giaglis et al. claim there are six different types of service uses for mobile positioning technology (see Table 4).

Geofencing applications (aka Location Based Services (LBS)) like Jiepang and Foursquare are useful services for sports book marketers as well. In his article *LBS Opportunities for Casino Marketers in Macau*[162], Chris Weiners offers the following ideas for casinos and/or sports books to get their LBS promotions rolling:

1. Pick your LBS service and claim your location.
2. Offer tips to customers via LBS.
3. Reward loyalty creatively. Start by offering your most loyal customers rewards, special access, and other promotions. Those who become your "Mayor"—or any other significant title—should be rewarded for their loyalty. This is a great way to identify potential social influencers and utilize them to further promote your venue.
4. Reward new customers: First time check-Ins should receive special promotions or incentives as it is important to give people a reason to continuously check in to your establishment.
5. Understand who your loyal customers are online, and work with them. Develop a plan to utilize these 'influencers' and tap into their social networks. "Casinos do it offline all of the time; develop a similar approach for high-valued customers online through social connections. Encourage your followers to promote their checked-in status to their friends via social networks and micro blogs like Sina and Twitter."[162]
6. Promote your services both on- and off-line.

Mobile marketing in general and OTT, MMS and SMS marketing in particular can help sports books create a one-to-one, two-way interactive experience with its patrons. These channels are not just about sending out a simple message, but rather they are about starting a customer relationship that can be analyzed so that the sports book has a 360-degree understanding of its patron. It is an understanding that includes his or her wants, desires and needs.

Besides geo-fencing applications, social media channels like Facebook, Instagram, Twitter, WeChat, as well as many others can reveal a patron's location. Instagram tracks a user's photos even if he or she doesn't geo-tag them. As Cadie Thompson warns in her article *Social media apps are tracking your location in shocking detail*[163], "While the picture sharing app does give users the option to name the location of where they are uploading an image, it also geotags an uploaded pic regardless if the user has selected the 'Add to Photo Map' function."[163]

Foursquare's check-in app Swarm also broadcasts users' location even if they have not selected a specific location for check-in.[163] Many live-streaming apps like Periscope, YouTube, and several Chinese ones will also show the location of the user and this is information that can be utilized by a sports book's marketing department if it can exploit the information quickly enough. Although YouTube doesn't have a filter for location, websites like geosearchtool.com allow users to search by location. Advanced filters allow searching by keyword and within a certain designated area.

Besides the normal geo-location apps, sports books should also look into the smaller ones such as Bizzy, Glympse, Neer (neerlife.com), and social gaming app Scvngr.

Facial Recognition

Facial recognition technology is the capability to identify or verify a person from a digital image or a video frame from a video source by comparing the actual facial features of someone on camera against a database of facial images, or faceprints, as they are also known.

As patrons enter a sports book, "security cameras feed video to computers that pick out every face in the crowd and rapidly take many measurements of each one's features, using algorithms to encode the data in strings of numbers,"[164] as explained in the *Consumer Reports* article *Facial Recognition: Who's Tracking Who in Public.*[164] These are called faceprints or templates.[164] The faceprints are compared against a database, and when there's a match, the system alerts hosts, sales people, or security guards.

Sports book personnel can receive alerts through a mobile app or an SMS when a member of a VIP loyalty program enters the store. A screen can display the patron's name, or a photo just taken from the video feed. Gambling preferences and other details, like a customer's average daily Theo or ADT can also be displayed.

Currently, facial recognition technology can be more useful for security departments than customer service.[164] At the 2014 Golden Globe Awards, facial recognition technology was used to scan for known celebrity stalkers.[164] The technology has also been used to bar known criminals from soccer matches in Europe and Latin America.[164] "Police forces and national security agencies in the U.S., the United Kingdom, Singapore, South Korea, and elsewhere are experimenting with facial recognition to combat violent crime and tighten border security."[164]

Facial recognition technology is becoming second nature to consumers, who are used to tagging themselves in photos on Facebook, Snapchat, Picasa, and/or WeChat. In 2015, Google launched a photo app that helped users organize their pictures by automatically identifying family members and friends.[164] Google, however, suffered a public relations and social media disaster when its system labeled a photo of two black people as gorillas.[164] The search giant quickly apologized profusely and promised to fix its algorithms[164], but this does show that the technology isn't foolproof and sensitivity is important.

Currently, MasterCard is "experimenting with a system that lets users validate purchases by snapping a selfie. Like fingerprint scanners and other biometric technologies, facial recognition has the potential to offer alternatives to passwords and PINs."[164]

This technology is moving so fast, privacy advocates are having trouble keeping up with it all. In this regard, today's facial recognition technology is reminiscent of the World Wide Web of the mid-1990s.[164] Back then, few people would have anticipated that every detail about what we read, watch, and buy online would become a commodity traded and used by big business and sometimes, more sinisterly, hacked and used by nefarious individuals to perpetrate crimes.[164]

Facial recognition technology "has the potential to move Web-style tracking into the real world, and can erode that sense of control."[164] Experts such as Alvaro Bedoya, the executive director of Georgetown Law's Center on Privacy & Technology, and the former chief counsel to the Senate's subcommittee on privacy, technology, and the law finds this attack on privacy alarming.[164]

"People would be outraged if they knew how facial recognition" is being developed and promoted, Bedoya states.[164] "Not only because they weren't told about it, but because there's nothing they can do about it. When you're online, everyone has the idea that they're being tracked. And they also know that there are steps they can take to counter that, like clearing their cookies or installing an ad blocker. But with facial recognition, the tracker is your face. There's no way to easily block the technology," warns Bedoya.[164]

Right now, facial recognition is largely unregulated and few consumers seem to even be aware of its use. "Companies aren't barred from using the technology to track individuals the moment we set foot outside. No laws prevent marketers from using faceprints to target consumers with ads. And no regulations require faceprint data to be encrypted to prevent hackers from selling it to stalkers or other criminals," says Bedoya.[164] This is true for both the United States, Asia, and

Europe.

Users might be happy to tag their face and the faces of their friends and acquaintances on a Facebook wall, but they might shudder if every mall worker was jacked into a system that used security-cam footage to access their family's shopping habits.[164] This could, however, be the future of retail, according to Kelly Gates, associate professor in communication and science studies at the University of California, San Diego.[165]

In her article *Our Biometric Future: Facial Recognition Technology and the Culture of Surveillance*[165], Gates argues that "Regardless of whether you want to be recognized, you can be sure that you have no right of refusal in public, nor in the myriad private spaces that you enter on a daily basis that are owned by someone other than yourself." Gates concluded that by entering a retail establishment filled with facial recognition technology, you are tacitly giving your consent to the retailer to use it, even if you are unaware of its use.[165]

"In a recent study of 1,085 U.S. consumers by research firm First Insight, 75 percent of respondents said they would not shop in a store that used the technology for marketing purposes. Notably, the number dropped to 55 percent if it was used to offer good discounts."[164]

However, consumers may warm to facial recognition technology once it becomes more widespread, especially if businesses offer enough incentives to make it worth their while. In some cases, full facial recognition isn't needed, some marketers just want to determine the age, sex, and race of shoppers.

In Germany, the Astra beer brand recently created an automated billboard directed solely at women, even to the point of shooing men away.[164] The billboard approximated the women's age, then played one of 80 pre-recorded ads to match.[164] For a sports book, this could help if they want to direct specific advertising towards women, or to men, or to a certain age group, i.e., only those old enough to bet.

Sports books can also utilize "facial recognition systems to see how long people of a particular race or gender remain in the shop, and adjust displays and the store layout to try to enhance sales."[164] They can also be used to spot people who aren't supposed to be there, like problem gamblers.

In 2014, Facebook announced a project it calls DeepFace, "a system said to be 97.35 percent accurate in comparing two photos and deciding whether they depicted the same person—even in varied lighting conditions and from different camera angles. In fact, the company's algorithms are now almost as adept as a human being at recognizing people based just on their silhouette and stance."[164]

"Entities like Facebook hold vast collections of facial images," says Gates, the UC, San Diego professor.[164] "People have voluntarily uploaded millions of images, but for their own personal photo-sharing activities, not for Facebook to develop its facial recognition algorithms on a mass scale."[164]

Potentially Facebook, Instagram, WeChat, Pinterest, Snapchat, Google, or a number of other social media companies could use their vast databases of faceprints to power real-world facial recognition.[164] "Hypothetically, a tech giant wouldn't need to share the faceprints themselves. It could simply ingest video feeds from a store and let salespeople know when any well-heeled consumer walked through the door."[164] It could also, potentially, do this for a sports book as well, to prevent money laundering, Know Your Customer (KYC), or AML activities.

Natural Language Processing

According to skymind.ai[34], "Natural language refers to language that is spoken and written by people, and natural language processing (NLP) attempts to extract information from the spoken and written word using algorithms."

In their article *How Artificial Intelligence and Machine Learning Can Impact Market Design*[166], Paul R. Milgrom and Steve Tadelis give some interesting use cases for NLP. Online marketplaces like eBay, Taobao, Airbnb, along with many others have seen exponential growth since their inception because they provide "businesses and individuals with previously unavailable opportunities to purchase or profit from online trading."[166] Besides the new marketplaces created for these wholesalers and retailers, "the so called 'gig economy' is comprised of marketplaces that allow individuals to share their time or assets across different productive activities and earn extra income."[166]

"The amazing success of online marketplaces was not fully anticipated," Milgrom and Tadelis surmise, "primarily because of the hazards of anonymous trade and asymmetric information. Namely, how can strangers who have never transacted with one another, and who may be thousands of miles apart, be willing to trust each other?"[166] "Trust on both sides of the market is essential for parties to be willing to transact and for a marketplace to succeed," claim Milgrom and Tadelis.[166]

eBay's early success is often attributed to its innovative feedback and reputation mechanism, which has been replicated by practically every other marketplace that came after eBay.[166] Milgrom et al. believe that these online feedback and reputation mechanisms provide a modern-day version of more ancient reputation mechanisms used in the physical marketplaces that were the medieval trade fairs of Europe.[167]

The problem for Milgrom and Tadelis is that "recent studies have shown that online reputation measures of marketplace sellers, which are based on buyer-generated feedback, don't accurately reflect their actual performance. [166] "For example, the average percent positive for sellers on eBay is about 99.4%, with a median of 100%. This causes a challenge to interpret the true levels of satisfaction on online marketplaces," state Milgrom and Tadelis.[166]

For Milgrom and Tadelis, a natural question emerges: "can online marketplaces use the treasure trove of data it collects to measure the quality of a transaction and predict which sellers will provide a better service to their buyers?"[166] Afterall, these online marketplaces and gig-economy sites collect vast amounts of data as part of the process of trade.[166] The millions of transactions, searches and browsing that occur on these marketplaces every day could be leveraged to create an environment that promotes trust, similar to the way institutions emerged in the medieval trade fairs of Europe that helped foster trust.[166] Milgrom and Tadelis believe that AI can be applied to these marketplaces to help create a more trustworthy and better buying experience to consumers.[166]

"One of the ways that online marketplaces help participants build trust is by letting them communicate through online messaging platforms," explain Milgrom and Tadelis.[166] On eBay, buyers question sellers about their products, "which may be particularly useful for used or unique products for which buyers may want to get more refined information than is listed."[166] Airbnb also "allows potential renters to send messages to hosts and ask questions about the property that may not be answered in the original listing."[166]

Using NLP, "marketplaces can mine the data generated by these messages in order to better predict the kind of features that customers value."[166] However, Milgrom and Tadelis claim, "there may also be subtler ways to apply AI to manage the quality of marketplaces."[166] The messaging platforms are not only restricted to pre-transaction inquiries, they also provide both parties the ability to send messages to each other post-transaction.[166] The obvious question that emerges for Milgrom and Tadelis is, "how could a marketplace analyze the messages sent between buyers and sellers post the transaction to infer something about the quality of the transaction that feedback doesn't seem to capture?"

This question was posed and answered in the paper *Canary in the e-commerce coal mine: Detecting and predicting poor experiences using buyer-to-seller messages*[168] by Masterov et al. Milgrom and Tadelis explain[166]:

> "By using internal data from eBay's marketplace. The analysis they performed was divided into two stages. In the first stage, the goal was to see if NLP can identify transactions that went bad when there was an independent indication that the buyer was unhappy. To do this, they collected internal data from transactions in which messages were sent from the buyer to the seller after the transaction was completed and matched it with another internal data source that recorded actions by buyers indicating that the buyer had a poor experience with the

transactions. Actions that indicate an unhappy buyer include a buyer claiming that the item was not received, or that the item was significantly not as described, or leaves negative or neutral feedback, to name a few."

The simple NLP approach Milgrom and Tadelis use "creates a 'poor-experience' indicator as the target (dependent variable) that the machine learning model will try to predict, and uses the messages' content as the independent variables."[166] "In its simplest form and as a proof of concept, a regular expression search was used that included a standard list of negative words such as 'annoyed,' 'dissatisfied,' 'damaged,' or 'negative feedback' to identify a message as negative," explain Milgrom and Tadelis.[166] Messages void of these designated terms were considered neutral.[166] Using this classification, the researchers grouped transactions into three distinct types: "(1) No post-transaction messages from buyer to seller; (2) One or more negative messages; or (3) One or more neutral messages with no negative messages."[166]

In the second stage of the analysis, using the fact that negative messages are associated with poor experiences, Masterov et al. constructed a novel measure of seller quality based on the idea that sellers who receive a higher frequency of negative messages are bad sellers.[168] According to Masterov et al., the measure, which is "calculated for every seller at any point in time using aggregated negative messages from past sales, and the likelihood that a current transaction will result in a poor experience,"[168] is a monotonically increasing relationship.[168]

This simple exercise shows that using a marketplace's message data and a simple NLP procedure, businesses could predict which sellers would create poor experiences better than one inferred from highly inaccurate and wildly inflated feedback data.[166] Of course, eBay is not unique in allowing "parties to exchange messages and the lessons from this research are easily generalizable to other marketplaces."[166] "The key is that there is information in communication between market participants, and past communication can help identify and predict the sellers or products that will cause buyers poor experiences and negatively impact the overall trust in the marketplace," conclude Milgrom and Tadelis.[166]

Creating a market for feedback

Besides the over-inflation of customer feedback as described above, another problem with customer feedback forums is the fact that few buyers even bother leaving feedback.[166] Milgrom and Tadelis argue, "through the lens of mainstream economic theory, it is surprising that a significant fraction of online consumers leave feedback. After all, it is a selfless act that requires time, and it creates a classic free-rider problem."[166] Additionally, because potential buyers are intereste in buying from sellers "that already have an established good track record, this creates a 'cold start' problem,"[166] i.e., new sellers with no feedback face a high barrier-to-entry because buyers are hesitant to try them out.[166]

Li et al. address this problem in their paper *Buying Reputation as a Signal of Quality: Evidence from an Online Marketplace*[169] by "Using a unique and novel implementation of a market for feedback on the huge Chinese marketplace Taobao where they let sellers pay buyers to leave them feedback."[166] Of course, it might be concerning to allow "sellers to pay for feedback as it seems like a practice in which they will only pay for good feedback and suppress any bad feedback, which would not add any value in promoting trust."[166] However, Milgrom and Tadelis explain that "Taobao implemented a clever use of NLP to solve this problem: it is the platform, using an NLP AI model, that decides whether feedback is relevant and not the seller who pays for the feedback."[166] "Hence, the reward to the buyer for leaving feedback was actually managed by the marketplace, and was handed out for informative feedback rather than for positive feedback," note Milgrom and Tadelis.[166]

"Specifically, in March 2012, Taobao launched a 'Rebate-for-Feedback' (RFF) feature through which sellers can set a rebate value for any item they sell (cash-back or store coupon) as a reward for a buyer's feedback," says Milgrom and Tadelis.[166] Sellers who choose this option guarantee that the rebate will be transferred from the seller's account to a buyer who leaves high-quality feedback that is, most importantly, informative, rather than whether the feedback is positive or negative.[166] The marketplace actually manages "the market for feedback by forcing the seller to deposit at Taobao a certain amount for a chosen period, so that funds are guaranteed for buyers who meet the rebate criterion, which itself is determined by Taobao."[166]

Taobao wanted to promote more informative feedback, but as Li et al. note, "economic theory offers some insights into how the RFF feature can act as a potent signaling mechanism that will further separate higher from lower quality sellers and products."[169]

Building upon the work of Philip Nelson in his influential article *Information and Consumer Behavior*[170] that suggested advertising acts as a signal of quality. "According to the theory, advertising—which is a form of burning money—acts as a signal that attracts buyers who correctly believe that only high-quality sellers will choose to advertise," say Milgrom and Tadelis.[166] "Incentive compatibility is achieved through repeat purchases: buyers who purchase and experience the products of advertisers will return in the future only if the goods sold are of high enough quality," argue Milgrom and Tadelis.[166] "The cost of advertising can be high enough to deter low quality sellers from being willing to spend the money and sell only once, because those sellers will not attract repeat customers, and still low enough to leave profits for higher quality sellers. Hence, ads act as signals that separate high quality sellers, and in turn attract buyers to their products," argue Milgrom and Tadelis.[166]

Li et al. believe that Taobao's "RFF mechanism plays a similar signaling role as ads do, which can be seen as signals that separate high quality sellers, and in turn attract buyers to their products."[169] Assuming "consumers express their experiences truthfully in written feedback, any consumer who buys a product and is given incentives to leave feedback, will leave positive feedback only if the buying experience was satisfactory."[166]

Li et al. believe that a seller will offer RFF incentives to buyers if he or she expects positive feedback, which usually only happens if the seller provides a high quality item and/or service.[166] "If a seller knows that their goods and services are unsatisfactory, then paying for feedback will generate negative feedback that will harm the low-quality seller," claim Milgrom and Taledis.[166] "Equilibrium behavior," Milgrom and Tadelis contend, "implies that RFF, as a signal of high quality, will attract more buyers and result in more sales."[166] "The role of AI was precisely to reward buyers for information, not for positive feedback," state Milgrom and Tadelis[166], and that is as it should be.

Li et al. analyzed data "from the period where the RFF mechanism was featured, and confirmed that first, as expected, more feedback was left in response to the incentives provided by the RFF feature."[169] Li et al. also discovered that "the additional feedback did not exhibit any biases, suggesting that the NLP algorithms used were able to create the kind of screening needed to select informative feedback."[169] Li et al. conclude that, "the predictions of the simple signaling story were borne out in the data, suggesting that using NLP to support a novel market for feedback did indeed solve both the free-rider problem and the cold-start problem that can hamper the growth of online marketplaces."[169]

Reducing Search Friction with A.I.

"An important application of AI and machine learning in online marketplaces is the way in which potential buyers engage with the site and proceed to search for products or services," note Milgrom and Tadelis.[166] At Google, Facebook, and Amazon AI-powered search engines are trained to maximize what the provider believes to be the right objective.[166] "Often this boils down to conversion, under the belief that the sooner a consumer converts a search to a purchase, the happier the consumer is both in the short and the long run," say Milgrom and Tadelis.[166] The rationale: "search itself is a friction, and hence, maximizing the successful conversion of search activity to a purchase reduces this friction."[166]

Although this is consistent with economic theory, which posits "search as an inevitable costly process that separates consumers from the products they want"[166] this isn't really the case. "Unlike the simplistic models of search employed in economic theory, where consumers know what they are looking for and the activity of search is just a costly friction, in reality, people's search behavior is rich and varied," claim Milgrom and Tadelis.[166]

In their paper *Returns to Consumer Search: Evidence from eBay[171]*, Blake, Nosko, and Tadelis use "comprehensive data from eBay to shed light on the search process with minimal modeling assumptions." Blake et al.'s data showed that consumers search significantly more than in previous studies, which were conducted with limited access to search behavior over time.[171]

"Furthermore, search often proceeds from the vague to the specific. For example, early in a search a user may use the query 'watch', then refine it to 'men's watch' and later add further qualifying words such as color, shape, strap type, and more," explain Blake et al.[171] This behavior suggests that consumers aren't looking specifically at first and are exploring their own tastes, and what product characteristics might exist, as part of their search process.[171] Blake et al. showed that the average number of terms in a user's query "rises over time, and the propensity to use the default ranking algorithm declines over time as users move to more focused searches like price sorting."[171]

"These observations suggest that marketplaces and retailers alike could design their online search algorithms to understand search intent so as to better serve their consumers," recommend Milgrom and Tadelis.[166] Consumers in the exploratory phases of the search process, should be provided some general offerings to better learn their tastes as well as all available options in the market.[166] Once the consumer shows the desire to purchase something in particular, the offering should be narrowed to a set of products that match the consumer's preferences.[166] "Hence, machine learning and AI can play an instrumental role in recognizing customer intent," contend Milgrom and Tadelis.[166]

Milgrom and Tadelis explain that, AI and machine learning not only helps "predict a customer's intent, but given the large heterogeneity on consumer tastes, AI can help a marketplace or retailer better segment the many customers into groups that can be better served with tailored information."[166] Using AI for more refined customer segmentation, or even personalized experiences, does raise price discrimination concerns.[166] "For example, in 2012 the Wall Street Journal reported[172] that 'Orbitz Worldwide Inc. has found that people who use... Mac computers spend as much as 30% more a night on hotels, so the online travel agency is starting to show them different, and sometimes costlier, travel options than Windows visitors see."[166]

Whether these practices of utilizing consumer data and AI to adjust pricing helps or harms consumers is up for discussion, but economic theory states that price discrimination can either increase or reduce consumer welfare.[166] "If on average Mac users prefer staying at fancier and more expensive hotels because owning a Mac is correlated with higher income and tastes for luxury, then Orbitz practice is beneficial because it shows people what they want to see and reduces search frictions. However, if this is just a way to extract more surplus from consumers who are less price sensitive, but do not necessarily care for the snazzier hotel rooms, then it harms these consumers," contend Milgrom and Tadelis.[166] Either way, price elasticity systems can be set up if brands to choose to set them up.

Conclusion

We live in a real-time, 24-7 world, a world where 280-character Twitter messages foment political revolutions; a world where marketers should fear not the power of the pen, but the destructive force of the critical tweet or the far-reaching viral impact of an inflammatory social media diatribe that can encircle the digital world in seconds, laying waste to a reputation that might have taken decades to develop. Conversely, it is also a world where an advertiser's message can go viral and reach more eyeballs in less than an hour than a multi-million dollar television commercial campaign can in a year. Customer intelligence is imperative in a world that moves so quickly and, thankfully for the sports betting industry, great strides have been made in developing tools and setting up architectures that simplify the customer intelligence and customer experience (CX) process.

The loyalty programs that started in the 80s and 90s should be morphing into complex data collecting and data crunching exercises that capture not just every dollar (or pound or euro or won or every mop even) that a customer spends within a sports book, but also every post they submit to their social channels so that an online psychometric profile can be built for each and every customer. This profile can be used to both keep track of each customer's behavior as well as create competitive intel, i.e., is this particular customer frequenting a competitor's betting shop?

These psychological profiles can also be the basis for micro and macro psychometric profiles that a sports book can utilize to understand the type of customer it is attracting, which is highly valuable information that can be utilized by the sports book's marketing department in future advertising campaigns. Better client understanding should also go a long way in closing the gap between customer service expectations and a company's delivery of service quality, which is currently quite divergent.

Sports books should recognize that the customer journey is an important concept to understand and implement. Each customer should be viewed through his or her unique customer experience maturity stage, which includes "initial", "developing", "defined", "managed", and "optimized". Questions of loyalty, customer satisfaction, and customer dissatisfaction should be viewed according to which maturity stage the customer has reached. A problem that arises for a new customer should be handled in a very different way as compared to an issue arising with a returning patron.

In this chapter, I delved into the history of analytics and it is important to understand what today's analytics environment was built upon to truly grasp where it might be going. In the next chapter, I break down the various analytical processes that are important to sports book executives; some of these are decades old, while others are quite new; more are surely on their way as computing power is increasing exponentially and software is getting much more powerful and much more sophisticated on a daily basis. Vast sets of data can be culled through and acted upon by cloud-based servers that can be spun up and turned off as needed, meaning numbers can be crunched only as needed, thereby reducing unnecessary costs.

Mobile marketing is important for a sports book not only because of the mobile phone's ubiquity, but also because of the mobile phone's data measurement capacity. The mobile ad of the future will be created by a sophisticated analytical-driven mobile advertisement system that juxtaposes relevant advertiser content that corresponds to the mobile user's personal profile and context variables.[37]

If a sports book wants to succeed in this new marketing environment, it must become an ally to the marketed individual, someone who is actually sought out as a person with cultural capital.[149] "Property exchanges", "social exchanges" and "cultural exchanges" are all paradigms that are "built on peer-to-peer interactivity motivated by the desire to exchange, to share information, or to express one's self," contend Deighton and Kornfeld.[149] Deighton and Kornfeld argue that of all the paradigms, "the most potent of the new media are those that enable cultural exchange, media currently exemplified by the functionality of YouTube and Facebook."[149]

In the next couple of chapters, I will look at how these technologies can shape the customer experience so that true personalization can be delivered to a market of one. Capturing a first time visitor's IP address can be an important— and necessary—first step in the customer relation and once a user signs up for a patron card all of his or her customer information becomes relevant, which means personalization marketing should be in the cards, so to speak.

Analyzing clickstream data, customer card data, marketing data, as well as social media data can help sports books develop three dimensional profiles on each of their customers and, once these profiles are perfected, the behavioral marketing work can begin to ensure that the sports book is bringing in the customers that will produce the highest ROI. Matching customer needs with the sports book's staffing and operation requirements then becomes an added cost reduction perk.

---

48 Reichheld, F. (1996). The loyalty effect. Harvard Business Press.

49 Ang, Lawrence and Buttle, Francis A. (2002). Macquarie Graduate School of Management. ROI on CRM: a customer-journey approach. www.impgroup.org/uploads/papers/4225.pdf (Accessed 19 January 2018).

50 Schell, C. (1996). "Corporate Banking", in F. Buttle (ed.). Relationship Marketing: Theory and Practice. Paul Chapman Publishing: London (pp. 91-103.)

51 Accenture, "Does CRM pay?" Report, 2001.

52 Henschen, D. 2014, March 2. In-Memory Databases: Do You Need The Speed? Retrieved from informationweek.com: http://www.informationweek.com/big-data/big-data-analytics/in-memory-databases-do-you-need-the-speed/d/d-id/1114076

53 Hauss, Debbie. (1 August 2017). ROI of AI: 5 Ways Retailers Are Embracing The Innovation. Retailtouchpoints.com http://www.retailtouchpoints.com/features/trend-watch/roi-of-ai-5-ways-retailers-are-embracing-the-innovation

54 Jones, Andrew (2015, December 15). Study finds marketers are prioritizing personalization...but are further behind than they realize, http://venturebeat.com/2015/12/14/study-finds-marketers-are-prioritizing-personalization-but-are-further-behind-than-they-realize/ (accessed 26 November 2016).

55 Vatash, Prateek. (2018). 2018 Digital Trends I Retail. Adobe. https://wwwimages2.adobe.com/content/dam/acom/uk/modal-offers/pdfs/Econsultancy-2018-Digital-Trends-Retail_EMEA.pdf (Accessed 6 August 2018).

56 Klein, Michael. Adobe. Machine Learning and AI: If Only My Computer Had a Brain Wired for Business. https://www.adobe.com/insights/personalization-with-machine-learning-and-ai.html (Accessed 7 April 2019).

57 Tractica. Artificial Intelligence Revenue to reach 36.8 Billion Worldwide by 2025. August 25, 2016. https://www.tractica.com/newsroom/press-releases/artificial-intelligence-revenue-to-reach-36-8-billion-worldwide-by-2025/ (Accessed 7 April 2019).

58 Goode, Lauren. (2019). 8 Things to Expect from CES, Consumer Tech's Big Shindig. Wired. January 4, 2019. https://www.wired.com/story/ces-2019-what-to-expect/ (Accessed 6 January 2019).

59 https://www.brightlocal.com/learn/voice-search-for-local-business-study/

60 https://www.youtube.com/watch?v=co3fdFNUaFA&feature=youtu.be&t=2m59s (Accessed 12 March 2019).

61 Jones, Andrew. (2015). VentureBeat. Marketing Personalization: Maximizing Relevance and Revenue. July 28, 2015. http://6ae7543f2267daab3ad5-4f1a402bff79f310bc7e3ee91a2ee421.r9.cf2.rackcdn.com/Marketing%20Personalization%20-%20VentureBeat%20Insight.pdf (Accessed 30 March 2017).

62 Abramovich, Giselle. (2018). CMO.com. 3 AI-driven strategies for retailers in 2019. 11 November 2018. https://www.cmo.com/features/articles/2018/11/15/3-ai-driven-strategies-for-retailers-in-2019.html#gs.COMQdxdU (Accessed 23 February 2019).

63 Eyefortravel Limited. (2017). https://www.eyefortravel.com/sites/default/files/data_in_travel_report_draft7.pdf (Accessed 30 March 2019).

64 Adobe Experience Cloud. (2018). Creating the Ultimate Single Customer View. Adobe. 10 October 2018. https://theblog.adobe.com/creating-the-ultimate-single-customer-view-with-adobe-campaign/ (Accessed 16 January 2019)

65 Forrester Research. (2013, November). Delivering New Levels of Personalization In Consumer Engagement. Retrieved from sap.com:

https://www.sap.com/bin/sapcom/he_il/downloadasset.2013-11-nov-21-22.delivering-new-levels-of-personalization-in-consumer-engagement-pdf.html

66 Adobe Experience Cloud. (2018) Adobe.com. Creating the Single Customer View with Adobe Campaign. https://theblog.adobe.com/creating-the-ultimate-single-customer-view-with-adobe-campaign/ (Accessed 12 January 2019).

67 Jones, Andrew (2015, December 15). Study finds marketers are prioritizing personalization...but are further behind than they realize, http://venturebeat.com/2015/12/14/study-finds-marketers-are-prioritizing-personalization-but-are-further-behind-than-they-realize/ (Accessed 26 November 2017).

68 Abramovich, Giselle. (2018). CMO. The 5 Biggest Marketing Trends for 2019. https://www.cmo.com/features/articles/2018/12/12/the-5-biggest-marketing-trends-for-2019.html#gs.GwcjmLKw (Accessed 11 January 2019).

69 CB Insights. (2019). What's Next in AI? Artificial Intelligence Trends. CB Insights. https://www.cbinsights.com/research/report/ai-trends-2019/ (Accessed 10 February 2019).

70 Enterprise Content Team. Adobe. Incredible content, incredible experiences. https://www.adobe.com/insights/deliver-experience-with-content-intelligence.html (Accessed 8 January 2019).

71 Adobe Retail Team. (2017). Adobe. Retailers: Adopt Artificial Intelligence Now for Personalized and Relevant Experiences. 22 June 2017. https://theblog.adobe.com/machine-learning-predictive-analytics-drive-todays-retail-personalization/ (Accessed 11 January 2019).

72 CMO Staff. Executives Are Eyeing These 2019 Consumer Trends. January 7, 2019. https://www.cmo.com/features/articles/2018/11/30/predictions-consumer-trends-2019.html#gs.QpPk92IO (Accessed 23 January 2019).

73 Forrester. 2015. How Analytics Drives Customer Life-Cycle Management. SAS.com. https://www.sas.com/content/dam/SAS/en_us/doc/analystreport/forrester-analytics-drives-customer-life-cycle-management-108033.pdf (Accessed April 15, 2019).

74 Chew, Christie. (2018). The Art and Science Behind Every "Add to Cart." Adobe Blog. https://theblog.adobe.com/the-art-and-science-behind-every-add-to-cart/ (Accessed 19 January 2019).

75 Hauser, John R., Urban, Glen, Liberali, Guilherme, Braun Michael. (2009). "Website Morphing." Marketing Science 28.2 (2009): 202-223. © 2009 Informs. https://www.researchgate.net/publication/41822749_Website_Morphing (Accessed 16 February 2019).

76 Hayes, J., C. W. Allinson. 1998. Cognitive style and the theory and practice of individual and collective learning in organizations. Human Relations 31(7) 847–871.

77 Witkin, H. A., C. Moore, D. Goodenough, P. Cox. 1977. Field dependent and field-independent cognitive styles and their educational implications. Rev. Educational Res. 47(1) 1–64.

78 Riding, R. J., S. Rayner. 1998. Cognitive Styles and Learning Strategies Understanding Style Differences in Learning and Behavior. David Fulton Publishers, London.

79 Ansari, A., C. F. Mela. 2003. E-customization. J. Marketing Res. 40(2) 131–145

80 Montgomery, A. L., S. Li, K. Srinivasan, J. Liechty. 2004. Modeling online browsing and path analysis using clickstream data. Marketing Sci. 23(4) 579–585.

81 Riding, Richard J., Rayner, Stephen (1998), Cognitive Styles and Learning Strategies: Understanding Style Differences in Learning and Behavior, (London, UK: David Fulton Publishers).

82 Allinson, Christopher W. and Hayes, John. (1996), "The Cognitive Style Index: A Measure of Intuition-Analysis for Organizational Research," Journal of Management Studies, 33, 1, (January), 119-135.
83 Kirton, Michael J. (1987), Adaption-Innovation Inventory (KAI) Manual (Hatfield, UK: Occupational Research Centre).
84 Riding, Richard J., and Indra Cheema (1991), "Cognitive Style: An Overview and Integration", Educational Psychology, 11, 3&4, 193-215.
85 Kopfstein Donald (1973), "Risk-Taking Behavior and Cognitive Style." Child Development, 44, 1, 190-192.
86 Siegelman, Ellen (1969), "Reflective and Impulsive Observing Behavior" Child Development, 40, 4, 1213-222.
87 Khatchadourian, Raffi. (2015). The New Yorker. We Know How You Feel. January 19, 2015. https://www.newyorker.com/magazine/2015/01/19/know-feel. (Accessed 24 February 2019).
88 Ford, Martin. (2018). Architects of Intelligence. The truth about AI from the people building it. Packt Publishing; 1 edition. November 23, 2018.
89 Lovelock, C. a. (2010). Services Marketing, People, Technology, Strategy, Seventh Edition. Prentice Hall.
90 https://en.wikipedia.org/wiki/Social_CRM
91 Greenberg, P. (2009, July 6). Time To Put a Stake in the Ground On Social CRM. Retrieved from ZDnet.com: http://www.zdnet.com/blog/crm/time-to-put-a-stake-in-the-ground-on-social-crm/829
92 Divol, R. E. (2012, April). Demystifying social media. Retrieved from Mckinsey.com: http://www.mckinsey.com/insights/marketing_sales/demystifying_social_media
93 The Customer Satisfaction-Loyalty Relationship from Thomas O. Jones and W. Earl Sasser, Jr., "Why Satisfied Customers Defect" Harvard Business Review, Nov.–Dec. 1995, p. 91. Reprinted by permission of Harvard Business School.
94 Wangenheim, F. v. (2005). Postswitching Negative Word of Mouth. Journal of Service Research, 8, No. 1, 67-78.
95 Rigby, Darrell. 2015. Management Tools 2015. An Executive's Guide. Bain & Company. http://www.bain.com/publications/articles/management-tools-customer-relationship-management.aspx
96 https://en.wikipedia.org/wiki/Market_segmentation
97 Urbanski, Al. At Caesars Digital Marketing Is No Crap Shoot. DMNews. February 01, 2013 www.dmnews.com/marketing-strategy/at-caesars-digital-marketing-is-no-crap-shoot/article/277685/ (Accessed 20 November 2017).
98 MIT Technology Review. (2016). Transforming Customer Experiences by Harnessing the Power of AI in CRM. www.technologyreview.com/media (Accessed 10 January 2018.
99 Reichheld, F. a. (1990). Zero defections: quality comes to services. Harvard Business Review, 105-111.
100 Stodder, David. TDWI Research. Best practices report, customer analytics in the age of social media. Third quarter 2012. https://tdwi.org/research/2012/07/best-practices-report-q3-customer-analytics-in-the-age-of-social-media.aspx?tc=page0 (Accessed 30 April 2019).
101 Cognizant. (2014, January). Retail Analytics: Game Changer for Customer Loyalty. Retrieved from congnizant.com: http://www.cognizant.com/InsightsWhitepapers/Retail-Analytics-Game-Changer-for-Customer-Loyalty.pdf (Accessed 20 November 2017).

102 Peterson, T. (2014, August 13). Facebook Now Tells Whether Mobile Ads Lead to Desktop Purchases. Retrieved from AdAge: http://adage.com/article/digital/facebook-makes-link-mobile-ads-desktop-purchases/294568/ (Accessed 20 November 2017).

103 Cook, Rick. Control Group Marketing—With or Without CRM Software Systems. crmsearch http://www.crmsearch.com/marketing-control-groups.php (Accessed 19 November 2017).

104 Huguesrey.com. 15 Applications of Artificial Intelligence in Marketing. October 26, 2017. https://huguesrey.wordpress.com/2017/10/26/15-applications-of-artificial-intelligence-in-marketing-source-robert-allen/ (Accessed 18 March 2019).

105 Vicioso, Sara. Seer Interactive. Programmatic Advertising 101: How it Works. August 27, 2015. https://www.seerinteractive.com/blog/programmatic-advertising-101-works/ (Accessed 26 March 2019).

106 Shaw, Allie. (2017). VentureBeat. AI could save television advertising with advanced personalization. October 28, 2017. https://venturebeat.com/2017/10/28/ai-could-save-television-advertising-with-advanced-personalization/ (Accessed 15 April 2018).

107 Kumar, V. V. (2006). Knowing What to Sell, When, and to Whom. Harvard Business Review.

108 Bea, Francis. March 25, 2012. Goodbye, anonymity: latest surveillance tech can search up to 36 million faces per second. www.digitaltrends.com http://www.digitaltrends.com/cool-tech/goodbye-anonymity-latest-surveillance-tech-can-search-up-to-36-million-faces-per-second/

109 Eckerson, Wayne. 2007. Predictive Analytics, Extending the Value of Your Data Warehouse Investment. TDWI Best Practices Report. https://www.sas.com/events/cm/174390/assets/102892_0107.pdf

110 https://www.chirpify.com/announcing-chirpify-moderation-brands-can-now-moderate-social-triggers/ (Accessed September 7, 2017).

111 http://www.chiefmarketer.com/pro-awards-winners-2017 (Accessed September 7, 2017)

112 Bartels, Robert (1988), The History of Marketing Thought, 3rd ed. Columbus, OH: Publishing Horizons.

113 Wedel, Michel and Kannan, P.K. (2016) Marketing Analytics for Data-Rich Environments. Journal of Marketing: November 2016, Vol. 80, No. 6, pp. 97-121. https://www.rhsmith.umd.edu/files/Documents/Departments/Marketing/wedel-kannan-jm-2016-final.pdf (Accessed 4 November, 2017).

114 Reilly, W.J. (1929), Marketing Investigations. New York: Ronal Press Company.

115 Starch, Daniel (1923), Principles of Advertising. Chicago: A.W. Shaw Company.

116 Nixon, H.K. (1924), "Attention and Interest in Advertising," Archives de Psychologie, 72 (1), 5–67.

117 Guadagni, Peter M. and John D.C. Little (1983), "A Logit Model of Brand Choice Calibrated on Scanner Data," Marketing Science, 2 (3), 203–38.

118 Shaw, Robert (1987), Database Marketing, Gower Publishing Co.

119 Winer, Russell S. and Scott A. Neslin, eds. (2014), The History of Marketing Science. Hackensack, NJ: World Scientific Publishing.

120 Ferber, Robert (1949), Statistical Techniques in Market Research. New York: McGraw-Hill.

121 Bartels, Robert (1988), The History of Marketing Thought, 3rd ed. Columbus, OH: Publishing Horizons.

122 Raiffa, Howard and Robert Schlaifer (1961), Applied Statistical Decision Theory. Boston: Clinton Press.

123 Green, Paul E. (1963), "Bayesian Decision Theory in Pricing Strategy," Journal of Marketing, 27 (January), 5–14.

124 Bass, Frank (1969), "A New Product Growth for Model Consumer Durables," Management Science, 15 (5), 215–27.

125 Massy, William F., David B. Montgomery, and Donald G. Morrison (1970), Stochastic Models of Buying Behavior. Cambridge, MA: MIT Press.

126 Little, John D.C. and Len M. Lodish (1969), "A Media Planning Calculus," Operations Research, 17 (1), 1–35.

127 Lodish, Leonard M. (1971), "CALLPLAN: An Interactive Salesman's Call Planning System," Management Science, 18, P-25–40.

128 Little, John D.C. (1970), "Models and Managers: The Concept of a Decision Calculus," Management Science, 16 (8), B-466–485.

129 Nakanishi, Masao and Lee G. Cooper (1974), "Parameter Estimation for a Multiplicative Competitive Interaction Model: Least Squares Approach," Journal of Marketing Research, 11 (August), 303–11.

130 Coombs, Clyde (1950), "Psychological Scaling Without a Unit of Measurement," Psychological Review, 57, 148–58.

131 Green, Paul E. and Srinivasan, V. (1978), "Conjoint Analysis in Consumer Research: Issues and Outlook," Journal of Consumer Research, 5 (2), 103–23.

132 Louvie're, Jordan J. and Woodworth, George. (1983), "Design and Analysis of Simulated Consumer Choice or Allocation Experiments: An Approach Based on Aggregate Data," Journal of Marketing Research, 20 (November), 350–67.

133 Luce, R. Duncan and John W. Tukey (1964), "Simultaneous Conjoint Measurement: A New Scale Type of Fundamental Measurement," Journal of Mathematical Psychology, 1 (1), 1–27.

134 Kannan, P.K. and Gordon P. Wright (1991), "Modeling and Testing Structured Markets: A Nested Logit Approach," Marketing Science, 10 (1), 58–82.

135 Gupta, Sunil (1988), "Impact of Sales Promotions on When, What, and How Much to Buy," Journal of Marketing Research, 25 (November), 342–55.

136 Schmittlein, David C. and Robert A. Peterson (1994), "Customer Base Analysis: An Industrial Purchase Process Application," Marketing Science, 13 (1), 41–67.

137 DeKimpe, Marnik G. and Dominique M. Hanssens (1995), "The Persistence of Marketing Effects on Sales," Marketing Science, 14 (1), 1–21.

138 Kamakura, Wagner A. and Gary J. Russell (1989), "A Probabilistic Choice Model for Market Segmentation and Elasticity Structure," Journal of Marketing Research, 26 (November), 379–90.

139 Wedel, Michel and Wayne S. DeSarbo (1995), "A Mixture Likelihood Approach for Generalized Linear Models," Journal of Classification, 12 (1), 21–55.

140 Rossi, Peter E., Robert E. McCulloch, and Greg M. Allenby (1996), "The Value of Purchase History Data in Target Marketing," Marketing Science, 15 (4), 321–40.

141 Andrews, Rick L., Andrew Ainslie, and Imran S. Currim (2002), "An Empirical Comparison of Logit Choice Models with Dis- crete Versus Continuous Representations of Heterogeneity," Journal of Marketing Research, 39 (November), 479–87.

142 Rossi, Peter E. and Greg M. Allenby (2003), "Bayesian Statistics and Marketing," Marketing Science, 22 (3), 304–28.

143 Wedel, Michel and Pieters, Rik (2000), "Eye Fixations on Advertisements and Memory for Brands: A Model and Findings," Marketing Science, 19 (4), 297–312. White, Percival (1931), Market

144 Ansari, Asim and Mela, Carl F. (2003), "E-Customization," Journal of Marketing Research, 40 (May), 131–45.

145 Montgomery, Alan L., Shibo Li, Kannan Srinivasan, and John C. Liechty (2004), "Modeling Online Browsing and Path Analysis Using Clickstream Data," Marketing Science, 23 (4), 579–95.

146 Moe, Wendy W. and Trusov, Michael (2011), "The Value of Social Dynamics in Online Product Ratings Forums," Journal of Marketing Research, 48 (June), 444–56.

147 Rutz, Oliver J., Michael Trusov, and Randolph E. Bucklin (2011), "Modeling Indirect Effects of Paid Search Advertising: Which Keywords Lead to More Future Visits?" Marketing Science, 30 (4), 646–65.

148 Kim, K. L. (2012). The typological classification of the participants' subjectivity to plan the policy and strategy for the smart mobile market. Korean Management Review, 367-393.

149 Deighton, J. & Leora Kornfeld. (2009). Interactivity's Unanticpated Consequences for Marketers and Marketing. Journal of Interactive Marketing, 23, 4 - 10.

150 Sharma, R. S. (2009). The Economics of Delivering. Journal of Media Business Studies, 1-24.

151 Dushinski, K. (2012). The Mobile Marketing Handbook. Information Today, Inc.

152 Nielsen Company. (2012). Global Trust in Advertising and Brand Messaging. Nielsen Company.

153 https://en.wikipedia.org/wiki/Proximity_marketing

154 Xu, H. T. (2003). "Foundations of SMS Commerce Success: Lessons from SMS Messaging and Co-opetition." Proceedings of 36th Hawaii International Conference on System Sciences (pp. 90-99). Los Angeles: IEEE Computing Society Press.

155 https://en.wikipedia.org/wiki/IBeacon

156 Hill, K. (2013, December 10). Your iPhone Is Now a Homing Beacon (But It's Ridiculously East to Turn Off). Retrieved from forbes.com: http://forbes.com/sites/kashmirhill/2013/12/10/your-iphone-is-now-a-homing-beacon

157 Neil, Shane Paul. June 17, 2016. Is iBeacon Marketing Finally Taking Off? The Huffington Post. http://www.huffingtonpost.com/shane-paul-neil/is-ibeacon-marketing-fina_b_10508218.html

158 McFarland, Matt. How iBeacons could change the world forever. January 7, 2016. Washington Post. https://www.washingtonpost.com/news/innovations/wp/2014/01/07/how-ibeacons-could-change-the-world-forever/?utm_term=.182e91de201b

159 TechTarget. (2011). Geofencing definition. Retrieved from TechTarget: http://whatis.techtarget.com/definition/geofencing

160 Berman, S. J., Battino Bill, Feldman, Karen. 2007. Executive Brief: Navigating the media divide: Innovating and enabling new business models. IBM Institute for Business Value.

161 Giaglis, G. M. (2002). On the Potential Use of Mobile Positioning Technologies in Indoor Environments. 15th Bled Electronic Commerce Conference eReality: Constructing the eEconomy. Bled, Solvenia.

162 Weiners, C. (2012, March 30). LBS Opportunities for Casino Marketers in Macau. Retrieved from clickz.com: http://www.clickz.com/clickz/column/2281870/lbs-opportunities-for-casino-marketers-in-macau

163 Thompson, Cadie. May 28, 2015. Social media apps are tracking your location in shocking detail. Business Insider. http://www.businessinsider.com/three-ways-social-media-is-tracking-you-2015-5

164 Facial recognition: Who's Tracking You In Public. (December 30, 2015) Consumer Reports. Online: http://www.consumerreports.org/privacy/facial-recognition-who-is-tracking-you-in-public1/

165 Gates, Kelly A. January 23, 2011. Our Biometric Future: Facial Recognition Technology and the Culture of Surveillance. NYU Press.

166 Milgrom, Paul R. and Tadelis, Steve. (2018). How Artificial Intelligence and Machine Learning Can Impact Market Design. 6 January 2018. https://www.nber.org/chapters/c14008.pdf (Accessed 20 January 2019).

167 Milgrom, P.R., North, D.C. and Weingast, B.R. (1990). The role of institutions in the revival of trade: The law merchant, private judges, and the Champagne fairs," Economics and Politics, 2(1):1-23.

168 Masterov, D. V., Mayer, U. F., and Tadelis, S. (2015) "Canary in the e-commerce coal mine: Detecting and predicting poor experiences using buyer-to-seller messages," In Proceedings of the Sixteenth ACM Conference on Economics and Computation, EC '15, pp81-93.

169 Li, L.I., Tadelis, S., and Zhou, X. (2016). Buying Reputation as a Signal of Quality: Evidence from an Online Marketplace. NBER Working Paper No. 22584.

170 Nelson, P. (1970). Information and Consumer Behavior. Journal of Political Economy, 78(2), 311-329. Retrieved from http://www.jstor.org/stable/1830691

171 Blake, Thomas, Nosko, Chris, and Tadelis, Steven. (2016), Returns to consumer search: Evidence from ebay. In Proceedings of the 2016 ACM Conference on Economics and Computation, pages 531–545. http://www.hbs.edu/faculty/conferences/2016-dids/Documents/Tadelis_BNT_search_EC_vST.pdf (Accessed 22 January 2019).

172 Mattolli, Dana. (2012). Wall Street Journal. On Orbitz, Mac users steered to higher pricier hotels. August 23, 2012. https://www.wsj.com/articles/SB10001424052702304458604577488822667325882 (Accessed 3 February 2019).

CHAPTER TWO

Analytics

"If the 20th Century was known in marketing circles as the advertising century, the 21st Century may be the advertising measurement century. Marketers are increasingly focused on the effectiveness of their pitches, trying to figure out the return on investment for ad spending...The ability of newer digital media to provide more precise data has led traditional media like television, radio, magazines and newspapers to try upgrading the ways they count consumers."

~Stuart Elliot, *NY Times*

Overview

As previously mentioned, Annie Eissler points out that, according to Nucleus Research "analytics and business intelligence solutions deliver, on average, $13.01 for every dollar spent."[20] She adds that, "We're at a point where the hype surrounding data analytics has converted into real, documented returns for companies of all sizes and across all industries. But the truth is, leading companies have been achieving double-digit return on investment (ROI) from their analytics investments for several years now."[20]

According to Nina Sandy, a Nucleus Research analyst, "Companies don't have the luxury anymore to wait weeks for reports on the profitability of business decisions in increasingly fast paced markets."[20] "New analytics solutions are being developed around this need where businesses can make better decisions, faster."[20]

The fact that so many software vendors are adding analytics to their standard data mining, CRM, social media, marketing automation, and other offerings is reducing prices across the board. For price, you obviously can't beat open source, but there is no free lunch in the software world and these open source products do require skilled consultants to write the code and build the systems, but these open source solutions can reduce the sting of the yearly license/maintenance fees that comes with commercial software.

Eissler warns that, "You need the technology to enable analytics, but if you don't understand the technology that enables the analytics—or the business application—then it won't provide any value,"[20] which is an accurate assessment; "junk in, junk out," as any good analyst will tell you. Eissler concludes that, "The real value comes when you take the technological component of analytics and apply it to a business component that—once optimized—produces a solid ROI that continues to pay off over time."[20]

Analytics is, of course, a huge field. In this chapter, I will mostly focus on customer analytics, which, when coupled with insights from social media data, can enable organizations to make faster strides in predicting retention, attrition, and return rates, with the goal of reducing customer churn, raising customer lift, and/or increasing a whole host of other metrics.[173]

Sources such as transactions data, clickstream data, as well as service and call center records are also important for customer analytics.[173] These can both improve how a sports betting organization decides on characteristics for customer segmentation, and also provide clues to emerging characteristics for the definition of new segments.[173] As David Stodder explains in his article *Customer Analytics in the Age of Social Media*[173], "Firms can employ predictive modeling to test and learn from campaigns so that they are able to select the most persuasive offers to put in front of the right customers at the right time."[173]

As Webopedia.com explains, customer analytics "exploits behavioral data to identify unique segments in a customer base that the business can act upon. Information obtained through customer analytics is often used to segment markets, in direct marketing to customers, predicate analysis, or even to guide future product and services offered by the business."[174]

In the most basic sense, customer analytics is made possible by combining elements of business intelligence, software such as IBM's cognos, SAP's Lumira and Business Object's suite, and Qlik's QlikView, amongst a whole host of others, with predictive analytics solutions like SAP's and SAS's suite of analytical tools, as well as R, Python, WEKA, etc., etc.

In IBM's *Achieving Customer Loyalty with Customer Analytics*[175], IBM argues that customer analytics can uncover "patterns and trends in customer behavior and sentiment hidden among different types of customer data such as transactions, demographics, social media, survey and interactions." "The results of the analysis are then used to predict future outcomes so businesses can make smarter decisions and act more effectively."[175] Results from these models can then be presented back to the business users in easily digestible dashboards and scorecards.[175] "Self-learning predictive models ensure that each new iteration of customer analytics insight and the business decisions it drives become more accurate and effective," argues IBM.[175]

Customer analytics can also help determine which of a sports book's advertising campaign or advertising partner's pages have the highest landing rates, as well as show conversion rates for all of a sports book 's advertising and marketing spend. Mobile analytics can also display how many visitors downloaded material from a site, which can help in factoring a company's advertising and marketing spend. And, finally, mobile analytics can display which pages have the highest exit rates. With this type of analysis, marketers can rapidly adjust marketing campaigns to exploit the most effective ones and, conversely, trim the non-performing ones.

The biggest problem with any analytics procedure is filtering out the noise associated with the data. Without clean data, "the trends, patterns, and other insights hidden in the raw data are lost through aggregation and filtering."[173] Organizations need an unstructured place "to put all kinds of big data in its pure form, rather than in a more structured data warehousing environment."[173] This is because what might be considered just "noise" in the raw data from one perspective could be full of important "signals" from a more knowledgeable perspective.[173] "Discovery, including what-if analysis, is an important part of customer analytics because users in marketing and other functions do not always know what they are looking for in the data and must try different types of analysis to produce the insight needed."[173] As per Stodder, among the most frequent targets for analysis are the following[173]:

- Understanding sentiment drivers.
- Identifying characteristics for better segmentation.
- Measuring the organization's share of voice and brand reputation compared with the competition.
- Determining the effectiveness of marketing touches and messages in buying behavior, i.e., attribution analysis.
- Using predictive analytics on social media to discover patterns and anticipate customers' problems with products and/or services.

TWDI's research[173] about the general purpose of customer analytics technology and methods (see Figure 11) discovered that "the business functions or operations for which respondents considered customer analytics most important were marketing (81%, with 52% indicating "very important"), sales and sales reporting (79%, with 45% "very important"), and campaign management (74%, with 47% "very important").[173] Market research (43% "very important") and customer services and order management (also 43% "very important") were also high among business functions regarded as critical to developers and consumers of customer analytics.[173]

The marketing department, "which in most organizations is empowered with the responsibility for identifying, attracting, satisfying, and keeping customers, is clearly the main stage for customer analytics."[173] Marketing departments and functions are becoming increasingly qualitative.[173] "Gut feelings" are being replaced by data-driven decision-making.[173] "Data drives the pursuit of efficiency and achievement of measurable results. Marketing functions are key supporters of 'data science,' which is the use of scientific methods on data to develop hypotheses and models and apply iterative, test-and-learn strategies to marketing campaigns and related initiatives."[173]

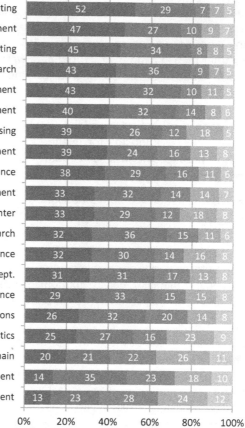

- Very important
- Somewhat important
- Somewhat unimportant
- Not important
- Don't know

	Very important	Somewhat important	Somewhat unimportant	Not important	Don't know
Marketing	52	29	7	7	5
Campaign management	47	27	10	9	7
Sales/sales reporting	45	34	8	8	5
Market research	43	36	9	7	5
Customer services/order management	43	32	10	11	5
Executive management	40	32	14	8	6
Advertising	39	26	12	18	5
Fraud/risk management	39	24	16	13	8
Finance	38	29	16	11	6
Product development	33	32	14	14	7
Call/contact center	33	29	12	18	8
Operations management/research	32	36	15	11	6
Web storefront/online presence	32	30	14	16	8
New media/social media dept.	31	31	17	13	8
Regulatory complaine/data governance	29	33	15	15	8
Public relations	26	32	20	14	8
Distribution, fulfillment, or logistics	25	27	16	23	9
Supply Chain	20	21	22	26	11
Event Management	14	35	23	18	10
Procurement	13	23	28	24	12

Figure 11: Importance of Customer Analytics Technology
Based on one answer per business function from 452 responses.
Source: TWDI Research[173]

"Customer analytics can be a very effective tool for micro-targeting customers with customized marketing offers and promotions.[175] Obviously, when an organization "attempts to cross-sell or up-sell a customer, a product or service they desire, it can enhance satisfaction."[175] However, unwanted marketing campaigns can do just the opposite, annoying customers, thereby eroding loyalty and, potentially, hurting sales.[175] Even worse, unwanted marketing campaigns can give customers the impression that the organization doesn't care about their wants, desires, needs and preferences."[175]

"Customer analytics can help determine which marketing interactions are likely to please individual customers and which will not."[175] Sales functions can be important beneficiaries of customer analytics as well.[173] Stodder argues that, "Sales reports typically focus on providing visibility into the pipeline. Managers can use data insights to improve sales forecasting of potential revenues based on deeper knowledge of priority opportunities, most valued customer segments, and more."[173]

"Customer service and order management can use customer analytics to get a more subtle and substantial view of what actions impact customer experiences and satisfaction."[173] Contact centers can utilize "customer analytics to help tune performance metrics closer to real time, so that each day's agents are guided, if not incentivized, to interact with customers in beneficial ways."[173]

Analytics can also "help service and order management functions move away from one-size-fits-all approaches to customers and instead tune and tailor interactions more personally based on knowledge of particular types or segments, such as regions or nationalities."[173] "Finally, through integrated views of customer data and analytics, service and order management functions are able to work in better synchronicity with the organization's marketing, sales, and other business functions."[173] Customer analytics can be used to understand where marketing campaigns are working as well.

In the words of business management guru Thomas Davenport, "Organizations are competing on analytics not just because they can—business today is awash in data crunchers—but also because they should."[176] Although these words were said more than ten years ago, they might be more relevant today than ever before. Davenport adds, "Business processes are among the last remaining points of differentiation. And analytics competitors wring every last drop of value from those processes."[176] "Customer analytics helps organizations determine what steps will give them competitive advantages, increase profitability, and identify waste in business processes," Davenport argues.[176]

With the steep drop in RAM prices, in-memory solutions are all the rage these days and they allow analytics to reach a whole new level. Today, creativity is becoming the differentiator; today's overriding philosophy might be "Those who analyze best win."

With products and services being commoditized at such a rapid rate today, customer loyalty has become more elusive than ever.[173] "Innovation must be constant and must immediately address why an organization is losing customers. Information insights from analytics can help an organization align product and service development with strategic business objectives for customer loyalty."[173] In addition, these insights can help sports betting organizations be selective in how they deploy marketing campaigns and customer-touch processes so that they emphasize features in new products and services that are important to customers.

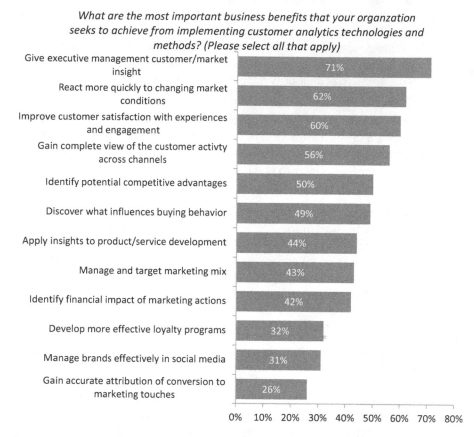

What are the most important business benefits that your organzation seeks to achieve from implementing customer analytics technologies and methods? (Please select all that apply)

Figure 12: What Are the Important Business Benefits of Customer Analytics?
Based on 2,573 responses from 454 respondents; almost six responses, on average.
Source: TDWI Research[173]

When TDWI Research examined the business benefits sought from customer analytics (see Figure 12), respondents cited giving executive management customer and market insight as the most important benefit (71%).[173] The second most important benefit was being able to react more quickly to changing market conditions (62%).[173]

Improving customer satisfaction and gaining a complete picture of a customer's activity across business channels—two areas that would be considered a part of the "Customer Experience Management" (CEM) process—are critical to identifying what steps an organization must take to build and retain customer loyalty.[173] The remaining items fall mainly into the categories of business intelligence, marketing, and brand management and they are extremely important to a sports book as well.

Organizations are becoming open to customer analytics because they are interested in discovering how a marketing department can be more effective, not just more efficient.[173] "Whereas other types of applications for e-commerce, fulfillment, or marketing automation help organizations determine how to get things done (e.g., getting goods delivered at the right time, executing a marketing campaign), customer analytics helps organizations answer who, what, when, where, and why questions," argues Scott Groenendal, program director of customer analytics market strategy for IBM Business Analytics.[173] "They can find answers to questions such as: What channel should I communicate through? When is the best time to target this person, and why would they be receptive to this message?" adds Groenendal.[173]

Individual creativity, personal experiences, customer behavior and marketing context are critical components of consumer marketing decisions.[173] "The role of customer analytics is not necessarily to replace these, but to help decision makers come to fact-based conclusions through better knowledge of the organization's customers and markets."[173] Just as importantly, analytics are needed for scalability.[173] "Just as automation is necessary to run hundreds or thousands of marketing campaigns, customer analytics processes are important for supplying intelligence and guidance to those automated routines. Customer analytics can provide the brains to match the marketing systems' brawn."[173] For a sports book, there's no point in advertising an upcoming football scorecast bet to a punter who only bets on basketball

With the commoditization of products and services, customer loyalty can be elusive; innovation must be constant and it should help to reveal why an organization might be losing its customer base.[173] "Information insights from analytics can help organizations align product and service development with strategic business objectives for customer loyalty."[173] These insights can also help an organization be selective about how they deploy their marketing campaigns and customer-touch processes so that they emphasize features in new products and services that are important to each specific customer.[173]

In its *Achieving Customer Loyalty with Customer Analytics*[175], IBM describes one of its studies that asked some of the world's leading company CEOs and CMOs what their number one priority was.[175] The CEOs answered that it was to engage customers, while the CMOs said it was to enhance customer loyalty.[175] The study argued that forward-thinking companies were using customer analytics to[175]:

- Guide front-line interactions with customers.
- Create and execute customer retention strategies.

- Prompt people or systems to proactively address customer satisfaction issues.
- Guide product planning to fulfill future customer needs.
- Hire and train employees to act upon customer insights and improve loyalty.
- Align operations to focus on satisfying customers.

The *Customer Analytics in the Age of Social Media*[173] report concluded that the importance of customer analytics is in the boardroom; "overwhelmingly, respondents cited giving executive management customer and market insight (71%) as the most important business benefit that their organization seeks to achieve from implementing customer analytics."[173] "This percentage rises to 81% when survey results are filtered to see only the responses from those who indicated 'strong acceptance' of data-driven customer analytics over gut feel."[173] The second highest benefit cited at 62% was "the ability to react more quickly to changing market conditions, which speaks to the need for customer data insights to help decision makers address competitive pressures from rapid product or service commoditization."[173]

Businesses can realize significant ROI from investing in customer analytics as it can improve the marketing department's efficiency and effectiveness.[173] However, customer analytics ROI is a difficult thing to fully quantify. Better customer knowledge equates to more optimized marketing spend because a business can focus its resources on those campaigns that have the highest predicted chances of success for particular segments, as well as cut off or avoid those that have the least.[173]

"By using analytics to eliminate mismatches of campaigns targeting the wrong customers or using the wrong messages and offers, marketing functions can reduce wasteful spending and increase gains relative to costs."[173] Customer segmentation allows organizations to move "away from one-size-fits-all, brand-level-only marketing and toward the 'market of one': that is, personalized, one-to-one marketing."[173]

Reaching a customization and customer service level that makes a customer feel as though he or she is a preferred customer is not easy, scaling that up so that an entire database of customers feel that they are unique and receiving outstanding customer service is even more challenging, but, in this day and age, it is almost a necessity if a company wants to provide good and engaging customer service.

In your organization, which of the following marketing objectives are most important to achieve for customer analytics to deliver a return on investment? (Please select all that apply.)

Figure 13: Which Are the Most Important Business Objectives When it Comes to Customer Analytics?
Source: TWDI Research[173], Based on 1,625 responses from 432 respondents; almost four responses per respondent, on average.

TDWI Research[173] examined the importance of accomplishing various objectives for gaining positive ROI from customer analytics (see Figure 13). "Using customer analytics to target cross-sell and up-sell opportunities was the objective cited by the biggest percentage of respondents (54%)."[173] This objective is about gaining more value from existing customers by understanding their purchasing habits and trying to get them to buy more products more often.[173] "Some organizations (18%) are implementing an advanced technique called 'uplift modeling' (also called incremental or true-lift modeling), which enables marketers to use data mining to measure the impact and influence of marketing actions on customers."[173] Insights such as these allow marketers to develop new kinds of predictive models to determine the best prospects for up-sell and cross-sell offerings.[173] "As firms scale up to execute large numbers of campaigns across multiple channels, the efficiency gained from predictive modeling can be critical to marketing spending optimization," argues Stodder.[173]

Analytics can improve marketing performance by quantifying a customer's lifetime value as well as customer worth at the many different stages in the customer's life cycle.[173] "If organizations can identify their most valuable customers they can determine if they are worthy of retention efforts and resources because of the returns they will provide."[175] For instance, it may not be worth the time, effort, and expense to retain a low value customer, unless customer analytics reveals that this low-spend customer actually has a lot of social influence.[175] Armed with this information, managers can align their deployment of resources to achieve the highest value, as well as avoid the costs and inefficiencies of marketing to the wrong people at the wrong time.[173]

Organizations have long used demographics such as gender, household size, education, occupation, and income to segment customers.[173] Data mining techniques let organizations segment much larger customer populations and, perhaps, more importantly, determine whether to apply new characteristics that refine segmentation to fit the specific attributes of the organization's products and services.[173]

"Customer analytics using data mining tools improves the speed of segmentation analysis over manual and spreadsheet efforts that are often used in less mature organizations."[173] Speed is a vital ingredient for marketing initiatives that are time sensitive, particularly for those companies that need to provide real-time cross-sell and up-sell offers to customers clicking through Web pages.[173] Today, personalized web pages can be rendered during the web page load and elements of the page can take into account past purchase history, clickstream information, as well as a whole host of other data points.

In its *Achieving Customer Loyalty with Analytics*[175], IBM argues that customer analytics can provide businesses with the ability to:

- Analyze all data types to gain a 360-degree view of each individual customer.
- Employ advanced algorithms that uncover relevant patterns and causal relationships that impact customer satisfaction and loyalty.
- Build predictive models that anticipate future outcomes.
- Learn from every customer interaction and apply lessons to future interactions and strategies.
- Deploy customer insights to decision-makers and front line systems.
- Improve sales forecasting and help minimize sales cycles.
- Measure and report on marketing performance.

"The next most common objectives in the research were predicting retention, attrition, and churn rates (47%) and determining lifetime customer value (42%)."[173] Churn can cost organizations heavily, both from the loss of profits from existing customers as well as in the high price of attracting new ones. "Attrition or churn analysis methods are aimed at discovering which variables have the most influence on customers' decisions to leave or stay."[173]

With data mining and predictive analytics, organizations can learn which attrition rates are acceptable or expected for particular customer segments and which rates could be highly detrimental to the bottom line.[173] "Predictive customer analytics can play a major role in enabling organizations to discover and model which customers are most likely to leave, and from which segments."[173]

"Advertising concerns are recording tens of millions of events daily that organizations want to mine in near real time to identify prospects," notes Stodder.[173] Businesses of all kinds want to use predictive models and score event and transaction details as fast as they come in so that they can gain insight into individual shopping behavior.[173] Insights that they hope will give them an advantage over their competitors, but this is dangerous and expensive territory to chart, especially if done incorrectly.

The "data sources most commonly monitored for customer analytics are customer satisfaction surveys (57%) and customer transactions and online purchases (55%). Just under half (44%) are monitoring Web site logs and clickstream sources. In addition to monitoring customer satisfaction surveys, about half (48%) of organizations surveyed are studying call and contact center interactions."[173] For a sports book, additional data sources would be gaming systems, facial recognition, RFID, PoS and credit card fraud systems, as well as mobile tracking and security systems, amongst many others.

Customer satisfaction surveys are usually conducted in person, on a website, over the phone or through traditional mail and e-mail channels.[173] Because this includes both semi-structured data and unstructured comments, data collection can be difficult.[173] "Standard questions inquire about a customer's satisfaction with purchases, the services they received, and the company's brands overall. Other questions address the customer's likelihood of buying from the company again and whether they would recommend the firm to others."[173]

As Wedel & Kannan explain in their article *Marketing Analytics for Data-Rich Environments*[113], surveys are simple to administer and data can be collected and analyzed very easily and quite quickly. "Firms continuously assess customer satisfaction; new digital interfaces require this to be done with short surveys to reduce fatigue and attrition. For example, loyalty is often evaluated with single-item Net Promoter Scores. As a consequence, longitudinal and repeated cross-section data are becoming more common," contend Wedel & Kannan.[113] Machine Learning can be utilized to create personalized surveys that customers are much more likely to answer because they will be based upon the customer's response to previous questions.[113]

Text analytics can be used to increase the speed, depth, and consistency of unstructured content analysis far greater than what can be done manually.[173] "More advanced analytics can look for correlations between satisfaction ratings, commented sentiments, and other records, such as first-call-resolution metrics."[173]

In its *Retail Analytics: Game Changer for Customer Loyalty,* Cognizant argues that in the retail industry, "predictive models can be used to analyze past performance to assess the likelihood that a customer will exhibit a specific behavior in order to improve marketing effectiveness."[177] This can help with "predicting customer reactions to a given product and can be leveraged to improve basket size, increase the value of the basket and switch the customer to a better and more profitable offering"[177] Predictive models can also help tailor pricing strategies that take into account both the need for competitive pricing and the bottom line.[177] What works in the retail industry should also work in the sports betting industry.

Predictive analytics and data mining are used to discover which variables out of possibly hundreds are most influential in determining customer loyalty within certain segments.[173] "Advanced analytics generally involves statistical, quantitative, or mathematical analysis and centers on developing, testing, training, scoring, and monitoring predictive models."[173]

Models can be created that will uncover patterns, affinities, anomalies, and other useful insights for marketing campaigns and for determining cross-sell and up-sell opportunities.[173] "The tools and techniques are also used for developing and deploying behavioral scoring models for marketing, deciding whether to adjust customers' credit limits for purchases, and a variety of highly time-sensitive analytic processes," notes Stodder.[173]

"As more online customer behavior is recorded in Web logs and tracked through cookies and other observation devices, sizeable amounts of information are becoming available to organizations that seek a more accurate view of a customer's path to purchase," states Stodder.[173] Attribution analysis is, first and foremost, a big-data problem, given the quantity and variety of data available from today's multiple platforms.[173]

Businesses that are performing attribution analysis will frequently employ Hadoop, MapReduce, with analytic software solutions such as R, SAS's eMiner, SAP's InfiniteInsights, Python, and IBM's SPSS, amongst others.[173] This allows a business to run sophisticated algorithms against detailed data to find the correct path of purchase. This analysis can then be integrated with analysis from other data types and sources, including those that might have been generated by any offline customer activity [173]

Attribution analysis can reveal such things as what kinds of campaigns most influence customer behavior.[173] "The analysis can help organizations determine where to allocate marketing resources to gain the highest level of success, as well as how to more accurately assign the percentage of credit due to specific marketing and advertising processes," concludes Stodder.[173]

On August 13, 2014, Facebook announced a major step forward in the area of attribution analysis. It said that it "would start telling advertisers on what device people saw an ad and on what device they took an action, such as buying a product or signing up for a test drive, as a result of seeing that ad. That means Facebook will be able to credit mobile ads that lead to desktop sales and desktop ads that result in mobile purchases."[178]

In his article *Facebook Now Tells Whether Mobile Ads Lead to Desktop Purchases*[102], Peterson notes that, "Advertisers can already track conversions through Facebook on desktop and on mobile, but to date Facebook hasn't broken out conversions by device type for advertisers to see. For example, advertisers have been able to see if their desktop and mobile ads lead to conversions, but they didn't know on which device type those conversions were taking place."[102]

However, Facebook's new cross-device conversion measurement only works for advertisers who place specific Facebook trackers on their websites and mobile apps.[102] "Without sharing users' personal information with the advertiser, those trackers can see that a Facebook user is checking out the advertisers' site or app and whether they've converted in the advertiser-specified fashion."[102] If the person does convert, "Facebook's trackers can trace back to see if that person has seen an ad from that advertiser on Facebook, which may have directly or indirectly led to the conversion."[102] Of course, nothing is 100% certain when it comes to attribution analysis, but this is a big step in the right direction of quantifying advertising spend.

With many of the following analytical marketing models, sports books should keep in mind that it is important to create control groups to measure the true effects of their models and marketing campaigns. Control groups are typical components in marketing analysis and are fundamental to statistical studies.[179] In his article *Control Group Marketing—With or Without CRM Software Systems*[179], Rick Cook states that:

> "The basic idea of a control group is simple. Select a random (or nearly random) sample from your campaign's marketing list and exclude them from promotion. Then measure the control group's activity and compare it to the activity of the group targeted via a campaign. The difference between the control and campaign group gives you a pretty good notion of how effective—and profitable—the campaign is.

"The theory is that a certain fraction of the customers in the campaign are going to purchase from you anyway during the campaign period. The control group lets you filter out that effect, as well as the effects of other channels which may be influencing behavior, such as display advertising, and shows you how much the campaign has affected customer behavior," argues Cook.[179]

Although they should be used to test out the effects of marketing campaigns, few companies include them in their marketing process.[179] "Marketing control groups become even more effective when combined with the customer analytics found in most marketing automation or customer relationship management systems," notes Cook.[179]

Cook argues that, "With a CRM system and a control group you can also detect the halo effect of your campaign. These are purchases and other actions which are influenced by the campaign but don't come in through the normal campaign channels."[179] For example, a customer could be so inspired by one particular campaign that he or she picks up the phone and orders products directly from the company instead of going through the call to action channel.[179] "Another example is the customer who doesn't use the promotional coupon you included in your marketing campaign but who purchases the product anyway."[179] Cook notes that marketers "can assume that customers in the test group who respond in unconventional methods are still influenced by the campaign and so should be counted as part of the campaign effect."[179] "Because CRM software lets you track all points of customer contact, and not just the direct response to the campaign, it can capture these halo customers," notes Cook.[179]

The size of the control group is usually 10 percent of the size of the campaign or test group.[179] Ideally you want the control group to be a truly random sample from the sports book's campaign list, but this is difficult to attain in practice as complete randomness is hard to achieve.[179] "Many companies select their control group by a simpler process, such as selecting every 10th name on the list to make up the control group," but there are other more scientific ways to choose the participants that should be utilized.

In the article *Artificial Intelligence Unlocks the True Power of Analytics,* Adobe explains that, "Descriptive analytics is the most basic of analysis functions. It summarizes and reports what has happened, such as click-throughs and revenue per visitor. This gives marketers historical context and prompts them to ask questions based on past customer behaviour."[18] For example, a marketer could use "descriptive analytics to dig into the various segments and get a good idea of all the behaviours and marketing touchpoints that led"[18] a user to buy something from an e-commerce website, let's say. Utilizing this information, the marketer could "make some educated guesses about how to appeal to similar audiences in the future."[18]

Simple cluster segmentation models could divide customers into their preferred choice of purchases. Market basket analysis, which utilizes association rules, would also be considered a descriptive analytics procedure.

Sports books could use market basket analysis to bundle offer promotions, as well as gain insight into its customers' buying habits. Detailed customer shopping and purchasing behavior could also be used to develop future products. I will go into further detail on this topic in chapter three. According to Adobe, "All users of analytics start by using descriptive analytics and it can lead to valuable insights, but it is limited by the imagination of the person using it. Because the analyst or marketer can only evaluate the data in front of them, they can only find answers to questions that focus on that limited dataset."[18]

"Whereas descriptive analytics is about prompting educated guesses and good questions, diagnostic analytics is about drilling down and filtering that descriptive data to figure out the why and the how of what has happened. Almost everyone who uses descriptive analytics asks, 'Why did this happen?' and uses diagnostic analytics to investigate by comparing different datasets."[18] Adobe believes questions likes "'Why Is revenue per visitor so low this week?' leads to 'Is it low for everyone or just for some groups?' which might lead to 'Has it been low all week or just for a few days?' and 'Is it getting better or worse?'"[18]

"As critical as this diagnostic process is to business, it too is limited," argues Adobe.[18] "As the amount of incoming data increases and the number of variables in customer behaviour grows, the power of diagnostic analytics becomes limited to specific situations, specific anomalies, leaving a vast sea of data questions unasked and unanswered."[18]

"Predictive analytics uses machine learning and other forms of artificial intelligence to meet this problem of scope head-on," argues Adobe.[18] "These technologies can recognise patterns, match events to the patterns and thereby predict the most likely next events. For example, based on how customers have responded to a campaign, predictive analytics will identify segments that respond in like ways, reaching the same outcome."[18] "It will identify what attributes of those groups are important in defining the segment, such as a particular past purchase or number of purchases or geography. It will then 'recognise' any visitor that matches that segment and predict the outcome that visitor will reach," explains Adobe.[18]

Prescriptive analytics, the pinnacle of the analytics pyramid, "applies prediction to suggest the best course of action."[18] "For example, having discovered a segment that almost always responds to a particular campaign by adding an item to the basket but not buying it, prescriptive analytics would suggest the most likely way to nudge those visitors to take the next step. In some cases, the nudge could be performed automatically—in real time," says Adobe.[18]

As to the "why" of analytics, in her article *How Much ROI Can Data Analytics Deliver?*[20], Annie Eissler makes quite a compelling case for analytics. According to Nucleus Research "analytics and business intelligence solutions deliver, on average, $13.01 for every dollar spent."[20] "Leading companies have been achieving double-digit return on investment (ROI) from their analytics investments for several years now," Eissler says.[20]

Data Mining

In his paper *The CRISP-DM model, the new blueprint for data mining[180]*, C. Shearer introduces the concept of the "Cross-industry standard process for data mining", which is more commonly known by its acronym CRISP-DM. It is a "data mining process model that describes commonly used approaches that data mining experts use to tackle problems."[180] It is currently the de facto standard for developing data mining and data discovery projects.[180]

In their paper *Methods for mining HTS data[181]*, Harper and Pickett break the CRISP-DM process of data mining into the following six major phases:

1. Business understanding—focuses on understanding the project objectives and requirements purely from a business perspective, and then "converting this knowledge into a data mining problem definition, and a preliminary plan designed to achieve the objectives."[181] "A decision model, especially one built using the *Decision Model and Notation* standard can be used."[181]
2. Data understanding—this starts with an "initial data collection and proceeds with activities in order to get familiar with the data, to identify data quality problems, to discover first insights into the data, or to detect interesting subsets to form hypotheses for hidden information."[181]
3. Data preparation—this phase covers "all activities to construct the final dataset (data that will be fed into the modeling tool(s)) from the initial raw data. Data preparation tasks are likely to be performed multiple times, and not in any prescribed order. Tasks include table, record, and attribute selection as well as transformation and cleaning of data for modeling tools."[181]
4. Modeling—various modeling techniques are selected and applied in this phase, and their parameters are calibrated to optimal values.[181] "Typically, there are several techniques for the same data mining problem type. Some techniques have specific requirements on the form of data. Therefore, stepping back to the data preparation phase is often needed."[181]
5. Evaluation—At this project stage, model (or models) that appear to have high quality from a data analysis perspective should have been made.[181] "Before proceeding to final model deployment, it is imperative to more thoroughly evaluate the model, and review the steps executed to construct the model, to be certain it dovetails with the business objectives."[181] A key objective here is to determine if any important key business objectives have been left out.[181] At the end of this phase, a decision on whether to use the data mining results should be reached.[181]

6. Deployment—Creation of the model is generally not the end in and of itself.[181] "Even if the purpose of the model is to increase knowledge of the data, the knowledge gained will need to be organized and presented in a way that is useful to the customer."[181] "Depending on the requirements, the deployment phase can be as simple as generating a report or as complex as implementing a repeatable data scoring (e.g. segment allocation) or data mining process."[181] "In many cases it will be the customer, not the data analyst, who will carry out the deployment steps. Even if the analyst deploys the model it is important for the customer to understand up front the actions which will need to be carried out in order to actually make use of the created models."[181]

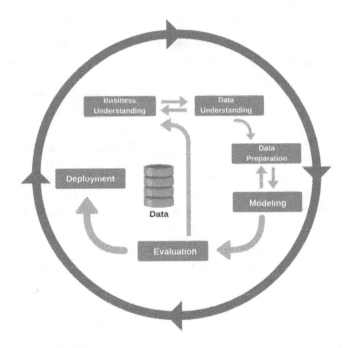

Figure 14: CRISP DM
Source: Wikipedia

The sequence of the phases (see Figure 14) is not strict and Harper and Pickett argue that moving back and forth between different phases is often required so flexibility is important.[181] "The arrows in the process diagram indicate the most important and frequent dependencies between phases," contend Harper and Pickett.[181] "The outer circle in the diagram symbolizes the cyclic nature of data mining itself," add Harper and Pickett.[181] The data mining processes continues long after a solution has been deployed, argue Harper and Pickett.[181] The "lessons learned during the process can trigger new, often more focused business questions and subsequent data mining processes will benefit from the experiences of previous ones," the writers conclude.[181]

In the SAS Institute Best Practices paper *Data Mining and the Case for Sampling[182]*, SAS defines data mining "as the process used to reveal valuable information and complex relationships that exist in large amounts of data."[182] For SAS, data mining is an iterative process, divided into five stages that are represented by the acronym SEMMA.[182] "Beginning with a statistically representative sample of data, the SEMMA methodology—which stands for Sample, Explore, Modify, Model, and Assess—makes it easy for business analysts to apply exploratory statistical and visualization techniques, select and transform the most significant predictive variables, model the variables to predict outcomes, and confirm a model's accuracy," argues SAS.[182] According to SAS, the SEMMA methodology is broken down into the following steps[182]:

- "Sample the data by creating one or more data tables. The samples should be big enough to contain the significant information, yet small enough to process quickly."[182]
- "Explore the data by searching for anticipated relationships, unanticipated trends, and anomalies in order to gain understanding and ideas."[182]
- "Modify the data by creating, selecting, and transforming the variables to focus the model selection process."[182]
- "Model the data by allowing the software to search automatically for a combination of data that reliably predicts a desired outcome."[182]
- "Assess the data by evaluating the usefulness and reliability of the findings from the data mining process."[182]

SEMMA is itself a cycle, in which the internal steps can be performed iteratively, as needed.[182] SAS advises that projects following SEMMA "can sift through millions of records and reveal patterns that enable businesses to meet data mining objectives such as" [182]:

- "Segmenting customers accurately into groups with similar buying patterns.
- Profiling customers for individual relationship management.
- Dramatically increasing response rate from direct mail campaigns.
- Identifying the most profitable customers and the underlying reasons.
- Understanding why customers leave for competitors (attrition, churn analysis).
- Uncovering factors affecting purchasing patterns, payments and response rates.
- Increasing profits by marketing to those most likely to purchase.
- Decreasing costs by filtering out those least likely to purchase.
- Detecting patterns to uncover non-compliance."[182]

AI, ML & Deep Learning

In the *AI Momentum, Maturity, & Models for Success*[183], a consortium of companies consisting of Accenture, Intel, Forbes Insight, and SAS polled 300 executives from a wide variety of industries about AI and discovered that it appears likely that we are on the verge of a radical momentum shift for the technology. As seen in many other leaps of technology over the years, greater familiarity is likely to lead to greater trust.[183] "Think about your first ride in a car sharing service, or the first time you used online banking," says Oliver Schabenberger, Chief Operating Officer and Chief Technology Officer for SAS.[183] So it will be with AI and machine learning. Schabenberger adds that[183]:

> "In a sense, those represented a leap of faith in newer technologies. That is where we are with AI right now. But even for many sophisticated users, AI still is a black box—they put data in, they get an output, and they do not understand the connections between the inputs and the outputs of AI systems. That is a fundamental challenge that has implications on everything from regulatory compliance to the customer experience it even affects how we respond to examining biases in our models. Organizations that have adopted AI can illuminate the black box by observing how the model responds to variations in the inputs, and adjusting accordingly."

The companies behind the study believe, "We are rapidly approaching a 'critical mass' moment in which the entire picture comes into view."[183] The responses submitted in the "What are the benefits of AI study" (see Figure 15) show "a level of enthusiasm and AI-focused activity that point to an explosion of AI adoption just around the corner, even as gaps in capabilities and strategy are revealed. Already, 72 percent of the organizations we surveyed have either deployed AI-based technology or are in the process of doing so."[183]

"A large percentage of survey respondents report having real success with AI. When looking at only those who have reported having deployed AI, 51 percent say the impact of deployment of AI-based technologies on their operations has been 'successful' or 'highly successful,'" claim the consortium.[183]

"It seems clear that the more experienced you are in AI, the more likely you are to appreciate the central role analytics will play in your efforts," argues the consortium.[183] "Among those who have deployed AI, they recognize that success in AI is success in analytics," says Schabenberger.[183] "For them, analytics has achieved a front and center role in AI. In fact, in many ways, AI is analytics."[183] Perhaps that is why 66 percent of respondents agree that "AI will enable us to mine massive volumes of data faster to inform business decisions."[183]

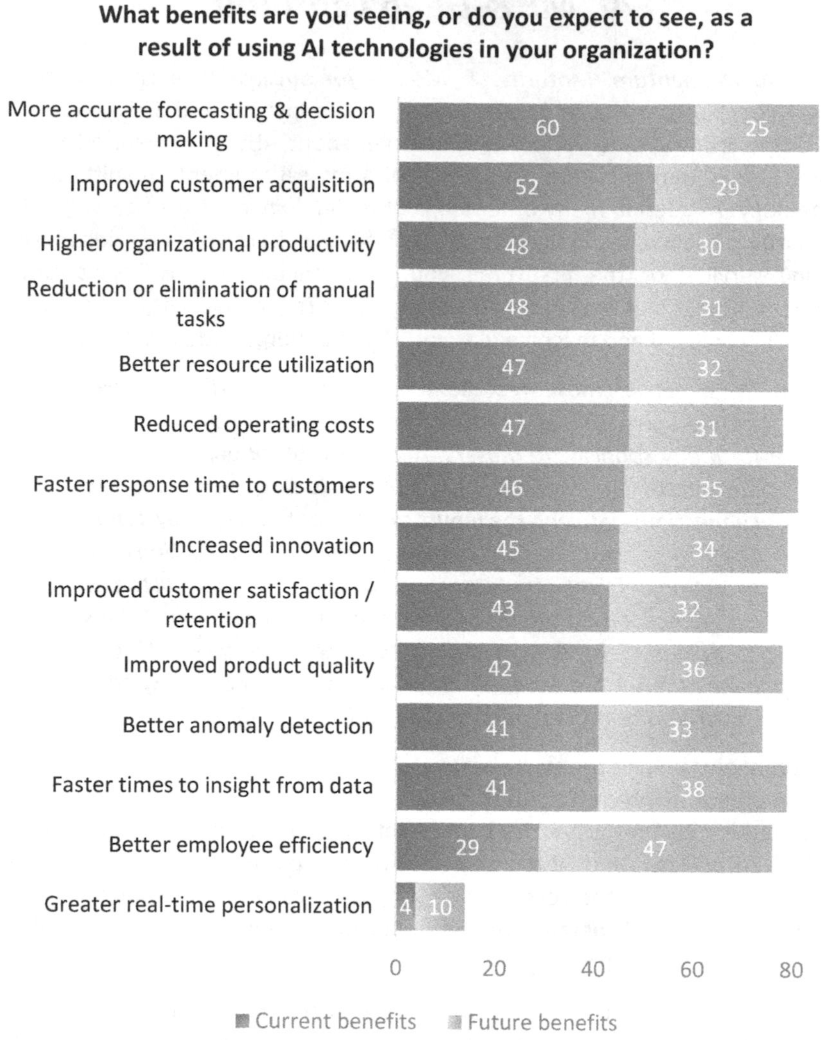

What benefits are you seeing, or do you expect to see, as a result of using AI technologies in your organization?

Benefit	Current benefits	Future benefits
More accurate forecasting & decision making	60	25
Improved customer acquisition	52	29
Higher organizational productivity	48	30
Reduction or elimination of manual tasks	48	31
Better resource utilization	47	32
Reduced operating costs	47	31
Faster response time to customers	46	35
Increased innovation	45	34
Improved customer satisfaction / retention	43	32
Improved product quality	42	36
Better anomaly detection	41	33
Faster times to insight from data	41	38
Better employee efficiency	29	47
Greater real-time personalization	4	10

■ Current benefits   ▨ Future benefits

Figure 15: Benefits of AI
Source: SAS.com

"Generally speaking, the progress of AI is unparalleled," says Intel's Melvin Greer.[183] "We've seen some very positive first impressions regarding how AI can actually be used – and we have a long way to go. We've seen more sophistication from our customers, who are looking for us to be much clearer in our explanations of AI, and in illuminating important differences between different types of AI and analytics technologies—from augmented reality and machine learning to deep learning, automated forecasting and many more—so we don't treat AI as the hammer to every nail."[183]

Despite the idea that suggests AI operates independently of human intervention, those responsible for putting AI to work in the polled organizations recognize that these technologies require rigorous oversight.[183] "In fact, nearly a quarter (23 percent) of AI adopters review or evaluate AI outputs at least daily," reports the consortium.[183]

The report "also suggests that companies that have been more successful with AI tend to have more rigorous oversight processes in place. For example, 74 percent of successful companies report that they review their AI output at least weekly, compared with 33 percent of those that are less successful."[183] Additionally, "43 percent of successful companies have a process in place for augmenting or overriding questionable results, compared with 28 percent of companies that haven't yet found success in their AI initiatives."[183]

"Many believe that despite these positive signs, oversight processes have a long way to go before they catch up with advances in AI technology," says the consortium.[183] "Although we are still in the very early phases of AI, the technology is already well ahead of the marketplace when it comes to the processes and procedures organizations have in place to provide oversight," says Oliver Schabenberger.[183] "For example, we would be seeing more widespread use of driverless cars if government oversight and automaker-level governance capabilities were able to keep up with the technology itself. The technical capabilities are ahead of our ability to cope with the technology."[183]

This does mean companies might find themselves in the unenviable position of waiting for slow moving governments to get on their initiatives, but I'd argue it's always better to be ahead of any government oversight task force than to be follower behind it.

According to Wikipedia, Machine Learning (ML) is the subfield of computer science that "explores the construction and study of algorithms that can learn from data. Such algorithms operate by building a model based on inputs and using that to make predictions or decisions, rather than following only explicitly programmed instructions."[184]

ML "evolved from the study of pattern recognition and computational learning theory in artificial intelligence."[184] It "explores the study and construction of algorithms that can learn from and make predictions on data—such algorithms overcome following strictly static program instructions by making data driven predictions or decisions, through building a model from sample inputs."[184]

As per Wikipedia, ML can be broken down into the following three categories[184]:

1. Supervised learning: The computer is presented with example inputs and their desired outputs, given by a "teacher", and the goal is to learn a general rule that maps inputs to outputs.

2. Unsupervised learning: No labels are given to the learning algorithm, leaving it on its own to find structure in its input. Unsupervised learning can be a goal in itself (discovering hidden patterns in data) or a means towards an end (feature learning).

3. Reinforcement learning: A computer program interacts with a dynamic environment in which it must perform a certain goal (such as driving a vehicle), without a teacher explicitly telling it whether it has come close to its goal or not. Another example is learning to play a game by playing against an opponent.

There are so many use cases for ML and deep learning for marketing departments that it is almost impossible to create an exhaustive list here, but it is particularly useful for marketing personalization, customer recommendations, spam filtering, network security, optical character recognition (OCR), voice recognition, computer vision, fraud detection, optimization, language translations, sentiment analysis, SEO, and online search, amongst many others use cases.

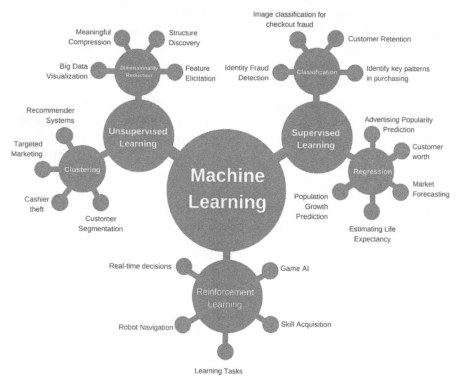

Figure 16: Machine Learning for marketers
Source: Artificial Intelligence in Logistics[185]

Figure 16 reveals how ML can be broken down into supervised and unsupervised learning, as well as reinforcement learning that is specific to a marketing department.

Machine-learning can also be used to spot credit card or transaction fraud in real-time. ML can build predictive models of credit card transactions based on their likelihood of being fraudulent and the system can compare real-time transactions against these models. When the system spots potential fraud it can alert either the bank, retail outlet or sports book where the transaction occurred. This is exceptionally important for businesses with online presences because online fraud is on the rise and this could be an additional security layer that ensures a purchase made is ultimately a purchase paid for.

Although ML and data mining often employ the same methods and overlap significantly, they do differ markedly. As Wikipedia explains[184]:

> *"While machine learning focuses on prediction, based on known properties learned from the training data, data mining focuses on the discovery of (previously) unknown properties in the data (this is the analysis step of Knowledge Discovery in Databases). Data mining uses many machine learning methods, but with different goals; on the other hand, machine learning also employs data mining methods as 'unsupervised learning' or as a preprocessing step to improve learner accuracy. Much of the confusion between these two research communities (which do often have separate conferences and separate journals, ECML PKDD being a major exception) comes from the basic assumptions they work with: in machine learning, performance is usually evaluated with respect to the ability to reproduce known knowledge, while in Knowledge Discovery and Data Mining (KDD) the key task is the discovery of previously unknown knowledge. Evaluated with respect to known knowledge, an uninformed (unsupervised) method will easily be outperformed by other supervised methods, while in a typical KDD task, supervised methods cannot be used due to the unavailability of training data.*

Another subset of AI and ML is deep learning, which, according to SAS[186] is "a type of machine learning that trains a computer to perform human-like tasks, such as recognizing speech, identifying images or making predictions. Instead of organizing data to run through predefined equations, deep learning sets up basic parameters about the data and trains the computer to learn on its own by recognizing patterns using many layers of processing."

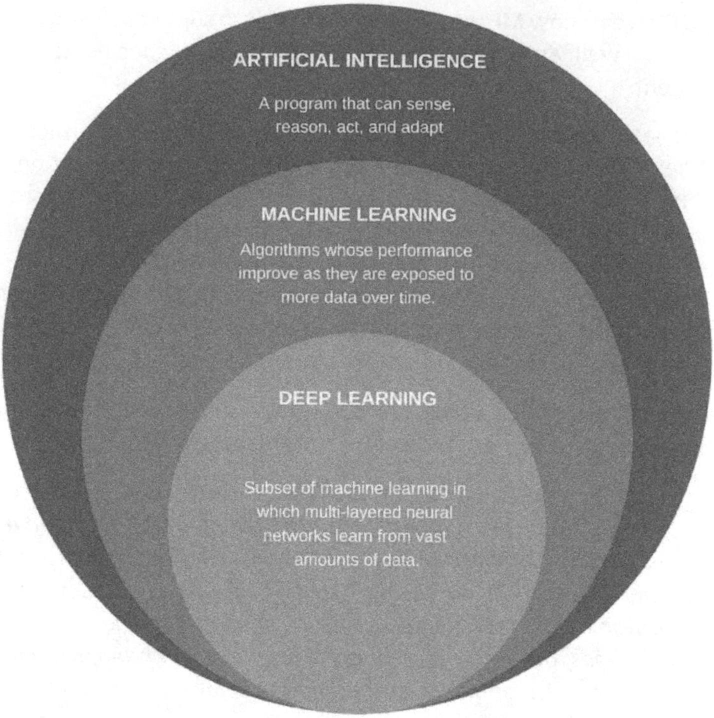

Figure 17: A.I., ML, and Deep Learning

Deep learning (see Figure 17) is a branch of machine learning and it seeks to imitate the neural activities of the human brain. Deep learning architectures have been applied to fields of computer vision, speech recognition, NLP, audio recognition, social network filtering, machine translation, bioinformatics and drug design, amongst others. In most cases, results have proven to be comparable, if not superior to human experts.[187]

In his blog[188], Ajit Jaokar explains that:

> "Deep learning refers to artificial neural networks that are composed of many layers. The 'Deep' refers to multiple layers. In contrast, many other machine learning algorithms like SVM are shallow because they do not have a Deep architecture through multiple layers. The Deep architecture allows subsequent computations to build upon previous ones. We currently have deep learning networks with 10+ and even 100+ layers. The presence of multiple layers allows the network to learn more abstract features. Thus, the higher layers of the network can learn more abstract features building on the inputs from the lower layers. A Deep Learning network can be seen as a Feature extraction layer with a Classification layer on

top. The power of deep learning is not in its classification skills, but rather in its feature extraction skills. Feature extraction is automatic (without human intervention) and multi-layered. The network is trained by exposing it to a large number of labelled examples. Errors are detected and the weights of the connections between the neurons adjusted to improve results. The optimisation process is repeated to create a tuned network. Once deployed, unlabelled images can be assessed based on the tuned network."

ML can help a sports book discover customer segments that they may not realize were there. Armed with this kind of information, sports books can understand what matters most to its customers at the individual and personalization level, which will enable them to anticipate their customer's needs before even the customers are aware of them. Even more, sports books can understand key characteristics of their most profitable customers and recognize the next important ones when he or she happens to log into their account or walk into a sports book branch.

The use of deep neural networks and image classifiers can analyze and parse images, which can enable sports book marketers to monitor the images that provide the highest selling and conversion rates through each ecommerce channel. ML can also be used to compute dynamic clusters of customers to create fluid segmentation in real-time.

Today, the importance of personalization in customer experience initiatives can't be underestimated. In his article *5 Ways AI Will Boost Personalization in Digital Marketing*[189], Dirk Vogel argues that AI will radically change the marketing landscape by allowing the following:

- Personal shopping for everyone.
- Utilizing chatbots to increase customer service.
- Seamless programmatic media buying.
- Predictive customer service.
- Optimizing marketing automation.

According to Vogel, "Shopping online creates rich data footprints regarding the individual preferences, spending habits and preferred channels of individual consumers. Feeding these digital breadcrumbs into an AI-engine helps bring curated shopping journeys to mass audiences."[189]

As Amazon, Pandora, and Netflix have proven, personalized shopping for everyone is a winning formula; "Using an advanced recommendation-AI, e-commerce leader Amazon creates more than 35% of its total revenues with personalized shopping recommendations," states Vogel.[189] "Taking personalization to the next level, artificial intelligence also allows for predicting the kinds of purchases consumers are going to make before they even know it," notes Vogel.[189]

"Customer service is still where today's brands are dropping the ball," Vogel believes, adding that, "Only 35% of companies are able to identify their customers at the moment of contact (Selligent survey)—with customers potentially unfriending brands and taking their business elsewhere."[189]

It may sound counter-intuitive, Vogel argues, "but automated bots can create lifelike, seamless customer service experiences, addressing the consumer on their purchase history and known preferences."[189] One of the standouts, Vogel notes is Facebook's "M" technology, which is embedded in the Messenger app.[189] "The AI delivers personalized product, travel and restaurant recommendations, while troubleshooting technical problems," explains Vogel.[189]

Although chatbots are cheaper than handling customer service inquiries over the phone, there's a catch as chatbots can only deliver highly personalized and contextual assistance if they have access to universal consumer profiles that are populated by real-time data.[189] This means, done correctly, developing chatbots is an expensive upfront investment, and it is an investment that should be done company-wide, not siloed by just the marketing or customer service department, as information that chatbots tap into are useful throughout an organization.

On the marketing side, AI may deliver that extra dash of relevancy programmatic advertising has been waiting for all these years.[189] "On the consumer side, AI helps create individualized display ads that website visitors want to see,"[189] while on the accounting side, "the bots handle invoicing and payment for these ad transactions, giving marketers more time to focus on the big picture."[189]

With AI, predictive customer service and marketing could be just around the corner.[189] "What may sound like a scenario from *Minority Report* is already being beta tested: Intel subsidiary Saffron has created an artificial intelligence that is able to predict with 88% certainty why, on which channel, and for which product individual customers will seek help next. 'We've been expecting your call,' never rang more true," states Vogel.[189]

One of the biggest problems in corporate marketing is hitting the customer with automated marketing offers too often.[189] In the future, AI will analyze a consumer's purchase history and email habits to choose the optimal time for hitting the inbox with content that's bound to boost open rates and conversions," contends Vogel.[189]

In its article *Sports trading and AI: Taking the human out of sports betting*[12], *Gambling Insider* argues that, "Just as more scientific analysis of sport is changing how coaches, trainers and clubs play their respective games, greater analysis of sporting events is helping odds making database operators evaluate the potential permutations of each sporting event, increasing the accuracy of that respective odd and thereby making the subsequent odds determination easier."[12]

Human traders simply cannot process the enormous amounts of sporting analysis data available to them the way AI can, especially in today's expansive betting market, where an increasing amount of games and bet types are offered to an increasingly insatiable betting public.[12]

"There is also a greater degree of accuracy to the odds calculations of AI based sport trader than a human sports trader, who will always be liable to human error regardless of their skill," notes *Gambling Insider*.[12] "An AI odds maker can make hundreds of thousands of calculations per second, leaving their human counterparts in the dust," they add.[12]

Connall McSorley, Commercial Director of Metric Gaming, believes AI-based trading "is vital in order to run the quantity of markets required to be seen in a competitive benchmark perspective because quite frankly human sports traders cannot manage that type of output."[12]

"AI in sports betting is still in its relative infancy, with programmers still developing the language that will ensure its security and accuracy," claim *Gambling Insider*.[12] However, "While they may be able to develop programming language and algorithms to replicate and exceed the knowledge of a human odds maker, AI still cannot currently replicate the experience of a human."[12]

Kambi's Head of Business Intelligence, Daniel Tidström, added: "Coming from a data and algorithmic side, AI is becoming more and more of an accepted practice in the sports betting industry, however the Holy Grail of a fully autonomous general artificial intelligence sports betting system is still some years away."[12]

"With the gap between the operational effectiveness of AI and human sports traders becoming smaller the role of human odds makers will inevitably have to change to one of risk management ensuring that the system remains free of potential corruption and that problem gamblers are identified/stopped, all things that AI systems cannot currently do without human intervention,"[12] adds *Gambling Insider*.

McSorley believes that the role of human sports traders will "morph more into one of risk management and price biasing, using AI algorithms as a tool in this role."[12]

Besides the setting of odds, AI can help with player analysis as well as risk management.[12] Kambi has utilized AI in this way, as Daniel explains: "We've developed fully automated player management systems that actively manage the profile of every player on our network, perhaps hundreds of thousands of players. This gives us the means to manage players in a way that a human operator could not in terms of speed and coverage."[12]

"We've been doing a lot of work aimed at removing the human element from player profiling in particular, however we do still retain an element of input from human risk assessors. The sheer number of players currently participating in sports betting necessitates the need for practical ways to assess every player on the network, which is only possible with a high degree of automation," adds Tidström.[12]

The world of odds-setting has evolved from an exercise where "an odds-maker starts with a blank sheet of paper and compiles prices/lines based on his own subjective skill and experience, and moved towards a role where the skill is in interpreting the market and positioning your firm within the boundaries that the market provides you," argues *Gambling Insider*.[12]

Langeland believes that there is a future for human traders "in designing and pricing unique markets, and also pricing events and markets early before a strong market has formed."[12] Langeland adds that, "Sports traders should also be able to have an active and valuable role in designing and programming the AI trading systems, so at least in the short-term sports traders should see AI as an opportunity not a threat."[12] Ultimately, putting AI odds makers in total control of a betting operator's books could expose it to an attack by hackers[12], which could be financially devastating. "Given the significant levels of revenue involved and the number of high profile corporate entities which have fallen victim to hackers over the last five years, betting operators may be reluctant to place the entirety of their odds making under AI control," warns *Gambling Insider*.[12]

"Traders are constantly monitoring the output of what AI is generating and if there is seen to be a denial of service or a system failure the markets are just pulled and voided," explains McSorley.[12] "There is an absolute requirement for the sort of monitoring and management of what content is being produced, the accuracy and sanity checking against other operators to ensure that you are in line and not creating arbitrage opportunities," adds McSorley.[12]

"There has always been a potential for hacking out there, with denial of service attacks being a feature of the industry for quite some time," warns Tidström.[12] Robust cyber security is paramount, he adds.[12]

One area where human intellect beats AI hands-down is in the ability to read subtle human behaviors and emotions, specifically those involved in a sporting event.[12] For example, *Gambling Insider* notes that, "no computer could understand the shock and resignation on David Luiz' face when Brazil were five-nil down at half time in the world cup semi-final, or see the pained body language of Rafael Nadal when he injured his back in the Australian Open final but carried on playing."[12]

Kambi has "human traders with decades of experience who are experts at reading body language," explains Tidström. "The statistical modelling and algorithms simply do not exist for these sorts of situations, so there will always be a requirement for an expert human trader who can read the body language of the participant and interpret the emotional aspect of the event," he adds.[12]

Connall McSorley concurs: "Human sports traders will never be replaced by AI, the overview component of their offering is absolutely huge, for example is a player crocked but has he stayed on the pitch because he is the team captain is just one example of all sorts of nuances and sentiment in sport that an algorithm will never get."[12] McSorley also notes that, "Human sports traders are also able to offer bettors a company's position from regionality or marketing perspective or a competitive one, all an algorithm can do is offer a price."[12]

"In betting there is a big incentive for people to look to manipulate the market with disinformation," Langeland explains, "so an AI social media monitor would need to learn which sources to trust, as well as how to weigh what is said.[12] "When police detectives can be replaced by AI we will know that AI bookmaker traders are ready to take over from human counterparts!" jokes Langeland.[12]

Tidström feels there is "a definite need for a human component, you simply cannot remove it, however what you need to do is to free up human sports traders to watch and interpret the sporting events rather than be constantly changing the prices and doing the manual tedious work that machines can be doing, instead allowing the human trader to concentrate on the things that machines cannot do."[12] "A modern trader requires a more diverse skillset than ever, he must speak a common language with developers, understand and help refine the mathematical models and have a fundamental understanding of the mechanics of both sporting events and betting markets," Tidström argues.[12] "You need to create a pipeline to develop talent with the right experience. Maths alone will only take you so far, you need experts who know when correlation is not causation," Tidström concludes.[12]

Gambling Insider concludes that, "the sports betting industry has accepted artificial intelligence algorithmic sports trading into the fold, but the nature of the relationship between human sports trader and AI algorithm will be an ever evolving one, with both seemingly being required to be of benefit to the industry."[12]

In her article *ROI of AI: 5 Ways Retailers Are Embracing The Innovation*, Debbie Haus lists five recent examples of retailers using AI[53]:

1. L'Occitane achieved a 15% life in mobile sales by using heat maps and artificial intelligence-powered technology from ContentSquare to analyze the checkout process and identify the 'struggle points' in each market."[53]
2. David's Bridal has seen "13 times more click-throughs across social platforms and a 40% decrease in bounce rate"[53] when using AI to improve social commerce with a tool that uses the technology to create pop-up landing pages for brands to link to on social media.[53]

3. "Earth Fare is boosting year-over-year topline sales by optimizing promotion with an AI solution from Daisy Intelligence. Earth Fare's category managers use weekly promotional recommendations to improve sales growth and guide go-forward decision-making."[53]

4. Amazon offers "Prime members the ability to complete purchases using the AI-powered Amazon Echo. Shoppers can ask Alexa to recommend products. The tool analyzes the user's order history to find relevant products before fulfilling the purchase command."[53]

5. Shop Direct is "working with IBM's Watson to develop AI that can perform sentiment analysis to detect a shopper's mood, based on word usage and message tone."[53]

The last example might be particularly interesting for the sports betting industry as it is an industry that incites a lot of emotion in its players and understanding a player's mindset before, during, and after they play could be beneficial in a multitude of ways. It would provide considerable behavioral information as well as potentially reveal gamblers who have problems and should be cut off.

WEKA, a comprehensive collection of machine-learning algorithms for data mining tasks written in Java and released under the GPL, contains tools for data pre-processing, classification, regression, clustering, association rules, and visualization. It has a very minimal learning curve compared to products like SAS's Enterprise Miner. However, unlike SAS, it can become quite inefficient with larger datasets.

Python and R are the most popular open sources solutions used for ML and they both have a large user base community. Scikit-learn combined with Pandas, Numpy, Seaborn and Matplotlib make implementing ML algorithms in Python very versatile and these provide more customization and utilization than R.

The R community has a large and active user base. R's libraries contain a wide variety of statistical and graphical techniques as well. These include linear and nonlinear modeling, classical statistical tests, time-series analysis, classification, clustering, amongst others. Due to its S heritage, R also has strong object-oriented programming capabilities.

Other ML software includes Matlab, Scikit, Accord, Apache's Mahout, Spark's MLLib, H2O on Hadoop, ConvNteJS, SPSS, SAP's Predictive Analytics library, even SQL Server is powerful enough to build some ML models.

ML can be used to compute dynamic clusters of customers to create fluid segmentation in real-time. As consumer buying habits evolve, fluid segmentation ensures the sports book continues to reach the right customer, at the right time, at the right price, through the right channels, with the right offer.

Although chatbots are cheaper than handling customer service inquiries over the phone, there's a catch as chatbots can only deliver highly personalized and contextual assistance if they have access to universal consumer profiles that are populated by real-time data.[189] This means, done correctly, developing chatbots is an expensive upfront investment, it is an investment that should be done company-wide, not siloed by just the marketing or customer service department as information that chatbots tap into are useful throughout the organization.

On the marketing side, AI may deliver that extra dash of relevancy programmatic advertising has been waiting for all these years. "On the consumer side, AI helps create individualized display ads that website visitors want to see,"[189] while on the accounting side, "the bots handle invoicing and payment for these ad transactions, giving marketers more time to focus on the big picture."[189]

With AI, predictive customer service and marketing could be just around the corner.[189] "What may sound like a scenario from the Minority Report movie is already in beta testing: Intel subsidiary Saffron has created an artificial intelligence that is able to predict with 88% certainty why, on which channel, and for which product individual customers will seek help next. 'We've been expecting your call,' never rang more true," Vogel predicts.[189]

One of the biggest problems in corporate marketing is hitting the customer with automated marketing offers too often.[189] In the future, AI will analyze a consumer's purchase history and email habits to choose the optimal time for hitting the inbox with content that's bound to boost open rates and conversions," Vogel contends.[189]

Another interesting use of AI is what Pinterest is doing with its visual serach technology. Accoridng to Lauren Johnson Adweek article *Pinterest Is Offering Brands Its Visual Search Technology To Score Large Ad Deals*[190], "The visual search technology is Pinterest's version of AI and human curation that lets consumers snap a picture of IRL things and find similar items online. Taking a picture of a red dress for example, pulls up posts of red dresses that consumers can browse through and shop," states Johnson.[190]

"The idea is to give people enough ideas that are visually related so that they have a new way to identify and search for things," said Amy Vener, retail vertical strategy lead at Pinterest.[190] "From a visual-discovery perspective, our technology is doing something similar where we're analyzing within the image the colors, the shapes and the textures to bring that to another level of dimension," Vener adds.[190]

Utilizing the technology, someone who points his or her phone's camera at a baby crib will receive recommendations for similar baby products.[190] "Eventually, all of Target's inventory will be equipped with Pinterest's technology to allow anyone to scan items in the real world and shop similar items through Target.com," states Johnson. "Target is the first retailer to build Pinterest's technology into its apps and website, though the site also has a deal to power Bixby, Samsung's AI app that works similarly."[190]

"We're now in a place where we're using Pinterest as a service to power some visual search for other products," Vener said. "I think there's an opportunity for retailers to be a little more of a prominent player when it comes to visual discovery."[190] Similarly, sports books can look at this technology to create a more interactive customer. Why shouldn't a bettor watching a football match not be able to raise their mobile phone up to the television and see the bets offered on particular player or team.

Deep Learning

Deep Learning is a branch of Machine Learning and it seeks to imitate the neural activity of the human brain. Deep learning architectures have been applied to the fields of computer vision, speech recognition, NLP, audio recognition, social network filtering, machine translation, bioinformatics and drug design, amongst others. In most cases, results have proven to be comparable, if not superior to human experts.[191]

In the ensuing pages, I'll break down the current offerings available in deep learning technology and try to give you the pros and cons of each system. This is, however, technology that changes by the day and, although I'll keep the discussion as updated as possible, much of this information will need to be updated in six months. (All the more reason to keep an eye on these editions, I usually update these book once every six months or so)

In their paper *Caffe2 vs. TensorFlow: Which is a Better Deep Learning Framework?*[192], Baige Liu and Xiaoxue Zang focus on the two most used deep learning programs, Caffe2 and Tensorflow, comparing five aspects of the software – the expressiveness, the modeling capability, the performance, help and support, and the scalability.[196] The authors chose "TensorFlow because it is currently the most widely-used deep learning framework."[196] The authors recognize that Caffe was an extremely popular framework before TensorFlow was introduced and the Caffe2 framework can build upon that potential, while gaining a lot of user preference in the near future.[196]

However, as Liu and Zang conclude:

> "in many aspects and as a result we find neither of these two has an [sic] dominating advantages over the other. Therefore, in practice, the choice between these two actually depends on the specific user tasks and the user preferences. Overall if the user need [sic] to pursue speed and has limited space restricted by the device, Caffe2 is a better choice since our experiments' results revealed that Caffe2 has a significant advantage over TensorFlow both in speed and space. Nevertheless, TensorFlow is still powerful and useful because there is a large number

> *official [six] and third-party resources, services, debugging tools, and a big supportive community that makes it easier to find reference codes."*

With software, there is not always a binary answer, i.e., "Is *x* piece of software better for my problem than *y* piece of software?" Caveats abound. Always. And Liu and Zang do seem to concur.

Tensorflow

In his article *Google Just Open Sourced TensorFlow, Its Artificial Intelligence Engine[193]*, Cade Metz explains that at its 2015 Google I/O conference Google open sourced its deep learning engine known as TensorFlow. In open sourcing TensorFlow, Google is freely sharing the underlying code with the world at large.[193] "In literally giving the technology away, Google believes it can accelerate the evolution of AI. Through open source, outsiders can help improve on Google's technology and, yes, return these improvements back to Google," explains Metz.[193]

"What we're hoping is that the community adopts this as a good way of expressing machine learning algorithms of lots of different types, and also contributes to building and improving [TensorFlow] in lots of different and interesting ways," says Jeff Dean, and a key player in the rise of Google's deep learning technology.[193]

Open sourcing AI has been a common practice over the past few years.[193] Facebook, Microsoft, and Twitter have all made huge strides in AI and some have open sourced software that is similar to TensorFlow, including Torch—a system originally built by researchers in Switzerland—as well as systems like Caffe and Theano.[193] However, Google's move is highly significant because Google's AI engine is considered to be the world's most advanced—and because, well, it is Google after all.[193]

Google, however, isn't giving away all its secrets.[193] As Metz explains[193]:

> *"At the moment, the company is only open sourcing part of this AI engine. It's sharing only some of the algorithms that run atop the engine. And it's not sharing access to the remarkably advanced hardward infrastructure that drives this engine (that would certainly come with a price tag). But Google is giving away at least some of its most important data center software, and that's not something it has typically done in the past."*

In the past, Google only shared its designs until after it had moved onto other designs, but it had never open sourced code.[193] With TensorFlow, however, the "company has changed tack, freely sharing some of its newest—and, indeed, most important—software."[193] Google open sources parts of its Android mobile operating system and several other smaller software projects, but this is far different.[193] With TensorFlow's release, "Google is open sourcing software that sits at the heart of its empire," states Metz.[193]

Deep learning relies on neural networks and Google typically "trains these neural nets using a vast array of machines equipped with GPU chips—computer processors that were originally built to render graphics for games and other highly visual applications, but have also proven quite adept at deep learning," explains Metx.[193]

GPUs are good at processing lots of little bits of data in parallel, and that's what deep learning needs, but after they've been trained, these neural nets work in different ways[193], often running on "traditional computer processors inside the data center, and in some cases, they can run on mobile phones," notes Metz.[193] The *Google Translate* app is a prime example of this. It runs entirely on a mobile device without a data center connection, letting users translate foreign text into their native language.[193]

TensorFlow is a way of building and running neural networks that are required for computations like this, both at the training stage and the execution stage.[193] It is basically a set of software libraries that users "can slip into any application so that it too can learn tasks like image recognition, speech recognition, and language translation."[193]

The underlying TensorFlow software was built in C++[193], but "in developing applications for this AI engine, coders can use either C++ or Python, the most popular language among deep learning researchers," adds Metz.[193] Google hopes that developers "will expand the tool to other languages, including Google Go, Java, and perhaps even Javascript, so that coders have more ways of building apps."[193]

According to Google's Jeff Dean, "TensorFlow is well suited not only to deep learning, but to other forms of AI, including reinforcement learning and logistic regression."[193] Tensorflow is twice as fast as Google's previous system, DistBelief, adds Dean.[193]

In open sourcing the tool, Google provides some sample neural networking models and algorithms, "including models for recognizing photographs, identifying handwritten numbers, and analyzing text."[193] "We'll give you all the algorithms you need to train those models on public data sets," Dean says.[193]

The major caveat to Google's seeming geneorisity is that the initial open source version of TensorFlow only runs on a single computer, you can't train models across a vast array of machines.[193] "This computer can include many GPUs, but it's a single computer nonetheless," notes Metz.[193] "Google is still keeping an advantage," Chris Nicholson, Chief Executive of AI startup Skymind, says.[193] "To build true enterprise applications, you need to analyze data at scale," he adds.

"At the execution stage, the open source incarnation of TensorFlow will run on phones as well as desktops and laptops, and Google indicates that the company may eventually open source a version that runs across hundreds of machines," notes Metz[193], so the technology is something to keep an eye on in terms of AI and ML options.

So why the change of heart at Google? Well, part of it has to do with the very nature of how the machine learning community operates.[193] "Deep learning originated with academics who openly shared their ideas, and many of them now work at Google—including University of Toronto professor Geoff Hinton, the godfather of deep learning," explains Metz.[193]

"TensorFlow was built at a very different time from tools like MapReduce and GFS and BigTable and Dremel and Spanner and Borg," notes Metz.[193] "The open source movement—where Internet companies share so many of their tools in order to accelerate the rate of development—has picked up considerable speed over the past decade. Google now builds software with an eye towards open source," adds Metz.[193] Many of Google's earlier tools were just too closely tied to Google's IT infrastructure to make them easily useful for outside developers.[193]

Unlike its competitors, Google has not handed the open source project to an independent third party, but will manage the project itself at Tensorflow.org.[193] The code is shared under an Apache 2 license, meaning anyone can use the code free of copyright issues.[193]

Any goodwill this generates for Google is less important than the projects it could potentially feed.[193] According to Dean, "you can think of TensorFlow as combining the best of Torch and Caffe and Theano. Like Torch and Theano, he says, it's good for quickly spinning up research projects, and like Caffe, it's good for pushing those research projects into the real world."[193]

However, even some within Google might disagree.[193] "According to many in the community, DeepMind, a notable deep learning startup now owned by Google, continues to use Torch—even though it has long had access to TensorFlow and DistBelief," notes Metz.[193] But, the writer concludes, "at the very least, an open source TensorFlow gives the community more options. And that's a good thing."[193]

Even utilizing TensorFlow's powerful AI and ML capabilities, building a deep learning app still requires some serious analytics and coding skills.[193] But this too may change in the years to come, Metz adds.[193] As Dean points out, "a Google deep-learning open source project and a Google deep-learning cloud service aren't mutually exclusive."[193]

For now, Google merely wants to generously share the code.[193] As Dean says, "this will help the company improve this code."[193] At the same time, other benefits will result from this, including improving machine learning as a whole, which will undoubtedly find its way back to the souce—Google. The circle of code continues...

"Google is five to seven years ahead of the rest of the world," argues Chris Nicholson, adding, "If they open source their tools, this can make everybody else better at machine learning"[193]; sports books included.

According to its article *Comparing Top Deep Learning Frameworks: Deeplearning4J, PyTorch, TensorFlow, Caffe, Kera, MxNet, Gluon & CNTK*[194], TensorFlow's pros and cons include:

- Python + Numpy.
- Computational graph abstraction, like Theano.
- Faster compile times than Theano.
- TensorBoard for visualization.
- Data and model parallelism.
- Slower than other frameworks.
- Much "fatter" than Torch; more magic.
- Not many pretrained models.
- Computational graph is pure Python, therefore slow.
- No commercial support.
- Drops out to Python to load each new training batch.
- Not very toolable.
- Dynamic typing is error-prone on large software projects.

Caffe2

At its F8 developer conference in San Francisco in 2018, Facebook announced the launch of Caffe2, an open source framework for deep learning.[195] In his article *Facebook-Open Sources Caffe2, a New Deep Learning Framwork,* Jordan Novet explains that the announcement "builds on Facebook's contributions to the Torch open source deep learning framework and more recently the PyTorch framework that the Facebook Artificial Intelligence Research (FAIR) group conceived."[195] However, Caffe2 does have several differences from PyTorch.[195]

"PyTorch is great for research, experimentation and trying out exotic neural networks, while Caffe2 is headed towards supporting more industrial-strength applications with a heavy focus on mobile," explains Yangqing Jia, Facebook AI Platform engineering lead.[195] "This is not to say that PyTorch doesn't do mobile or doesn't scale or that you can't use Caffe2 with some awesome new paradigm or neural network, we're just highlighting some of the current characteristics and directions for these two projects," notes Jia. "We plan to have plenty of interoperability and methods of converting back and forth so you can experience the best of both worlds," adds Jia.

In their paper *Caffe2 vs. TensorFlow: Which is a Better Deep Learning Framework?*[196], Liu and Zang discovered that while Caffe2 and TensorFlow do not differ much in expressiveness, modeling capability, and scalability, Caffe2 significantly performs better than TensorFlow in both speed and space aspects, therefore it is a better choice for people who pursue speed or are limited by the device restrictions.[196] However, "TensorFlow provides more services and tools, such as Tensorboard, TensorFlow serving, TensorFlow Lite."[196] Caffe2 has a strong advantages in help and support.[196] "It is a better choice if people want to implement new or complicated models and do not know how to implement exactly yet," argue Liu and Zang.[196]

Torch

Officially released in October 2002, Torch is an open source machine learning library, computing framework, and a script language based on the Lua programming language. According to Collobert, Kavukcuoglu and Farabet, "Its goal is to provide a flexible environment to design and train learning machines

According to its article *Comparing Top Deep Learning Frameworks: Deeplearning4J, PyTorch, TensorFlow, Caffe, Kera, MxNet, Gluon & CNTK*[194], deeplearning4j states that while Torch is powerful, "it was not designed to be widely accessible to the Python-based academic community, nor to corporate software engineers, whose lingua franca is Java."

Keras

Created by Google software engineer Francois Chollet, Keras is a deep-learning library that sits atop TensorFlow and Theano, providing an intuitive API inspired by Torch.[194] According to Deeplearning4j it is "perhaps the best Python API in existence."[194] Deeplearning4j "relies on Keras as its Python API and imports models from Kera and through Keras from Theano and TensorFlow."[194]

- Intuitive API inspired by Torch.
- Works with Theano, TensorFlow and Deeplearning4j backends (CNTK backend to come).
- Fast growing framework.
- Likely to become standard Python API for NNs.

Pytorch

According to its article *Comparing Top Deep Learning Frameworks: Deeplearning4J, PyTorch, TensorFlow, Caffe, Kera, MxNet, Gluon & CNTK*[194], deeplearning4j states that "A Python version of Torch, known as Pytorch , was open-sourced by Facebook in January 2017. PyTorch offers dynamic computation graphs, which let you process variable-length inputs and outputs, which is useful when working with RNNs, for example." Since it's introduction, Deeplearning4J claims that "PyTorch has quickly become the favorite among machine-learning researchers, because it allows certain complex architectures to be built easily."[194]

According to Deeplearning 4J, these are the pros and cons of Torch and PyTorch[194]:

- Lots of modular pieces that are easy to combine.
- Easy to write your own layer types and run on GPU.
- Lots of pretrained models.
- You usually write your own training code (Less plug and play).
- No commercial support.
- Spotty documentation.

Deeplearning4j

Deeplearning4j was written in Java to reflect its focus on industry and ease of use.[194] Deeplearning4J believes "usability is the limiting parameter that inhibits more widespread deep-learning implementations."[194] "They believe scalability ought to be automated with open-source distributed run-times like Hadoop and Spark. And we believe that a commercially supported open-source framework is the appropriate solution to ensure working tools and building a community."[194]

CNTK

The "Computational Network Toolkit" or CNTK is an open-source deep-learning framework from MIcrosoft.[194] "The acronym stands for The library includes feed-forward DNNs, convolutional nets and recurrent networks. CNTK offers a Python API over C++ code."[194]

Sports Betting Analytics

In his article *Patron Analytics in the Casino and Gaming Industry: How the House Always Wins*[197], Scott Sutton lays out the backstory of how analytics is currently used in the casino and gaming industry, much of which is relevant to the sports betting industry. Sutton writes:

> *"In the 1980's and 1990's, casino patron loyalty programs, originally called 'slot clubs', started popping up in many of the larger casinos. These slot clubs encouraged customers to sign up for player cards and, in return for loyalty to the casino, patrons would receive rewards such as complimentary rooms, access to special events, and other offers. This was revolutionary, as it allowed casinos to track gaming behavior down to the individual level, leading to more accurate information about patrons' gaming behavior and interests. The information could then be used to better segment customers,*

predict future behavior, and improve marketing outcomes. As casino analytics advanced, casino resorts started incorporating the relevant data from hotel, dining, retail, entertainment, and other outlets to get a more complete view of a patron's behaviors. A recent development is that many of the major gaming loyalty programs, especially those in competitive markets such as Las Vegas, are now also rewarding non-gaming spending in order to encourage customers to keep non-gaming spending at their respective properties, in addition to providing additional data about non-gaming behavior."

This book is an attempt to chart the next course of analytics for sports books by utilizing IoT, geo-location capabilities, ML, facial recognition, AR, psychometrics, chatbots, etc., as well as many of the other technologies discussed here.

It could be argued that the most valuable use of predictive analytics at a sports book would be by the marketing and sales department, but that's not the whole story. Being able to accurately predict not only who are a sports book's best leads and prospects, but when and how it is best to engage them is nice, but understanding how their acceptance of these marketing offers will affect the overall sports book's bottom line is what *The A.I. Sports Book* is all about.

This ability will not only empower marketers and salespeople in the coming seasons to be radically more productive and profitable than they are today, but also give multiple sports book departments visibility on their micro and macro needs. Used properly, AI and predictive analytics can transform the science of sales forecasting from a dart-throwing exercise to a precision instrument.

The concept of sales and marketing automation has already produced some of the highest-flying successes in high-tech. Companies like Salesforce have been wildly successful in automating the sales process for salespeople and managers. Big software vendors likes SAP and Oracle are vying for supremacy with smaller players like Pega Systems, SugarCRM, Netsuite, and Sage, but no one seems to have captured the essence or fulfilled all of the needs of the sports betting industry.

Today, the software analytics space is more crowded than it has ever been before. Standard ETL-solution providers are adding analytics to their multitude of offerings. Many of the new players in the Master Data Management (MDM) field have BI platforms that combine integration, preparation, analytics and visualization with data governance and security features.

Such standard analytics processes as column dependencies, clustering, decision trees, and recommendation engines are all included in many of these software offerings. Instead of forcing clients to purchase modules on top of modules on top of modules, new software companies are creating packages that contain many built-in analytical functions. Thanks to software connectors, open source products like R, Python, and the WEKA collection can easily be slotted into many ETL, MDM, BI, CI and MA software solutions, thereby reducing costs as well as the need for expensive code translation layers.

Before going any further, I believe one of the first questions that needs to be answered in this chapter is: "What exactly is analytics?" The standard answer is that there are four different types of analytics and they are:

- Descriptive analytics – What happened?
- Diagnostic analytics – Why did it happen?
- Predictive analytics – What will happen?
- Prescriptive analytics – How can we make it happen again?

Figure 18 contains examples of how each of these types of analytics can be utilized by a sports book .

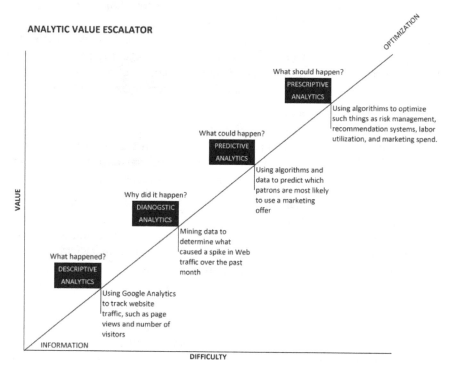

ANALYTIC VALUE ESCALATOR

Figure 18: Analytics Value Escalator
Source: www.intelligencia.co

For a sports book, descriptive analytics could include pattern discovery methods such as customer segmentation, i.e., culling through a customer database to understand a customer's preferred game of choice. Simple cluster segmentation models could also divide customers into their preferred choice of purchases.

Market basket analysis, which utilizes association rules, would also be considered a descriptive analytics procedure. Sports books should use market basket analysis to bundle and offer promotions as well as gain insight into its customers' buying habits. Detailed customer shopping and purchasing behavior could also be used to develop future products.

Diagnostic analytics is a form of advanced analytics that examines data or content to answer the question, "Why did it happen?" It attempts to understand causation and behaviors by utilizing such techniques as drill-down, data discovery, data mining and correlations. Building a decision tree atop a web user's clickstream behavior pattern could be considered a form of diagnostic analytics as these patterns might reveal why a person clicked his or her way through a website.

In his seminal article *Predictive Analytics White Paper*[198], Charles Nyce states that, "Predictive analytics is a broad term describing a variety of statistical and analytical techniques used to develop models that predict future events or behaviors. The form of these predictive models varies, depending on the behavior or event that they are predicting. Most predictive models generate a score (a patron rating, for example), with a higher score indicating a higher likelihood of the given behavior or event occurring."

Data mining, which is used to identify trends, patterns, and/or relationships within a data set, can then be used to develop a predictive model.[198] Prediction of future events is the key here and these analyses can be used in a multitude of ways, including forecasting behavior that could lead to a competitive advantage over rivals. Gut instinct can sometimes punch you in the gut and predictive analytics can help factor in variables that are inaccessible to the human mind and often the amount of variables in an analytical problem are beyond human comprehension.

Predictive analytics Is the use of statistics, machine learning, data mining, and modeling to analyze current and historical facts to make predictions about future events. Said another way, it gives mere mortals the ability to predict the future like Nostradamus. In recent years, data-mining has become one of the most valuable tools for extracting and manipulating data and for establishing patterns in order to produce useful information for decision-making.

Whether you love it or hate it, predictive analytics has already helped elect presidents, discover new energy sources, score consumer credit, assess health risks, detect fraud, and target prospective buyers. It is here to stay, and technological advances, ranging from faster hardware to software that analyzes increasingly vast quantities of data, are making the use of predictive analytics more creative and efficient than ever before.

Predictive analytics is an area of data mining that deals with extracting information from data and using it to predict trends and behavioral patterns.

Often the unknown event of interest is in the future, but predictive analytics can be applied to any type of unknown, whether that is in the past, the present, or the future.

Predictive analytics uses many techniques from data mining to analyze current data to make predictions about the future, including statistics, modeling, machine learning, and artificial intelligence. For example, logistic regression can be used to turn a market basket analysis into a predictor so that a sports book can understand what items are usually purchased together. This could be useful information when a patron is having a run of bad luck on his or her favorite type of bet. Perhaps a marketing offer for a bet type he or she sometimes plays would be appreciated rather than an offer on his or her favorite bet type, as that might not be seen in such a positive light while the patron is in the midst of a losing run.

For a sports book, predictive analytics can also be used for CRM, collection analysis, cross-sell, customer retention, direct marketing, fraud detection, product prediction, project risk management, amongst many other things.

Predictive analytics utilizes the following techniques:

- Regression
- Linear regression
- Discrete choice models
- Logistic regression
- Multinomial logistic regression
- Probit regression
- Time series models
- Survival or duration analysis
- Classification and regression trees
- Multivariate adaptive regression splines
- Machine learning
- Neural networks
- Naïve Bayes
- K-nearest neighbors

Continuing with an example from the sports betting industry, whereas an RFM (Recency-Frequency-Monetary) model would be more of descriptive analytics procedure that tells you all about a player's behavior, predictive analytics would allow you to predict when the player might return and how much he or she will spend on any future trip.

Prescriptive analytics tries to optimize a key metric, such as profit, by not only anticipating what will happen, but also when it will happen and why it happens. Wikipedia states that, "Prescriptive analytics suggests decision options on how to take advantage of a future opportunity or mitigate a future risk and shows the implication of each decision option. Prescriptive analytics can continually take in new data to re-predict and re-prescribe, thus automatically improving prediction accuracy and prescribing better decision options."[199]

In its *Prescriptive Analytics Makes Waves with Retail & CPG*[200], Profitect has one of the best descriptions of prescriptive analytics, i.e., it is the "application of logic and mathematics to data to specify a preferred course of action. The most common examples are optimization methods, such as linear programming; decision analysis methods, such as influence diagrams; and predictive analytics working in combination with rules." Profitect argues that prescriptive analytics differs from descriptive, diagnostic and predictive analytics in that its output is a decision.[200]

Prescriptive analytics can ingest a mixture of structured, unstructured, and semi-structured data, and utilize business rules that can predict what lies ahead, as well as advise how to exploit this predicted future without compromising other priorities. Stream processing can add an entirely new component to prescriptive analytics.

In his book *Business Analytics*[201], Jay Liebowltz states that prescriptive analytics can help customers in the following ways:

1. Discover best options or approaches that might be imperceptible because of the number of choices or the amount of data that is being analyzed.
2. Automate routine decision-making tasks such as staff scheduling, vehicle and/or parts routing.
3. Gain further insights in the trade-offs that must be made since optimization of one resource can either negatively or positively affect another one.

The analytics powerhouse SAS is finding its vaunted place atop the analytics pyramid challenged not just by their typical acronymed competitors—SAP, IBM, EMC, HDS, and the like—but also by the simpler visualization toolmakers like Tableau, Qlik, and Alteryx, who are muscling their way into the mix, with offers that include data blending and in-memory technology that allows business users to access complete datasets at the touch of a button.

Throughout the rest of this chapter, I will break down many of the different types of analytical models that can be used to strengthen the customer experience for sports books.

In its conference paper *How Predictive Analytics is Changing the Retail Industry*[202] from the International Conference on Management and Information Systems, the writers argue that predictive models incorporate the following steps:

- Project Definition: Define the business objectives and desired outcomes for the project and translate them into predictive analytic objectives and tasks.
- Exploration: Analyze source data to determine the most appropriate data and model building approach, and scope the effort.
- Data Preparation: Select, extract, and transform data upon which to create models.
- Model Building: Create, test, and validate models, and evaluate whether they will meet project metrics and goals.
- Deployment: Apply model results to business decisions or processes. This ranges from sharing insights with business users to embedding models into applications to automating decisions and business processes
- Model Management: Manage models to improve performance (i.e., accuracy), control access, promote reuse, standardize toolsets, and minimize redundant activities.

Even though this was a paper on the subject of retail, it can be utilized for model building in the sports betting industry as well.

Analytical Models

Decision Trees

According to Wikipedia, a decision tree is "a decision support tool that uses a tree-like graph or model of decisions and their possible consequences, including chance event outcomes, resource costs, and utility. It is one way to display an algorithm."[203]

Lucidchart[204] states that, "A decision tree is a map of possible outcomes of a series of related choices. It allows an individual or organization to weigh possible actions against one another based on their costs, probabilities, and benefits. They can be used either to drive informal discussion or to map out an algorithm that predicts the best choice mathematically." Lucidchart also adds: "A decision tree typically starts with a single node, which branches into possible outcomes. Each of these outcomes leads to additional nodes, which branch off into other possibilities. This gives it a treelike shape."[204]

Decision trees are used to identify the strategy that is most likely to reach a goal. It is a decision support tool that uses a graph or model of decisions and their possible consequences, including chance event outcomes, resource costs, and utility. Decision trees are sequential partitions of a set of data that maximize the differences of a dependent variable (response or output variable). They offer a concise way of defining groups that are consistent in their attributes, but which vary in terms of the dependent variable.

A decision tree (See Figure 19) consists of three types of nodes[204]:

1. Decision nodes—represented by squares, which shows a decision to be made.
2. Chance nodes—represented by circles, which shows the probabilities of the certain results.
3. End nodes—represented by triangles, which reveals the final outcome of a decision path.

The construction of a decision tree is based on the principle of "divide and conquer": through a supervised learning algorithm, successive divisions of the multivariable space are carried out in order to maximize the distance between groups in each division (that is, carry out partitions that discriminate). The division process finalizes when all of the entries of a branch have the same value in the output variable, giving rise to the complete model. The further down the input variables are in the tree, the less important they are in the output classification (and the less generalization they allow, due to the decrease in the number of inputs in the descending branches).

For a sports books, decision trees can be utilized in operations management and marketing, where they can be used to predict whether a person will respond to an offer or not, or whether they are likely to abuse a marketing offer.[197]

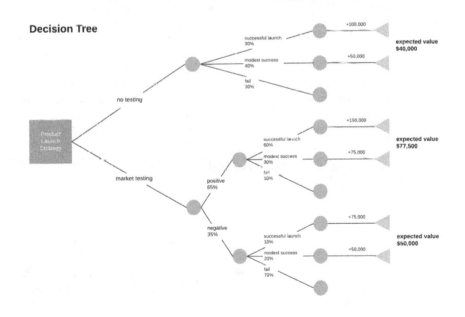

Figure 19: Decision Tree
Source: Lucid Chart

In their paper *Building a Big Data Analytics Service Framework for Mobile Advertising and Marketing*[205], Deng et al. state that the decision tree algorithm is:

> "Used to classify the attributes and decide the outcome of the class attribute. In order to construct a decision tree both class attribute and item attributes are required. Decision tree is a tree like structure where the intermediate nodes represent attributes of the data, leaf nodes represents the outcome of the data and the branches hold the attribute value. Decision trees are widely used in the classification process because no domain knowledge is needed to construct the decision tree."

The main step in the decision tree algorithm is to identify the root node for any given set of data.[205] "Multiple methods exist to decide the root node of the decision tree. Information gain and Gini impurity are the primary methods used to identify the root node. Root node plays an important role in deciding which side of the decision tree the data falls into. Like every classification method, decision trees are also constructed using the training data and tested with the test data."[205]

Advantages	Disadvantages
• Simple and robust • Useful to predict the outcomes of future data • Little cleansing is enough to remove the missing values data • Useful for large data sets • Decision trees can handle both categorical and numerical data	• Possibility of creating complex decision trees for simple data • Replication problem makes the decision trees complex. So remove the replicated data before constructing a decision tree • Pruning is required to avoid complex decision trees • It is hard to find out the correct root node

Table 5: Advantages and disadvantages of decision trees
Source: Researchgate[205]

k-Means Cluster

As its name suggests, the *k*-Means cluster is a clustering algorithm and it is one of the most commonly used analytical models because of its simplicity and ease of use. The fact that it is still going strong 50 years after it was introduced speaks as much to its ease-of-use as it does to the difficulty of designing a general purpose clustering algorithm.

According to Telgarsky and Vattani, "The goal of cluster analysis is to partition a given set of items into clusters such that similar items are assigned to the same cluster whereas dissimilar ones are not. Perhaps the most popular clustering formulation is *K*-means in which the goal is to maximize the expected similarity between data items and their associated cluster centroids."[206]

Hartigan and Wong explain that the: "aim of the *k*-means algorithm is to divide *M* points in *N* dimensions into *k* clusters so that the within-cluster sum of squares is minimized. It is not practical to require that the solution has minimal sum of squares against all partitions, except when *M, N* are small and *k* = 2. We seek instead 'local' optima, solutions that no movement of a point from one cluster to another will reduce the within-cluster sum of squares."[207]

k-Means clustering identifies and classifies items into groups based on their similarity. *K* is the number of clusters that needs to be decided upon before the clustering process begins.[205] "The whole solution depends on the *K* value. So, it is very important to choose a correct *K* value. The data point is grouped into a cluster based on the Euclidean distance between the point and the centroid of the cluster," explains Deng et al.[205] With sports books and casinos, the *K* value is pretty self-explanatory should you want to create groups of gamblers by their preferred game.

For Deng et al., initial clustering can be done in one of the following three ways[205]:

1. "Dynamically Chosen: In this method, the first *K* items are chosen and then assigned to *K* clusters.
2. "Randomly Chosen: In this method, the values are randomly selected and then assigned to *K* clusters.
3. "Choosing from Upper and Lower Boundaries: In this method, the values that are very distant from each other are chosen and they are used as initial values for each cluster."[205]

According to Deng at al., the *k*-Means methodology is as follows[205]:

- Step 1: Choose the initial values using one of the above three methods.
- Step 2: For each additional value:
- Step 3: Calculate the Euclidean distance between this point and centroid of the clusters.
- Step 4: Move the value to the nearest cluster.
- Step 5: Calculate the new centroid for the cluster.
- Step 6: Repeat steps 3 to 5.
- Step 7: Calculate centroid of the cluster.
- Step 8: For each value:
- Step 9: Calculate the Euclidean distance between this value and the centroid of all the clusters.
- Step 10: Move the value to the nearest cluster.

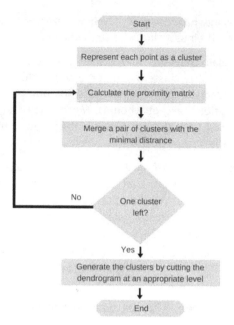

Figure 20: Clustering Algorithm
Source: Researchgate[205]

Advantages	Disadvantages
<ul><li>Faster computations than hierarchical clustering</li><li>It produces tighter clusters than other clustering techniques</li><li>Gives best result when data sets are distinct</li><li>Easy to understand</li></ul>	<ul><li>Sensitive to noise</li><li>Numbers of clusters must be decided before starting clustering</li><li>Choosing correct initial clustering process</li><li>Choosing correct number of clusters</li><li>The centroid of the group changes because we calculate centroid every time a new item joins the cluster</li><li>Large data sets needed to cluster the data correctly</li></ul>

Table 6: Advantages and disadvantages of decision trees
Source: Researchgate[205]

k-Nearest Neighbors

First described in the early 1950s, the *k*-nearest neighbors method is a classification (or regression) algorithm that, in order to determine the classification of a point, combines the classification of the *K* nearest points. It is supervised because you are trying to classify a point based on the known classification of other points. It is labor intensive when given large training sets, and it did not gain popularity until the computer revolution in the 1960s brought processing power that could handle vast data sets.[205] Today, it is widely used in the area of pattern recognition.[205]

As Deng et al. explain[205]:

> "Nearest-neighbor classifiers are based on learning by analogy, that is, by comparing a given test tuple with training tuples that are similar to it. The training tuples are described by n attributes. Each tuple represents a point in an n-dimensional space. In this way, all of the training tuples are stored in an n-dimensional pattern space. When given an unknown tuple, a k-nearest-neighbor classifier searches the pattern space for the k training tuples that are closest to the unknown tuple. These k training tuples are the k 'nearest neighbors' of the unknown tuple. When the 'k' closest points are obtained, the unknown sample is then assigned to the most common class among those k-points. In case of k=1, the unknown sample is assigned to the closest point in the pattern space. The closeness is measured using the distance between the two points."

the k-means clustering and k-nearest neighbor methodologies seek to accomplish different goals; k-nearest neighbors is a classification algorithm, which is a subset of supervised learning, while k-means is a clustering algorithm, which is a subset of unsupervised learning.

K-nearest neighbor techniques can be used to prevent theft in the retail and gaming business. Modern surveillance system are intelligent enough to analyze and interpret video data on their own, utilizing k-nearest neighbor for visual pattern recognition to scan and detect hidden packages in the bottom bin of a shopping cart at check-out, for example.

As she explains in her article *Solving Real-World Problems with Nearest Neighbor Algorithms*[208], Lillian Pierson states that, "If an object is detected that's an exact match for an object listed in the database, then the price of the spotted product could even automatically be added to the customer's bill. While this automated billing practice is not used extensively at this time, the technology has been developed and is available for use."

The K-nearest neighbor algorithm can also be used to detect patterns in credit card usage to root out credit card fraud. "Many new transaction-scrutinizing software applications use kNN algorithms to analyze register data and spot unusual patterns that indicate suspicious activity," Pierson adds.[208]

"If register data indicates that a lot of customer information is being entered manually rather than through automated scanning and swiping, this could indicate that the employee who's using that register is in fact stealing customer's personal information," warns Pierson.[208] Another example would be "if register data indicates that a particular good is being returned or exchanged multiple times, this could indicate that employees are misusing the return policy or trying to make money from doing fake returns."[208]

*k*NN is not just about fraud. It can also be used to increase retail sales. "Average nearest neighbor algorithm classification and point pattern detection can be used in grocery retail to identify key patterns in customer purchasing behavior, and subsequently increase sales and customer satisfaction by anticipating customer behavior," explains Pierson.[208]

Advantages	Disadvantages
• It produces tighter clusters than other clustering techniques • Gives best result when data sets are distinct • Easy to understand	• *K*NN neither doesn't follow any nor have any standard for selecting the value '*k*', which is one of the key factors in the success of an algorithm • As *K*NN is a Lazy Learner algorithm, it has high storage requirements and requires efficient indexing techniques • The efficiency of the *K*NN algorithm also depends on the choice of the distance metric used. The results of the algorithm differ for each similarity metric

Table 7: Advantages and disadvantages of decision trees
Source: Researchgate.[205]

Logistic Regression

According to Wikipedia, logistic regression is a regression model where the dependent variable (DV) is categorical, i.e., a variable that can take on one of a limited, and usually fixed, number of possible values.[209] This compares to a variable that would be continuous.

Developed in 1958 by statistician David Cox, "The binary logistic model is used to estimate the probability of a binary response based on one or more predictor (or independent) variables (features). It allows one to say that the presence of a risk factor increases the probability of a given outcome by a specific percentage," explains Cox.[209]

In his article *Using Logistic Regression to Predict Customer Retention*[210], Andrew Karp explains that:

> *"Logistic regression is an increasingly popular statistical technique used to model the probability of discrete (i.e., binary or multinomial) outcomes. When properly applied, logistic regression analyses yield very powerful insights in to what attributes (i.e., variables) are more or less likely to predict event outcomes in a population of interest. These models also*

> *show the extent to which changes in the values of the attributes may increase or decrease the predicted probability of event outcomes."*

Logistic regression techniques may be used to classify a new observation whose group is unknown in one of the groups, based on the values of the predictor variables. According to Karp, "Logistic regression models are frequently employed to assess the chance that a customer will: a) re-purchase a product, b) remain a customer, or c) respond to a direct mail or other marketing stimulus."[210]

Karp adds that "Economists frequently call logistic regression a 'qualitative choice' model, and for obvious reasons: a logistic regression model helps us assess probability which 'qualities' or 'outcomes' will be chosen (selected) by the population under analysis."[210] As can be expected, Karp argues that, "When proper care is taken to create an appropriate dependent variable, logistic regression is often a superior (both substantively and statistically) alternative to other tools available to model event outcomes."[210]

Karp uses a health care example to make his point that the analyst has several independent variables to use in the modeling process, but this example can be illustrative of how they could be used in the sports betting industry.[210] Karp explains that "An analyst developing a model predicting re-enrollment in a health insurance plan may have data for each member's interaction with both the health plans administrative apparatus and health care utilization in the prior 'plan year.'"[210]

The analyst can then construct variables such as the "number of times member called the health plan for information, number of physician office visits, whether or not the member changed primary care physicians during the previous 'plan year,' and answers to a customer satisfaction survey."[210] These can be employed in the modeling process and, once the model has been constructed, the analyst must decide which variable can be employed as the "outcome" or the "dependent" variable.[210]

In logistic regression analyses "it is often the analyst's responsibility to *construct* the dependent variable based on an agreed-upon definition of what constitutes the 'event of interest' which is being modeled."[210]

In the health care re-enrollment example, "a health plan's management team may define 'attrition' or 'failure to re-enroll' as situations where a member fails to return the re-enrollment card within 30 days of its due date. Or, in a response modeling scenario, a direct mail firm may define 'non-response' to an advertisement as failure to respond within 45 days of mailout."[210]

Logistic regression models can be powerful tools to build models that understand customer retention.[210] "When applied properly, logistic regression models can yield powerful insights into why some customers leave and others stay. These insights can then be employed to modify organizational strategies and/or assess the impact of the implementation of these strategies," adds Karp.[210]

A/B Testing

Also known as split testing or bucket testing, A/B testing is a method of marketing testing by which a baseline control sample is compared to a variety of single-variable test samples in order to improve response rates.

A classic direct mail tactic, this method has recently been adopted within the interactive space to test tactics such as banner ads, emails, and landing pages. As Scott Sutton explains in his article *Patron Analytics in the Casino and Hospitality Industry: How the House Always Wins*[197], for casino marketers, A/B Testing is the most effective way to identify the best available marketing offer.[197] It can test "two different offers against one another in order to identify the offer that drives the highest response and the most revenue/profit."[197] The same is, obviously, true for sports book marketers.

As Dan Siroker and Peter Komen explain in their book *A/B Testing: The Most Powerful Way to Turn Clicks Into Customers*[211], "The hardest part of A/B testing is determining what to test in the first place. Having worked with thousands of customers who do A/B testing every day, one of the most common questions we hear is, 'Where do I begin?'"

The mistake many companies make is they jump in head first without any detailed planning. Siroker and Komen propose the following deliberate five-step process[211]:

1. Define success
2. Identify bottlenecks
3. Construct a hypothesis
4. Prioritize
5. Test

A/B testing is particularly good for website marketing, especially for uncovering a company's best landing pages. As Siroker and Komen explain, "Defining success in the context of A/B testing involves taking the answer to the question of your site's ultimate purpose and turning it into something more precise: *quantifiable success metrics*. Your success metrics are the specific numbers you hope will be improved by your tests."[211]

Whereas an e-commerce site could easily define its success metrics in terms of revenue per visitor[211], a sports betting website could look at purchased bets for A/B testing. It is also important to understand such things as traffic sources, bounce rate, top pages, conversion rates, conversion by traffic source, amongst other things.

Site Type	Common Conversion & Aggregate Goals
e-Commerce A site that sells things for users to purchase online.	• Completed purchase • Each step within the checkout funnel • Products added to cart • Product page views
Media/Content A site focused on article or other content consumption.	• Page views • Articles read • Bounce rate (when measuring within an A/B testing tool, this is often measured by seeing if the user clicked anywhere on the page)
Lead Generation A site that acquires business through name capture.	• Form completion • Clicks to a form page (links may read "Contact us" for example)
Donation	• Form completion • Clicks to a form page (links may read "Send a donation" for example)

Table 8: Typical A/B conversion & aggregate goals
Source: A/B Testing: The Most Powerful Way to Turn Clicks Into Customers[211]

As Siroker and Komen state:

> *"Part of building out your testing strategy is identifying what constitutes—and does not constitute—a "conversion" for your particular site. In online terms, a conversion is the point at which a visitor takes the desired action on your website. Pinpointing the specific actions you want people to take most on your site and that are most critical to your business will lead you to the tests that have an impact."[211]*

Once the site's quantifiable success metrics are agreed upon, attention can be paid trying to discover where the bottlenecks are.[211] These are the places where users are dropping off, or the places where momentum in moving users through the desired series of actions weakens.[211]

Time Series Analysis

A time series is an ordered sequence of values of a variable at uniformly spaced time intervals. A Time Series model can be used to predict or forecast the future behavior of a variable.

In his article *Time Series Analysis*, Muhammad Imdadullah explains that, "Time series analysis is the analysis of a series of data-points over time, allowing one to answer question such as what is the causal effect on a variable Y of a change in variable X over time? An important difference between time series and cross section data is that the ordering of cases does matter in time series."[212]

These models account for the fact that data points taken over time may have an internal structure (such as autocorrelation, trend or seasonal variation) that should be taken into account. For the sports betting industry, a time series analysis can be used to forecast sales, project yields and workloads, as well as analyze budgets.

Time series can be broken down into two variations:

- Continuous Time Series—"A time series is said to be continuous when observation are made continuously in time. The term continuous is used for series of this type even when the measured variable can only take a discrete set of values."[212]
- Discrete Time Series—"A time series is said to be discrete when observations are taken at specific times, usually equally spaced. The term discrete is used for series of this type even when the measured variable is a continuous variable."[212]

As Sang and Dong explain in their *Determining Revenue-Generating Casino Visitors Using a Vector Autoregressive Model: The Case of the G Casino in Korea*[213], time-series data was analyzed to:

> "investigate the characteristics of casino visitors that affect casinos' revenue generation. Exchange rates—a traditional measure relevant to tourism—and customer types and nationalities were empirically analyzed with a vector autoregressive model using data acquired from all branches of Korea's G casino. The results suggest that the casinos' revenues were affected by the customers' type and nationality: VIP customers were very important factors in the casinos' revenue generation; moreover, the revenue impact of Russian visitors was quite strong despite their small numbers."

Time series can be used to compare seasonal estimation and trend estimation in forecasting models on both a state or a national level.

Neural Networks

Artificial Neural Networks (ANN) or just "Neural Networks" are the building blocks of AI. They are non-linear statistical data modeling tools that are used when the exact nature of a relationship between input and output is unknown. In their article *Neural Networks in Data Mining*[214], Singh and Chauhan claim that a neural network is:

> "A mathematical model or computational model based on

> biological neural networks, in other words, is an emulation of a biological neural system. It consists of an interconnected group of artificial neurons and processes information using a connectionist approach to computation. In most cases an ANN is an adaptive system that changes its structure based on external or internal information that flows through the network during the learning phase."

Jim Gao expounds upon this description in his article *Machine Learning Applications for Data Center Optimization.*[215] Goa writes215:

> "Neural networks are a class of machine learning algorithms that mimic cognitive behavior via interactions between artificial neurons. They are advantageous for modeling intricate systems because neural networks do not require the user to predefine the feature interactions in the model, which assumes relationships within the data. Instead, the neural network searches for patterns and interactions between features to automatically generate a best fit model. Common applications for this branch of machine learning include speech recognition, image processing, and autonomous software agents. As with most learning systems, the model accuracy improves over time as new training data is acquired."

As previously mentioned, there are three types of training in neural networks; reinforcement learning, supervised and unsupervised training, with supervised being the most common one. Their fundamental characteristics include parallel processing, distributed memory and adaptability to their surroundings.

In her article *A Beginners Guide To AI: Neural Networks*[216], Tristan Greene puts it in simpler terms, stating that, "Scientists believe that a living creature's brain processes information using a biological neural network. The human brain has as many as 100 trillion synapses—gaps between neurons—which form specific patterns when activated. When a person thinks about a specific thing, remembers something, or experiences something with one of their senses, it's thought that specific neural patterns 'light up' inside the brain."

Greene continues, "when you were learning to read you might have had to sound out the letters so that you could hear them out loud and lead your young brain to a conclusion. But, once you've read the word cat enough times you don't have to slow down and sound it out."[216] At that point, Greene contends, "you access a part of your brain more associated with memory than problem-solving, and thus a different set of synapses fire because you've trained your biological neural network to recognize the word 'cat.'"[216]

"In the field of deep learning a neural network is represented by a series of layers that work much like a living brain's synapses," explains Greene.[216] 'Researchers teach computers how to understand what a cat is—or at least what a picture of a cat is—by feeding it as many images of cats as they can."[216] The neural network analyzes those images and "tries to find out everything that makes them similar, so that it can find cats in other pictures," adds Greene.[216]

There are many kinds of deep learning and many types of neural networks, but here I will focus upon generative adversarial networks (GANs), convolutional Neural Networks (CNNs), and recurrent neural networks (RNNs).

GANs were invented by Ian Goodfellow, one of Google's AI gurus, in 2014.[216] To put it simply, "a GAN is a neural network comprised of two arguing sides—a generator and an adversary—that fight among themselves until the generator wins."[216] Greene gives the example that, "If you wanted to create an AI that imitates an art style, like Picasso's for example, you could feed a GAN a bunch of his paintings."[216]

According to Greene, the process works in the following way, "One side of the network would try to create new images that fooled the other side into thinking they were painted by Picasso. Basically, the AI would learn everything it could about Picasso's work by examining the individual pixels of each image."[216] One side would create the image, while the other side would determine if it was a Picasso.[216] "Once the AI fooled itself," Greene claims, "the results could then be viewed by a human who could determine if the algorithm needed to be tweaked to provide better results, or if it successfully imitated the desired style."[216]

Convolutional Neural Networks (CNNs) are among the most common and robust neural networks around, which have, at least theoretically, been in use since the 1940s.[216] Thanks to advanced hardware and efficient algorithms, they can now be used on a wide scale.[216] "Where a GAN tries to create something that fools an adversary, a CNN has several layers through which data is filtered into categories," explains Greene.[216] "These are primarily used in image recognition and text language processing," notes Greene.[216]

"If you've got a billion hours of video to sift through, you could build a CNN that tries to examine each frame and determine what's going on," explains Greene.[216] "One might train a CNN by feeding it complex images that have been tagged by humans," adds Greene.[216] "AI learns to recognize things like stop signs, cars, trees, and butterflies by looking at pictures that humans have labelled, comparing the pixels in the image to the labels it understands, and then organizing everything it sees into the categories it's been trained on," says Greene.[216]

So how can images be used by a marketer? Well, in his Adobe blog *See It, Search It, Shop It: How AI is Powering Visual Search*[217], Brett Butterfield explains how visual search could become a big part of a buyer's shopping future. "You spot something you love on a passerby. That stranger walking past you is wearing the perfect pair of sneakers. You want them. But you have no idea what brand they were or where to buy them. Even without those essential details, you figure you can go online and search—but you get just a few, mostly irrelevant, results, and you aren't any closer to getting your next favorite pair of shoes. Enter visual search," says Butterfield.[217] Talk about seamless. *Gartner* predicts that image search will be a lucrative technology.[217] Even with visual search still in its early stages, *Gartner* says early adopters will experience a 30 percent increase in e-commerce revenue by 2021.[217]

RNNs are "primarily used for AI that requires nuance and context to understand its input."[216] "An example of such a neural network is a natural language processing AI that interprets human speech," such as Google's Assistant and Amazon's Alexa.[216]

"To understand how an RNN works, let's imagine an AI that generates original musical compositions based on human input," explains Greene.[216] "If you play a note the AI tries to 'hallucinate' what the next note 'should' be. If you play another note, the AI can further anticipate what the song should sound like. Each piece of context provides information for the next step, and an RNN continuously updates Itself based on its continuing input—hence the recurrent part of the name," explains Greene.[216] Scientists use neural nets to teach computers how to do things for themselves.

Neural nets are extremely good at finding patterns in data. A key feature of neural networks is that they learn the relationship between inputs and outputs through training. For marketing purposes, neural networks can be used to classify a consumer's spending pattern, analyze a new product, identify a customer's characteristics, as well as forecast sales.[217] The advantages of neural networks include high accuracy, high noise tolerance and ease of use as they can be updated with fresh data, which makes them useful for dynamic environments.[217]

In her article *How DeepMind's AlphaGo Zero Learned all by itself to trash world champ AI AlphaGo*[218], Katyanna Quach explains how neural networks can work when training computers to play board games. According to Quach, the board game *Go* is considered a "difficult game for computers to master because, besides being complex, the number of possible moves—more than chess at 10^{170}—is greater than the number of atoms in the universe."[218]

"AlphaGo, the predecessor to AlphaGo Zero, crushed 18-time world champion Lee Sedol and the reigning world number one player, Ke Jie," explains Quach.[218] The next generation of DeepMind's technology, AlphaGo Zero, beat "AlphaGo 100-0 after training for just a fraction of the time AlphaGo needed, and it didn't learn from observing humans playing against each other—unlike AlphaGo. Instead, Zero's neural network relies on an old technique in reinforcement learning: self-play."[218]

As Quach notes about the process[218]:

"Essentially, AlphaGo Zero plays against itself. During training, it sits on each side of the table: two instances of the same software face off against each other. A match starts with the game's black and white stones scattered on the board, placed following a random set of moves from their starting positions. The two computer players are given the list of moves that led to the positions of the stones on the grid, and then are each told to come up with multiple chains of next moves along with estimates of the probability they will win by following through each chain.

"So, the black player could come up with four chains of next moves and predict the third chain will be the most successful. The white player could come up with its own chains and think its first choice is the strongest.

"The next move from the best possible chain is then played, and the computer players repeat the above steps, coming up with chains of moves ranked by strength. This repeats over and over, with the software feeling its way through the game and internalizing which strategies turn out to be the strongest."

This methodology differs from the old AlphaGo, which "relied on a computationally intensive Monte Carlo tree search to play through Go scenarios."[218] "The nodes and branches created a much larger tree than AlphaGo practically needed to play."[218] "A combination of reinforcement learning and human-supervised learning was used to build 'value' and 'policy' neural networks that used the search tree to execute gameplay strategies," explains Quach.[218] "The software learned from 30 million moves played in human-on-human games, and benefited from various bodges and tricks to learn to win. For instance, it was trained from master-level human players, rather than picking it up from scratch," adds Quach.[218]

"Self-play is an established technique in reinforcement learning, and has been used to teach machines to play backgammon, chess, poker, and Scrabble," says Quach.[218] David Silver, a lead researcher on AlphaGo, explains that it is an effective technique because the opponent is always the right level of difficulty.[218]

"So it starts off extremely naive," Silver says, adding that "at every step of the learning process it has an opponent—a sparring partner if you like—that is exactly calibrated to its current level of performance. To begin with these players are very weak but over time they get progressively stronger."[218]

Tim Salimans, a research scientist at OpenAI, explains that self-play means "agents can learn behaviours that are not hand coded on any reinforcement learning task, but the sophistication of the learned behavior is limited by the sophistication of the environment. In order for an agent to learn intelligent behavior in a particular environment, the environment has to be challenging, but not too challenging."[218]

"The competitive element makes the agent explicitly search for its own weaknesses. Once those weaknesses are found the agent can improve them. In self-play the difficulty of the task the agent is solving is always reasonable, but over time it is open ended: since the opponent can always improve, the task can always get harder," adds Salimans.

Self-play does have its limitations.[218] Right now, there are "problems that AlphaGo Zero cannot solve, such as games with hidden states or imperfect information, such as StarCraft, and it's unlikely that self-play will be successful tackling more advanced challenges."[218]

Self-play will be worthwhile in some areas of AI, argues Salimans.[218] "As our algorithms for reinforcement learning become more powerful the bottleneck in developing artificial intelligence will gradually shift to developing sufficiently sophisticated tasks and environments. Even very talented people will not develop a great intellect if they are not exposed to the right environment," he warns.[218]

DeepMind, the company behind AlphaGo Zero and its predecessor, believes that "the approach may be generalizable to a wider set of scenarios that share similar properties to a game like Go."[218]

In his article *Is AI Riding a One-Trick Pony?*[219], Somers explains that Geoffrey Hinton, the man who is considered to be the father of deep learning, published a breakthrough paper in 1986, with colleagues David Rumelhart and Ronald Williams that "elaborated on a technique called backpropagation, or backprop for short."

According to Jon Cohen, a computational psychologist at Princeton, backprop is "what all of deep learning is based on—literally everything."[219] "In fact, nearly every achievement in the last decade of AI—in translation, speech recognition, image recognition, and game playing—traces in some way back to Hinton's work."[219] "For decades," Somers explains, "backprop was cool math that didn't really accomplish anything. As computers got faster and the engineering got more sophisticated, suddenly it did."[219]

When you boil it down, Somers claims, "AI today is deep learning, and deep learning is backprop—which is amazing, considering that backprop is more than 30 years old."[219] Somers adds that, "It's worth understanding how that happened—how a technique could lie in wait for so long and then cause such an explosion—because once you understand the story of backprop, you'll start to understand the current moment in AI, and in particular the fact that maybe we're not actually at the beginning of a revolution. Maybe we're at the end of one."[219] Figure 21 shows a diagram of a neural net from Hinton's paper.

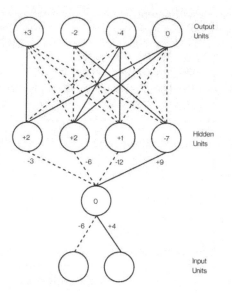

Figure 21: A diagram from the seminal work on "error propagation" by Hinton, David Rumelhart, and Ronald Williams.
Source: Is AI Riding a One-Trick Pony? [219]

According to Somers[219]:

> *"A neural net is usually drawn like a club sandwich, with layers stacked one atop the other. The layers contain artificial neurons, which are dumb little computational units that get excited—the way a real neuron gets excited—and pass that excitement on to the other neurons they're connected to. A neuron's excitement is represented by a number, like 0.13 or 32.39, that says just how excited it is. And there's another crucial number, on each of the connections between two neurons, that determines how much excitement should get passed from one to the other. That number is meant to model the strength of the synapses between neurons in the brain. When the number is higher, it means the connection is stronger, so more of the one's excitement flows to the other."*

One of the most successful applications of deep neural nets is in image recognition, which HBO's *Silicon Valley* so hilariously spoofed when Jian Yang's Hot Dog app was able to decipher between images of "hot dogs" and "not hot dogs."[219] The first step in the image recognition process is to show the machine a picture.[219] Somers gives the example of "a small black-and-white image that's 100 pixels wide and 100 pixels tall. You feed this image to your neural net by setting the excitement of each simulated neuron in the input layer so that it's equal to the brightness of each pixel. That's the bottom layer of the club sandwich: 10,000 neurons (100x100) representing the brightness of every pixel in the image."[219]

Somers continues: "You then connect this big layer of neurons to another big layer of neurons above it, say a few thousand, and these in turn to another layer of another few thousand neurons, and so on for a few layers."[219] "The idea is to teach the neural net to excite only the first of those neurons if there's a hot dog in the picture, and only the second if there isn't."[219] "Backpropagation—the technique that Hinton has built his career upon—is the method for doing this," explains Somers.[219] "Backprop is remarkably simple, though it works best with huge amounts of data," says Somers.[219] "That's why big data is so important in AI—why Facebook and Google are so hungry for it," he adds.[219]

"In this case, the data takes the form of millions of pictures, some with hot dogs and some without; the trick is that these pictures are labeled as to which have hot dogs," says Somers.[219] "When you first create your neural net, the connections between neurons might have random weights—random numbers that say how much excitement to pass along each connection. It's as if the synapses of the brain haven't been tuned yet," notes Somers.[219] "The goal of backprop," Somers explains, "is to change those weights so that they make the network work: so that when you pass in an image of a hot dog to the lowest layer, the topmost layer's 'hot dog' neuron ends up getting excited."[219]

"Suppose you take your first training image, and it's a picture of a piano. You convert the pixel intensities of the 100x100 picture into 10,000 numbers, one for each neuron in the bottom layer of the network. As the excitement spreads up the network according to the connection strengths between neurons in adjacent layers, it'll eventually end up in that last layer, the one with the two neurons that say whether there's a hot dog in the picture," details Somers.[219] "Since the picture is of a piano, ideally the 'hot dog' neuron should have a zero on it, while the 'not hot dog' neuron should have a high number."[219] However, sometimes it doesn't quite work out this way. Hypothetically, the network could be wrong about the picture and this is where the backprop procedure comes in as it can be rejiggered so that the strength of every connection in the network can be tweaked, thereby fixing the error for a given training example.[219]

"The way it works is that you start with the last two neurons, and figure out just how wrong they were: how much of a difference is there between what the excitement numbers should have been and what they actually were? When that's done, you take a look at each of the connections leading into those neurons—the ones in the next lower layer—and figure out their contribution to the error," explains Somers.[219] This continues all the way to very bottom of the network.[219] At that point, it's clear "how much each individual connection contributed to the overall error, and in a final step, you change each of the weights in the direction that best reduces the error overall."[219] The technique is known as "backpropagation" because you are literally "propagating" errors back (or down) through the network, starting from the output.[219]

"The incredible thing is that when you do this with millions or billions of images, the network starts to get pretty good at saying whether an image has a hot dog in it," notes Somers.[219] Even more remarkable is the fact that "the individual layers of these image-recognition nets start being able to 'see' images in sort of the same way our own visual system does."[219] "That is, the first layer might end up detecting edges, in the sense that its neurons get excited when there are edges and don't get excited when there aren't; the layer above that one might be able to detect sets of edges, like corners; the layer above that one might start to see shapes; and the layer above that one might start finding stuff like 'open bun' or 'closed bun,' in the sense of having neurons that respond to either case," explains Somers.[219] "The net organizes itself, in other words, into hierarchical layers without ever having been explicitly programmed that way," notes Somers.[219]

As Somers explains it[219]:

> "This is the thing that has everybody enthralled. It's not just that neural nets are good at classifying pictures of hot dogs or whatever: they seem able to build representations of ideas. With text you can see this even more clearly. You can feed the text of Wikipedia, many billions of words long, into a simple neural net, training it to spit out, for each word, a big list of numbers that correspond to the excitement of each neuron in a layer. If you think of each of these numbers as a coordinate in a complex space, then essentially what you're doing is finding a point, known in this context as a vector, for each word somewhere in that space. Now, train your network in such a way that words appearing near one another on Wikipedia pages end up with similar coordinates, and voilà, something crazy happens: words that have similar meanings start showing up near one another in the space. That is, "insane" and "unhinged" will have coordinates close to each other, as will "three" and "seven," and so on. What's more, so-called vector arithmetic makes it possible to, say, subtract the vector for "France" from the vector for "Paris," add the vector for "Italy," and end up in the neighborhood of "Rome." It works without anyone telling the network explicitly that Rome is to Italy as Paris is to France."

"It's amazing," says Hinton, the father of AI.[219] "Neural nets can be thought of as trying to take things—images, words, recordings of someone talking, medical data—and put them into what mathematicians call a high-dimensional vector space, where the closeness or distance of the things reflects some important feature of the actual world," adds Somers.[219] Hinton believes this is how the brain works.[219] "If you want to know what a thought is," he says it can be expressed in a string of words such as, "John thought, 'Whoops.'"[219] But if you ask, 'What is the thought? What does it mean for John to have that thought?', it's not that inside his head there's an opening quote, and a 'Whoops,' and a closing quote, or even a cleaned-up version of that. Inside his head there's some big pattern of neural activity."[219] "Big patterns of neural activity, if you're a mathematician, can be captured in a vector space, with each neuron's activity corresponding to a number, and each number to a coordinate of a really big vector," says Somers.[219] "In Hinton's view, that's what thought is: a dance of vectors," states Somers.[219]

Although this all sounds rather clever, what shouldn't be lost in all of this is the fact that deep learning systems are still pretty dumb, despite how smart they might appear sometimes.[219] The most amusing moment in that *Silicon Valley* episode was when the rest of Jian Yang's team understood how limited his program really was—it could only really distinguish hot dogs and thousands of hours of training would be needed for it to understand only a limited number of other food types.[219]

"Neural nets are just thoughtless fuzzy pattern recognizers, and as useful as fuzzy pattern recognizers can be," explains Somers.[219] This is why there is a "rush to integrate them into just about every kind of software—they represent, at best, a limited brand of intelligence, one that is easily fooled."[219] "A deep neural net that recognizes images can be totally stymied when you change a single pixel, or add visual noise that's imperceptible to a human," warns Somers.[219] The limitations of deep learning are becoming quite apparent; "Self-driving cars can fail to navigate conditions they've never seen before; Machines have trouble parsing sentences that demand common-sense understanding of how the world works."[219]

"Deep learning in some ways mimics what goes on in the human brain, but only in a shallow way—which perhaps explains why its intelligence can sometimes seem so shallow," says Somers.[219] Backprop itself "wasn't discovered by probing deep into the brain, decoding thought itself; it grew out of models of how animals learn by trial and error in old classical-conditioning experiments;"[219] think Pavlov's dog and that ringing bell. On top of that, "most of the big leaps that came about as it developed didn't involve some new insight about neuroscience; they were technical improvements, reached by years of mathematics and engineering."[219] "What we know about intelligence is nothing against the vastness of what we still don't know"[219] i.e., we're still very much deep in the middle of Socrates' "I know that I know nothing" territory, especially with AI.

"It can be hard to appreciate this from the outside, when all you see is one great advance touted after another," says Somers.[219] However, "the latest sweep of progress in AI has been less science than engineering, even tinkering. And though we've started to get a better handle on what kinds of changes will improve deep-learning systems, we're still largely in the dark about how those systems work, or whether they could ever add up to something as powerful as the human mind," adds Somers.[219]

Somers concludes with the troubling thought that, "It's worth asking whether we've wrung nearly all we can out of backprop. If so, that might mean a plateau for progress in artificial intelligence."[219] That also means that, when it comes to AI, creativity might be the great differentiator between companies; if the tools are limiting, creativity becomes much more important.

Survival or Duration Analysis

As per Wikipedia, "Survival analysis is a branch of statistics for analyzing the expected duration of time until one or more events happen, such as death in biological organisms and failure in mechanical systems. This topic is called reliability theory or reliability analysis in engineering, duration analysis or duration modeling in economics, and event history analysis in sociology."[220] Survival analysis attempts to answer questions such as[220]:

- What is the proportion of a population which will survive past a certain time?
- Of those that survive, at what rate will they die or fail?
- Can multiple causes of death or failure be taken into account?
- How do particular circumstances or characteristics increase or decrease the probability of survival?

A branch of statistics that deals with death in biological organisms and failure in mechanical systems, survival analysis involves the modeling of time to event data; in this context, death or failure is considered an "event" in the survival analysis literature—traditionally only a single event occurs, after which the organism or mechanism is dead or broken. Survival analysis is the study of lifetimes and their distributions. It usually involves one or more of the following objectives:

1. To explore the behavior of the distribution of a lifetime.
2. To model the distribution of a lifetime.
3. To test for differences between the distributions of two or more lifetimes.
4. To model the impact of one or more explanatory variables on a lifetime distribution.

In they offer casino games, sports books can apply survival analysis to revenue management models to gain a truer picture of their table games revenue.[221]

There are several other data mining techniques that can be used but the ones listed above are the industry's most common ones and much of what you will need to glean from your data can be discovered by using these. Once the data has been mined, a business intelligence solution can help visualize what's going on with your data, while a predictive analytics program can actually analyze current and historical trends to make predictions about future events.

Sports Betting Analytical Models

The following models have been implemented in the gaming and sports betting industries, but this should not be considered an authoritative list, as creative sports book executives should be able to easily come up with many more.

First Bet Scoring Model

The purpose of this model is to score new customers for a sports book so that it can understand the betting ability of its customers. The purpose of these models will be for the sports book to have an intimate understanding of its clientele so that they will know how aggressively they should allow a customer to place their desired bets.

With the highly competitive nature of the sports betting business and the tight margins that sports betting websites are operating under, competition is fierce and knowing the likely profile of a customer in their infancy would be crucial in mitigating losses. In some cases, a sophisticated bettor can take a naïve sports book for thousands of dollars or more before the sports book has been alerted to the bettor's skill. Traditional logic only allows for profiling after a certain number of bets, but it may be too late by this stage as a punter could already be far ahead of the game by the time the sports book gets a full picture of the bettor's behavior.

A first bet scoring model scores a customer after his or her initial wagers or time with the business. The model attempts to extract significant predictors of long-term success/value using beginning of lifecycle metrics/data. With any data-mining problem, the nature of the data and its richness is what's going to decide the best approach to take, so there will need to be preliminary analysis of the input data to understand what is available, such as a derivation of metrics. These metrics can then be tested for their likelihood of predicting punter success/profitability. The inputs would then be narrowed down to significant predictors that could be fed into a prediction algorithm. The first bet scoring model will investigate such predictive analytical processes as neural networks, decision trees and logistic regression, amongst others.

Customer Segmentation

A customer segmentation model provides a view of the sports book from a customer perspective: such models have many and varied applications.

Customers are segmented according to what they present to the sports book. Views include:

1. Game preference: the games offered by a sports book are grouped according to business needs and customer turnover by game is analyzed to derive a preferential game for every customer above a certain threshold turnover.
2. Day of week: customer turnover is analyzed by day of the week and clusters are derived in line with how the sports book is visited. It is often the case that customers group into single day segments, as well as some longer segments, such as weekend players, midweek players, etc., etc.
3. Time of day: split the 24 hours of the day into meaningful segments and analyze customer turnover by time period from when a bettor's session began. This creates a view of the customer according to when they are most likely to frequent the sports book.
4. Length of session: this view clusters customers according to how long their play session is likely to be. While this isn't usually as pure a view as the above models, it can give an idea of impulse players and session players.
5. Size of stake: the size of a customer's stake can be an important view for planning. Depending on how granular the venue information is, individual stakes or the table limit or credits played per hand on a slot machine are used to segment customers according to their stakes.

Generally, the data is used to determine the appropriate segments for these views. However, the sports book has the ability to select the intervals that are preferential and relevant to their venue. For example, it may be desirous to split time of day into three, eight-hour periods or six, four-hour periods.

The results of this analysis presents a detailed view of how the sports book is populated at different times and can allow for appropriate strategic decisions to be made. These decisions could be a function of marketing, operations or strategy. The output is also used for the building of acquisition models as discussed below.

Other potential for analysis would be a master segmentation model that uses the preference results described above. Customers are clustered based on their preferences to gain a global view of the sports book that is concise and understandable. Furthermore, such models can help measure the impact of strategic decisions, e.g. the addition or removal of a sports or lottery game can be measured against how particular metrics are affected.

Customer Acquisition Model

Just like every other business, sports books are always looking for new customers. With the gaming market getting more and more competitive and saturated by the day, there is always a constant need to know where to attract customers from and what type of customers to target.

The results of the segmentation modeling previously described can be used to build a predictive model that identifies likely characteristics of attractive customers. Obviously the sports book will have no internal data available on customers they don't already have on their books so the analysis becomes a data mining exercise using publicly available input variables. Sports books can then target these customers with a view to attracting those who have the traits that they see in their already valuable customers.

The best external data to use would be population census data, linked to the internal customers by a location identifier, such as postcode or mesh block. It is acknowledged that in some jurisdictions robust and accurate census data may not be available so the model would be relying on whatever information the sports book records on its customers from a demographic and lifestyle point of view.

This approach becomes a classical data-mining problem, where a pool of independent variables would be tested for the strength of association with the response variable. Once the relevant predictors are identified and the characteristics and traits are defined, marketing and acquisition campaigns could be targeted at the population towards these kinds of people.

This would be something that looks to predict a metric derived from current/past customers. Such a metric could come from a segmentation model that identified the high value customers that are most attractive to the sports book. There are several approaches that can be used and once the target has been defined, this allows for a parametric equation to be derived. This equation attempts to predict the characteristics that distinguish the desirable customers from the rest.

This model can only use publicly available information (although other sports book information might be acceptable) as that is how a potential customer would be identified. Current information that the company would have on hand would be age, nationality, gender, and address.

Where available, third party data should be looked at to further enhance the findings. This could be census data that gives an indication of further customer demographics and this enhances the ability to hone in on customer sweet spots.

Recency-Frequency-Monetary (RFM) Models

First and foremost, the goal of this RFM modeling process is to increase sales for a sports book. This is done by gaining deep insights into a sports book's database of customers, which will not only provide information about who a sports book's best and worst customers are but will also provide a starting point for a sports book to understand each one of their Customer's Lifetime Value (CLV) as well as, potentially, improve its marketing process.

Sports betting customers are not static and one dimensional, so it is important to look at them as they go through phases and change specific to their unique customer lifecycles. A sports book needs to implement behavior analytics that can reveal how customers change over time, not just at a point in time, such as when a player last transacts. Time-series, path and graph analytics can help plot the journey of a sports book's customers as well as, more importantly, anticipate when they might bet. RFM is a good starting point for all of this customer and marketing analysis, it can also reveal the true value of each customer.

RFM Analysis is extremely useful to discover the following:

- Who are the sports book's best customers?
- Who are the sports book's most loyal customers?
- Which customers are on the verge of churning?
- Who has the potential to be converted into a more profitable customer?
- Who are the lost customers that a sports book doesn't need to pay much attention to?
- Which customers must be retained?
- Which group of customers is most likely to respond to a marketing campaign?

While there are countless ways to perform segmentation, RFM analysis is popular for three main reasons:

- It utilizes objective, numerical scales that yield a concise and informative high-level depiction of customers.
- It is simple—marketers can use it effectively without much need for data scientists or sophisticated software.
- It is intuitive—the output of this segmentation method is easy to understand and interpret, even for a layman.

The goal is to produce RFM Segments that reflect the following types of customers:

1. Champions
2. Loyal Customers
3. Potential loyalists
4. New customers
5. Promising
6. Customers needing attention
7. About to sleep
8. At Risk
9. Can't lose
10. Hibernating

11. Lost

Many people associate the RFM principle with the 80/20 rule (or Pareto's Law). The process does condense the customers purchasing patterns in some form of an 80/20, whereby 80% of the sales come from 20% of the customers and this is a further extension of analysis that a sports book can derive from this process, but the RFM process can be more nuanced than that.

The important thing here is not to lose focus on the customers that have a lower ranking (the 80%). A sports book should focus its efforts on nurturing these customers into the higher rankings. This can be achieved by:

- Targeted promotions.
- Increased call cycle activity.
- Increased email marketing broadcasts.

The most important thing to understand about the RFM model is that it produces information that can best be utilized by the company's marketing department.

RFM is a method used for analyzing customer value. It is commonly used in database marketing and direct marketing and has received particular attention in the gambling and retail industries. RFM stands for:

- **Recency**: How much time has elapsed since a customer's last activity or transaction with the sports book? Activity is usually a bet, although variations are sometimes used, e.g., the last visit to sports book's website or use of its mobile app. In most cases, the more recently a customer has interacted or transacted with the sports book, the more likely that customer will be responsive to communications from the company, including marketing communications.
- **Frequency**: How often has a customer transacted or interacted with a sports book during a particular period of time? Clearly, customers with frequent activities are more engaged, and probably more loyal, than customers who rarely do so. A one-time-only customer is in a class of his or her own.
- **Monetary**: Also referred to as "monetary value," this factor reflects how much a customer has spent with the brand during a particular period. Big spenders should usually be treated differently than customers who spend little. Looking at monetary divided by frequency indicates the average purchase amount—an important secondary factor to consider when segmenting customers.

Most businesses will keep scores of data about a customer's purchases. All that is needed is a table with the customer name, date of purchase and purchase value. One methodology is to assign a scale of 1 to 10, whereby 10 is the maximum value and to stipulate a formula by which the data suits the scale. For example, in a service based business like the gambling business, you could have the following:

- Recency = 10—the number of months that have passed since the customer last purchased.
- Frequency = number of purchases in the last 12 months (maximum of 10).
- Monetary = value of the highest order from a given customer (benchmarked against $10k).

Alternatively, one can create categories for each attribute. For instance, the 'Recency' attribute might be broken into three categories: customers with purchases within the last 90 days; purchases between 91 and 365 days; and purchases longer than 365 days. Such categories may be arrived at by applying business rules, or using a data mining technique to find meaningful breaks.

Once each of the attributes has appropriate categories defined, segments are created from the intersection of the values. If there were three categories for each attribute, then the resulting matrix would have twenty-seven possible combinations (one well-known commercial approach uses five bins per attribute, which yields 125 segments).

Segments could also be collapsed into sub-segments, if the gradations appear too small to be useful. The resulting segments can be ordered from most valuable (highest recency, frequency, and value) to least valuable (lowest recency, frequency, and value). Identifying the most valuable RFM segments can capitalize on chance relationships in the data used for this analysis. For this reason, it is highly recommended that another set of data be used to validate the results of the RFM segmentation process.

Once the RFM data has been developed, a sports book can utilize this data to easily develop a customer loyalty program based on the purchasing patterns of its passengers, this is one of the best reasons to develop an RFM model. Where a sports book has points assigned for Recency, Frequency and Monetary Value, the sports book can assign the same amount of points, or a different points concept, for loyalty to its products and/or services. Sports books should consider using a range of customer loyalty concepts to develop and measure customer loyalty, and then reward customers who choose to fraternize the sports book, rather than one its competitors.

Advocates of this technique point out that it has the virtue of simplicity: no specialized statistical software is required, and the results are easily understood by business people. In the absence of other targeting techniques, it can provide a lift in response rates for promotions.

Whichever approach is adopted, profiling will be done on the final results to determine what makes up group membership. Categorical factors such as gender, nationality/locality can be used as well as age (or, indeed, any other demographic feature that is available) to understand the "type" of customer that resides in each group. These factors can be used for each segment and applied against the population metrics to determine how much more or less likely a segment is to exhibit a particular feature or type of behavior when compared to the customer base as a whole.

Propensity to Respond Model

A Propensity to Response model is the theoretical probability that a sampled person will become a respondent in an offer or survey. They are especially useful in the marketing field.

A response likelihood model can have substantial cost savings as it can lead to lower mailing costs by identifying patrons who are very unlikely to respond to a particular offer. After segmenting these people out, the sports book can then focus on only those most likely to take up the offer. A sports book can identify the likelihood of response from all eligible patrons.[197] After that, it can identify the most valuable patrons that are most likely to respond.[197] This allows the sports book to estimate the expected response from the most valuable patrons and eliminate mailing(s) to the patrons that are of lower worth and/or are unlikely to respond.[197]

Sutton warns that, "Occasionally, response likelihood models will lead to easy decisions, such as cutting out low worth patrons with a low likelihood of responding. However, more complex situations might arise since response models are never perfect."[197] It doesn't matter how good a model is or how accurate the historical data is, there is always a chance that a patron identified as unlikely to respond will respond.[197] "Thus, when making a decision about patrons identified as unlikely to respond to an offer, it is also important to balance that likelihood of response with the potential return on response," advises Sutton.[197]

A propensity to respond model would be built using historical information around marketing campaigns and it looks at predicting the likelihood a customer will respond to a marketing communication. The advantage of this model is that it strengthens the marketing strategy even more, beyond purely segmenting the customer base. It can further allow for improved ROI on the marketing budget, by identifying the likely number of respondents to be returned by a campaign.

Often a business' marketing department will have an expected number of respondents or an expected response rate.[197] By identifying those who are most likely to respond, the chances of meeting that expected number or rate of response is greatly improved.[197] Gone are the days of marketing to an entire customer base. This is an unnecessary waste of the marketing budget and also runs the risk of annoying customers by touching them too often or with the wrong offer.[197]

Again, a predictive model would be built which identifies those most likely to respond through to those least likely to respond. This would be done using customer metrics and historical campaign/marketing information that identifies those who responded and those who didn't. Variables that have a significant association with the customer action are extracted and these form part of the prediction algorithm. Every customer is then given a score according to how likely they are to respond to a marketing campaign.

This information can be used for strategies such as extracting the top 40% of customers most likely to respond, or a fixed number of customers. The end result is the marketing function becomes more efficient and effective, with better returns for the company's marketing dollar.

Customer Conversion Model

To identify the relationships that may exist between how the customer comes to the sports book and his or her desirability metric, information would be extracted from the sports book's source systems. For a sports book, this would include information such as source of betting, channel of betting, lead-time for betting and the incentives offered to attract the customer. Basically, anything that can be attributed to the initial transaction the customer has with the sports book would be used as a potential input.

The major advantage of a predictive model with this intention would be that it allows the sports book to identify customers that they need to interact with once they browse to the sports book's webpage. This would give the sports book's hosts the potential to get the required information they need to successfully foster a strong customer relationship.

Furthermore, if every potential customer has a score associated with him or her as to his or her long-term likelihood of being attractive, the sports book can further home in on its customers by monitoring their behavior once they are on the sports book's website. It is imperative that the sports book interact with desirable customers before they have left the website. If customers are made to feel like they are valuable and worthwhile, the likelihood of them returning under their own volition significantly increases.

Identify When a Patron is Likely to Return

Besides knowing which offers a customer is most likely to respond to, it would also be good to know exactly when a customer was planning to make his or her next bet.[197] Although it might not be possible to know exactly when a customer plans to return, the sports book's marketing department might be able to make an accurate prediction around it.[197]

"There are a variety of methods that range in complexity that can be used to assess when a patron will return to bet, including frequency analysis, regression, and survival analysis. Knowing when a patron is likely to bet is beneficial as it helps to identify patrons that haven't made a trip in the expected amount of time and are at risk of leaving," advises Sutton.[197] "First, the business needs to have an idea of the average or median time between trips. This might need to be segmented based on geography, worth, or even historical frequency," recommends Sutton.[197] Patrons who haven't made a bet within the set amount of time for his or her segment will be flagged and dealt with appropriately, perhaps marketed to more aggressively, perhaps given marketing content referencing "We haven't seen you in a while", or "Last chance type of offers."[197]

"Historical data can help to identify segments of patrons that are expected to make bets weekly, monthly, quarterly, annually, bi-annually"[197], or around specific events such as the FIFA World Cup, the Euro championships, or the Champions League tournament, say for a sports book.

"Marketing can integrate information from predicted worth, optimal offers, and time to next trip to maximize campaign success in a number of ways," says Sutton.[197] "The business can save money by adjusting the frequency of offers for patrons that are not identified as likely to bet on rarer events. Instead of sending the patron monthly offers, they can send quarterly offers with longer validation windows that allow more time to bet. Conversely, campaigns might be created with the goal of increasing the frequency of bets from higher worth patrons," recommends Sutton.[197]

The goal of the sports book's marketing department should be to generate customer bets sooner than expected and converting patrons into more frequent bettors or perhaps manipulating behavior so that bettors could spread out their bets and use their typical weekly bet bankroll over the course of several days, rather than blowing it all at once.[197]

Patron Worth Model

As Sutton explains, "Most industry experts would agree that determining a patron's worth is the first and foremost responsibility of patron analytics in the casino industry."[197] Same holds true for the sports betting industry. Of course, predicting a patron's future behavior is not easy and it is affected by a number of variables, "many of which are outside factors that the business might not have insight into, including total income, expendable income, ethnicity, reasons for a trip to the casino, etc., etc."[197] Even where a patron lives or information gleaned from his or her social media accounts could be very revealing. There is also "plenty of information to be found with in-house data that can be used to build models and metrics to predict a patron's future worth."[197] Once patron worth has been determined, "patrons can then be segmented into groups based on other behaviors and effective marketing campaigns can be developed around those behaviors."[197]

The first thing to do is to "determine what worth is, as the definition of worth is critical for deciding how valuable a patron is and how much to reinvest in the patron in the future."[197] As Sutton explains, "There are two main components of worth—the financial sources of worth (i.e., gambling) and the unit of time to which it refers (daily, weekly, monthly, etc.). Additionally, worth can refer to historical worth, which is already known, or future worth, which is unknown."[197]

"The definition of worth will likely depend on both the various financial sources of revenue that affect the business directly and the exact business problems that are being addressed. Gambling worth can also be broken down into various sources (i.e., what types of betting does the patron like to do) depending on the business issues being addressed," explains Sutton.[197]

In the gaming industry, there are "two important measures used to assess a patron's gaming worth—actual and theoretical loss. Actual loss is how much money the patron actually lost (or won), whereas theoretical loss usually refers to the amount of money a patron is expected to lose based on the amount of money wagered, the time spent playing, and the probability associated with type of games played."[197] Theoretical loss or Theo loss "tends to be more heavily relied upon for predictive analysis and is a much stronger predictor of future behavior, as actual loss is usually used to measure campaign performance and profitability."[197] Actual win could be heavily affected by a lucky winning streak, while Theo win would not.

"Once patron worth has been defined, the business can then use data mining and modeling to estimate predicted worth into the future," states Sutton.[197] "There are a variety of techniques that are used to develop models to predict future worth, the most common being regression models. Multiple regression models are the most common because they utilize a variety of predictors and the relationships between those predictors to predict future worth," adds Sutton.[197]

"Regression models can also be built using such categorical variables predictors as gender, ethnicity, age range, or other demographic variables. Developing separate models based on categorical variables, such as separate models predicting worth for slot and table players, might produce models with less error and better predictions."[197] "Regression models are particularly effective because the model can be used to score historical data to predict an unknown outcome, which is worth in this case, within a certain degree of confidence," adds Sutton.[197]

All sports betting analytics departments should have a solid method for predicting the various types of patron worth based on the sources and time periods they need for making informed marketing decisions. For instance, daily gambling worth would be most useful for building a campaign with a daily free play offer.

Customer Churn Model

Arguably, customer retention is both one of the cornerstones of any CRM system, as well as being the most important component of the customer lifetime value (CLV) framework.[222]

In their article *In pursuit of enhanced customer retention management*[223], Ascarza, Neslin, Netzer, Lemmens, & Aurélie highlight "the importance of distinguishing between which customers are *at risk* and which *should be targeted*—as they aren't necessarily the same customers."

There are indications that companies have problems managing customer retention. According to Handley[224], from the point of view of the customer, 85% report that companies could do more to retain them. A *Forbes Insight*[225] study found that from the company's point of view, a vast majority of top executives report that customer retention is a priority for their organization, only 49% believe their company has the ability to support their retention goals.

Ascarza et al. suggest that "an inordinate amount of effort has been devoted to predicting customer churn"[223], but less attention has been afforded to "elements of campaign design such as whom to target, when to target, and with what incentives, as well as the broader issues of managing multiple campaigns and integrating retention programs with the firm's marketing activities and strategies."[223]

Ascarza et al. propose the following definition: "First, the central idea that customer retention is *continuity*—the customer continues to interact with the firm. Second, that customer retention is a form of customer behavior—a behavior that firms intend to manage. Accordingly, we propose that '*Customer retention is the customer continuing to transact with the firm.*'"[223]

Sports books and casinos are unique from many other industries in that their customers are not tied into contracts, but "many of the retention metrics relevant for contractual firms are also relevant for non-contractual firms" state Ascarza et al.[223] A simple 0/1 indicator of transaction, and a measure of recency are appropriate for both types of companies.[223] However, on its own recency is not a good indicator of customer retention, argue Ascarza et al.[223] They provide the following example[223]:

> Customers A and B last purchased 6 months ago. On the one hand, Customer A typically purchases once a year (i.e., her inter-purchase time is 12 months), thus a recency of 6 months should not be taken as an indication of churn because it is well within the customer's purchase cycle. On the other hand, Customer B usually purchases every month, in which case a recency of 6 months should be worrisome for the firm. We thus recommend calculating a recency/inter-purchase ratio, where

a ratio larger than one is an indication of a retention problem. Regarding the examples above, Customer A's recency/inter-purchase times is 6/12 = 0.5, whereas Customer B's ratio is 6/1 = 6.

Ascarza et al. warn there are two caveats that should be kept in mind when creating the recency/inter-purchase-time ratio[223]; "First, it requires observing a reasonable number of transcation to reliability calculate the average inter-purchase time. Second, even for those customers for whom one observes a sufficient number of transactions, the inter-purchase time measure might be biased due to the right censoring nature of the data—the time between the last purchase and the last observation is ignored."[223]

Ascarza et al. propose the following process to develop and evaluate a single retention campaign[223]:

1. Identify customers who are at risk of not being retained.
2. Diagnose why each customer is at risk.
3. Decide when to target these customers and with what incentive and/or action.
4. Implement the campaign and evaluate it.

For Ascarza et al., "these steps are applicable to both proactive and reactive campaigns."[223] "Reactive campaigns are simpler because the firm doesn't need to identify who is at risk—the customer who calls to cancel self-identifies. 'Rescue rates' can readily be calculated to evaluate the program, and subsequent behavior can be monitored."[223] The incentive should be substantial because the company is pretty certain the customer will churn.[226] Reactive campaigns, however, can be challenging because not all customers can be rescued, and, because we're dealing with human nature here, customers learn that informing the firm about their intentions to churn can be richly rewarded with valuable incentives, which can endanger the long-run sustainability of reactive churn management.[227]

"Proactive campaigns are more challenging starting from the basic task of identifying who is at risk," argue Ascarza et al.[223] Balancing the cost of false positives (targeting a customer who has no intention to leave) against false negatives (failing to identify a customer who is truly at risk) requires sophisticated analytics.[228]

To discover who is at risk, a predictive model must be built that identifies customers at risk of not being retained, or in general of generating lower retention metrics.[223] "The dependent variable could be 0/1 churn or any measure of retention."[223] Table 9 summarizes variables predictor variables for several different industries, all in contractual settings, but many will be useful for the sports betting industry. "These include well-researched predictors like customer satisfaction, usage behavior, switching costs, customer characteristics, and marketing efforts, as well as more recently explored factors such as social connectivity," explain Ascarza et al.[223]

Factors	Example	Method
Customer Satisfaction	1. Emotion in emails	1. Logistic, SVM, Random Forests
	2. Customer service calls	2. SVM + ALBA
	3. Usage trends	3. Logistic, NN, SVM, Genetic
	4. Complaints	4. Logistic, NN, SVM, Genetic
	5. Previous non-renewal	5. Logistic, SVM, Random Forests
Usage Behavior	1. Usage levels	1. SVM with ALBA
	2. Usage levels	2. Logistic, NN, SVM, Genetic
Switching Costs	1. Add-on services	1. Logistic, NN, SVM, Genetic
	2. Pricing plan	2. Dec Tree, Naïve Bayes, Logistic, NN, SVM
	3. Ease of switching	3. Graphical comparison
Customer Characteristics	1. Psychographic Segment	1. Logistic, NN, SVM, Genetic
	2. Demographics	2. Logistic, NN, SVM, Genetic
	3. Customer tenure	3. Logistic, Decision Tree
Marketing	1. Mail responders	1. Bagging and Boosting
	2. Response to direct mail	2. Logistic, SVM, Random Forests
	3. Previous marketing campaigns	3. Decision rules
	4. Acquisition method	4. Probit
	5. Acquisition channel	5. Logistic
Social Connectivity	1. Neighbor churn	1. Hazard
	2. Social network connections	2. Random Forests, Bayesian Networks
	3. Social embeddedness	3. Decision rules
	4. Neighbor/connections usage	4. Logistic

Table 9: Predictors of Churn in Contractual Settings
Ascarza, Neslin, Netzer, Lemmens, Aurelie[223]

According to Ascarza et al., "Social connectivity factors can predict churn."[223] Studies in the telco industry have shown that high 'social embeddness', i.e., the extent to which the customer is connected to other customers within the network, is negatively correlated with churn.[229] Additionally, "the behavior of customer's connections also affects her own retention."[223] Two studies[230][231] found that a customer is more likely to churn from a service or company if his or her contacts within the company has churned. Conversely, an Ascarza, Ebbes, Netzler and Danielson study[232] found that a customer is less likely to churn if his or her contacts increase use of the service. Due to network externatlities, Ascarza et al. argue, "the service becomes less valuable to the customer if her friends are not using it."[223] "These social-related factors are more likely to predict churn for network oriented services such as multi-player gaming, communications, shared services, since customers exert an externality by using the service," state Ascarza et al.[223] Ascarza et al. conclude that, "If ones goes beyond the predictive power of social connections and towards understanding the social effect, it is imperative to consider the similarity among connected customers (homophily), correlated random shocks among connected customers (e.g., a marketing campaign that is geographically targeted and hence affects connected customers), and true social contagious effects."[223]

Ascarza et al. also consider whether using ultra-fine grained "big data" can be used to improve churn prediction.[223] According to Ascarza et al., these include "actions consumers take such as visiting a web page, visiting a specific location, 'Liking' something on Facebook, etc,"[223] but the researchers have found no evidence of this sort of data improving retention.[223] However, this type of data has been found to improve the prediction of customer acquisition[233] [234] and cross-selling[235] so Ascarza et al. believe it could be considered for churn prediction as well.

The main goal of a retention program is obviously to prevent churn, therefore understanding the causes of such churn behavior is imperative if you are to design an effective retention program.[223] Ascarza et al. believe that, "There is a difference between determining the best predictors of churn and understanding *why* the customer is at risk of churning."[223] "For example, demographic variables might predict churn, but these variables rarely cause customers to leave the company."[223] "The distinction becomes less clear when we consider factors like past consumption or related behaviors. Are heavy users more likely to be retained *because* they consume more or is it that satisfaction with the service is driving both behaviors?" ask Ascarza et al.[223]

Additionally, "identifying specific causes for an individual customer is quite different from identifying general causes in a population."[223] To identify the potential causes of churn for an individual customer, the variables or combinations of variables that are both viable causes and for which the customer exhibits a risky behavior must be discovered.[223] A competing risk hazard model could be used "to predict which of the possible reasons of churn are most likely to cause churn at any point in time."[223]

Once the causes of churn are identified, the sports book needs to isolate those thare are controllable and those that are not.[223] Both correlates of low retention and also the causes of it need to be identified.[223]

Ascarza et al. argue that it's not always the customers who are at the highest risk that should be targeted.[223] In her article *Retention Futility: Targeting High Risk Customers Might Be Ineffective*[236], Eva Ascarza argues that the highest risk customers may not be receptive to retention efforts. As Ascarza et al. put it, "They might be so turned off by the company that nothing can retain them."[223] Ascarza et al. advise focusing on customers who are at risk of leaving *and* are likely to change their minds and stay if targeted.[237]

Although research on customer *response* to retention programs is scarce, Ascarza's *Retention Futility: Targeting High Risk Customers Might Be Ineffective*[236], which advocates for the use of "uplift" models. "In the jargon of customer-level decision models, uplift modeling recognizes customer *heterogeneity* with respect to the incremental impact of the test," states Ascarza.[236] Incremental impact can be modeled in many different way, including by utilizing interactions models and machine learning methods.[238] [239] [236]

Even customers who are likely to both churn and respond still might not be worth rescuing because they might have low lifetime values.[223] Sports books should always consider the potential profit that a retention action can generate, which depends on "the likelihood of churning, the incremental likelikhood or responding, the customer's CLV, and the incentive cost.[236] [237] [240]

In the majority of cases, most of the customer targeted in a proactive campaign will be those whom the company would have retained anyway.[223] In their paper *Building Data Applications for CRM*[241], Berson et al. discovered that "customers targeted by a retention campaign who did not accept the retention offer ended up with a higher churn rate than average." Ascarza et al. speculate this is because "the offer triggered these customers to examine whether they wanted to stay with the company, and the answer turned out to be 'no.'"[223] Although Ascarza et al. found the study provocative, they did also point out that, the data did "not permit rejection of the alternative explanation that the retention offer bifurcated non-churners (satisfied customers who therefore accepted the offer) and churners (dissastisfied customer who therefore churned without accepting the offer)."[223]

More troublingly, in their article *The Perils of Proactive Churn Prevention Using Plan Recommendations: Evidence froma Field Experiment*[242], Ascarza, Iyengar and Schleicher showed that some would-be non-churners could be provoked by the retention effort to churn. "Non-churners may be continuing to transact with the firm partly out of habit or inertia,"[242] and the retention efforts may inadvertently make people realize they are unhappy with the status quo, and paradoxically cause churn.[242]

According to Ascarza et al., another factor to consider in deciding whom to target is the position of the customer in the firm's social network."[223] "Taking a social perspective, a customer with many contacts, or highly connected with customers who themselves are highly connected, can be very valuable because his/her defection could cause others to churn," warn Ascarza et al.[223] Individuals who are central in a network might have a lower risk of churning because of the high social cost of leaving.[243] Because of the tendency of individuals to be in social networks with others like them, high profitability customers may have a strong effect on each other, which provides even more of an incentive to target high CLV customers, as well as to provide channels to market virally.[244] Hogan, Lemon and Libai point out that product life cycle should also be kept in mind as "socially related monetary loss due to customer churn would be much higher early in the product life cycle, when social influence is critical in driving product growth."[245]

One important consideration that needs to be kept in mind is the selection of the best action to take to prevent churn.[223] Price incentives are one of the top considerations and they can be effective in the short term, but they are easily replicated by competitors.[223] This might put pressure on margins as customers can become overly price sensitive. Ascarza et al. argue that "non-price incentives, such as product improvements (e.g., a gaming company adds additional levels in a game) may work better in the long term."[223]

Another approach is to let customers pick the incentive amongst a set of options.[223] Research by Shrift and Parker[246] has shown that including in that set the option of no-choice (i.e., doing nothing) increases persistence among customers, which would likely results in higher retention. Sports book can also "design the retention effort in a way that it will mainly affect customers at high risk of churn and/or in a way that all customers, targeted or not, would appreciate it (e.g., product or service improvement)."[223]

The element of surprise has proven to be quite positive for customer retention as well. Research by Oliver, Rust and Varki[247] showed that surprising positive events attach a customer to the company. This is particularly important because the retention campaign will most likely target many non-would-be churners and it should enhance retention in the long run even among those uninterested in churning.[223]

Ascarza et al. argue that "the best way to conceptualize when-to-target is to consider the different type of marketing campaign throughout the customer's lifecycle: acquisition => pre-emptive => proactive => reactive => win-back => post win-back"[223] (see Figure 22). Although it won't be necessary to target immediately after customer acquisition, this is the time a company needs to start thinking about retention.[223] Ascarza et al. give an example from the telco industry in which the provider would make sure the customer is on the right data plan from the very beginning, thereby ensuring there won't be any nasty bill surprises.[223]

"Pre-emptive timing would be to target the customer before the customer shows any sign of diminished retention,"[223] while proactive timing would be the lauching of a "campaign targeted at customers who are identified as a retention risk based on predictive models."[223] "Reactive timing is when the firm tries to prevent the customer from churning, while that customer literally is in the act of churning."[223] Win-back is when the customer has churned and the company attempts to re-acquire that customer.[223] Post win-back actions refers to contacts initiated after the customer has rejected a win-back offer.[223]

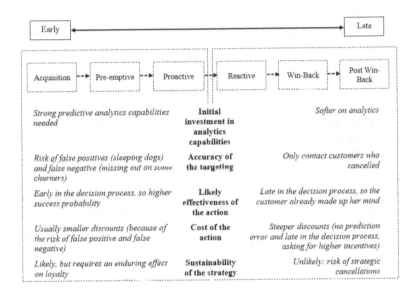

Figure 22: Alternative Timing of Retention Campaigns
Ascarza, Neslin, Netzer, Lemmens, Aurelie[223]

Once campaigns have been initiated they need to be evaluated, if possible by using a control group randomly selected not to be targeted.[223] "This allows top-line results to be compiled easily without formal causal modeling," note Ascarza et al.[223] Overall profitability metrics and various retention measures should be calculated.[223] The rescue rate should be calculated for all of the sports book's retention campaigns.[223] This will allow the sports book to "undertake a meta-analysis across multiple campaigns to understand which factors influence rescue rates (incentive characteristics, characteristics of customers targeted, the match between these two, etc.)."[223] This meta-analysis could reveal both immediate insights as well as long-term trends that affect the sports book's business.

Long-term impacts of the campaign should also be part of the evaluation.[223] As Ascarza et al. note, "'Yes, the customer might have been retained this time, but what impact did that have on the customer's future profitability? What happened to the customer's retention rate after the campaign? Did it increase because the customer was more satisfied, or decrease because now the customer expected if not demanded incentives?"[223]

Multiple campaign management is similar to single campaigns except now the following questions need to be asked in a dynamic setting across several campaigns:

1. Who is at risk?
2. Why are they at risk?
3. Who should be targeted?
4. When should they be targeted?
5. With what efforts?
6. What was gained by these actions?[223]

In their article *Database Marketing: Analyzing and Managing Customers*[248], Blattberg, Kim, and Neslin discuss two key issues in multiple CRM campaign management: wear-in and wear-out. As Ascarza et al. note, "A campaign may take time before it reaches its maximal impact (wear-in) and then decline at some rate afterwards (wear-out). These concepts have important implications for the spacing of retention campaigns."[223]

On the individual level, multiple campaign management is tricky because any current campaign can influence what "state" a customer might be in for the next campaign.[223] A customer who receives an incentive that is clearly of lesser value than a previous incentive might be offended and so put off by the offering that the incentive works against the giving company. This, Ascarza et al. suggest that dynamic optimization is required.[223]

In terms of integrating strategy, it is important to coordinate both the company's acquisition and retention as well as its retention spending with the company's marketing strategy and its segmentation, targeting and positioning (STP) approach.[223] Optimizing both acquisition and retention can be a tricky endeavor, but it is important to do.[223]

Ascarza et al. provide an example from the financial services industry that show how easy it is for things to get out of sync.[223] They consider the STP of a financial services company that may be trying to segment the market by customer value and also wants to target high-value customers with premium products and services.[223] A retention campaign emphasizing promotional discounts would then be "off-strategy."[223]

Ascarza et al. believe that emotions and social connections are important when it comes to identifying who is at risk of churn, but what's more important is understanding *why* the customer is at risk and *whom should be targeted*.[223] "Social connections data could be particularly important for key 'influencers', i.e., customers that provide network value to other customers, as Ascarza, Ebbes et al. put it.[232]

"Emotional and other indicators gleaned from text data should provide key insights on why customers churn," argue Ascarza et al.[223] They add, "Textual analysis approaches such as Linguistic Inquiry and Word Count (LIWC) and topic modeling may be used to extract measures of emotions and other useful insights from consumer data and leverage these for churn prediction and management."[223]

Engagement metrics do have the potential to identify what retention actions need to be taken.[223] For example, measures of how a customer plays a slot machine could provide a hint of what incentive (monetary or not) the customer needs to keep playing.[223] Ascarza et al. conclude that, "knowledge management will be necessary to ensure the firm's entire experience base in retention management is codified and accessible to planners. This is especially important for planning multiple campaigns and integrating strategy, since these tasks require a broad understanding of the firm's experiences."[223]

When it comes to building the actual models, Ascarza et al. proffer that, tried and true regression-based predictive modeling is useful for constructing the following[223]:

1. "Predictive models for identifying who is at risk and who will respond to targeting.
2. "Meta analyses of field data that provide insights needed for multiple campaign planning.
3. "Marketing mix model that can drive strategy integration."[223]

Deep learning has been used to uncover the probability that a customer might defect[249] and it may also help in modeling response to retention offers.[223] Ascarza et al. add that, boosted varying-coefficient regression models have been studied for dynamic predictions and optimization in real time[250], which have shown to offer major improvements over the classic stochastic gradient boosting algorithm currently used for churn prediction.[251][240] Ascarza et al. see these methods as promising discoveries for retention management.

"Dimensionality reduction and variable selection techniques form another major development in the machine learning field, and may be useful for retention research and practice, which face an overflow of potential defection predictors," add Ascarza et al.[223] Companies wanting to build models predicting *who is at* risk, *whom to target*, and *when to target* should look at modern regularization techniques like Lasso[252], elastic net[253], and adaptive regularization[254]. Churn modelers should consider the Cox proportional hazard models[255][256] as it has been proven particularly effective, and it is available in the R package 'glmnet'.[223]

"State-of-the-art regularization models, which systematically control for overfitting and thus allow modeling with larger feature sets, also offer the potential to expand the set of predictors to include interactions between churn predictors," explain Ascarza et al.[223] They also believe that when estimating the effects of churn incentives it helps to include "interactions between the treatment variable (i.e., being targeted with a retention action) and customer or campaign design covariates."[223]

The use of analytics and data management to help detect and avoid the act of attrition is something that can benefit all sports books. Churn questions that a sports book should be asking include:

- How is the sports book detecting behaviorial changes in its patrons?
- Does the sports book have steps in place to identify when the customer experience is going wrong, or when the customer is about to leave?

Sports betting operators can use Master Data Management (MDM) techniques to communicate important customer preference information to staff who sit at interaction points throughout the sports betting operation.

To ensure customer retention is front and center, sports books should be scoring their databases on a regular basis in order to understand the likelihood of a customer churning from their venue. This kind of modeling is prevalent in the telecommunications, finance, and utilities industries, and should be utilized in the gaming industry as well. While a slightly different set up due to those industries mostly having their customers locked into contracts, gaming companies need to stay ahead of the game in retaining their customers.

Anecdotal evidence collected in our discussions with gaming companies have indicated a tendency to ignore customers until they have not been seen for up to two years. At this stage, there might be a marketing activity targeted at the customer for up to 12 months. It could be proffered that, by this stage, it is too late to win the customer back; the customer has probably already made up his or her mind and, once a decision like that has been made, it is almost impossible to reverse it, no matter how attractive any competing offer might be.

One of the hardest parts for a gaming company to determine—as opposed to commercial entities that have their customers on contract and definitely know they are tied down—is whether the customer has categorically churned. It may be that a change in location, circumstances or something else has caused a customer to disappear from the sports book, with every intention of returning. However, statistical measures could be used to identify customer's whose behavior has changed and the change wouldn't be attributed to chance.

Historical internal data can be used to model the difference between a churned customer and one who is still engaged. There would be significant metrics in the data that identify the likelihood of churning. Similar to the acquisition model described above, a parametric equation could be constructed that elicits the association and relationship between the target variable and the predictors.

This model would serve as an early warning system for the sports book. It would also be a strategic tool useful to predict whether a customer was deemed worth retaining or not. The model should be run on a regular basis across the entire customer database to understand which customers have reached or are reaching a critical value in their churn score. The theory: these customers would then be targeted with an offer to return to the sports book, in the process avoiding the likelihood of them churning. Alternatively, if the customer is deemed to be of little or no value, there would be no offer forthcoming to entice them to return.

Optimizing Offers

As Sutton explains, "In addition to predicting the future worth of patrons, it is important to know which marketing campaigns are the most effective for driving response, revenue, and profit. In general, certain offers are better than others, and specifically certain offers will be better for certain patrons."[197]

"While knowing the probable future worth of a patron is critical for determining the reinvestment level for which a patron is eligible, patrons' behaviors and interests can be used to identify the offer(s) that will be most appealing to each patron as well as the ones generating the most profitable response," explains Sutton.[197] By analyzing the likelihood that a patron will respond to a certain offer or offers, sports book analysts can optimize the offer that each patron is given in order to maximize the amount of revenue and profit driven by the marketing campaign as a whole.[197]

As previously mentioned, A/B testing is one of the best ways to identify which offers work best. A/B testing involves "testing two different offers against one another in order to identify the offer that drives the highest response and the most revenue/profit," says Sutton.[197] "More advanced statistical methods can be used to generate likelihood of response scores and classification scores. Some of the more common statistical approaches are logistic regression, decision trees, and discriminant analysis," Sutton states.[197]

"Essentially, these statistical methods use historical data to find the factors that are related as to why a patron responds. Those factors can then be used to assess the likelihood of response based on the similarity of a patron profile to that of responders," adds Sutton.[197]

"These methods have historically been used in direct marketing analysis to identify the best types of offers and the most likely responders," says Sutton.[197] "In order to build accurate and predictive response models, historical data about response is required. The likelihood of response might be a broad measure of response that refers to the likelihood a patron will respond to any offer, or it might be specific to the likelihood of response to a specific type of offer."[197]

In addition, Sutton adds, "it's a good idea to select test segments of customers for the purpose of continually testing new offers. Doing so will help to ensure that there is a large amount of response data that can be used to build models and continually improve the efficacy of marketing."[197] "Effective response models will help identify which patrons are most likely to respond to an offer, and in turn to which offer patrons are most likely to respond," concludes Sutton.[197]

Chronological View of a Sports Book's Analytics Implementation

1. Data reduction via cluster analysis and segmentation is a logical starting point and the initial work should be around identifying patron preferences. Reducing the customer database into more manageable and meaningful segments has many advantages; the preferences that can be derived are dependent on the availability of meaningful distinguishing factors.

2. *Segmentation models* use customer metrics that help reduce and profile the customer database and should be constructed as this information can be the underpinning for further analyses, such as patron acquisition worth models.

3. *First Trip Scoring Model* would give the sports book a view of the customer across the entire business and a rich history of engaged customers. The sports book would then need to build a modeling data set that is adequate to investigate the relationship between a metric for "valuable" and the inputs that are extracted, derived, and constructed from the first trip of each customer.

4. *A Propensity to Respond Model* is heavily dependent on the marketing data and the veracity and richness of it. The sports book would need to develop the whole view of the customer first, but, once developed, this is one of the most powerful marketing models available.

5. *Customer Conversion Model* could be viewed as an extension of a number of the above models, with the idea to derive a data driven metric that scores a customer's likelihood of returning after his or her first trip.

6. *Patron Likelihood to Return Model* requires a complete view of the customer along with considerable marketing data. This would help with offers sent, who was sent offers, who responded to the offers, etc., etc. The derived metric on its own would have value, but it could also be a significant input into a two stage model to predict next trip value and worth.

7. A *Patron Worth Model* would identify the sports book's most valuable patrons. The assumption is that a sports book would be looking to predict different metrics, such as worth on the next trip, worth over the next 12 months, lifetime value, etc., etc.

8. *RFM* is a method used for analyzing customer value and it is commonly utilized in database marketing and direct marketing and has received particular attention in the casino industries. A sports book should keep scores of data about a customer's purchases that includes a table with

the customer name, date of purchase and purchase value. From this data, the sports book can score the true value of a customer and this information can be fed to the marketing department, which can decide to send an offer to the client if it is worth it.

9. A *Customer Acquisition Model* would then be built by using the results of the segmentation modeling models (or a different metric for desirable customers). A deeper investigation of a sports book's source systems is needed and this could be part of the analysis to help understand what is available, and what might be able to be used from external parties. Different jurisdictions would have different models.

10. *Customer Churn Models* would require preliminary analysis to extract only engaged customers. The sports book would need to derive a statsitcially dirven metric that indicated whether a customer had churned or not. The sports book could then build models to detect upcoming patron attrition.

11. An *Identifying Patrons at Risk of Abuse Model* would likely take into account the factors that predict whether a guest will play on a future trip, but it also makes sense to build a separate model to identify patrons who are likely to use a future offer and not play at all.

Edge Analytics

The driving concept behind edge analytics is the fact that data loses its value as it ages. As previously mentioned, the concept of "Edge Analytics"—i.e., the processing of analytics at the point or very close to the point where the data is being collected—exponentially increases one's ability to use predictive analytics where it can be utilized best.

As Patrick McGarry explains in his article *Why Edge Computing is Here to Stay*[257], Edge analytics is easier to implement than ever before because in the field micro data centers use a fraction of the space, power and cost of a traditional analytics infrastructure, but they can provide massive performance gains. These systems use "hybrid computing technology, seamlessly integrating diverse computing technologies, whether they are x86, GPU or FPGA technologies, or any combination thereof. They are extremely compact in space and require very little power, yet still provide performance that is several orders of magnitude more than what today's traditional systems can provide."[257] "It's a win/win situation for all involved; insights come faster than ever before, operational expenses are lower, [sic] power and administration needed to run the systems," McGarry adds.[257]

"Emergency repair work and equipment down-time can be reduced when manufacturers build edge-based analytical systems into machinery and vehicles, allowing them to decide for themselves when it is time to reduce power output or send an alert that a part may be due for replacement."[21] Sports books can connect their IoT devices into their data warehouses and enact predictive asset maintenance to reduce equipment costs.

Although building an edge analytics platform does require a shift in corporate thinking, the ROI benefits can far outweigh the costs. "The cost savings by scaling back central data analytics infrastructures to handle non-time sensitive analysis while installing cost-efficient platforms purpose-built for edge analytics can have a real impact on an organization's budget," McGarry notes.[257] The value of near-instant analysis and insight cannot be underestimated in a business so dependent on customer excellence like the sports betting business. Avoiding latency and eliminating the time and costs associated with transporting the data to and from the edge is a major step toward achieving that goal.[257]

IoT sensors can help spot patrons arriving in a sports betting shop, or track employees, suppliers, and supplies throughout the operation, as well as help save energy and water usage. Edge analytics can help analyze a sports betting shop's customer behavior, as well as spot upcoming equipment malfunction. Other areas where it can help include compliance analysis and mobile data thinning, i.e., the culling of mobile data noise from social media or direct mobile streams.

Sentiment Analysis

In the TDWI *Customer Analytics in the Age of Social Media*[173] Research report about the same percentage (30%) of respondents sought to monitor and measure sentiment drivers. "Sentiment analysis enables organizations to discover positive and negative comments in social media, customer comment and review sites, and similar sources."[173]

Sentiment analysis often focuses on monitoring and measuring the 'buzz' value, usually through volume and frequency of comments around a topic."[173] However, it is not just the buzz that is important, many organizations want more analytical depth so that they can understand what the buzz is all about, where it comes from, and who is benefiting the most from it.[173]

For more sophisticated sentiment analysis, text analytics tools that use word extraction, natural language processing, pattern matching, and other approaches to examine social media users' expressions are employed.[173] "Sentiment analysis can give organizations early notice in real time of factors that may be affecting customer churn; the research shows that 14% are interested in monitoring and analyzing social activity in real time."[173]

In 2011, Toyota started testing social media monitoring and sentiment-analysis tools. After a few years of research they discovered that by filtering for such words as "Lexus", "decide", "buy" and "BMW", they were able to quickly identify active shoppers who were choosing between theirs and their competitor's brands.[258]

Today, Toyota uses social media data analysis across many areas—sales, service, quality, marketing and product development.[258] For example, if a customer expresses interest in a car, Toyota "can determine engagement by analyzing the frequency of dealership visits via their Foursquare check-ins, understand their dealership experiences, and even understand what features may have sparked their interest in a competitor's product."[258]

Armed with this information, Toyota stratifies its leads based on their readiness to buy, moving stronger leads to the top of the funnel and weaker ones to the bottom.[258] By analyzing free-form text, Toyota can learn what customers think of specific vehicles.[258] In the quality area, "Toyota can look for information like whether new-car owners are hearing a slight rattle and pass that on to their quality engineers."[258] They are also working on using sentiment analysis to increase the accuracy of their sales predictions; an important goal, if ever there was one.[258]

Sports betting operators should keep these ideas in mind when developing their own use cases. A "rattle" for a sports book wouldn't be an engine problem, of course, but rather a poor customer experience on the company's website.

Toyota also wants to deepen its understanding of its customers' other interests, like what a Camry owners' favorite TV show might be, as well as which other brands they might like.[258] This can help with product placement and brand tie-ins down the line.[258]

Sentiment analysis is also key to understanding a competitors' relative strengths and weaknesses in the social sphere.[173] The TDWI research found that "18% of respondents are examining social media data to analyze a competition's 'share of voice.'"[173]

As Joe Mullich explains in his article *Opposition Research: Sentiment Analysis as a Competitive Marketing Tool*[259]:

> *"When a leading bank wanted to find out how it stacked up against competitors, it assumed customers would focus on lending terms and interest rates. To the bank's surprise, the most enthusiastic discourse on blogs and specialized financial forums related to a smartphone app a competing financial institution had just put out. The bank had dismissed apps as a generic marketing gimmick, like the old custom of giving away a toaster for opening an account. After learning how much customers valued the app, the bank quickly created its own with the same prized features as its competitor."*

"You get the benefits of corporate espionage without doing corporate espionage," notes Joseph Carrabis, founder of NextStage Evolution, the company that did the analysis for the bank.[259]

Sentiment analysis can also provide early insight into a competitor's new product initiatives.[259] "Very often companies will test market before they release a product," says Mullich.[259] "And no matter what you get people to sign saying that they won't share information, they'll go online and talk about products they're excited about," warns Mullich.[259] You can't change human nature, but sometimes you can make it work for you.

In addition, sentiment analysis can alert companies about new competitors who are bubbling up to the surface or even coming out of left-field.[259] Ford would obviously consider Chevy a competitor, but it might not think of public transport as being troubling competition.[259] However, Carrabis argues that a car company should realize that it needs to analyze online discussion boards to try to understand why people are making different transportation choices so it can change its product offerings or marketing campaigns to emphasize their customers' growing environmental concerns.[259] "We have to think broader and wider than we used to," Carrabis advises.[259] The lesson here is, don't just look at your closest competitors as your competition, widen your view. Gambling's gambling and sports books and lottery companies are as much of a competitor for a casino gambler's dollar as is a competing casino.

This is why it is so imperative for a sports book to understand how and why people discuss competitors online. "When car shoppers talk online they don't talk about 'quality,'" says Susan Etlinger, an analyst with the Altimeter Group.[259] "They'll say, 'I love the leather interior' or 'the cup holder fell out.' It takes meticulous work to roll together all the indicators of quality."[259]

Etlinger suggests that "social-media listening teams work with the groups in the organization that handle keyword search terms and search-engine optimization effort, since they have a solid grasp on how people online actually talk about the industry and products."[259]

Another thing to keep in mind: "At any point in time, the way people feel about a brand can be distorted online, because things like Twitter are so volatile and affected by the news of the day," warns Etlinger.[259] "But over time, you can get directional trends—why do people love or hate you, how do they feel about your product compared to the competitor's products."[259]

"My belief is that the sweet spot for social media is not conversion, but nurturing," said Brian Ellefritz, vice president of global social media at SAP.[173] "Whether it's in your community, through Twitter, or through Facebook pages, you want to build an increasing conviction that your company is the one to do business with," says Ellefritz.[173] "It's about establishing a belief system that becomes robust with the support of fans and followers. The question is how you measure that and create value out of that investment," he adds.[173]

When it comes to setting strategies for customer and social media analytics, Stodder recommends the following[173]:

- Use social media data to support an active, not passive social media strategy. "In competitive, fast-moving markets, organizations cannot just passively listen to and analyze social media data. The analytics should plug into strategies for engaging users and customers on social networks and comment sites. Predictive analytics can help organizations anticipate the results of active strategies. Special events such as tweet-ups can build on customer data analysis and create positive exchanges and engagement."[173]
- Take a holistic view of the potential contributions of social media data analytics. "Understanding behavior in the social sphere can have a positive impact, not just on marketing and sales functions, but also on services and other processes in the organization. Marketing executives should use social media insights to improve brand awareness and reputation throughout the organization."[173]
- Give CMOs and marketing executives the ability to understand the financial impact of certain decisions.
- Apply analytics to gain a more accurate understanding of marketing attribution. "Last-touch" attribution may be easy to affix, but it is not always reliable. Powerful analytics, along with big data, can help organizations get a better understanding of what truly affects a customer's purchase decision.

Clickstream Analysis

When a person browses a website, he or she leaves behind a digital trail, which is known as a "clickstream." Clickstream analysis is the process of collecting, aggregating, reporting and analyzing the browsing behavior of a web surfer to better understand the intentions of users and their interests in specific content or products on a website. Clickstream analysis is the process of collecting, analyzing and reporting aggregate data about which pages a website browser visits—and in what order. The path the visitor takes though a website is, basically, the clickstream.

There are two levels of clickstream analysis: traffic analytics and e-commerce analytics. Traffic analytics operates at the server level and tracks how many pages are served to the user, how long it takes each page to load, how often the user hits the browser's back or stop button and how much data is transmitted before the user moves away from the website. E-commerce-based analysis uses clickstream data to determine the effectiveness of a website as a channel-to-market. It is concerned with what pages the browser lingers on, what he or she puts in or takes out of a shopping cart, what items are purchased, whether or not the buyer belongs to a loyalty program, whether the buyer uses a coupon code, as well as his or her preferred methods of payment.

Utilizing clickstream analysis, a casino can help build a Master Marketing Record for each customer in real-time. This allows the sports book to test scenarios and options for the website, as well as develop personalized responses for individuals. The system should include a combination of social listening, analytics, content publication and distribution, and tracking, as well as a strong workflow and rules engine that is geared around strong governance. All of these applications are built to ultimately feed a Master Marketing Profile—a centralized customer record that pulls in all data based on digital activity that can be identified by a single customer ID.

Figure 23 shows the customer funnel that takes an anonymous web browser to a known patron. Through clickstream analytics, personalization marketing can begin, and associating this activity with a customer once he or she walks through the sports book's front door or browses onto its website should be a sports book's primary goal. This can be done by enabling new users to log into his or her account via web or mobile applications, like a sports book's mobile app.

Figure 23: Customer funnel

In their article *Big Data and Competition Policy: Market Power, personalised pricing and advertising[260]*, Marc Bourreau et al. explain that firms may collect personal and non-personal data about users, as well as machines, in several different ways, including:

- Publicly observed through device, operating system, IP address, etc.
- Voluntarily provided by the consumer, "either with knowledge when registering to a website, such as name, data of birth, email or postal address for delivery, etc., or often without knowledge when logging into a website (login-based data) such as products the consumer is looking for, purchases, etc."[260]

- Tracking the consumer online, which can be achieved in different ways, such as:
  - "tracking cookies, which are a specific type of cookie that is distributed, shared, and read across two or more unrelated websites for the purpose of gathering information or presenting customized data to a consumer."[260]
  - "Browser and device fingerprinting, which is a method of tracking web browsers by the configuration and settings information they make visible to websites."[260]
  - "History sniffing, which is the practice of tracking which sites a user has and has not visited (by hacking its browser history list)."[260]
  - "Cross-device tracking offers the ability to interact with the same consumer across her desktop, laptop, tablet, wearable, and smartphone, using both online and offline information."[260]
  - "Through the use of applications by the user, this information is accessible for the Operating System owner as well as for the developer of the application."[260]

Of all the available marketing and customer channels, social media represents the biggest issue due to the sports book's inability to track the value of social connections.[97] In his article, *At Caesar's Digital Marketing Is No Crap Shoot*[97], Al Urbanski explains that at Caesar's, they "wanted to make better use of the social space, but one of the overwhelming problems had been, 'How do you measure the effectiveness?' Not a lot of organizations are able to measure it effectively."[97] "Caesars marketers didn't want to create a social island that communicated with customers separately and distinctly from all other channels," Urbanski explains.[97]

"Each channel is tracked and rated for its ability to turn engagements into booked rooms, and Caesars had been flying blind in the region of social media."[97] "Top management wants to know, 'How did this perform?' 'What's the return on ad spend?' and how can we tell the path to purchase from first touch point to last touch point, even if the starting point was in social media," Kahle, Caesars' Web Analytics Manager, explains.[97] "Before, we couldn't understand social's role in the transaction. You could track it to a degree, but you built a social island and there was some guessing involved. You could end up double counting social's contribution," he warned.[97]

"To support these efforts, Caesars invested in Adobe's Digital Marketing Suite, which includes real-time tracking and segmentation of digital site visitors, analysis of social media's role in purchasing, and content testing by segment or individual visitor," explains Kahle.[97]

The problem with driving online conversions among Frequent Independent Travelers (FITs), however, is that—based on their online behaviors—they're not loyal to a particular casino.[97] "They're on Kayak; they're on other casinos' sites. They're looking for a deal," says Kahle, who adds that Caesars regularly targets these travelers with offers, such as free meals and free gaming play.[97]

As noted in the article[97]:

> "Kahle's staff conducted A/B analysis aimed at presenting the company's individual properties with the best option for increasing Total Rewards memberships. Half the people who searched Total Rewards online were sent to the main Caesars Entertainment homepage, while the other half was sent to the homepage of a specific property. While the conversion rate for room reservations was the same for both groups, the latter group signed up for the loyalty program at a significantly higher rate. The practice was adopted across the Caesars Web network and resulted in a 10% increase in sign-ups."

"A similar test was used to maximize business from Total Rewards members, testing its old website interfaces against a new design. The difference was an eye-opener. The conversion rate for the newer interface option was 70% higher," Kahle explains.[97]

"In the past, when planning changes to web page design or elements, the winning design was often decided by the highest-ranking person in the office," Kahle says.[97] "With Adobe testing, people's personal opinions aren't the deciding factor. We can look at the numbers, see the results, and clearly identify the best-performing design."[97] Kahle adds that Caesars deployed these new capabilities without having to increase its IT staff.[97]

"Caesars went from a culture of opinion to a culture of data. We essentially gave them the...flexibility to test so that the [end-user's] experience is optimized," says Matt Langie, senior director of product marketing at Adobe.[97]

As per Paul Greenberg states in his article *Is Adobe a Marketing Player Now?*[261]:

> "First thing to know about Adobe is that they are a tools company—and this is both good and bad. For the most part and for the purposes of this discussion, the products are a good thing. The second thing to know about Adobe (and the Marketing Cloud) is that what they are currently offering is a significant piece of a digital engagement platform. Keep in mind this is for the marketing side—the first line of engagement—the first place that the customer comes into contact with the brand and either starts interacting or doesn't."

The Master Marketing Record is the core around which Adobe's Marketing Cloud is built and this goes to the heart of two of Adobe's themes, one of which is as old as modern man—the single view of the customer—and the other is the Real Time Enterprise, the set-up of which I detail in chapter five.

Just to step into the MCM (Multi-Channel Marketing) arena for a moment, as Greenberg explains, "The Adobe Marketing Cloud essentially consists of a basket of applications and services. At the highest level it is:

- Adobe Analytics—A strong package focused around digital analytics, mobile and web in particular. They also, wisely, have predictive analytics as part of the core offering.
- Adobe Campaign—For now, this is where the core Neolane integration has occurred. They have done a remarkable job of taking that piece of Neolane's capabilities and making it seamless in a short period of time. There are still parts of Neolane to be integrated into other areas and here too.
- Adobe Target—This allows you to test scenarios and options for the web and develop personalized responses for individuals. It's one of the most popular and powerful of Adobe's tools. It's as close as Adobe gets to what Epiphany and Exact Target does.
- Adobe Experience Manager—This is Adobe's digital experience management; its purpose is to manage the assets and create and manage the communities needed to optimize the customer journey across digital channels and media.
- Adobe Social—This is a combination of social listening, analytics, content publication and distribution, tracking (which they oddly call "campaign") as well as a strong workflow and rules engine geared around governance and protocols.
- Adobe Media Optimizer—The idea is simple: Who's your audience, what ads will appeal to them the most and what media mix should we use to maximize that appeal? To do that is complex and difficult, but the tools in Media Optimizer are designed to make it as accurate as possible, while not necessarily as easy as possible."[261]

All of these applications are built to ultimately feed what Adobe calls the "Master Marketing Profile"—a centralized customer record that pulls in all data based on digital activity that can be identified by a single customer ID. "That means that John Smith's record will have his social profile data, his transactional data, his response to campaigns, his click-throughs, his web browsing, etc. This goes to the heart of their effort—the personalization of the response to individual customers. The Master Marketing Profile is where you find all that data."[261]

To Adobe's credit, Greenberg feels that the software vendor has done some solid integration of the entire portfolio.[261] The total package, if viewed as an advanced digital marketing cloud, some believe it could very well be the best of its kind on the market. However, Adobe is "competing with other Marketing Clouds—

notably, if the name Marketing Cloud is meaningful, salesforce.com and Oracle. If the name Marketing Cloud isn't—add Marketo, Microsoft, Teradata Applications, SAS, IBM Unica, and Infor to the mix. If niche players count, there are dozens and dozens out there chomping off pieces of the potential revenue stream. This is a hot competition."[261]

A word of caution here: the sports betting industry does seem to be struggling with CRM and marketing automation solutions because none of the big players have produced a product that fulfills all of the industry's unique needs. From my experience, sports betting companies are cobbling together a multitude of products to capture certain elemental needs, but the addition of unstructured data and real-time streaming is only adding to the complexity and it'll be interesting to see which company, if any, can create a solution that checks off all the CRM, MA, and analytics boxes for a sports book.

In his article *Google Attribution Allows Clear, Seamless Campaign Analysis for Marketers*[262], Matthew Bains explains that Google has released a new tool called Google Attribution that "uses machine learning and data to help marketers measure the impact of each of their marketing touch points, across multiple channels, and across multiple devices." "It uses data that's already there from Adwords and Google Analytics; it just takes that data and shows you how each customer moved through their buyer's journey and attributes those conversions respectively. It provides a single view of the path to purchase to help marketers learn what is actually working compared to what seems to be working,"[262] adds Bain.

Wanamaker would be ecstatic as "marketers can finally begin to answer the age-old question that is typically at the forefront of their minds—is my marketing working?", as Bains puts it[262]

Moving away from the flawed last-click attribution idea, "Google Attribution uses machine learning and data to help marketers measure the impact of each of their marketing touch points, across multiple channels, and across multiple devices."[262] Google Attribution shows users how each customer moves through his or her buyer's journey and attributes those conversions respectively.[262] "It provides a single view of the path to purchase to help marketers learn what is actually working compared to what seems to be working," Bains explains.[262]

As Bains warns[262]:

> *"With last click, the reward for the conversion often went to the last touch point that the user made, often with a sale after a click on an ad. This could lead to false impressions about the effectiveness of an ad campaign versus display ads, organic search, social, email affiliates, and many other interactions that a customer made with a business along the buyer's journey. Maybe organic search is actually more important than*

display ads or vice versa."

"The aim of Google Attribution is to simplify the complex problem of multichannel, multi-device attribution by leveraging data advertisers already have in Google Analytics, AdWords, or DoubleClick Search," adds Kishore Kanakemedela, director of product management at Google.[262]

With Attribution, users can see how effective each step of a campaign is, whether that step is a video ad, a banner ad, a carousel ad, an email, a social campaign, or any other quantifiable digital content.[262] Attribution will show users how these micro-moments worked together to spot leads and drive them to conversions.[262] Marketers will now have much more transparency on what is actually driving their business, which in turn, can help them better allocate their resources between channels[262]; quantifiable success on one channel leads to increased budget spend on that channel, that is until numbers drop off, then reallocation commences.

Location Analytics

Location analytics is a technology that enables firms to capture and analyze location data on customers who are at a physical venue. In his article *How Location Analytics Will Transform Retail[263]*, Tony Costa argues that, "By leveraging connected mobile devices such as smartphones, existing in venue Wi-Fi networks, low cost Bluetooth-enabled beacons, and a handful of other technologies, location analytics vendors have made it possible to get location analytics solutions up and running fast at a minimal cost." "Customer tracking data is typically sent to the location analytics vendor where it is analyzed and accessed via online dashboards that provide actionable data tailored to the needs of specific employees—from the store manager to the executive C-suite," adds Costa.[263]

Already, the scale of data collected by early adopters is venturing into "Big Data" territory. Location analytics firm RetailNext currently "tracks more than 500 million shoppers per year by collecting data from more than 65,000 sensors installed in thousands of retail stores. A single customer visit alone can result in over 10,000 unique data points, not including the data gathered at the point of sale."[263]

RetailNext is not alone; Euclid Analytics—one of the biggest players in this space—"collects six billion customer measurements each day across thousands of locations, and multiple location analytics firms surveyed said they are adding hundreds of new venues each month."[263]

As Costa explains, venue owners are applying insights gathered from location analytics to help in all aspects of their business, including[263]:

1. Design. "After analyzing traffic flows in their stores, a big box retailer realized that less than 10% of customers visiting their shoe department engaged with the self-service wall display where merchandise was stacked. The culprit turned out to be a series of benches placed in front of the wall, limiting customer access."[263] Simply relocating the benches to enhance accessibility increased sales in the department by double digits.[263]

2. Marketing. A restaurant chain wanted to understand whether or not sponsoring a local music festival had a measurable impact on customer visits. After collecting data on 15,000 visitors passing through the festival entrances and comparing it to customers who visited their restaurants two months before and after the festival, they concluded that the festival resulted in 1,300 net new customer visits.[263]

3. Operations. "A grocery store chain used location analytics to understand customer wait times in various departments and check-out registers. This data not only enabled the company to hold managers accountable for wait times, but it gave additional insight into (and justification for) staffing needs."[263]

4. Strategy. A regional clothing chain was concerned that opening an outlet store would cannibalize customers from its main stores. "After analyzing the customer base visiting each store, they discovered that less than 2% of their main store customers visited their outlet. The upside: the outlet gave them access to an entirely new customer base with minimal impact to existing store sales."[263]

Just as web analytics is an essential tool on the web, location analytics will become a must-have for designing, managing, and measuring offline experiences.[263] Location analytics is set to have a profound impact on how businesses operate in the very near future. Costa adds that, "Beyond creating more efficient, effective and meaningful services, firms will begin to rethink the notion of customer value."

Costa argues that having the ability "to identify, track, and target customers in physical locations will enable companies to extend preferential status and rewards to customers based on their behaviors, rewarding them on the number and frequency of visits, where they go in venues, and their exclusive loyalty (i.e., not visiting competitor venues)."[263]

If you want to see where the future of location analytics might be headed, Foursquare's 'Hypertrending' application, which was rolled out at SXSW 2019, would be a good place to start. As Dennis Crowley, executive chairman of Foursquare, explains in his company blob *Introducing Hypertrending, Where 10 Years of Foursquare Has Led Us*[264]:

> *Hypertrending is a top-down view of all the places and phones that Foursquare knows about in Austin. The "Map" view gives*

you a real-time look at how people are spread throughout the city—each dot represents a different place, the size of each dot corresponds to the number of people at each place, and each color represents a different type of place. If you see it on the map, you're seeing it live. The "Top 100" view charts places and events as they trend up or down in busy-ness (based on the number of phones inside those places) while the up/down arrows represent whether that place or event has become more or less busy in the past 30 minutes.

Hypertrending is powered by Foursquare's "Pilgrim" technology, which allows Foursquare to understand how phones move in and out of more than 100 million places around the world.[264] The data in Hypertrending comes from Foursquare's "first-party panel"—"a mix of data from our own apps and other apps that use our technology."[264] As all the data flowing through Hypertrending is anonymized and aggregated, Crowley claims that, "Hypertrending lets you see the movement of the panel population as a whole, without showing you anything about any of the individuals in the panel."[264]

"Foursquare's approach to analytics focuses on visits (not location trails), and aggregated and anonymized data (not individuals' location data)," states Crowley.[264] "Hypertrending only sees phones that are stopped at a specific place (e.g. the convention center, the bar at the Driskill Hotel, Lamberts BBQ), so the map won't show people walking, driving, or otherwise in-between places," explains Crowley.[264] Foursquare also filtered out stops at what it calls 'sensitive' areas, like homes or apartments, religious centers, divorce lawyers' offices, etc.[264] This means users won't see these types of places in Hypertrending.[264]

Foursquare only released Hypertrending during SXSW 2019 and hoped the demo would pique the interest of developers and entrepreneurs, as well as inspire them to build things with the tool.[264] As Crowley explains, "Building city guides and data viz comes naturally to us—but we want to see what the urban planners, the game developers, the folks innovating with AR, etc. would do with a Hypertrending-esque data set."[264]

Conclusion

In this chapter, I wanted to lay out the many ways in which *The A.I. Sports Book* can track and understand its customer base on both a micro and a macro level. Sports books should look to do what Caesars did when its company culture went from a culture of opinion to a culture of data. Many of the analytical models I mention in this chapter have been around for decades and every sports book should be aware that creativity with these models is what will separate them from their competitors and positively affect their bottom line.

With today's IT budgets in the millions of dollar per year, every sports books can afford to buy software that segments its customers, creates marketing campaigns and predicts customer churn, but it's what it does with this information that matters most. Customers want to be wowed and this is not an easy thing to do.

Analytics can be useful for the entire customer journey process, from the initial moment a customer is picked up in a clickstream, through the descriptive analytics process of understanding website traffic, to data mining and diagnostic analytics utilized to understand customer spend. Predictive analytics can help forecast which offers a customer might use, while prescriptive analytics can optimize the sports book's offerings and operation in a multitude of ways.

---

173 Stodder, D. (2012). Customer Analytics in the Age of Social Media. Retrieved from Business Times: http://www.businesstimes.com.sg/archive/monday/sites/businesstimes.com.sg/files/Customer%20Analytics%20in%20the%20Age%20of%20Social%20Media.pdf

174 http://www.webopedia.com/TERM/C/customer_analytics.html

175 IBM. (2013). Achieving Customer Loyalty with Customer Analytics. Retrieved from adma.com: http://www.adma.com.au/assets/Uploads/Downloads/IBM-Achieving-Customer-Loyalty-with-Analytics.pdf

176 Davenport, T. (January 2006). Competing on Analytics. Harvard Business Review.

177 Cognizant. (2014, January). *Retail Analytics: Game Changer for Customer Loyalty.* Retrieved from congnizant.com: http://www.cognizant.com/InsightsWhitepapers/Retail-Analytics-Game-Changer-for-Customer-Loyalty.pdf

178 Peterson, T. (2014, August 13). Facebook Now Tells Whether Mobile Ads Lead to Desktop Purchases. Retrieved from AdAge: http://adage.com/article/digital/facebook-makes-link-mobile-ads-desktop-purchases/294568/

179 Cook, Rick. Control Group Marketing—With or Without CRM Software Systems. crmsearch http://www.crmsearch.com/marketing-control-groups.php (Accessed 19 November 2017).

180 Shearer C., The CRISP-DM model: the new blueprint for data mining, J Data Warehousing (2000); 5:13—22.

181 Harper, Gavin; Stephen D. Pickett (August 2006). "Methods for mining HTS data". Drug Discovery Today. 11 (15–16): 694–699.

182 SAS Institute. Data Mining and the Case for Sampling. http://sceweb.uhcl.edu/boetticher/ML_DataMining/SAS-SEMMA.pdf (Accessed November 21, 2017).

183 SAS, Accenture Applied Intelligence, and Intel, with Forbes Insights. (2018). AI Momentum, Maturity, & Models for Success. sas.com.

184 https://en.wikipedia.org/wiki/Machine_learning (Accessed 20 November 2017).

185 UPS Customer Solutions & Innovations. (2018). Artificial Intelligence in Logistics, a collaborative report by DHL and IBM on implications and use cases for the logistics industry. https://www.logistics.dhl/content/dam/dhl/global/core/documents/pdf/glo-ai-in-logistics-white-paper.pdf (Accessed 29 April 2019).

186   https://www.sas.com/en_us/insights/analytics/deep-learning.html   (Accessed   4 January 2019).

187 Krizhevsky, Alex; Sutskever, Ilya; Hinton, Geoffrey. (2012). ImageNet Classification with Deep Convolutional Neural Networks. NIPS 2012: Neural Information Processing Systems, Lake Tahoe, Nevada.

188 Jaokar, Ajit. (2017). Twelve Types of Artificial Intelligence (AI) Problems. 5 January 2017.   https://www.datasciencecentral.com/profiles/blogs/twelve-types-of-artificial-intelligence-ai-problems (Accessed 7 October 2018).

189 Vogel, Dirk. (6 September 2017). 5 Ways AI Will Boost Personalization in Digital Marketing. Selligent. https://www.selligent.com/blog/contextual-marketing/5-ways-ai-will-boost-personalization-in-digital-marketing (Accessed 24 October 2017).

190 Johnson, Lauren. 2017. Pinterest Is Offering Brands Its Visual Search Technology To Score   Large   Ad   Deals.   Adweek.   October   2,   2017. http://www.adweek.com/digital/pinterest-is-offering-brands-its-visual-search-technology-to-score-large-ad-deals/ (Accessed 18 November 2017).

191 Krizhevsky, Alex; Sutskever, Ilya; Hinton, Geoffry. (2012). ImageNet Classification with Deep Convolutional Neural Networks. NIPS 2012: Neural Information Processing Systems, Lake Tahoe, Nevada.

192 Liu, Baige, Zang, Xiaoxue. (2017). Caffe2 vs. TensorFlow: Which is a Better Deep Learning   Framework?   Stanford   University. http://cs242.stanford.edu/assets/projects/2017/liubaige-xzang.pdf (Accessed 1 May 2018).

193 Metz, Gade. (2015). Google Just Open Sourced TensorFlow, its Artificial Intelligence Engine. Wired.com. 9 November 2015. https://www.wired.com/2015/11/google-open-sources-its-artificial-intelligence-engine/ (Accessed 1 May 2018).

194 Deeplearning4j.org. Comparing Top Deep Learning Frameworks: Deeplearning4J, PyTorch,   TensorFlow,   Caffe,   Kera,   MxNet,   Gluon   &   CNTK. https://deeplearning4j.org/compare-dl4j-tensorflow-pytorch (Accessed 3 May 2018).

195 Novet, Jordan. (2017). Facebook Open Sources Caffe2, a New Deep Learning Framework.   Venturebeat.   18   April   2017. https://venturebeat.com/2017/04/18/facebook-open-sources-caffe2-a-new-deep-learning-framework/ (Accessed 1 May 2018).

196 Liu, Baige, Zang, Xiaoxue. (2017). Caffe2 vs. TensorFlow: Which is a Better Deep Learning   Framework?   Stanford   University. http://cs242.stanford.edu/assets/projects/2017/liubaige-xzang.pdf (Accessed 1 May 2018).

197 Sutton, Scott. 2011. Patron Analytics In the Casino and Gaming Industry: How the House Always Wins. SAS. http://support.sas.com/resources/papers/proceedings11/379-2011.pdf

198   Nyce,   Charles.   2007.   Predictive   Analytics   White   Paper. https://www.scribd.com/document/200505883/Predictive-Analytics-White-Paper

199 https://en.wikipedia.org/wiki/Prescriptive_analytics

200 Profitect. Prescriptive Analytics Makes Waves with Retail & CPG. https://bbc604576ecf2bcb1563-2fd6af82f3627aa26d05cd090ce38fd1.ssl.cf5.rackcdn.com/profitect-1-422FA4M.PDF (accessed 26 October 2017).

201 Liebowitz, Jay. (2015). Business Analytics. Suerbach Publications. September 15, 2015.

202 How Predictive Analytics is Changing the Retail Industry. International Conference on Management and Information Systems. September 23-24, 2016. http://www.icmis.net/icmis16/ICMIS16CD/pdf/S154.pdf

203 https://en.wikipedia.org/wiki/Decision_tree

204 https://www.lucidchart.com/pages/decision-tree (Accessed 22 January 2018).

205 Deng, L., Gao, J., Vuppalapatie, C. Building a Big Data Analytics Service Framework for Mobile Advertising and Marketing. March 2015. https://www.researchgate.net/profile/Jerry_Gao/publication/273635443_Building_a_Bi g_Data_Analytics_Service_Framework_for_Mobile_Advertising_and_Marketing/links/5 508de220cf26ff55f840c31.pdf

206 Telgarsky, Matus, and Andrea Vattani. "Hartigan's Method: k-means Clustering without Voronoi." *AISTATS*. 2010.

207 Hartigan, J.A., Wong, M.A. A *K*-Means Clustering Algorithm. Journal of the Royal Statistical Society. Series C (Applied Statistics), Vol. 28, No. 1 (1979) http://www.cs.otago.ac.nz/cosc430/hartigan_1979_kmeans.pdf

208 Pierson, Lillian. Solving Real-World Problems with Nearest Neighbor Algorithms. www.dummies.com. http://www.dummies.com/programming/big-data/data-science/solving-real-world-problems-with-nearest-neighbor-algorithms/

209 https://en.wikipedia.org/wiki/Logistic_regression

210 Karp, A. H. (2009). Using Logistic Regression To Predict Customer Retention. New York. Sierra Information Service, Inc. http://www.lexjansen.com/nesug/nesug98/solu/p095.pdf

211 Siroker, Dan, Koomen, Pete. *A/B Testing: The Most Powerful Way to Turn Clicks Into Customers*. Google Books.

212 Imdadullah, Muhammad, December 27, 2013. Time Series Analysis and Forecasting. http://itfeature.com/time-series-analysis-and-forecasting/time-series-analysis-forecasting

213 Sang, Hyuck Kim, Dong Jin Kim. March 23, 2016 Determining Revenue-Generating Casino Visitors Using a Vector Autoregressive Model: The Case of the G Casino in Korea. *Journal of Quality Assurance in* Hospitality & Tourism.

214 Singh Y, Chauhan AS. Neural Networks in Data Mining. Journal of Theoretical and Applied Information Technology. 2009; 5:37-42 http://jatit.org/volumes/research-papers/Vol5No1/1Vol5No6.pdf (Accessed 20 November 2017).

215 Goa, Jim. Machine Learning Applications for Data Center Optimization. https://static.googleusercontent.com/media/www.google.com/en//about/datacenters/ efficiency/internal/assets/machine-learning-applicationsfor-datacenter-optimization-finalv2.pdf (Accessed 20 November 2017).

216 Greene, Tristan. (2018). A Beginner's Guide to AI: Neural Networks. The Next Web. July 2018. https://thenextweb.com/artificial-intelligence/2018/07/03/a-beginners-guide-to-ai-neural-networks/ (Accessed 13 August 2018).

217 Butterfield, Brett. (2018). Adobe. See It, Search It, Shop It: How AI is Powering Visual Search. 12 December 2018. https://theblog.adobe.com/see-it-search-it-shop-it-how-ai-is-powering-visual-search/ (Accessed 20 January 2019).

218 Quach, Katyanna. (2017). How DeepMind's AlphaGo Zero learned all by itself to trash world champ AI AlphaGo. The Register. 18 October 2017. https://www.theregister.co.uk/2017/10/18/deepminds_latest_alphago_software_does nt_need_human_data_to_win/ (Accessed 21 January 2018).

219 Somers, James. (2017) MIT Technology Review. Is AI Riding a One-Trick Pony? 29 September 2017. https://www.technologyreview.com/s/608911/is-ai-riding-a-one-trick-pony/ (Accessed 8 January 2019).

220 https://en.wikipedia.org/wiki/Survival_analysis

221 Peister, Clayton. 2007. Table-games revenue management: Apply- ing survival analysis. Cornell Hotel and Restaurant Administration Quarterly 48 (1): 70-87.

222 Gupta, Sunil, Lehmann, Donald R., and Stuart, Jennifer Ames. (2004), Valuing Customers. *Journal of Marketing Research*, 41(1), 7-18.

223 Ascarza, Neslin, Netzer & Lemmens, A. (2017). In pursuit of enhanced customer retention management: Review, key issues, and future directions. Customer needs and solutions, 1-17. DOI: 10.1007%2Fs40547-017-0080-0#citeas.

224 Handley, Lucy (2013). Customer Retention: Brave New World of Consumer Dynamics. Marketing Week Online Edition, 21. March 20, 2013.

225 Forbes Insight. (2014). Company struggling to win customers for life, says new study by Forbes Insight and Sitecore. https://www.forbes.com/sites/forbespr/2014/09/10/companies-struggling-to-win-customers-for-life-says-new-study-by-forbes-insights-and-sitecore/#6c4d57741407 (Accessed 21 April 2018).

226 Springer, Tom, Kim, Charles, Azzarello, Domenico, and Melton, Jeff. (2014). Service Quality: The Impact of Frequency, Timing, Proximity, and Sequence of Failures and Delights. Journal of Marketing, 78(1), 41-58.

227 Lewis, Michael. (2005). Incorporating Strategic Consumer Behavior into Customer Valuation. Journal of Marketing, 69(4), 230-238.

228 Blattberg, Robert C., Getz, Gary, and Thomas, Jacqueline S. (2001). Customer Equity: Building and Managing Relationships as Valuable Assets, Boston, MA: Harvard Business Press.

229 Benedek, Gabor, Lubloy, Agnes, Vastag, Yule. (2014). The Importance of Social Embededness: Churn Models at Mobile Providers. Decision Sciences, 45(1), 175-201.

230 Nitzan, Irit, Libai, Barak. (2011). Social Effects of Customer Retention. Journal of Marketing, 75(6), 24-38.

231 Verbeke, Wouter Martens, David, Mues, Christopher, and Baesens, Bart. (2011). Building Comprehensive Customer Churn Predictions Models with Advanced Rule Induction Techniques. Expert Systems with Applications, 38(3), 2354-2364.

232 Ascarza, Eva, Ebbes, Peter, Netzer, Oded, and Danielson, Matt. (2017). Beyond the Target Customer: Social Effects of CRM Campaigns. Journal of Marketing Research: June 2017, Vol. 54, No. 3, pp. 347-363.

233 Provost, Foster, Dalessandro, Brian, Hook, Rod, Zhang, Xianhan, and Murray, Alan. (2009). Audience Selection for On-line Brand Advertising: Privacy-friendly Social Network Targeting. In Proceedings of the Fifteenth ACM SIGKDD International Conference on Knowledge Discovery and Data Mining, 707-716.

234 Perlich, Claudia, Delessandro, Brian, Stitelman, Ori, Raeder, Troy, and Provost, Foster. (2014). Machine Learning for Targeted Display Advertising: Transfer Leaning in Action. Machine Learning 95(1), 103-127.

235 Martens, David, Provost, Foster, Clark, Jessica, de Fortuny, Enric Junque. (2016). Mining Massive Fine-Grained Behavior Data to Improve Predictive Analytics. MIS Quarterly, 40(4) 869-888.

236 Ascarza, Eva. (2016). Retention Futility: Targeting High Risk Customers Might Be Ineffective. Social Sciences Research Network 2759170.

https://papers.ssrn.com/sol3/papers.cfm?abstract_id=2759170 (Accessed 22 April 2018).

237 Provost, Foster, and Fawcett, Tom. (2013). Data Science for Business: What You Need To Know About Data Mining and Data Analytic Thinking. O'Reilly Media, 2013.

238 Guelman, Leo, Montserrat Guillen, and Ana M. Pérez-Marín. 2012. Random forests for uplift modeling: An insurance customer retention case. In Modeling and Simulation in Engineering, Economics and Management. Springer, pp. 123–33.

239 Athey, Susan and Imbens, Guido W. (2016). Recursive partitioning for heterogeneous causal effects. PNAS 113(27), 7353-7360.

240 Lemmens, Aurélie, and Gupta, Sunil. (2013). Managing Churn to Maximize Profits. Harvard Business School (working paper).

241 Berson, Alex, Smith, Stepthen, and Thearling, Kurt. (2000). Building Data Applications for CRM. New York, NY. McGraw-Hill.

242 Ascarza, Eva, Iyengar, Raghuram, and Schleicher, Martin. (2016). The Perils of Proactive Churn Prevention Using Plan Recommendations: Evidence from a Field Experiment. Journal of Marketing Research, 52(1), 46-60.

243 Giudicati, Gianna, Massimo Riccaboni, and Anna Romiti (2013), "Experience, Socialization and Customer Retention: Lessons from the Dance Floor," Marketing Letters, 24(4), 409–422.

244 Haelein, Michael, and Libai, Barak. (2013). Targeting Revenue Leaders for a New Product. Journal of Marketing, 77(3), 65-80.

245 Hogan, John E., Katherine N. Lemon, and Barak Libai (2003), What Is the True Value of a Lost Customer? Journal of Service Research, 5(3), 196–208.

246 Schrift, Rom Y., and Parker, Jeffrey R. (2014). Staying the Course: The Option of Doing Nothing and Its Impact on Postchoice Persistence. Psychological Science, 25, 3, 772–780.

247 Oliver, Richard L., Rust, Roland T., and Vaarki, Sajeev. (1997). Customer Delight: Foundations, Findings, and Managerial Insight. Journal of Retailing, 73(3), 311–336.

248 Blattberg, Robert C., Kim, Byung-Do, and Neslin, Scott A. (2008). Database Marketing: Analyzing and Managing Customers, New York, NY: Springer.

249 Castanedo, Federico, Valverde, Gabriel, Zaratiegui, Jamie and Vazquez, Alfonso. 2014. Using Deep Learning to Predict Customer Churn in a Mobile Telecommunication Network. www.wiseathena.com/pdf/wa_dl.pdf (accessed 22 April 2018).

250 Wang, Jianqiang C. and Hastie, Trevor. 2014. Boosted Varying-Coefficient Regression Models for Product Demand Prediction. Journal of Computational and Graphical Statistics, 23(2), 361–382.

251 Lemmens, Aurélie, and Croux, Christophe. (2006). Bagging and Boosting Classification Trees to Predict Churn. Journal of Marketing Research, 43(2), 276–286.

252 Tibshirani, Robert J. (1996). Regression Shrinkage and Selection via the Lasso. Journal of the Royal Statistical Society. Series B (Methodological), 267–288.

253 Zou, Hui and Hao Helen Zhang (2009). On the Adaptive Elastic-net with a Diverging Number of Parameters. Annals of statistics, 37(4), 1733–1751.

254 Crammer, Koby., Kulesza, Alex and Dredze, Mark. (2009). Adaptive Regularization of Weight Vectors. Advances in Neural Information Processing Systems, 22, 414–422.

255 Zou, Hui, and Trevor Hastie (2005), "Regularization and Variable Selection via the Elastic Net. Journal of the Royal Statistical Society: Series B (Statistical Methodology), 67(2), 301–320.

256 Simon, Noah, Friedman, Jerome, Hastie, Trevor and Tibshirani, Rob. (2011). Regularization Paths for Cox's Proportional Hazards Model via Coordinate Descent. Journal of Statistical Software, 39(5), 1–13

257 Patrick McGarry. Why Edge Computing Is Here to Stay: Five Use Cases. https://www.rtinsights.com/why-edge-computing-is-here-to-stay-five-use-cases/

258 Hicks, Z. (2013, August 28). Toyota Goes All-in With Social Media Monitoring. Retrieved from CIO.com: http://www.cio.com/article/2383143/social-media/toyota-goes-all-in-with-social-media-monitoring.html

259 Mullich, J. (2012, December 10). *Opposition Research: Sentiment Analysis as a Competitive Marketing Tool.* Retrieved from Wellesley Information Services: http://data-informed.com/opposition-research-sentiment-analysis-as-a-competitive-marketing-tool/

260 Borreau, Marc, de Streel, Alexandre, and Graef, Inge. (2017). Big Data and Competition Policy: Market power, personalised pricing and advertising. Centre on Regulation in Europe. 16 February 2017. http://www.crid.be/pdf/public/8122.pdf (Accessed January 25, 2017).

261 Greenberg, Paul. March 31, 2014. Is Adobe a Marketing Player Now? http://www.zdnet.com/article/is-adobe-a-marketing-player-now/

262 Bains, Matthew. (July 28, 2017) . Search Influence. http://www.searchinfluence.com/2017/07/google-attribution-allows-clear-seamless-campaign-analysis-for-marketers/ (accessed 25 August 2017).

263 Costa, T. (2014, March 12). *How Location Analytics Will Transform Retail.* Retrieved from Harvard Business Review: http://blogs.hbr.org/2014/03/how-location-analytics-will-transform-retail/

264 Crowley, Dennis. Foursquare.com. Introducing Hypertrending. March 8, 2019. https://enterprise.foursquare.com/intersections/article/introducing-hypertrending/ (Accessed 21 August 2019).

CHAPTER THREE

Marketing

"Personalization is table stakes for today's retailers, who are increasingly competing to be relevant in the hearts and minds of shoppers."

~Giselle Abramovich, Adobe

Overview

One of the recurring themes of this book is self-reliance. I'm trying to lay out a case for sports books to become much more self-reliant than they currently are. Software companies are providing the tools for sports book to become self-sufficient in areas like CRM, SEO, marketing, website personalization, social media, even programmatic advertising.

Today's advertising environment is nothing like the advertising environment of just a few short years ago, as Dan Woods showed in his amusing comparison of the differing environments that marketers face today as compared to what their 1980s counterparts might have faced back then.[36] Right now, there is a radical realignment going on in the advertising industry. As Derek Thompson points out in his *The Atlantic* article *The Media's Post-Advertising Future Is Also Its Past[265]*, it might be tempting to blame media's advertiser problem and the current state of its demise as the inevitable end game of the Google and Facebook's duopoly because the two companies already receive more than half of all the dollars spent on digital advertising, as well as command 90 percent of the growth in digital ad sales in 2017[266]. However, what's happening in media right now is more complex, Thompson argues.[265] He sees the convergence of the following four trends[265]:

1. Too many players.
2. Not enough saviors.
3. No clear playbook.
4. Patrons with varying levels of beneficence.

It isn't just Facebook and Google, Thompson states[265], adding that, "just about every big tech company is talking about selling ads, meaning that just about every big tech company may become another competitor in the fight for advertising revenue."[265]

"Amazon's ad business exploded in the past year; its growth exceeded that of every other major tech company, including the duopoly," notes Thompson.[265] Wanting to move beyond just selling people iPhones, Apple is shifting its growth strategy to selling services not just phones.[267] Meanwhile, "Microsoft will make about $4 billion in advertising revenue this year, thanks to growth from LinkedIn and Bing."[265] "AT&T is building an ad network to go along with its investment in Time Warner's content, and Roku, which sells equipment for streaming television, is building ad tech," adds Thompson.[265]

As Sara Fischer explains in her article *The Next Big TV Tech Platform: Roku*[268], "Roku, the connected TV hardware company, is quietly building a large software business, driven mostly by advertising revenue." Fischer adds: "Roku typically doesn't sell advertising through an open exchange (open bidding system), like some of the big tech companies do, but it does use programmatic infrastructure to digitally target those ads—a tactic commonly referred to as 'programmatic direct' or 'programmatic reserved.'"[268]

At the Adobe Summit in March 2019, Adobe announced[269] a new partnership with Roku that would help advertisers engage with Roku's 27 million OTT viewers. These kinds of deals, which allow businesses to directly connect with consumers are the wave of the future. According to *Adweek*, "marketers can now use elements of the Adobe Advertising Cloud to match their own audience data with Roku's in a way that provides an unprecedented degree of targeting granularity for those eager to engage with the streaming provider's 27 million viewers."[269]

"Keith Eadie, VP and general manager of Adobe Advertising Cloud, said the partnership would enable advertisers to better manage elements of their cross-screen campaigns such as frequency capping and that it would also help them to better measure the outcomes of their media buys on OTT—the fastest-growing channel on the Adobe media buying platform."[269]

Meanwhile, Scott Rosenberg, general manager, business platform, Roku, added, "Programmatic trading is already a material part of our business, but it is still a minority but some of that is a function of the fact that TV marketers are not by and large as yet trading programmatically."[269]

This is because the majority of TV ad space is still traded manually, rather than programmatically. However, Rosenberg explained to *Adweek* that "this is about to change. 'Programmatic is not the predominant methodology for TV marketers, but it's coming in strong … this partnership is so important because one of the friction points, that holds programmatic trading of OTT back is scale.'"

The standard ad business methodology is also rapidly evolving. As Sara Fischer points out in her *Axios* article *How Media Companies Lost the Advertising Business*[270], the great irony is that "many of the tech companies began with an aversion to advertising, fearing it would be a disruption towards the consumer experience." Fischer notes that Google initially feared that advertising-based search engines were "inherently biased towards the advertisers and away from the needs of consumers."[270] "Facebook CEO Mark Zuckerberg reportedly only accepted advertising on his platform initially so he could pay the bills."[270] "Snapchat boss Evan Spiegel initially criticized some targeted ads as 'creepy,' but four years later, 90% of the ads sold on Snap's platform are sold in an automated fashion."[270]

Today, most tech companies are embracing the advertising model in one form or another. Fischer adds that, "Some publishers are banding together to offer marketers to [sic] cheaper advertising against traditional media content at scale." Fischer's examples include[270]:

- Several digital websites, such as Quartz, New York Media, PopSugar and Rolling Stone are all joining Concert, a digital advertising marketplace operator whose stated goal is to combat the tech giants' ad dominance.
- News Corp launched a global digital ad network in 2018 called News IQ, which will pull audience data from sites like *The Wall Street Journal*, *New York Post* and *Barron's*, as well as give advertisers a way to reach highly specific audiences.
- AT&T is hoping to create a similar type of ad network through its Time Warner partnership, with plans to bring on other media and technology partners in time.
- Disney and Verizon are looking into building their own ad networks.

Fischer adds that, "It's not just tech firms, but retail and consumer package goods companies, too. Ad-serving has become so democratized that any company with an audience is now able to steal advertising dollars away from traditional media companies. Kroger has an ad business and so does its grocery rival Albertsons. Target has a media network and so does Walmart."[270]

Thompson notes that, "These tech companies have bigger audiences and more data than just about any media company could ever hope for. The result is that more advertising will gravitate not only toward 'programmatic' artificial-intelligence-driven ad sales but also toward companies that aren't principally (or even remotely) in the news-gathering business."[265]

In his *Where Did All the Advertising Jobs Go?*[271] Derek Thompson explains that, "The emergence of an advertising duopoly has coincided with the rise of 'programmatic advertising,' a torpid term that essentially means 'companies using algorithms to buy and place ads in those little boxes all over the internet.'" Thompson adds that, "advertising has long been a relationship-driven business, in which multimillion-dollar contracts are hammered out over one-on-one meetings, countless lunches, and even more-countless drinks. With programmatic technology, however, companies can buy access to specific audiences across several publishing platforms at once, bypassing the work of building relationships with each one."[271] Because advertising has become more automated, more ads can be produced with fewer people.[271] AI needs be a part of this programmatic advertising process because it could become overwhelming otherwise.

In her article *Experts Weight in On the Future of Advertising*[272], Giselle Abramovich quotes Keith Eadie, VP and GM of Adobe Advertising Cloud, who argues that, "Programmatic advertising is no longer a silo or a distinct media channel—it's simply how brands are buying ads." "As a result," Eadie says, "the focus is shifting from execution to strategy and better connecting marketing and advertising."[272]

"With programmatic, the big lure for advertisers is its efficiency, according to Amy Avery, Droga5's chief intelligence officer."[272] "But it also needs to be about effectiveness, too," Avery argues.[272] "I don't think we will ever go to 100% [programmatic ad buying]. But I do think it can increase to much more than it is now once the effectiveness variables come into play."[272] Avery believes this will happen once AI is integrated to help understand context and uses this information to inform messaging.[272]

Eadie believes the $70 billion TV advertising market is a great example of progress on this front.[272] Specifically, NBCUniversal recently "made its full portfolio of broadcast and cable television available to advertisers through a DSP, essentially automating ad buying for its TV market."[272]

"The old story about programmatic advertising was that both marketers and digital publishers—think AOL, or any news site—embraced the technology, as it allowed companies to cheaply target specific audiences on a budget," explains Thompson.[271] However, Thompson notes that, "the new reality is that programmatic advertising has placed many advertisements in controversial places, next to low-quality news sources or outright offensive content."[271] This has caused marketers to both cut back on running programmatic ad campaigns, as well as bringing their operations in-house, where they have more control over both who sees their ads and where they are seen.[271] "The upshot," Thompson concludes is that, "Programmatic ads have been a double blow to media agencies, first automating their function and then encouraging companies to insource the work."[271]

Becoming more self-sufficient may not be a bad thing for typical sports betting brand marketers. Throughout this book I try to make the argument that marketing departments should be more self-reliant. Software that does everything from automating marketing campaigns, to inexpensively segmenting customers, to simplifying the mundane and repetitive processes of producing and categorizing content can help marketers speed up the creative process enormously.

Thompson argues that currently there is a "merging of the advertising and entertainment businesses."[271] "As smartphone screens have edged out TV as the most important real estate for media, companies have invested more in 'branded content'—corporate-sponsored media, such as an article or video, that resembles traditional entertainment more than it does traditional advertising."[271] Thompson concludes that, "In short, the future of the advertising business is being moved to technology companies managing ad networks and media companies making branded content—that is, away from the ad agencies."[271] These are cross-currents that brands need to be aware of because they are not just radically changing the marketing landscape but also offering huge marketing opportunities to brands willing to embrace them.

If software products can alleviate the mundane and repetitive tasks humans are currently doing—and they most definitely can—then businesses can redeploy their staff to handle the more interesting and probably profitable work, like programmatic functions.

According to Lewnes and Keller, "Perceived value—especially with complex technological products—can be difficult for customers to assess."[16] "Formally, perceived value is all the different benefits gained by customers from purchasing and using a product as well as all the different costs saved. These are not just financial benefits and costs but also psychological, social, emotional, and other types of benefits and costs," claim Lewnes and Keller.[16] For the writers, "Value creation is only necessary, but not sufficient, for marketing success. Value must also be effectively and efficiently communicated and delivered."[16]

Psychology of Personalization

So, what does personalization really mean? It is a word that has been kicking around the marketing community for at least a decade or two now. The underlying psychology of the individual being marketed to is one of the key elements of personalization marketing. In his Buffer article *15 Psychological Studies That Will Boost Your Social Media Marketing*[273], Kevan Lee lists several psychological techniques that marketers should be using to reach today's audience. Lee's list is as follows[273]:

1. The endowment effect—the hypothesis that people ascribe more value to things merely because they own them.[274]
2. Reciprocity—in social psychology, reciprocity is a social norm of responding to a positive action with another positive action, rewarding kind actions.[275]
3. Consistency principle—People like to be consistent with the things they have previously said or done.[276]
4. Foot-in-the-door technique—"a strategy used to persuade people to agree to a particular action, based on the idea that if a respondent will comply with a small initial request then they will be more likely to agree

to a later, more significant, request, which they would not have agreed to had they been asked it outright."[277]

5. Framing effect—a cognitive bias where people decide on options based on if the options are presented with positive or negative semantics; e.g. as a personal loss or gain.[278]

6. Loss aversion—the disutility of giving up an object is greater than the utility associated with acquiring it, i.e., you're leery of giving something up once you have it, as compared to seeing that something as gain if you don't have it in the first place.[279]

7. Conformity and social influence—the theory that people will conform their ideas to the ideas of a group under social pressure.[280]

8. Acquiescence effect—a tendency to respond in the affirmative to survey items irrespective of substantive content.[281]

9. Mere exposure effect—the more often a person sees something new, the more positive meaning they will give it.[273]

10. Informational social influence—social influence occurs when a person's emotions, opinions or behaviors are affected by others intentionally or unintentionally.

11. The decoy effect—the phenomenon whereby consumers will tend to have a specific change in preference between two options when also presented with a third option that is asymmetrically dominated.[282]

12. Buffer effect or social support—the process in which a psychosocial resource reduces the impact of life stress on psychological well-being.[283]

13. Propinquity effect—the tendency for people to form friendships or romantic relationships with those whom they encounter often, forming a bond between subject and friend.[284]

14. Availability heuristic—"a mental shortcut that relies on immediate examples that come to a given person's mind when evaluating a specific topic, concept, method or decision."[285]

15. Scarcity principle—"economic theory in which a limited supply of a good, coupled with a high demand for that good, results in a mismatch between the desired supply and demand equilibrium."[286]

Throughout the rest of this chapter, I will break down the 15 principles that can be utilized by sports book marketers. In the ensuing chapters, I will dive deeper into how technology and psychology can be used together to increase personalization.

The endowment effect was revealed in a famous study from Duke University, which discovered that students who had won some coveted basketball tickets in a raffle valued the tickets at $2,400, while those who had not won the tickets would only agree to pay $170 for them.[273]

The marketing takeaway here is that a brand's customers will attribute a higher value to things they already own.[273] Sports books should try to increase their customer's ownership in their products by encouraging feedback and making it easier to upload suggestions and comments through social media.[273]

In terms of reciprocity, a 2002 research found that "waiters could increase tips with a tiny bit of reciprocity."[273] Tips rose by 3 percent when diners were given an after-dinner mint, but went up to 20 percent, when the server delivered the mint while looking the customers in the eye and telling them the mint was specifically for them.[273]

In another example, "BYU sociologist Phillip Kunz sent Christmas cards to 600 completely random strangers. He received 200 Christmas cards back in response."[273]

The consistency principle was displayed in a study where "Princeton researchers asked people if they would volunteer to help with the American Cancer Society. Of those who received a cold call, 4 percent agreed. A second group was called a few days prior and asked if they would hypothetically volunteer for the American Cancer Society. When the actual request came later, 31 percent agreed."[273]

The marketing takeaway here is for sports books to "help current customers and potential users create an expectation of what they may say or do. For instance, get users to opt-in to a marketing course and offer tools at the end that are used by expert marketers. Subscribers may wish to stay consistent with their stated goal of improving their marketing, and signing up for recommended tools will fall right in line with this expectation."[273]

According to Lee, "The first study on the foot-in-the-door method was performed in the 1960s by Jonathan Freedman and Scott Faser."[273] Researchers called several homemakers to inquire about the household products they used.[273] Three days later, the researchers called again, this time asking to send a group of workers to the house to manually note the cleaning products in the home. The research found that "the women who responded to the first phone interview were two times more likely to respond to the second request."[273]

The marketing takeaway here: provide strong enough content that customers will be motivated to frequently open your brand emails, as well as download your content or generally go along with your requests.[273] The more little things they do, the more likely they are to comply with a larger request, like sharing your content and inviting their friends to join in the brand conversation.[273]

Researchers Amos Tverksy and Nobel prize winning Daniel Kahneman found the way they framed a question was more important than the question itself.[273] The researchers "polled two different groups of participants on which of two treatments they would choose for people infected with a deadly disease.

- Treatment A: '200 people will be saved.'

- Treatment B: 'a one-third probability of saving all 600 lives, and a two-thirds probability of saving no one.'[273]

The majority of participants picked Treatment A because of the clear and simple gain in saving lives. However, in Group 2, participants were told the following:

- Treatment A: '400 people will die.'
- Treatment B: 'a one-third probability that no one will die, and a two-thirds probability that 600 people will die.'[273]

According to Lee, "The majority of participants picked Treatment B because of the clear negative effect of Treatment A."[273]

The marketing takeaway here is that the "words you use and the way you frame your content has a direct impact on how your readers will react."[273] Lee recommends that, whenever possible, brands "frame things in a positive light so that readers can see a clear gain."[273]

According to Decision Lab, "The framing effect has consistently proven to be one of the strongest biases in decision making. The ways in which framing can be used are nearly unlimited; from emotional appeals to social pressure to priming."[287]

When a positive frame is presented people are more likely to avoid risks but will be risk-seeking when a negative frame is presented. The effect does seem to increase with age, which could be highly important when designing health and financial policies, as well as marketing to an older audience.[287]

In a famous loss aversion study, several Chicago Heights teachers were split into two groups.[273] "One group of teachers stood to receive bonuses based on the performance of their students on standardized testing. Another group received their bonus at the beginning of the year and stood to either keep it or lose it based on the results of their students' tests," explains Lee.[273] The results showed that "the prepaid bonuses—the ones that could have been lost—had a bigger impact on teachers."[273]

The marketing takeaway here is that brands need to discover their customer's challenges and reservations, and then try to alleviate those concerns up front.[273] "Risk-free trials and money-back guarantees are one way to deal with loss aversion," argues Lee, since it removes the fear of loss from the equation.[273]

In 1951, social psychologist Solomon Asch conducted an experiment to investigate whether an individual would conform under social pressure.[280] As detailed in Saul McLeod *Solomon Asch—Conformity Experiment*[280], Solomon Asch experimented on 50 male students from Swarthmore College to study whether they would allow peer pressure to affect their judgment. "Using a line judgment task, Asch put a naive participant in a room with seven confederates/stooges. The confederates had agreed in advance what their responses would be when presented with the line task."[280]

According to McLeod, "The real participant did not know this and was led to believe that the other seven confederates/stooges were also real participants like themselves."[280] "Each person in the room had to state aloud which comparison line (A, B or C) was most like the target line. The answer was always obvious. The real participant sat at the end of the row and gave his or her answer last."[280]

In 12 of the 18 trials, the confederates gave the wrong answer.[280] "On average, about one third (32%) of the participants who were placed in this situation went along and conformed with the clearly incorrect majority on the critical trials," says McLeod.[280]

After the test, the subjects were asked why they conformed and most of them "said that they did not really believe their conforming answers, but had gone along with the group for fear of being ridiculed or thought 'peculiar.'"[280] Asch concluded that, "Apparently, people conform for two main reasons: because they want to fit in with the group (normative influence) and because they believe the group is better informed than they are (informational influence)."[280] The key takeaway for marketers here is that, "influencers and industry leaders can help your product appear more valuable to others."[273]

According to the psychology website Changing Minds[288] there are three scenarios in which we are most likely to acquiesce to the request of others:

- They seem to be a superior in some way.
- They have a need whereby we can easily help them.
- Answering the question fully seems like hard work.

Lee states that, "Leading questions are one way that the acquiescence effect impacts the answers that one gives."[273]

The marketing takeaway here is that brands should be aware of the leading questions they may be asking in customer development calls, surveys, or questionnaires.[273] "People can be easily swayed to answer in a certain way if the question seems tilted in a certain direction," warns—and recommends—Lee.[273]

Robert Zajonc's Chinese character study showed how the mere exposure to something could increase positive feelings about it. Zajonc showed several Chinese characters to non-Chinese-speaking participants, either once or up to 25 times, then asked the participants to guess the meaning of the characters.[273] The study revealed that the "more often a participant saw a character, the more positive meaning they gave."[273]

The marketing takeaway here is brands shouldn't be afraid to repeat their messaging.[273] Social media is the perfect channel for brands to share their content, as reposting helpful content can have a direct impact on an audience.[273]

The repetition seen here probably goes unnoticed because customers can easily surf away from a brand's messaging by visiting other social media pages and/or websites.

In an effort to curtail energy usage, Alex Lasky of Opower ran an experiment to study how messaging could best encourage others to save energy.[289] Opower sent customers one of the following four messages[273]:

- You can save $54 this month.
- You can save the planet.
- You can be a good citizen.
- Your neighbors are doing better than you.

Only the fourth message worked, leading to a 2 percent reduction in household energy usage.[273] The study showed that brands should use the experience of others to help people see the benefits of their product or services.[273] There's a close correlation between informational social influence and social proof.[273]

The decoy effect can be seen in an old subscription advertisement for *The Economist*, which stated[273]:

- Web Subscription – $59
- Print Subscription – $125
- Web and Print Subscription – $125

When Professor Dan Ariely tested this model with his students at MIT, he asked them to choose a subscription option among the three choices.[273] The results were as follows[273]:

- Web Subscription – $59 (16 students)
- Print Subscription – $125 (0 students)
- Web and Print Subscription – $125 (84 students)
- *Total revenue: $11,444*

When the print subscription was removed, the results looked like this[273]:

- Web Subscription – $59 (68 students)
- Web and Print Subscription – $125 (32 students)
- *Total revenue: $8,012*

Obviously, adding the decoy increases sales and the marketing takeaway is for brands to add a decoy in their pricing.[273] Lee concludes that, "The inclusion of an option that is 'asymmetrically dominated' (a plan that seems out of whack or a feature list that doesn't quite add up) will make the other options more appealing."[273]

In terms of the buffer effect, in a study of pregnant women, "researchers found that 91 percent of those with high stress and low social support suffered complications whereas only 33 percent of pregnant women with high stress and high social support suffered complications."

The marketing takeaway here is for brands to be consistent with availability and support for their customers.[273] "Constant support—in the form of email communication, blogging, in-app messages etc.—may help others feel more comfortable and less stressed," advises Lee.[273]

For the propinquity effect, researchers discovered that "tenants in a small two-floor apartment had closer friendships with their immediate neighbors. Least likely friendships were between those on separate floors. And tenants who lived near staircases and mailboxes had friendships on both floors."[273]

The marketing takeaway here is for brands to be a constant presence on social media, as well as in the inbox of its customers and subscribers.[273]

In the late 1960s, Amos Tversky and Daniel Kahneman began their work on "heuristic and biases." [285] They discovered "that judgment under uncertainty often relies on a limited number of simplifying heuristics rather than extensive algorithmic processing."[285] Tversky and Kahneman coined the term "availability heuristic" to explain these biases. According to Wikipedia, an "availability heuristic is a mental shortcut that relies on immediate examples that come to a given person's mind when evaluating a specific topic, concept, method or decision. As follows, people tend to use a readily available fact to base their beliefs about a comparably distant concept."[285]

In their *New Yorker* article, *The Two Friends Who Changed How We Think About How We Think*[290], Cass Sunstein and Richard Thaler explain that there were two distinct themes in the work of Tverksy and Kahneman – judgment and decision-making. "Judgment is about estimating (or guessing) magnitudes and probabilities. *How likely is it that a billionaire businessman from New York with no experience in government gets elected President?* Decision-making is about how we choose, especially when there is uncertainty (meaning almost all the time). *What should we do now?*" say Sunstein and Thaler.[290]

"Kahneman and Tversky showed that, in both of these domains, human beings hardly behave as if they were trained or intuitive statisticians. Rather, their judgments and decisions deviate in identifiable ways from idealized economic models," explain Sunstein and Thaler.[290] "Most of the importance of Kahneman and Tversky's work lies in the claim that departures from perfect rationality can be anticipated and specified. In other words, errors are not only common but also predictable," they say.[290]

Sunstein and Thaler explain the heuristic principle as such[290]:

> *For instance: ask people what they think is the ratio of gun homicides to gun suicides in the United States. Most of them will guess that gun homicides are much more common, but the truth is that gun suicides happen about twice as often. The*

explanation that Kahneman and Tversky offered for this type of judgment error is based on the concept of "availability." That is, the easier it is for us to recall instances in which something has happened, the more likely we will assume it is. This rule of thumb works pretty well most of the time, but it can lead to big mistakes when frequency and ease of recall diverge. Since gun homicides get more media coverage than gun suicides, people wrongly think they are more likely. The availability heuristic, as Kahneman and Tversky called it, leads people to both excessive fear and unjustified complacency—and it can lead governments astray as well.

"The influence of their work has been immense—not only in psychology and economics, where it has become part of the normal conversation, but in every other field of social science, as well as medicine, law, and, increasingly, business and public policy," note Sunstein and Thaler.[290]

The marketing takeaway here is for brands to make their products or services easy to grasp by providing examples of the actions you want users to take.[273]

Also known as the 'Fear of missing out' syndrome, the scarcity principle plays upon the idea that people covet things that are scarce. As Investopedia explains it, "Consumers place a higher value on goods that are scarce than on goods that are abundant. Psychologists note that when a good or service is perceived to be scarce, people want it more. Consider how many times you've seen an advertisement stating something like: limited time offer, limited quantities, while supplies last, liquidation sale, only a few items left in stock, etc. The feigned scarcity causes a surge in the demand for the commodity."[286]

"Marketers use the scarcity principle as a sales tactic to drive up demand and sales," says Investopedia.[286] The psychology behind the scarcity principle dovetails well with social proof and commitment.[286] "Social proof is consistent with the belief that people judge a product as high quality if it is scarce or if people appear to be buying it. On the principle of commitment, someone who has committed himself to acquiring something will want it more if he finds out he cannot have it," argues Investopedia.[286]

Another term for the scarcity principle is the 'Fear of missing out' syndrome. The FYRE festival played up the fear of missing out principle as well as any promotional event ever, promising concert-goers the experience of a lifetime in the Bahamas. Having now been dubbed 'the best festival that never was', Fyre Festival was then touted by hip hop mogul JaRule as being the 'cultural experience of the decade'. It has now become both legendary and the most talked about festival flop ever.[291]

As explained in *The Tonic Communications Fyre Festival: How Millennial FOMO Enabled High-end Fraud*, "A promotional video was produced with the specific intent of giving audiences FOMO (Fear of Missing Out), a form of social anxiety rooted in the concern that others might be having rewarding experiences that the individual is not a part of."[291] "The video combined persuasive messaging such as 'immersive', 'transformative', 'remote and private island' with imagery of supermodels living their best lives—a carefully crafted illusion of what was in store for attendees, should they be willing to spend thousands of dollars to partake."[291]

Billy McFarland, the CEO of the festival's production company, "commented that the video's release would be known as the 'Best coordinated social influencer campaign ever'. 400 of the 'hottest' celebrities around the world including artists, comedians, influencers and models posted an ambiguous burnt orange 'Fyre tile' across their Instagram accounts using the #FyreFestival and each inviting their followers to 'join me'. That was it."[291] The campaign amazingly "garnered over 300 million impressions within 24 hours."[291] The event immediately "sold out and rival festival organisers were stunned as investors tried to pull money out of their events to put into Fyre."[291]

As two documentaries of the event have shown, it was all a scam. McFarland defrauded investors to the tune of $27.4M and he is currently serving six years in prison for these and other offenses.[291] Thanks to the fear of missing out and a brilliant social media marketing campaign, thousands of unwitting concert-goers descended upon a little known island in the Bahamas for what turned out to be the experience of a lifetime all right, just not quite the one they were expecting.

As the world becomes numb to advertising, marketers need to find a way to connect with an audience on a visceral and emotional level and utilizing the above psychological methods could be a good first step in the long process of customer personalization.

Besides the 15 psychological methodologies described above, there are a few others to consider, including social proof as well as the principle of authority. "Think of it as building the foundation for massively scalable word-of-mouth"—these are the words of venture capitalist and blogger Aileen Lee describing the concept of social proof in her article *Social Proof Is The New Marketing*.[292] Lee believes that the best way to market a product or service "is by harnessing a concept called social proof, a relatively untapped gold mine in the age of the social web."[292] Lee contends social proof can generate sharing on a viral level through social channels that can multiply the discovery of a brand and add to its influence.[292]

Wikipedia describes social proof as "a psychological phenomenon where people assume the actions of others reflect the correct behavior for a given situation... driven by the assumption that the surrounding people possess more information about the situation."[293] In other words, "people are wired to learn from the actions of others, and this can be a huge driver of consumer behavior."[292]

Eric Hoffer's quote that, "when people are free to do as they please, they usually imitate each other" is quite amusing and, unquestionably, true. It speaks volumes about the herd mentality humans seem to succumb to as individuals take cues for proper behavior in most situations from the behavior of others. Psychologists call it the "conformity bias" and it is something that politicians and marketers have tapped into to enormous effect for centuries.

Oscar Wilde's quip that, "Most people are other people. Their thoughts are someone else's opinions, their lives a mimicry, their passions a quotation" strikes a similar chord and it's an idea that brands should keep in mind as they devise marketing plans aimed at the market of one. According to Robert Cialdini, who studied the principle of social proof in-depth in his book *Influence: The Psychology of Persuasion*[294], "we view a behavior as more correct in a given situation to the degree that we see others performing it."

In his article *The Psychology of Marketing: 18 Ways Social Proof Can Boost Your Results*[295], Alfred Lua concurs, stating, "So often in situations where we are uncertain about what to do, we would assume that the people around us (experts, celebrities, friends, etc.) have more knowledge about what's going on and what should be done." Besides that, "we often make judgments based on our overall impression of someone—A.K.A. the halo effect (named by psychologist Edward Thorndike)."[295]

In general, Lua claims there are six types of social proof, including[295]:

1. Expert: an expert in one's industry recommends your products and/or services or is associated with your brand.
2. Celebrity: a celebrity endorses your products.
3. User: current users recommend your products and/or services based on personal experiences with your brand.
4. The wisdom of the crowd: a large group of people endorse your brand for a myriad of reasons.
5. The wisdom of your friends: people see their friends approve of a product or service.

In his influential *Harvard Business Review* paper *Harnessing the Science of Persuasion*[296], Robert B. Cialdini looked at the science behind the power of persuasion and, since advertising is little more than trying to persuade a person to choose one's product and/or service over another, I think it is important to explore persuasion through the lens of social media. Cialdini contends that[296]:

> *"For the past five decades, behavioral scientists have conducted experiments that shed considerable light on the way certain interactions lead people to concede, comply or change. This research shows that persuasion works by appealing to a limited set of deeply rooted human drives and needs, and it does so in predictable ways. Persuasion, in other words, is*

governed by basic principles that can be taught, learned and applied."

Cialdini's six principles are[296]:

1. Like: People like those who like them.
2. Reciprocity: People repay in kind.
3. Social proof: People follow the lead of similar others.
4. Consistency: People align with their clear commitments.
5. Authority: People defer to experts.
6. Scarcity: People want more of what they can have less of.

For the reciprocity principle, people tend to give what they want to receive.[296] Praise is likely to have a warming and softening effect on people because there is a human tendency to treat people the way they are themselves treated.[296] All kinds of companies use this concept in their marketing to customers and brands should emulate these offerings.

For the principle of social proof, people tend to follow the lead of similar others.[296] People use peer power whenever it's available.[296] Cialdini adds that, "Social creatures that they are, human beings rely heavily on the people around them for cues on how to think, feel, and act."[296] We know this intuitively, Cialdini says "because intuition has also been confirmed by experiments, such as the one first described in 1982 in the *Journal of Applied Psychology*."[296] In that study, "A group of researchers went door-to-door in Columbia, South Carolina, soliciting donations for a charity campaign and displaying a list of neighborhood residents who had already donated to the cause. The researcher found that the longer the donor list was, the more likely those solicited would be to donate as well."[296]

"To the people being solicited, the friends' and neighbors' names on the list were a form of social evidence about how they should respond. But the evidence would not have been nearly as compelling had the names been those of random strangers," explains Cialdini[296] The lesson here is that "persuasion can be extremely effective when it comes from peers."[296] Cialdini argues that, "The science supports what most sales professionals already know: Testimonials from satisfied customers work best when the satisfied customer and the prospective customer share similar circumstances."[296]

For the principle of consistency, brands should make their commitments active, public, and voluntary. Cialdini states that, "Liking is a powerful force, but the work of persuasion involves more than simply making people feel warmly toward you, your idea, or your product. People need not only to like you but to feel committed to what you want them to do. Good turns are one reliable way to make people feel obligated to you. Another is to win a public commitment from them."[296]

For the principle of authority, people defer to experts, so brands should relay their expertise and not assume things are self-evident.[296] As Lee explains, "Approval from a credible expert, like a magazine or blogger, can have incredible digital influence."[292] Her examples include the following[292]:

- "Visitors referred by a fashion magazine or blogger to designer fashion rentals online at Rent the Runway drive a 200% higher conversion rate than visitors driven by paid search."[292]
- "Klout identifies people who are topical experts on the social web. Klout invited 217 influencers with high Klout scores in design, luxury, tech and autos to test-drive the new Audi A8. These influencers sparked 3,500 tweets, reaching over 3.1 million people in less than 30 days—a multiplier effect of over 14,000x."[292]
- "Mom-commerce daily offer site Plum District also reached mom influencers thru Klout, and found customers referred by influential digital moms shop at 2x the rate of customers from all other marketing channels."[292]

However, Lee warns that[292]:

> "I don't think a social proof strategy will be effective if you don't start with a great product that delights customers, and that people like well enough to recommend. How do you know if you have a great product? Track organic traffic growth, reviews, ratings and repeat rates. And measure your viral coefficient—if your site includes the ability to share, what percentage of your daily visitors and users share with others? How is the good word about your product being shared outside your site on the social web? Do you know your Net Promoter Score, and your Klout score?"

In his *Fast Company* article *How to use the psychology of social proof to your advantage[297]*, Ed Hallin argues that, "A lot of things go into a person's decision to purchase a product, and social proof is certainly one of those important factors. Studies show that 70% of consumers say they look at product reviews before making a purchase, and product reviews are 12x more trusted than product descriptions from manufacturers."[297] This isn't really that surprising.

One subset of social proof is celebrity social proof. This is, of course, "celebrity approval of your product or endorsements from celebrities."[297] However, Hallin warns that, "Celebrity endorsement is always a double-edged sword. If the celebrity is properly matched to the brand, it can do wonders for the company. If it's a mismatch, it may produce a bad image of the company and its brand."[297] Celebrities are also human beings and there can be a flavor-of-the-month aspect to them, especially amongst athletes, but, for every Aaron Hernandez disaster there might be a William Shatner Priceline endorsement that strikes internet and financial gold, for both parties involved.

As Hallin explains, "To understand why celebrity endorsements work from a psychological perspective, it's important to familiarize yourself with the concept of the extended self."[297] "The extended self," Hallin contends, "is made of up the self (me) and possessions (mine). It suggests that intentionally or unintentionally we view our possessions as a reflection of ourselves. This is why consumers look for products that signify group membership and mark their position in society."[297]

"User social proof is approval from current users of a product or service," explains Hallin.[297] This includes customer testimonials, case studies, and online reviews and it is particularly effective when storytelling is involved.[297]

Hallin believes that "We tend to imagine ourselves in other people's shoes when we read or hear a story. This is why stories are so persuasive and often more trustworthy than statistics or general trends. Individual examples stick with us because we can relate to them. Although statistics can be effective, it can be tougher to really see yourself in the aggregate the way you can with a personal account."[297]

'Wisdom of the Crowds' social proof is "approval from large groups of other people. It's showing evidence that thousands, millions, or even billions have taken the action that the company wants you to take—making a purchase, subscribing, etc."[297]

Hallin argues, "We kind of joke about FOMO in pop culture, but actually the Fear of Missing Out is a real thing. It's a form of social anxiety, and it's a compulsive concern that one might miss out on an opportunity. This anxiety is especially relevant for social media, as the sharing of what's going on in our daily lives means you can constantly compare your status to others on these platforms."[297]

Unsurprisingly, Hallin contends, "Social media has sparked dozens of different ways to provide this kind of social proof. Facebook widgets that show other Facebook friends that 'like' a brand, Twitter's display of people you follow that also follow another person, and the various ways that company offer rewards for referring others to the brand are all examples of this."[297]

Social proof is a powerful marketing tool and one that brands of all kinds need to exploit. "One study of 10,000 accounts at a German bank revealed that customers who came from customer referrals had 16% higher lifetime value than those who came from other acquisition sources. Additionally, the customers churned 18% less," says Hallin.[297]

"The concept of implicit egotism is that most people subconsciously like things that 'resemble' them in some way," explains Hallin.[297] He adds that, "Studies show that we value the opinions of people we perceive as most like us. We tend to become friends with people that we have a lot in common with, so it makes sense that social triggers like Facebook's Like Box or referral programs are successful."[297]

Aileen Lee concludes that, "In the age of the social web, social proof is the new marketing. If you have a great product waiting to be discovered, figure out how to build social proof around it by putting it in front of the right early influencers. And, engineer your product to share the love. Social proof is the best way for new users to learn why your product is great, and to remind existing users why they made a smart choice."[297]

SEO

A web search engine is a software system designed to search for information on the web and the search results are generally presented in a line of results often referred to as search engine results page (SERPs).[298] "The information may be a mix of web pages, images, and other types of files. Some search engines also mine data available in databases or open directories. Unlike web directories, which are maintained only by human editors, search engines also maintain real-time information by running an algorithm on a web crawler."[298]

In the US, Google is, by far, the biggest search engine around.[299] Outside the U.S., Google's main competitors are "Baidu and Soso.com in China; Naver.com and Daum Communications in South Korea; Yandex in Russia; Seznam.cz in Czech Republic; Yahoo! in Japan, Taiwan [sic]."[299]

Bit players like Bing compete with Google on standard search, but today Apple and Amazon are making inroads into Google's dominance, with Facebook set to be a challenger in the not-too-distant future as well. With those latter two, search is organically included within their platforms, i.e., when someone searches for an item to buy on Amazon, it gets included in the overall search rankings, ergo, an ecommerce site has become an important search engine.

Why is search so influential? Because users flock to search engines to organize the vast amounts of information most buyers need to make purchase decisions. "The main purpose of Google Search is to hunt for text in publicly accessible documents offered by web servers, as opposed to other data, such as with Google Image Search."[299] "The order of search on Google's search-results pages is based, in part, on a priority rank called a 'PageRank.'"[299] As Sharma et al. state in their book *Mobile Marketing*, "Search is one of the best ways to find content and the absolute best way for a marketer to determine consumer intent."[37]

Google Search "provides at least 22 special features beyond the original word-search capability, and language translation of displayed pages."[299] "In June 2011, Google introduced 'Google Voice Search' and 'Search by Image' features for allowing the users to search words by speaking and by giving images. In May 2012, Google introduced a new Knowledge Graph semantic search feature to customers in the U.S."[299]

"When Google was a Stanford research project, it was nicknamed BackRub because the technology checks backlinks to determine a site's importance."[299] Backlinks—and the quality of them—are very important for search engine optimization (SEO). The higher the quality of backlinks, the higher a website's ranking.

Even today, backlinks count, and they likely count prominently for SEO and, although backlinks are not always within a company's control, they are highly important due to their stature as the earliest persisting Google ranking factor. According to the *Moz 2015 Ranking Survey*, "the data continues to show some of the highest correlations between Google rankings and the number of links to a given page."[300] Today, *quality* backlinks are of the utmost importance and Google is the one who decides the quality of those backlinks; links from known spammy sites or sites associated with them, or merely hosted on servers that also host spammy content negatively affect rankings.[300]

In the early days of the battle for internet search supremacy, "previous keyword-based methods of ranking search results, used by many search engines that were once more popular than Google, would rank pages by how often the search terms occurred in the page, or how strongly associated the search terms were within each resulting page."[301] Google's PageRank algorithm instead "analyzes human-generated links assuming that web pages linked from many important pages are themselves likely to be important. The algorithm computes a recursive score for pages, based on the weighted sum of the PageRanks of the pages linking to them."[301] As a result, PageRank is thought to correlate well with human concepts of importance.[301]

Today, Google wants site owners to focus on developing great content—clear, accurate, highly-readable content that other site owners want to link to.[300] The way modern engines make this determination is by using advanced natural language processing, artificial intelligence and machine learning.[300] These evolving technologies enable the search engines to understand content without relying on a small set of specific keywords and phrases.[300] Google has invested heavily in this area, as evidenced by the plethora of white papers and research posted on its 'Machine Intelligence' website.[300]

As Brian Alpert argues in his article *Search engine optimization in 2017: A new world where old rules sill matter*[302], "One aspect of today's search engines that makes them very different from their predecessors is that advances in artificial intelligence and machine learning have enabled them to understand content and its underlying concepts independently of specific keywords."[302] Alpert adds: "This renders null and void the old concept that one must focus on keywords specific to a certain kind of content in order to be found via search engines. In today's landscape, exact keyword matches are less influential than ever before as engines can understand the relationships between words that are semantically related."[302]

With the introduction of its Knowledge Graph, Google is attempting to give users answers instead of just links.[299] "If you want to compare the nutritional value of olive oil to butter, for example, Google Search will now give you a comparison chart with lots of details. The same holds true for other things, including dog breed and celestial objects. Google says it plans to expand this feature to more things over time."[299]

Knowledge Graph also allows users to filter results.[299] "Say you ask Google: 'Tell me about Impressionist artists.' Now, you'll see who these artists are, and a new bar on top of the results will allow you to dive in to learn more about them and to switch to learn more about abstract art, for example," explains Lardinois.[299]

Search advertising falls into two main types—natural search results, and paid sponsorship based on keywords.[303] "Natural search requires high-quality, constantly updated content and search engine optimization (SEO). Paid search requires work to optimize keyword choice and messaging, but can be phenomenally expensive."[303] When not optimized for conversion, this can be a very pricey channel to use, with low conversion rates as well.[303]

Brands should constantly be testing their web pages for the most searched for and/or visited pages. As Siroker and Komen explain, A/B testing is particularly good for website marketing, especially for uncovering a website's best landing pages.[211] "Defining success in the context of A/B testing involves taking the answer to the question of your site's ultimate purpose and turning it into something more precise: *quantifiable success metrics*. Your success metrics are the specific numbers you hope will be improved by your tests," argue Siroker and Komen.[211] An e-commerce website could easily define its success metrics in terms of revenue per visitor[211], but it is still important to understand such things as traffic sources, bounce rate, top pages, conversion rates, conversion by traffic source, amongst other things.

In his article *Supercharging Your SEO with AI Insights, Automation, and Personalization*[304], Jim Yu believes that, "Artificial intelligence is making search more human. Although search does not yet 'speak' to users in the same way the Google Duplex demo could, its objective is very similar." He adds, "Google's RankBrain technology uses machine learning to understand the meaning of the content it crawls; it infers intent from ambiguous search queries; and it uses feedback data to improve the accuracy of its results. In other words, it listens and it learns."[304]

Research by BrightEdge "into a dataset of over 50 million keywords revealed that 84.4 percent of queries return universal search results. This occurs as Google uses AI to match the layout of search results pages to the user's intent."[304] According to BrightEdge, "There are now 37 different search engine result page (SERP) categories, a number that will only increase over the coming months and years."[304] These are:

Standard	Category	Weather
Taller Organic Cards	Images	Game scores
Local 3-pack	Video / Trailers	Twitter Tweets
Quick answers	Live	Discover more places
Shopping/PLA	Top sights	Send to Google home
Rich snippets	Reviews	People also search for
Site carousel	Blogs	See results about
Site links	Knowledge panel	Widgets
Site image carousel	Carousel	Found in related search
Top stories/News	Apps	Quotes
AMP	Google for jobs	Events
Google flights	Recipes	People also ask
Scholarly research		

Table 10: Search Engine keywords
Source: BridgeEdge[304]

"The potential for personalization has not yet been truly tapped, but Google's Sundar Pichai recently made public its goal to be an 'AI-first' company."[304] This means, "we should all expect the search landscape to change dramatically as AI takes center stage in the way it has already done in products like Google Photos and Google Lens.[304] As co-founder Sergey Brin put it: "AI touches every single one of our main projects, ranging from search to photos to ads."[304]

The pace of development on this front is accelerating, as everything at Google seems to have something to do with AI.[304] "Google is all too aware that AI can simply deliver better, more personalized experiences for consumers," says Yu.[304] "However, search marketers need to pay close attention to these technological advancements if they are to avail themselves of these opportunities for SEO," claims Yu.[304]

There are three key areas in which AI can improve SEO performance[304]:

1. Insights
2. Automation
3. Personalization

AI can process and analyze data at a scale simply not possible for humans.[304] "This makes it an essential complement to any search strategist, as AI can deliver the information we need to make informed decisions out of noisy, unstructured data," claims Yu.[304]

AI can be used to glean SEO insights in the following ways[304]:

- Understand underlying need in a customer journey.
- Identify content opportunities.
- Define opportunity space in the competitive context.
- Map intent to content.
- Use structured data and markup.
- Invest in more long-tail content.
- Ensure content can be crawled and surfaced easily by all user-agents.
- Automation.

"SEO is a labor-intensive industry that requires a huge amount of attention over the long term. Where we can automate tasks to receive the same output we could produce ourselves, we should make this a top priority. The time saved through automation can be applied to the areas that require our skills, like strategy and creative content," advises Yu.[304]

AI can be used for SEO personalization in the following ways[304]:

- Create content by persona, customer journey stage and delivery mechanism.
- Enhance user experience and conversion through personalization.
- Use semantically specific pages to associate query and intent.
- Use personalization and audience lists to nurture leads across search and social.
- Use AI to help publish content at the right times on the right networks.

Content Intelligence

In its article *The Magic of AI in a content-driven world. Using AI to create content faster*[305], the Adobe Enterprise Content Team argues that we're currently in the midst of a content explosion. Perhaps because of this, it is also a time when "Consumers expect to have personalized, relevant experiences at all times, in all places, and on all platforms."[305] "An IDC survey cites that 85 percent of marketing professionals feel under pressure to create assets and deliver more campaigns, more quickly. In fact, over two-thirds of respondents are creating over ten times more assets to support additional channels. This increased level of complexity is driving volume and associated costs."[305]

When thinking about what is needed to create this kind of content for thousands or even millions of customers at the near real-time speed that is necessary, doing it manually is impossible.[305] Adobe's *State of Creativity in Business 2017* survey found that "40 percent of creatives are using AI in photo and design retouching,"[305] so it's already happening. Currently, it can take hours for a designer to find just the right image to use in a piece of marketing collateral, and that's not counting the time required to manipulate the image, to crop it, to find the right layout scenario, and then to publish it to an online catalog and/or social media channel.[305] Serving the right content to the right person at the right time adds more time.[305] The cost for all this work adds up, as does the cost of photo shoots to create new assets.[305] AI and machine learning can help marketers find and reuse assets more efficiently, as well as deliver new and personalized content at scale, thereby helping a brand get a better return on its marketing investments.[305]

According to the Adobe Sensei Team, "AI can help you create more relevant content and more engaging experiences across the customer journey at the speed your customers expect. On the creative side, AI can speed up all kinds of tedious tasks, from identifying and organizing assets to adjusting and refining for specific channels."[17] "On the audience level, AI can help you better understand which audiences respond to which content, or how often people prefer to receive emails, so you can deliver the experiences your customers want while respecting their preferences and privacy," says the Sensei team.[17]

Klein concurs, stating "because the technology becomes smarter and more intuitive as it ingests more data, AI also can play a valuable role in automating the content creation process."[56] AI "offers capabilities for marketers that range from choosing the best image for a campaign or optimizing the content in a creative based on real-time user interactions," says Klein.[56] "For example, from a content creation perspective, this allows the ability to understand the focal— or sellable—point of hero images, and then to auto-crop them for best performance based on an understanding of millions of assets with similar meta-data," explains Klein.[56] "In this way, AI enhances creativity and enables a level of responsiveness and efficiency that until very recently was unachievable for marketers," concludes Klein.[56]

"Designers simply don't have time to tag the hundreds of images uploaded from every photo shoot. Even if they did, the list of keywords probably wouldn't be as exhaustive as it should be. But when a photo isn't tagged, it's virtually impossible to find by searching in an image bank of thousands," contend the Adobe Experience Cloud team.[305] "According to IDC, marketers report that one-third of marketing assets go unused or underutilized with the average organization creating hundreds of new marketing assets each year."[305] Repurposing images is unlikely, which means ROI suffers.

To try to tackle this issue, Adobe has created "Auto Tag", an Adobe Sensei capability that automatically tags images with key words.[305] For example, a marketer might have a picture of a young girl on a beach under a clear blue sky, which could be tagged with keywords like "beach", "girl", "dancing", "sundress", "blue sky", "white sand", or even a place like "Aruba."

"The Auto Tag service is used to power the Smart Tags features in Adobe Experience Manager, Photo Search in Adobe Lightroom, and Visual Search in Adobe Stock," explains the Enterprise Content Team.[305] "It's exciting to see the capabilities of auto-tagging," says Jonas Dahl, product manager for Adobe Experience Manager.[305] "We did several manual search queries against a customer's repository and showed the assets we were able to find. Then we applied Smart Tagging and did the same searches. This time the results were significantly better and much more comprehensive. And in a fraction of the time," says Dahl.[305]

"Adobe Sensei uses a unified AI and machine-learning framework, along with Adobe's deep domain expertise in the creative, marketing, and document segments, to harness the company's massive volume of content and data assets—from high-resolution images to customer clicks," says the Enterprise Content Team.[305]

"Adobe Sensei technology has learned to automatically identify what is in a photo. And not just an object like a car or a girl, but the concept of the photo, including context, quality, and style."[305] Theoretically, someone could search for an image with the words "walking" and "slow" and "the search might result in an image of an elderly man using a walker, because the technology made the connection between slow and walker."[305] Sensei's auto-phrasing service could tell you how each tag scored for prominence because the machine differentiates between the primary and secondary objects.[305] "This enables the technology to build a simple sentence or caption that more accurately describes the photo, such as 'An elderly man walking with a walker in a park.'"[305]

Using the Sensei framework, sports betting marketers could train the AI and machine learning models to create their own unique auto tags.[305] Many sports books take action on hundreds of games a week, in a multitude of sports and images for football are commonly sent to clients, but an image of a netball player would be noticed by someone who prefers betting on that particular sports. Identifying brand characteristics like the company logo could help the designers adhere to specific brand standards, or training it to identify a company's products so that they can be tagged in pictures on social media, which helps identify true reach.[305]

Custom auto tagging not only has the potential to increase a marketing team's efficiency, but it could lead to image-based shopping.[305] If a customer who is looking for a new couch uploads a photo of one they like and then shop for something similar based solely on the image, that's metadata the brand can use.[305] "Auto tagging identifies what is in the photo and finds the best matches for the customer. Auto tagging also allows brands to gain a deeper understanding of their audience and can help uncover market trends on social media, without the brand having to rely on tags and text. "If you run a social media feed through Adobe Sensei, it will tag places your brand is pictured—even if it's not mentioned or tagged—allowing you to see what is trending," explains the Enterprise Content Team.[305]

As any marketer can tell you, locating an image is simply step one in a multi-step process.[305] Unless, that is, you're using AI.[305] With products like Adobe's Deep Cutout, designers "can automatically remove an image's background and replace it with one that fits the brand guidelines."[305] Soon, designers will "be able to mask out an area such as a highway, and in just a few clicks, see what it looks like with a river, neighborhood, or other background—completely reinventing the photo in seconds."[305]

Auto Crop is another Adobe tool that can automate the cropping and sizing of images for different aspect ratios. The Enterprise Content Team gives the example of a shoe manufacturer who "may have guidelines that require only the shoe be shown, so they can automatically have all photos cropped accordingly."[305]

The AI can be trained on image aesthetics as well, so it automatically selects the best image and rejects anything that is below a certain quality standard and/or criterion.[305]

Time savings in any one of these areas could be quite substantial, but combined together, the velocity of creating and delivering content gets faster and faster.[305] The real power of this technology comes from creating custom workflows that allow brands to search, mask, crop, and publish in a fraction of the time it took in the past.[305]

For brands creating international marketing campaigns, this type of custom workflow can eliminate or reduce "the tedious, manual work involved in creating all of the different assets."[305] It allows brands to scale their campaigns to as many countries as needed.[305] When a "designer uploads a file to Adobe Creative Cloud, a custom workflow kicks off a series of Adobe Sensei Content AI Services that expedites the entire process from tagging, to cropping, to delivery of your production-ready asset to Adobe Experience Manager."[305] Adobe claims all of this can happen in a matter of hours instead of days.[305] Once again, creatives are allowed to focus on being creative, a place they would, undoubtedly, prefer to be anyway.

When this type of AI is coupled with a brand's content and audience data, its value increases exponentially.[305] "When you can combine what you know about the image with what you know about the customer from online and offline behaviors, you can micro-target customers with content that is truly relevant," says Richard Curtis, principal solutions consultant for Adobe.[305] "Furthermore, the machine will continue to learn customer patterns that help you fine-tune your personalization even further."[305] As Richard notes, "More personalization leads to more clicks,"[305] to say nothing of stronger brand loyalty bonds.[305]

According to Adobe's *Indelible content, incredible experiences*[70] article, the Adobe Enterprise Content team says that, "marketers are competing with brands that lure their customers not only with products and services, but also with individual experiences. And they're setting some healthy expectations, from recommending a film that customers will love, including a personal treat in their orders."

"To meet those expectations, marketers need to develop a steady flow of compelling content. You start the content journey with ideas and concepts, then create and manage assets, deliver and personalise experiences and finally analyse performance," says the Adobe Enterprise Content team.[70] "And you need to do all of this fast enough for the experiences to adapt instantly to every channel and screen your customer may use. The goal is achieving what McKinsey calls marketing's holy grail: digital personalization at scale."[70]

Machine learning is quickly becoming the "go-to tool to help marketers connect content with data and analytics, everywhere from lead scoring and retargeting to personalization and segmentation." According to the Adobe Enterprise Content team, the following three ways can make content more potent[70]:

1. Automate tedious tasks: "The complex, data-driven tasks that once only humans could perform are now in the realm of machines. They can easily and accurately handle repetitive tasks in specific contexts, like categorizing or scheduling, and can free humans for more value-added activities."[70]
2. Gain insights from big data: "Humans can't readily process massive amounts of data. Computers can. They can analyze big data—even unstructured data—to discover patterns, trends, and associations, and then offer actionable insights."[70]
3. Improve prediction accuracy: "Not only can computers analyze data, they can learn from it. And the more data they have, the savvier they become at making on-target recommendations and predictions."[70]

"Creating authentic one-to-one experiences requires extensive resources and an investment that your budget may not support. Even if you're flush with cash, you can't scale manually—you simply cannot hire that many people or analyse such vast datasets," warns the Adobe Enterprise Content team.[70] The solution lies at the intersection of content marketing and AI—content intelligence."[70]

With machine learning, software can analyse images imported into an editor "to detect facial features, similar images and even which way the subject is looking," claims the Adobe Enterprise Content team.[70] A designer can swap out images in real time to quickly preview as many options as a client might want to see.[70] If it doesn't look quite right, no problem, the editor can go back to any point in the process and see how a different decision—perhaps a young couple in a mortgage ad look excitedly at each other rather than at their new home—and then judge how it impacts the emotional experience of the ad.[70]

"AI can serve as your creative assistant, quickly assembling suggested content for audiences at every touchpoint and even optimizing it, so the burden's not on you. If your AI application supports voice recognition, you can even tell your assistant what you want—like making the mountains disappear in a climbing shot to focus on the gear," explains the Adobe Enterprise Content team.[70]

"You want one place where everyone—marketers, creatives and outside agencies—can find approved images and video to ensure experiences will remain consistent across channels," advises the Adobe Enterprise Content team.[70] "But manually tagging images with descriptive and contextual metadata is tedious, inconsistent and often incomplete. It's the type of job where machines excel. AI-powered smart tags automatically provide consistent, content-based metadata in seconds—saving you hours," they claim.[70] As Adobe's Senior Product Marketing Manager Elliot Sedegah succinctly puts it, "Computers will not complain about having to add metadata, they will not try to avoid it and they will work just as hard on the hundred thousandth image as on the first."[70]

Adobe allows for personalised customer treatment as well. "You can introduce as many experience variations as you choose for your digital properties to personalise customer experiences. By evaluating all behavioural and contextual variables, machine learning can determine the best experience for each consumer—regardless of channel, device or screen. As machine learning learns what works with each customer, predictive analytics can tell you what each one wants to see and buy—so you'll know whether they'll be excited by the image of the hotel on the island beach in Phuket or the snowy slopes at Whistler."[70]

"Just as a doctor must address each patient's issues and concerns, you must appreciate each customer's needs and desires," argues the Adobe Enterprise Content team.[70] Meeting the expectations of each customer calls for new tools, "You can't win in the digital era with industrial-age technology."[70] Integrating AI will help brands "deliver the truly surprising and delightful experiences that keep customers feeling on top of the world," concludes the Adobe Enterprise Content team.[70]

Measurement

In her article *Future of Advertising: Automated, Personalized, and Measurable*[306], Giselle Abramovich details an Adobe Think Tank panel discussion at Advertising Week 2017, in which "Phil Gaughran, U.S. chief integration officer at agency McGarryBowen, made a bold prediction: By 2022, he said, 80% of the advertising process will be automated, 'a threshold that will never be surpassed.'" The remaining 20%, Gaughran claims, "will comprise such elements as brand value, storytelling, and other more experiential tactics that will always need a human driver."[306]

According to Gaughran, this means a "changing job description in terms of what it means to work in advertising, unlocking a huge well of opportunity for advertisers."[306] "He reminded the audience that data doesn't deliver insights— people do."[306] "The more automated we become, the more we need humanity," he said.[306] Keith Eadie, VP of Adobe Advertising Cloud, agreed, "adding that as automation becomes mainstream, the big differentiator for brands will be human insight and creativity."[306] "Brands will always need human capital to innovate," he said.[306]

"Measurement, the panelists agreed, is a huge topic in advertising today, and one that's growing in importance as more advertising becomes measurable," says Abramovich.[306]One big hurdle to measurement is the concept of the "walled gardens" and the dark social of Facebook, Instagram, WeChat, and Google, which, according to Eadie, "have scaled media properties and tons of data, but the data and its ability to be activated stays within these platforms."[306] However, Eadie believes these walls "will start to come down in as little as five years, as Facebook and Google gear up to compete against newer entrants."[306] Time to plan for this change is now.

"Amazon is a rising walled garden, and this rise will mean a new set of competition to the media landscape," Eadie says.[306] "If companies can't get a sense of which garden is most impactful, they will move dollars to the platforms that do provide understanding of impact."[306] Facebook has proven to be very accommodating in this area any time advertisers are willing to put money on the table. This is a scenario that won't be ending any time soon, no matter how much privacy trouble Facebook gets into.

Will Warren, EVP, digital investment, at Zenith Optimedia, argues that measurement has improved with the onset of automation, because it allows companies to have a single view of their media, not just a single view of their customer.[306] "Further digitization will allow more user level data, and we can tie that to an outcome," he says.[306] "[Automation essentially brings] multitouch attribution across the digital landscape. Consolidated ad buying means better measurement."[306]

Jill Cress, National Geographic CMO, "believes the current state of measurement is more about 'measure what you can' than 'measure what you need to measure.'"[306] "Today, [advertisers] are focused a lot on the vanity metrics, like views, impressions, and clicks. But we need to figure out how far down the funnel these things are taking people," she says. "We feel like we are at a moment where we will see an ambition and a shift to emotional connection and the psychology of the consumer. That's how brands will differentiate."[306]

Another panelist, Aubrey Flynn, SVP and chief digital officer of REVOLT TV &

Media, believes Millennials and Gen Z not only want purpose in their lives, but they want the brands they use to share that purpose.[306] "To understand each person's individual purpose, brands need to move away from demographics and get closer to psychographics," says Flynn.[306] "In order to know people on an intimate level, companies will likely start investing in the study of human behavior to find authentic ways of personalizing experiences," explains Abramovich.[306]

Today, Facebook is far down the psychographics road. Although Facebook and the now defunct Cambridge Analytica got into a lot of trouble by harvesting Facebook data to sway political elections, the lessons and tactics learned there are far too powerful to be ignored by future advertisers. There is a way to utilize Facebook data that is either considerate of privacy concerns or anonymized all-together and advertisers are currently salivating at the prospect of getting their hands on all that highly important psychographic detail.

Authenticity also is key when it comes to advertising to the Millennial and Gen Z demographic, Flynn believes.[306] "We market a lifestyle, and bringing that to life means different things to different people," she says.[306] "Telling people about your company is one thing, she adds, but empowering audiences to successfully pursue the purposes that are important to them is a totally different type of engagement."[306] As companies learn about the drives and motivations of their customers, personalization will be key.[306]

"Most of the solutions to measure emotions are in beta, so it's still the early stages," says Abramovich. However, "the ability to understand not only how long someone engaged with an ad for but also how it made them feel is going to give advertisers an unprecedented understanding of the effectiveness of their ads," concludes Abramovich.[306]

Conclusion

More than ever before, AI allows marketers to reach consumers at every stage of the buying process based on their interests and demographics. In his article *How AI Will Change Marketing as We Know It*[307], Amine Bentahar claims that, "One particular example of how AI increases the efficiency of marketing is by making it easier to put customers into distinct groups that will allow for added segmentation to highly targeted niches." This means that, "Rather than creating one ad campaign that you hope will reach your target customers, marketers will instead be able to create more personalized, natural marketing content that will be unique for each targeted customer segment."[307]

AI will also "allow for more truly data-driven marketing campaigns, where AI will allow data to be more properly used and integrated into each ad campaign."[307]

The flip side of collecting as much data as a company possibly can is brands are collecting more data than they can actually use and here, too, AI can help by giving brands "the ability to seek out and identify patterns that will be beneficial for marketers in their campaigns."[307]

From a content standpoint, AI can help brands keep track of what type of content consumers are most interested in, information that can then be used to curate a website for each individual user.[307] This should help with customer conversions and should be a part of any brand customer personalization initiatives.

Overall, AI can help marketers "look at things through a broader, more big-picture lens."[307] Increased AI use won't necessarily replace marketing teams, it will simply allow them to work proactively, as well as help them focus on big-picture decisions and strategies.[307] Creatives will be allowed to be creative once again.

AI will unquestionably be changing the marketing world as we know it, but change can be good.[307] "AI will allow marketers to create more educated, personalized campaigns to reach consumers, all while viewing their work through a big-picture focus that will allow them to be more creative. That is how the biggest gains possible will be captured through AI," concludes Bentahar.[307]

Brands should recognize that there is a radical reorganization of platforms and delivery channels going on right now as well. All the major software, analytics, and tech vendors are looking at new ways to monetize their businesses and marketing is something they are taking a very close look at. Besides Amazon, Microsoft, AT&T, AOL, Verizon, new players like Roku are getting into the direct advertising business. Even companies like the now publicly traded company Uber are getting into the ad business.

---

265 Thompson, Derek. (2018) The Atlantic. The Media's Post-Advertising Future Is Also Its Past. December 31, 2018. https://www.theatlantic.com/ideas/archive/2018/12/post-advertising-future-media/578917/ (Accessed 1 January 2019).
266 Ballentine, Claire. (2018) New York Times. 12 August 2018. Google-Facebook Dominance Hurts Ad Tech Firms, Speeding Consolidation. https://www.nytimes.com/2018/08/12/technology/google-facebook-dominance-hurts-ad-tech-firms-speeding-consolidation.html (Accessed 1 January 2019).
267 Mickel, Tripp & Wells, Georgia. (2018) Wall Street Journal. Apple Looks to Expand Advertising Business with New Network for Apps. June 1, 2018. https://www.wsj.com/articles/apple-looks-to-expand-advertising-business-with-new-network-for-apps-1527869990?utm_source=newsletter&utm_medium=email&utm_campaign=newsletter_axiosmediatrends&stream=top (Accessed 1 January 2019).

268 Fischer, Sara. (2018) Axios. The Next Big TV Tech Platform: Roku. 22 May 2018. https://www.axios.com/roku-is-trying-to-become-software-platform-e8602b67-5af4-443e-affc-634b8d553aea.html (Accessed 1 January 2019).

269 Shields, Ronan. Adweek. Adobe's New Partnership with Roku Will Help Advertisers Engage with 27 Million OTT Viewers. https://www.adweek.com/programmatic/adobes-new-partnership-with-roku-will-help-it-engage-with-27-million-ott-viewers/ (Accessed 27 March 2019).

270 Fischer, Sara. (2018). Axios. How Media Companies Lost the Advertising Business. June 5, 2018. https://www.axios.com/facebook-google-duopoly-advertising-tech-giants-media-e382e5e2-21eb-4776-93c0-7d942ba80ada.html (Accessed 1 January 2019).

271 Thompson Derek. (2018). The Atlantic. Where Did All the Advertising Jobs Go? February 7, 2018. https://www.theatlantic.com/business/archive/2018/02/advertising-jobs-programmatic-tech/552629/ (Accessed 1 January 2019).

272 Abramovich, Giselle. (2018). Experts Weight in On the Future of Advertising. CMO. September 19, 2019. https://www.cmo.com/features/articles/2018/6/14/welcome-to-the-future-of-advertising-cannes18.html#gs.4BvSdQHt (Accessed 15 February 2019).

273 Lee, Kavan. Buffer. (2014) Psychological Studies That Will Boost Your Social Media Marketing. 17 November 2014. https://blog.bufferapp.com/psychological-studies-marketing (Accessed 14 February 2019).

274 https://en.wikipedia.org/wiki/Endowment_effect (Accessed 14 February 2019).

275 https://en.wikipedia.org/wiki/Reciprocity_(social_psychology)

276 https://www.influenceatwork.com/principles-of-persuasion/

277 Psychologist World. Foot-in-the-door technique as a Persuasive Technique. https://www.psychologistworld.com/behavior/compliance/strategies/foot-in-door-technique (Accessed 14 February 2019).

278 Plous, Scott (1993). The psychology of judgment and decision making. McGraw-Hill. ISBN 978-0-07-050477-6.

279 Kahneman, Daniel, and Amos Tversky, "Choices, Values and Frames," American Psychologist, April 1984, 39, 341–350.

280 McLeod, Saul. Solomon Asch – Conformity Experiment. Simply Psychology. December 28, 2018. https://www.simplypsychology.org/asch-conformity.html (11 March 2019).

281 Watson, Dorothy (1992). "Correcting for Acquiescent Response Bias in the Absence of a Balanced Scale: An Application to Class Consciousness". Sociological Methods & Research. 21 (1): 52–88.

282 Huber, Joel; Payne, John W.; Puto, Christopher (1982). "Adding Asymmetrically Dominated Alternatives: Violations of Regularity and the Similarity Hypothesis". Journal of Consumer Research. 9 (1): 90-98.

283 https://psychology.iresearchnet.com/social-psychology/emotions/buffering-effect/ (Accessed 11 March 2019).

284 https://en.wikipedia.org/wiki/Propinquity (Accessed 11 March 2019).

285 https://en.wikipedia.org/wiki/Availability_heuristic (Accessed 11 March 2019)

286 https://www.investopedia.com/terms/s/scarcity-principle.asp (Accessed 11 March 2019).

287 https://thedecisionlab.com/bias/framing-effect/ (Accessed 11 March 2019).

288 http://changingminds.org/explanations/theories/acquiescence_effect.htm (Accessed 11 March 2019).

289 Thu-Huong Ha. (2013). TED blog. The psychology of saving energy. February 27, 2013 https://blog.ted.com/the-psychology-of-saving-energy-alex-laskey-at-ted2013/ (Accessed 11 March 2019).

290 Sunstein, Cass and Thaler, Richard. (2016). The New Yorker. The Two Friends Who Changed How We Think About How We Think. December 7, 2016. https://www.newyorker.com/books/page-turner/the-two-friends-who-changed-how-we-think-about-how-we-think (Accessed 2 May 2019).

291 The Tonic Communications. (2018). Frye festival: how millennial FOMO enabled high end fraud. https://thetoniccomms.co.uk/fyre-festival-how-millennial-fomo-enabled-high-end-fraud/ (Accessed 12 March 2019).

292 Lee, Aileen. (2011). Social Proof Is The New Marketing. Techcrunch. https://techcrunch.com/2011/11/27/social-proof-why-people-like-to-follow-the-crowd/ (Accessed 16 August 2018).

293 https://en.wikipedia.org/wiki/Social_proof (Accessed 16 August 2018).

294 Cialdini, Robert B. (2006). Influence: The Psychology of Persuasion. Harper Business; Revised edition (December 26, 2006).

295 Lua, Alfred. The Psychology of Marketing: 18 Ways Social Proof Can Boost Your Results. https://www.upwork.com/hiring/for-clients/the-psychology-of-marketing-18-ways-to-use-social-proof-to-boost-your-results/ (Accessed 6 March 2019).

296 Cialdini, Robert B. Harnessing the Science of Persuasion. Harvard Business Review. October 2001. http://www.coachfinder.club/downloads/Influence%20by%20Cialdini.pdf (Accessed 15 August 2018).

297 Hallin, Ed. (2014). Fast Company. How to use the psychology of social proof to your advantage. 05 May 2014. https://www.fastcompany.com/3030044/how-to-use-the-psychology-of-social-proof-to-your-advantage (Accessed 14 August 2018).

298 https://en.wikipedia.org/wiki/Web_search_engine (Accessed 13 November 2017).

299 Lardinois, F. (2013, September 26). Google improves knowledge graph with comparisons and filters, brings cards & cross-platform notifications to mobile. Retrieved from TechCrunch: http://techcrunch.com/2013/09/26/google-improves-knowledge-graph-with-comparisons-and-filters-brings-cards-to-mobile-search-adds-cross-platform-notifications/

300 Moz (2015) 'Search Engine Ranking Factors 2015 Expert Survey and Correlation Data', available at: https://moz.com/search-ranking-factors (Accessed 15th August 2017). Moz's rankings survey consists of the compiled results of 150 SEP expert opinions as to what influences Google's secret algorithm. It is largely a technical document and relies heavily on (defined) technical terms, such as 'Domain-Level-Keyword-Agnostic-Features', but it is worth a look nevertheless.

301 https://en.wikipedia.org/wiki/Google_Search (Accessed 13 November 2017).

302 Alpert, Brian. (Spring 2017). Search engine optimization in 2017: A new world where old rules still matter. Journal of Digital & Social Media Marketing, Volume 5, Number 1, Spring 2017, pp. 39 – 60 (22). Henry Stuart Publication.

303 Vindicia. (2014). Digital Age/Digital Goods. Retrieved from vindicia: http://info.vindicia.com/White-Paper---Digital-Age-Digital-Goods-9essentials_for_acquiring_subscription_and_recurring_revenue_customers.html (Accessed 15 August 2018).

304 Yu, Jim. Searchengingland.com. Supercharging Your SEO with AI Insights, Automation, and Personalization. June 12, 2018. https://searchengineland.com/supercharging-your-seo-with-ai-insights-automation-and-personalization-299900 (Accessed February 19, 2019).

305 Enterprise Content Team. The Magic of AI in a content-driven world. Using AI to create content faster. https://www.adobe.com/insights/the-magic-of-AI-in-a-content-driven-world.html (Accessed 15 February 2019).

306 Abramovich, Giselle. (2017). CMO. Future of Advertising: Automated, Personalized, and Measureable. 26 September 2017. https://www.cmo.com/features/articles/2017/9/25/the-future-of-advertising-automated-personalized-and-measurable-.html
307 Bentahar, Amine. (2018). Forbes. How AI Will Change Marketing as We Know It. May 23, 2018. https://www.forbes.com/sites/forbesagencycouncil/2018/05/23/how-ai-will-change-marketing-as-we-know-it/#52bb93278b78 (Accessed 6 April 2019).

CHAPTER FOUR

Social Business

"When people are free to do as they please, they usually imitate others."

~Eric Hoffer

Overview

"Social Media" is a generic term that refers to websites that allow one or more of the following services: social networking, content management, social bookmarking, blogging and micro-blogging, live video-casting, and access into virtual worlds. Social Media—the technology as we know it today—has its roots in Usenet, a worldwide discussion system that allowed users to post public messages to it.[44]

Social also refers to online resources that people use to *share* content. This content can include images, photos, videos, text messages, pins, opinions and ideas, insights, humor, gossip, and news of almost any kind.[308] Drury's list of social media includes the following[308]:

> Blogs, vlogs, social networks, message boards, podcasts, public bookmarking and wikis. Popular examples of social media applications include Flickr (online photosharing); Wikipedia (reference); Bebo, Facebook and MySpace (networking); del.icio.us (bookmarking) and World of Warcraft (online gaming).

Unlike traditional marketing models that are nothing more than one-way delivery systems from a company to its consumers, social media is about building a relationship with an audience and starting a two-way dialogue between the company and that consumer.[308] In this new environment, marketing becomes a multi-dimensional discipline that is about receiving and exchanging perceptions and ideas.[308] The consumer is seen as a participant rather than as a "target audience." The old Source-Message-Channel-Receiver model[309] is evolving into "a collaborative and dynamic communication model in which marketers don't design 'messages' for priority audiences but create worlds in which consumers communicate both with the company and with each other."[310]

The most important thing to recognize about social media is the fact that most social media content is user generated. Social networks provide all of the tools their members require to become content producers and social network members submit photos, videos, and other forms of multimedia as well as provide customer reviews, content for blogs and vlogs and links to other social networking websites that they find noteworthy.[311] The content comes from the users themselves, not from the publishers, and this is an important distinction.[311] The publisher supplies all of the necessary tools for the content's distribution, but it must remain at arm's length from the actual content to ensure the integrity's content.

Business.com's *Top Tools to Measure Your Social Media Success*[312] states that there are five Ws that must be kept in mind when devising a social media strategy. These are:

1. Who within the company will be using this tool? Will one person or several people be using the tools and will they be inside or outside the organization? Will the primary user be tech savvy or will he or she require an intuitive interface?

2. What key performance indicators (KPI) are to be measured with this tool? It is imperative to know how you are going to measure and benchmark your social media efforts as this will dictate what social media monitoring tools are the best to use. If sales revenue is a key KPI, businesses should invest in a tool that integrates with a CRM system to track impact.

3. Where on the web will the business be engaging customers, and where does it plan to monitor its social media conversations? If a business is only interested in tracking specific channels such as Facebook or Twitter, tools such as Facebook (obviously), 48ers.com and socialmention.com can help with the former, while Twazzup, TweetEffect and Twittercounter can track the latter. All-encompassing tools that monitor new sites and forums are useful to monitor mentions from across the entire web.

4. When should the company be alerted of conversations and mentions within the social media sphere? Options here include general reporting dashboards or instant notifications via e-mail alerts or RSS feeds.

5. Why is the company engaging in social media? This is, perhaps, the most important question of all, and a sports book must decide whether it is turning to social media to manage its online brand reputation, to engage its customers and/or potential customers, to provide real-time customer service, or simply to drive traffic to its website to influence SEO.

Drury argues that confusion exists when pundits talk about social media because the emphasis is often placed on the "media" aspect of social media rather than the "social" aspect, where he feels it correctly belongs.[308] By giving people a platform to share and interact with each other, social media allows "content" to become more democratized than ever before.[308]

In their influential article *Users of the World, Unite! The Challenges and Opportunities of Social Media*[44], Kaplan and Haenlein explain that a formal definition of social media first requires an understanding of two related concepts that are often referred to when describing it: Web 2.0 and User Generated Content.[44] As Kaplan and Haenlein see it[44]:

> *"Web 2.0 is a term that was first used in 2004 to describe a new way in which software developers and end-users started to utilize the World Wide Web; that is, as a platform whereby content and applications are no longer created and published by individuals, but instead are continuously modified by all users in a participatory and collaborative fashion. While applications such as personal web pages, Encyclopedia Britannica Online, and the idea of content publishing belong to the era of Web 1.0, they are replaced by blogs, wikis, and collaborative projects in Web 2.0. Although Web 2.0 does not refer to any specific technical update of the World Wide Web, there is a set of basic functionalities that are necessary for its functioning."*

The "basic functionalities" that Kaplan and Haenlein refer to are; Adobe Flash, the popular animation tool, interactivity, and web streaming audio/video program, Really Simple Syndication (RSS), a family of web feed formats used to publish frequently updated works—such as blog entries or news headlines, as well as audio and video—in a standardized format; and Asynchronous Java Scrip (AJAX), a group of web development methods that can retrieve data from web servers asynchronously, allowing the update of one source of web content without interfering with the display and behavior of an entire page.[44] This is important because it means that a web page for a sports book could, while it is loading onto a customer's computer or mobile phone, be accessing and returning specific personalized customer content, including appropriate coupons that have been chosen because they are highly likely to be used and, potentially, could cost the sports book the least to redeem.

For Kaplan and Haenlein, Web 2.0 represents the ideological and technological foundation, while "User Generated Content (UGC) can be seen as the sum of all the ways in which people make use of social media. The term, which achieved broad popularity in 2005, is usually used to describe the various forms of media content that are publicly available and created by end-users."[44]

Also known as Consumer-Generated Media (CGM), User-Generated Content (UGC) refers to a wide range of applications, including blogs, news, digital video, podcasting, mobile phone photography, video, online encyclopedias and user reviews. According to Juniper Research, User Generated Content can be broken down into the following three categories[313]:

1. Mobile dating and chat room services—destinations for people to meet.
2. Personal content distribution—audio and video files uploaded onto third party sites for other mobile users to consume.
3. Social networking—social structures made of nodes "that are tied by one or more specific types of interdependency, such as values, visions, ideas, financial exchange, friendship, kinship, dislike, conflict or trade."[314]

UGC can be seen as the sum of all the ways in which people make use of social media and, according to the Organisation for Economic Cooperation and Development, UGC needs to fulfill the following three basic requirements in order to be considered as such[315]:

1. It must be published either on a publicly accessible website or on a social networking site accessible to a selected group of individuals.
2. It must show a certain amount of creative effort.
3. It must have been created outside of professional routines and practices.

For Kaplan and Haenlein, the first condition can't include content exchanged in e-mails or instant messages; the second precludes mere replications of already existing content (e.g., posting a copy of an existing newspaper article on a personal blog without any modifications or commenting); and the third condition implies that all created content must exclude a commercial market context.[44]

Kaplan and Haenlein believe that social media isn't just "a group of Internet-based applications that build on the ideological and technological foundations of Web 2.0, and that allow the creation and exchange of User Generated Content."[44] For Kaplan and Haenlein, this general definition should be broken down further because such disparate sites as Facebook, LinkedIn, Wikipedia, Weibo, and yy.com have little in common with each other when their offered services are looked at individually.[44]

As new sites are also popping up on a daily basis, a classification system created for social media should be able to include any future applications that are developed as well.[44] To create such a classification system, Kaplan and Haenlein rely on a "set of theories in the field of media research (social presence, media richness) and social process (self-presentation, self-disclosure), the two key elements of Social Media."[44] "Regarding the media-related component of Social Media, social presence theory[316] states that media differ in the degree of 'social presence'—defined as the acoustic, visual, and physical contact that can be achieved—they allow to emerge between two communication partners."[44]

Kaplan and Haenlein argue that: "Social presence is influenced by the intimacy (interpersonal vs. mediated) and immediacy (asynchronous vs. synchronous) of the medium, and can be expected to be lower for mediated (e.g., telephone conversations) than interpersonal (e.g., face-to-face discussions) and for asynchronous (e.g., e-mail) than synchronous (e.g., live chat) communications."[44] The higher the social presence, the more social influence the communication partners will have on each other.

Media Richness Theory[317] is a framework to describe a communications medium by its ability to reproduce the information sent over it and it implies that "the goal of any communication is the resolution of ambiguity and the reduction of uncertainty."[44] For Daft & Lengel[317], Media Richness is a function of:

- The medium's capacity for immediate feedback
- The number of cues and channels available
- Language variety: and
- The degree to which intent is focused on the recipient.

Regarding the social dimension of social media, the concept of self-presentation states that when an individual comes in contact with other people, that individual will attempt to guide or control the impression that others form of them and all participants in social interactions are attempting to avoid being embarrassed or embarrassing others.[318] "Usually such a presence is done through self-disclosure; that is, the conscious or unconscious revelation of personal information (e.g., thoughts, feelings, likes, dislikes) that is consistent with the image one would like to give."[44] This is important for sports books because someone's gambling isn't always something that patrons want to share with his or her friends. Although gamblers love to trumpet their winning bets, the MO seems to be keep losses—and news of those loses—to a minimum.

Applied to the context of social media, a classification is made based on the richness of the medium and the degree of social presence it allows.[44] Kaplan and Haenlein create the *Classification of Social Media by social presence/media richness and self-presentation/self-disclosure* table reveals (see Table 11)[44]:

- Low: Collaborative projects such as Wikipedia and blogs score the lowest, mostly because they are text based and only allow relatively simple exchanges. Blogs usually score higher than collaborative projects because the former aren't focused on specific content domains.
- Medium: Content communities and social networking sites allow users to share text-based communication, as well as other forms of media. Social network sites score higher than content communities because they allow more self-disclosure.
- High: Virtual games and social worlds attempt to replicate face-to-face interactions in a virtual environment. Virtual social worlds score higher on the self-presentation scale as the latter are ruled by strict guidelines that users have to either follow.

		Social Presence/ Media Richness		
		Low	Medium	High
Self-presentation/ Self-disclosure	High	Blogs	Social networking sites (e.g., Facebook)	Virtual social worlds (e.g., Second Life)
	Low	Collaborative projects (e.g., Wikipedia)	Content communities (e.g., YouTube)	Virtual game worlds (e.g., World of Warcraft)

Table 11: Classification of Social Media by social presence/media richness and self-presentation/self-disclosure
Source: *Users of the world unite! The challenges and opportunities of Social Media.*[44]

User Generated Content can be very useful in website Search Engine Optimization (SEO). Search engines are constantly looking for updated information on websites and adding such things as blogs and customer forums can be a cheap and effective way to get customers and/or clients to generate new content for you, which should increase search engine rankings.

Sports betting operators should look beyond the most well-known social platforms as well and try to be creative. For example, in 2014, Snapchat teamed up with Betfair to offer "self-destructing" odds to gamblers during two football games in February 2014.[319] "The offer was extended to anyone following the company's official Shapchat account, betfairofficial, during the Chelsea versus Everton and Crystal Palace versus Manchester United Premier League fixtures"[319] and enhanced odds were given to bettors. This may seem like a gimmick but, in this day and age, this is the kind of thing that gets companies noticed.

Sports betting operators should already be using social media to manage their brand, to enhance brand loyalty, as well as engage both their current customers and their potential customers. Most sports books are using social media, but in a limited way. Not only the perfect avenue to reach customers, the social media world is also the perfect place to harvest customer feedback, provide real-time customer service, build fanbases, and drive traffic to a sports book's website. Social media can have a predictive quality as well, i.e., it can be used to discover patterns that reveal upcoming customer problems with products and services. It can reveal brand sentiment as well show what drives that sentiment. Customer churn could be spotted early enough to head it off, as well.

Social media is a great place to get competitive intel, as well. Benchmarking a competitor's social media footprint and sentiment can help a sports book understand how its products and services measure up to its competitors and this is unfiltered information, coming directly from the voice of the customer, so it is trustable.

Sports books should not be reluctant to dive into social media because of its unfiltered nature. These forums will exist with or without the sports book's involvement, therefore it is better to stay ahead of the game rather than to be painfully stuck behind it.

Regarding social media, engagement is the key when it comes to successful ROI and profitable customer relations. To compete in this highly competitive industry, sports betting companies should recognize the importance of personalization when it comes to customer interactions. Most sports books today have customer loyalty programs that are a part of a CRM and/or a SCRM initiative to provide their customers with an intimate experience that will make them want to return again and again and again. Mobile and social media channels are some of the best ways to reach these customers.

Blogs and micro-blogging sites are also important mobile and social media channels and sports books should monitor Twitter feeds for both their satisfied and dissatisfied customers. This is where brand and anti-brand management comes into play. The invert of that old Paul Newman gambling chestnut that "Money won is twice as sweet as money earned" is probably, "Money gambled away is twice as painful as money spent on life's necessities," so sports books should be cognizant of the emotional toll that gambling losses can induce upon players. Monitoring what losing gamblers are saying on social media is paramount to any good CRM strategy.

Real time technology gives sports books the ability to see—and know—what is going on in real time around them, and this allows them to instantly counter negative brand perceptions. Social media marketing makes good economic sense as well. Given the explosive growth of social media sites, "these might become more cost-effective than using traditional advertising and marketing methods."[320]

In the article *The marketing of wagering on social media: An analysis of promotional content on YouTube, Twitter and Facebook*[321], Thomas et al. state that, "Social media is increasingly used as a platform to promote products and services. Research on tobacco and alcohol has shown the extent to which dangerous consumption industries are moving from traditionally highly regulated media platforms, such as television, to marketing channels that are not subject to existing government regulation, and which governments appear much more reluctant to regulate."

"On one level it seems intuitive that sports betting, an industry highly dependent on mobile internet devices and online wagering as platforms for engaging customers in gambling services, would also turn to these same media platforms to promote its products," argue Thomas et al.[321]

The Thomas et al. study "conducted a mixed methods interpretive content analysis of social media promotions on YouTube, Twitter, and Facebook to explore the written, verbal and visual communication strategies used within the advertisements."[322] The researchers "focused on content posted in September 2014 and April 2015 to represent the end and start of the Australian Football League (AFL) and National Rugby League (NRL) seasons."[322]

The study focused on the marketing activities of seven wagering brands, including Crownbet.com.au, Ladbrokes.com.au, Sportsbet.com, Tab.com.au, TomWaterhouse.com.au, Unibet.com.au, and WilliamHill.com.au. [322]

The researchers were "interested in the range of different types of creative strategies that were used in social media promotions."[322] The researchers used an "inductive approach to identify the categories used for the content analysis."[322] The following categories were identified and included for each platform:[322]

- YouTube: "wagering promotion; game commentary; advertisement; comedy/parody video; Corporate Social Responsibility (CSR) video; stunt; competition."[322]
- Twitter: "game statistics/news/commentary; wagering promotions and/or information; comedy/satire; cartoons; sporting nostalgia/history."[322]
- Facebook: "wagering information; game statistics/news/commentary; fan engagement strategies; comedy/satire; tributes; cartoons; sporting nostalgia/history."[322]

The researchers were then "interested in the specific content of wagering promotions across the social media platforms."[322] Thomas et al. included the following items in the content analysis for each platform:

- YouTube: "odds; tipping; mobile betting; prompts to bet; refund information; live betting; bonus bets; cash out; winner's information; responsible gambling message."[322]
- Twitter: "prompts to bet; odds information; refund information; bonus bets; tipping; winner's information; cash out; multi-bets; responsible gambling message." [322]
- Facebook: "prompts to bet; tipping; odds information; insider information; responsible gambling message; competitions; refund information; winner's information and; multi-bets."[322]

Thomas et al. discovered that[322]:

> *"YouTube had the least active subscribers to the channel, users had engagement with the channel through video views. Some*

industry content was viewed more often than others, with content viewed the most on Sportsbet.com.au (441,768 views of 6 videos posted across two months); Ladbrokes.com.au (832,363 views of 15 videos posted across two months); and WilliamHill.com.au (179,270 views of 3 videos posted across one month). In contrast, some brands (Tab.com.au; Crownbet.com.au and TomWaterhouse.com.au) had very limited engagement with users via YouTube, as determined by number of views, subscribers and likes."

To break it down, "Sportsbet.com.au, WilliamHill.com.au and Ladbrokes.com.au posted more advertising and promotional content, whilst Crownbet.com.au and Tab.com.au posted more specific tipping and odds based videos relating to particular sporting or horse racing events. The latter also posted significantly more content."[322]

According to the research, "191,074 accounts followed sports wagering companies on Twitter."[322] "All sports wagering brands posted multiple tweets per day during the data collection period, ranging from an average of 58 tweets per day (WilliamHill.com.au) to 4.3 tweets per day (Unibet.com.au)."[322] Tweets varied in content, with over half of the tweets featuring a picture, and about one in nine tweets including video, note Thomas et al.[322]

Thomas et al. concluded that, "User engagement with tweets varied according to brand. Tweets from Sportsbet.com.au were the most shared (total of 783 retweets, an average of 5 retweets per tweet), while most other brands averaged 1 or less retweets per tweet."[322]

Of all three social media platforms, sports betting dedicated Facebook pages had the highest number of 'likes', with a total of 1,372,707 'page likes' across the seven wagering brands.[322] There was "substantial difference in likes, ranging from the most 'liked' wagering brand 512,245 (Sportsbet.com.au) to 11,200 (Crownbet.com.au) which had the least page likes," state Thomas et al.[322]

Unibet.com.au did particularly stand out as it had limited user engagement on Twitter and no Australian YouTube channel, but it had 434,578 'page likes' on Facebook.[322] However, this brand had the fewest Facebook post likes (574) or shares (7) of the brands despite posting the most content on average/month of any of the brands. "Sportsbet.com.au and Tab.com.au had the most user engagement as measured through total number of Facebook post shares and likes with 29,034 shares and 174,865 likes for Sportsbet.com.au, and 12,539 shares and 75,007 likes for Tab.com.au."[322]

The Four Steps of Social Media

In their book *Online Marketing Inside Out: Reach New Buyers Using Modern*

Marketing Techniques[323], Eley & Tiley state that, when a company is first delving into social media, there are four steps of social media that should be followed—listen, join, participate and create—and these steps must be strictly followed in that specific order.

Listening is the most important step. People online are frequently mentioning and making comments about a company and its products, so all one has to do is listen. Even if a sports book does not choose to participate in the discussion itself, it will discover valuable information about the company by just listening.[323]

Instead of doing expensive surveys, focus groups or other experiments, the best information is often found right there in front of you at minimal or maybe even at no cost.[323] A sports book can find out what its customers think of its services, as well as what they might want improved. Problems and frustrations that might not make it onto corporate surveys might be detailed enough on blogs to affect real change.

In her article *50 ways to drive traffic to your website with social media*[324], Amanda Nelson recommends, listening can be used in the following ways:

1. Monitor for buying indication terms and reply with helpful links.
2. Listen for recommendation requests and share helpful links.
3. Listen for discussions of your product or category and provide web links.
4. Share relevant web content with prospects.
5. Discover relevant blogs and ask for backlinks.

To understand how important this process can be for a company, I'd like to take the example of one bourbon manufacturer who found itself in the midst of a self-created social media disaster. In February, 2013, because it was faced with both a high demand for its product and a low supply of bourbon whiskey, Maker's Mark announced plans to cut the amount of alcohol in its drink from 45 to 42 percent.[325] Needless to say the Internet wasn't pleased. As Laura Stampler explains in her article *Makers Mark Turned Watered Down Whiskey Debacle Into a Social Media Win*[325], "It's the age of social media, so consumers were tweeting and Facebooking their complaints to any and everyone who would listen."[325]

There were angry tweets as well as Facebook petitions against the company.[325] A normal Valentine's Day post on the company's Facebook page was flooded with negative comments about the shift.[325] Immediately realizing that it had made a huge mistake, the brand decided to embrace the social media platforms where they have been receiving such negativity and they quickly put out the message that it had made a huge mistake, it was sorry and that it was reversing its decision about lowering the alcohol content.[325] The link to the company's Facebook apology soon became a popular hashtag.[325] "Customers went from feeling abandoned to listened to and respected in record time."[325] The apology noted that even though the social media reaction was highly negative, the company wanted the conversation to continue.[325]

Maker's Mark even took this conversation into their print advertising using the tagline line: "You spoke. We listened. Here's proof", with an arrow cleverly pointing to the label, which showed that the alcohol content (or proof) was still 45%.

By listening, joining, participating and creating, Maker's Mark built its online brand and it now has an audience to share its content with, an audience which should help them spread their content far and wide, as well as, more importantly, sell a lot more 45 proof whiskey to.

Once a sports book understands the community and what it is all about, it is time to join a social network. Many networks require that you have an account on their site to participate in the discussions and the sports book should sign up for the account as it is always better to have an account even if it is not required to have one because one always wants to claim its brand and/or company name to gain credibility.

A sports book should also join communities where it is most likely to find its customers.[323] If you start out by listening, you will know where your customers tend to congregate online. Facebook, LinkedIn, YouTube, Flickr, Delicious, Digg and Twitter are big networks which should be on your radar.[323] Many of these sites can be used to listen to your audience or to start a discussion. Chinese listening social media sites include Sina Weibo, Tencent Weibo, and Netease Weibo, amongst others.

Sports betting operators should set up accounts at all the major social networking sites and link back to their website(s), as well as link content and similar keywords throughout their social channels.

Once the discussion has been joined, then it is time to participate in the community. Participating includes replying and posting to online forums and blogs, reviewing products and services and bookmarking sites that are like-minded.[323]

By participating, sports books will build their online brand and people will start to respect them as a valuable contributor to the community.[323] When respected, others will help to promote the company and, possibly, the sports books without even being asked to do so, which, as most marketers will tell you, is some of the best marketing around. Not only is word-of-mouth marketing one of the most trusted forms of marketing, but it can also spread virally. Two words of warning, however; your role models should always be very experienced and remain very active users in the community; and, most importantly of all, remember that it is never okay to spam.[323]

In her article *50 Ways to Drive Traffic to Your Website*[324], Nelson recommends using the following methods to increase participation:

1. Ask readers to sign up for an RSS feed.

2. Answer all questions and share peer referrals.
3. Feature community members on your site.
4. Share customer stories.
5. Ask influencers to share your web links.
6. Interview an influencer for web content.
7. Have an influencer guest blog.
8. Help an influencer write content about the brand.
9. Share products with influencers for feedback and web content.

Finally, it is time to create. Once a sports book has built itself an online brand by listening, joining and participating, it is time to create its own content.[323] It will now have an audience to share its content with and they will help the sports book spread its content far and wide. It should be noted here that the sports book has to create value; ads are not generally seen as valuable.[323] Posting "buy my stuff" on twitter will fail to achieve the results you want, and this practice may even get you banned.[323] By making beneficial contributions to the community, people will notice you and want to know more about the company.[323] If you have listened properly, you should have a solid idea of the type of content people would like to see.[323] Then, simply, give it to them. Nelson recommends companies be creative in the following ways[323]:

1. Divide a piece of content into multiple Slideshare presentations that link to your site.
2. Start a LinkedIn group.
3. Tie content together so an ebook links to a relevant blog post, which, in turn, links to a topical webinar.
4. Build a forum or community section on the company website.
5. Create referral programs.

Social Media Hierarchy

In his article *The Hierarchy of Social Marketing*[326] John Jantsch argues that, when venturing into social media, businesses should be following six distinct steps (see Figure 24). Using Abraham Maslow's *Hierarchy of Needs*[327] as a blueprint to look at social marketing, Jantsch states implicitly that each step should be fully understood and implemented before any ensuing step is undertaken.[326] Just as Maslow claimed that "Self-Actualization" can only be reached after all the needs below it have been fulfilled, so too does Jantsch believe that, without a mastery of the first five steps, the sixth step–"Micro"–will be useless because engagement with the intended audience will be shallow.[326]

Figure 24: Jantsch's Hierarchy of Social Media

Jantsch's breaks the hierarchy down into the following steps[326]:

1. Blogging: The pyramid's foundation and the doorway through which all other social marketing should flow. Sports books should read blogs, comment on blogs, and then blog themselves.
2. RSS: Aggregate and filter content around subjects and use RSS technology as a tool to help repurposing, republishing, and creating content.
3. Social Search: participation is important at this stage as is stimulating and managing one's reputation.
4. Social Bookmarking: Tagging content to and participating in social bookmarking communities can both open up more channels for a sports book as well as generate extra search traffic to a site.
5. Social Networks: Creating profiles on any social networking site will prove frustrating if the steps below it haven't been completed. These networks take time to understand and they thrive on ideas and content, therefore a lot of content is needed to build a strong business case.
6. Micro: With their instant tracking, joining, and engagement capabilities, platforms such as Twitter, Thwirl, Plurk and FriendFeed are very important elements of a social media strategy. They are atop the pyramid because, without content created below them, engagement will be superficial, at best.

Although this hierarchy is an interesting framework, it should be taken with a grain of salt. Social and mobile media is moving at such a high rate of speed, as well as splintering off in a thousand different directions, that nothing in this field is set in stone.

To create an effective and engaging marketing campaign, a marketer must understand the individual being marketed to as best as he or she can. As there are literally billions of people using social media, categorizing them into a simple classification system is not easy, but Li and Bernoff circumvent this problem by differentiating social media users into six different categories and they have created the *Participation Ladder for Social Media* (see Table 12).[328] As the "Inactives" at the bottom rung do not use social media, they can be ignored, but the other five types should be looked at and marketed to appropriately. It should also be noted that there are two other superficial types; the "contributors," who actively participate by starting their own conversations or replying to other threads and the "lurkers," who only read and follow content created by others.[329]

TYPE OF PARTICIPATION	ACTIVITY
Creators	Publish a blog
	Publish your own Web page
	Upload video you created
	Upload audio music you created
	Write articles or stories and post them
Critics	Post ratings/reviews of products or services
	Comment on someone else's blog
	Contribute to online forums
	Contribute to/edit articles in a wiki
Collectors	Use RSS feeds
	"Vote" for Web sites online
	Add "tags" to Web pages or photos
Joiners	Maintain profiles on a social networking site
	Visit social networking sites
Spectators	Read blogs
	Listen to podcasts
	Watch video from other users
	Read online forums
	Read customer ratings/reviews
Inactives	None of the above

Table 12: Participation Ladder for Social Media
Source: Harvard Business Review[328]

It is important to recognize that the vast majority of social media users fall into the "lurkers" category and these people are highly influenced by the "contributors"[329], so reaching the contributors is imperative. Sports book operators should recognize the unique symbiotic relationship between "contributors" and "lurkers" that is similar to a political commentator and his or her reading public.[329] These commentators do have enormous sway over their audience.

Dovetailing Li and Bernoff's participation ladder is the 1:9:90 rule, which as Paul Bates states in his article *Social Media Theory the 1:9:90 rule*[330] the 1:9:90 rule is not really a rule, but, rather, it is a useful concept to help understand how social media selling works. The theory proposes that for a mature website, just 1% of its website or social media visitors will actually produce original material or user generated content.[330] Meanwhile, 9% of visitors "will be editors or more likely commentators on that material and 90% of visitors will only ever read the material without ever making a comment."[330] Respectively, these groups are known as:

1. Originators—1%
2. Editors (or Commentators)—9%
3. Lurkers—90%

Bates points out that, "UGC is a very desirable thing on a social media site and If you can get your audience participating and creating original content, it will allow you to punch considerably above your weight and appear to have a large and active user base."[330] As previously mentioned, UGC can be a very good thing in terms of SEO and allowing users to add comments and/or create original content will go a long way to increase SEO rankings.

Bates also recommends that social media managers and professionals go out of their way to produce content that will attract comments and readership, but "it is even more profitable if social media managers or business owners can persuade others to create relevant and original content"[330]; getting such comments helps businesses gain credibility, especially if the comments are positive. A Facebook "like" is nice, but it doesn't take a lot of effort to "like" a Facebook page, whereas a comment is much more valuable because someone actually went through the process of explaining why they might recommend a product or a service, or both.[330]

The "lurker" category is the one Bates believes should not be taken for granted, though.[330] "This is the pay dirt for a social media based sales strategy," Bates argues, adding that this is where the big numbers lie.[330] By definition, lurkers have no engagement with a business and social media theory suggests that engagement must first be developed before any sale can be made.[330] However, the good news is that, although the ratios remain relatively stable, the individuals within these groups are constantly in flux.[330] "A lurker might indeed get interested and become a commentator before eventually buying and then just disappear or go back to lurking, or your 1% of originators might suddenly stop creating content and become lurkers" argues Bates.[330] What the 1:9:90 theory fails to address is that beyond the active user base is a whole world of potential prospects that you hope one day, at the very least, become lurkers.[330]

Social media listening can provide a sports book with an ongoing real-time window into customer sentiment, as well as give the sports book verifiable information about the company's marketing campaigns, brands, and services.

In chapter one, I mentioned Paul Greenberg stated that social CRM was "a philosophy and a business strategy supported by a technology platform, business rules, workflow, processes, and social characteristics, designed to engage and reach accordingly in a collaborative conversation."[91] *The A.I. Sports Book* must add social media elements to its CRM systems to give its customers a complete personalization experience. Continuous customer engagement can be fostered through a multitude of social channels and they are cheap to use, if not free, in some cases.

The beauty of a system like this is that it can be a real win-win situation when it comes to a company's marketing plan as customers who are happy with a business's products and/or services will often comment and blog about the products and/or services they like, while those who aren't happy with it can be reached out to and, hopefully, converted into satisfied customers. Often, the simple act of responding to a customer's comments can turn the tide of negativity and, as long as the remedies are constructive, can turn a hostile customer into a positive one, and, possibly, one who might even tout the company's excellent customer service at a later date.

Mullich offers the following tips on how to get the low-down on competitors[259]:

1. Understand that day-to-day online chatter can be misleading, but, over time, a sports book can find directional trends important to its business and industry.
2. The deepest insights often come not from general sources, like Facebook and Twitter, but from blogs and forums that are specific to an industry.
3. Think broadly about the nature of one's "competitors"—sentiment analysis can help a business prepare for unexpected entries that might be preparing to take a piece of its business. Keyword search terms can help.
4. The information you can gain online about a competitor is limited, and often must be combined with your own internal data to create actionable insights.

There are, of course, limits to what competitive sentiment analysis can provide. "The challenges you might address, using your company's own customer, product, and transactional data, are far more extensive than those you can tackle via available competitor data," says Seth Grimes, an analyst who runs the annual

Social Analysis Symposium.[259] "For instance, you're not going to have access to your competitors' contact-center notes and warranty claims, or to your competitors' customer profiles and transaction records. But with your own company's, you can create some very rich analyses," he adds.[259]

For the above reasons, competitive analysis is usually just one piece of the vast data mosaic.[259] For example, one company that noticed a drop in sales of its flagship product analyzed online chatter and found customers were talking enthusiastically about a new product a competitor had just released.[259] "When the company analyzed its contact-center data, it found that returns correlated to discontent about an attribute its own product lacked, but the new competing product offered."[259] The company was quickly able to identify the problem and by using a combination of competitive sentiment analysis, discovery from its own internal data, it was able to tweak its own product to make it much more competitive.[259]

As Grimes says, "Sentiment analysis can help you understand how the market perceives you and your competitors' products and services, but keep in mind that sentiment is only an indicator, useful in measuring and projecting market impact, not a substitute for strong human judgment."[259]

There is a dark side to all of this tracking as the case of IFA and Shopsense showed. Health Insurer IFA Insurance teamed up with Shopsense, a grocery chain in Midwest America, and bought their loyalty card customer data.[331] The insurance company discovered some intriguing patterns in the loyalty card data, such as the correlation between condom sales and HIV-related claims, for example.[331] It also discovered such things as households that buy cashews and bananas quarterly are the least likely to develop symptoms of Alzheimer's.[331] Although this information did prove to be highly profitable for IFA, I believe it is a clear violation of customer trust and privacy.

As Katherine Lemon explains in her article, *How Can These Companies Leverage the Customer Data Responsibly*[332], "Customer analytics are effective precisely because firms do *not* violate customer trust. People believe that retail and other organizations will use their data wisely to enhance their experiences, not to harm them. Angry customers will certainly speak with their wallets if that trust is violated."

Another concern for consumers is what Lemon calls "battered customer syndrome."[332] She explains that, "Market analytics allow companies to identify their best and worst customers and, consequently, to pay special attention to those deemed to be the most valuable."[332]

"Looked at another way, analytics enable firms to understand how poorly they can treat individuals or groups of customers before those people stop doing business with them. Unless you are in the top echelon of customers—those with the highest lifetime value, say—you may pay higher prices, get fewer special offers, or receive less service than other consumers," Lemon adds.[332] "Despite the fact that alienating 75% to 90% of customers may not be the best idea in the long run, many retailers have adopted this 'top tier' approach to managing customer relationships. And many customers seem to be willing to live with it—perhaps with the unrealistic hope that they maybe reach the upper echelon and reap the ensuing benefits."[332]

"Little research has been done on the negative consequences of using marketing approaches that discriminate against customer segments. Inevitably, however, customers will become savvier about analytics. They may become less tolerant and take their business (and information) elsewhere," Lemon warns.[332]

A word of warning here: don't set up fake accounts to try to get your marketing message out. There are people out in the blogosphere who would love nothing more than to uncover the latest social media scam, especially in China, and they probably have access to some of the most sophisticated tools to ferret out dishonest behavior.

Don't pick fights with customers on social media either. Threatening customers with legal action is never a good idea. The old rule that you shouldn't whip out a gun unless you're willing to pull the trigger should be kept in mind when it comes to social media as well. Use the threat of legal action cautiously and only as a last resort.

Social Media Analytics

As Melville and Lawrence explain in their article Social Media Analytics: Channeling the Power of the Blogosphere for Marketing Insight[333], social media analytics is "the practice of gathering data from blogs and social media websites and analyzing that data to make business decisions."

The most common use of social media is to mine customer sentiment." Social media analytics evolved out of the disciplines of social network analysis, machine learning, data mining, information retrieval (IR), and Natural Language Processing (NLP).

According to Melville and Lawrence, the automotive analysis of blogs and other social media sites raise the following intriguing marketing questions[333]:

1. Given the enormous size of the blogosphere, how can we identify the subset of blogs and forums that are discussing not only a specific product, but higher level concepts that are in some way relevant to this product?
2. Having identified this subset of relevant blogs, how do we identify the most authoritative or influential bloggers in this space?

3. How do we detect and characterize specific sentiment expressed about an entity (e.g., product) mentioned in a blog or a forum?
4. How do we tease apart novel emerging topics of discussion from the constant chatter in the blogosphere?

As Margaret Rouse explains in her article *Social Media Analytics*[334], step one of a social media analytics initiative is "to determine which business goals the data that is gathered and analyzed will benefit. Typical objectives include increasing revenues, reducing customer service costs, getting feedback on products and services and improving public opinion of a particular product or business division." Once these business goals have been identified, "key performance indicators (KPIs) for objectively evaluating the data should be defined. For example, customer engagement might be measured by the numbers of followers for a Twitter account and number of retweets and mentions of a company's name," states Rouse.[334]

Through social networks like Twitter and Weibo, organizations can pick up customer satisfaction in real time.[173] "Social media is enabling companies such as Coca-Cola, Starbucks, and Ford to go beyond standard customer satisfaction data gathering to innovate by setting up and participating in communities to gain feedback from customers."[173] A good example is MyStarbucksIdea.com, it is a website where "Starbucks customers can relate their experiences and offer ideas about how to improve the Starbucks experience, from drinks to foods to ambiance."[173]

When looking at what objectives companies were seeking when implementing customer analytics technologies with social media data (see Figure 25), TDWI Research found that gaining a "deeper customer understanding" topped the list at 56%[173] "Social media listening can provide an unprecedented window into customer sentiment and the reception of an organization's marketing, brands, and services."[173]

Besides the broad objective of gaining deeper customer understanding, nearly one-third (31%) of companies seek to identify attribution, or paths to buying decisions, which can be done on a limited scale with services like Google Analytics as well as other Web site analysis applications.[173] Google webmaster tools also allow sports books to understand the organic search traffic that is linking customers to them.

30% or respondents sought to discover customer sentiment, which is important because it helps companies discover positive and negative comments in social media channels, on customer comment and review sites.[173] "Sentiment analysis often focuses on monitoring and measuring the 'buzz' value, usually through volume and frequency of comments around a topic."[173]

Simply deciding which social media sites' data to analyze can be one of the biggest challenges facing businesses going down the analytics path.

"Organizations have to research where their customers are most likely to express themselves about brands and products. They need to spot influencers who have networks of contacts and take it upon themselves to play an advocacy role."[173]

Which of the following objectives does your organization seek to achieve by implementing customer analytics technologies and methods with social media data? (Please select all that apply.)

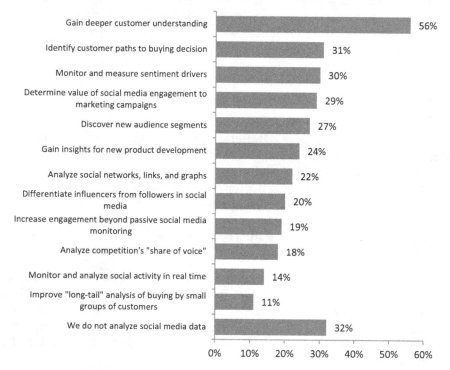

Figure 25: Customer Analytics and Social Media Objectives
Based on 1,546 respondents from 418 respondents; a bit more than three responses per respondent, on average.
Source: TDWI Research

"About 20% of respondents are interested in differentiating influencers from followers in social media.[173] "Link analytic tools and methods specialize in identifying relationships between users in social communities and enabling organizations to measure users' influence."[173] "With some tools, data scientists and analysts can test variables to help identify social communities as 'segments'. Then, as they implement segmentation models for other data sources, they can integrate these insights with social media network analysis to sharpen models and test new variables," explains Stodder.[173]

Analytics are critical in helping organizations "make the right decisions about when, where, and how to participate in social media. It isn't enough to just listen; organizations must insert themselves and become part of the conversation."[173] When doing so, however, companies should keep in mind advice from *The Cluetrain Manifesto*[335]—"Conversations among human beings sound human. They are conducted in a human voice," as well as this: "When delivering information, opinion, perspectives, dissenting arguments or humorous asides, the human voice is typically open, natural, uncontrived."[335]

Klear, a social media and social data platform that focuses on influencer marketing, offers a product that can help companies understand the effects of their influencer marketing. Klear's campaign reports contain the following summaries[336]:

- How many influencers participated in the campaign.
- Number of updates the influencers posted during the campaign.
- Engagements metrics.
- Number of people who saw the content.

The report also includes a drill-down analysis for each and every influencer. For each influencer the report will show[336]:

- Who is the influencer.
- The influencer's expertise.
- Fanbase across different social networks.
- Top posts during the campaign.
- Engagements for these updates.
- A direct link to the influencer's profile on Klear.

This is a paid service, but most of the information is publicly available and this is something a sports book could build up in-house, should they want a customized solution.

Influencer marketing taps directly into what Deighton and Kornfeld call the five paradigms of digital interactive marketing, i.e., social exchanges—building identities within virtual communities—and cultural exchanges—firms offering culture products that will compete in buzz markets.[149] This peer-to-peer interactivity should motivate the desire to exchange and share information, which should help market any sports book event.[149]

Social Media Monitoring

It is high time to revise Wanamaker's oft-made quote that he didn't know which half of his marketing spend was useful (as it is probably the most over-quoted quote in the history of marketing) because now we not only have the ability to figure out which advertisement works for which customer, but we can also extrapolate how that advertising will work on customers similar to the ones we might want to target.

Today, digital advertising should employ a multi-screen strategy that follows its audience throughout his or her digital day. As previously mentioned, successful mobile advertising requires three things—reach, purity and analytics. Analytics "involves matching users' interests—implicit and explicit, context, preferences, network and handset conditions—to ads and promotions in real time."[37]

In their *Measuring Social Media Performance and Business Impact (Part 1)*[337], Hamill and Stevenson put forth their '6Is' of social media monitoring framework that include:

1. Involvement—the number and quality of customers involved in your various online networks.
2. Interaction—the actions taken by online network members, who read, post, comment, review, recommend, etc.
3. Intimacy—the brand sentiments expressed, level of brand 'affection' or 'aversion'.
4. Influence—advocacy, viral forwards, referrals, recommendations, retweets, etc.
5. Insights—the level of customer/actionable insight delivered from monitoring online conversations.
6. Impact—business impact of your social media activities benchmarked against core business goals and objectives.

In 1999, *The Cluetrain Manifesto*[335] warned that "Reviews are the new advertising." Today, this is truer than ever before. There are a multitude of platforms that allow users to rate or comment on a sports book, a restaurant, a retail establishment, a hotel, a casino property, or even a local handyman or plumber. Nothing galvanizes people like sports and sports books should recognize the inherent marketing opportunities in connecting with people who are motivated to follow the teams and athletes they love.

Used properly, reviews can also be the new advertising currency for a sports book's marketing department. Companies such as Dell, Cisco, Salesforce.com, the American Red Cross, and Gatorade are creating Social Media command centers that monitor the social conversations about their companies. These social media centers enable company employees to monitor conversations from the social web on channels such as Twitter, Facebook, and YouTube, amongst others, in an attempt to keep track of the health of a company's social brand.

In December 2010, Dell became one of the first companies to launch a social media command center. Based at company HQ in Round Rock, TX, twelve full-time employees monitor conversations about Dell and its products around the globe, responding via @DellCares or forwarding the post to the right internal Dell team.[338] Through Dell's Social Media Listening and Command Center, Dell aggregates and culls through the 25,000 conversations about Dell every day (more than 6 million every year).[338]

"We're monitoring conversations in 11 languages 24/7, and each one is an opportunity to reinforce our brand," explains Karen Quintos, Dell CMO.[338] Quintos explains that[338]:

> "With the tremendous amount of information being generated, we can track basic demographics, reach, sentiment, subject matter of the discussions, the sites where conversations are happening, and more. We leverage these analytics to identify customer support needs as they happen, influence product development, insert ourselves into conversations with IT decision makers and connect with people having the most impact on these conversations."

In his article *Taking Back The Social-Media Command Center*[339], Scott Gulbransen argues that, "To do the command-center model right, a setup has to envision a real-time workflow empowered to take action on all of the relevant content being analyzed, whether it be insights derived from real-time monitoring, opportunities to respond, or great discovered content to feature that elevates you and your fans." Gulbransen recommends breaking down a command center into the following critical functions[339]:

1. Identify trends and insights—track not only the key themes, but also how they evolve over time.
2. Review the content—monitor a wide variety of terms that are meaningful to the brand and assign employees to sort through the responses, deciding which one warrants a response, and what might interest the community at large.
3. Curate the best stuff—leverage the great content that is being said about the company as well as champion those great content providers.
4. Listen and Respond—this is a two-way conversation, listen and respond quickly and accordingly.

Unlike casual conversations, comments, updates, likes and dislikes uploaded to social networks are collected and, therefore, analyzable and measurable. This results in "a data tsunami: the actions and content generated by participants in social media create 'Big Data' sources that are full of potential for tracking and understanding behavior, trends, and sentiments."[173] Remember, this can be highly quantifiable data. Sports betting operators should be studying attribution analysis for its social media campaigns on platforms like Facebook, YouTube, Twitter, Weibo, etc., etc.

Getting people to actually state their feelings and opinions about a product is paramount and it can help with attribution analysis, which can reveal such things as what kinds of campaigns most influence customer behavior.[173] In digital advertising, attribution is traditionally done at a user-specific level, where a consistent user identifier can be established across all analyzed events. In traditional media, attribution is generally done at the macro, user-group level, as there is no consistent user identifier available.

In its *Social Media Analytics: Making Customer Insights Actionable*[340], IBM believes that the "mistake many organizations make is to treat social media as distinct and separate from other customer data and divorced from revenue generating imperatives." IBM recommends companies venturing into the social media space do the following[340]:

- Integrate company-wide information from different data sources to drive the business through deeper consumer insight.
- Define the real value of the company's brand—its equity, reputation and loyalty—at any moment in time, in any place in the world; and
- Understand emerging consumer trends, both globally and locally and apply predictive models to determine actions with the highest probability of increasing relevance and maximizing marketing campaign ROI.

IBM also recommends businesses ask the following questions when devising a social media plan[340]:

- Assess—also referred to as "listening," at this stage a company should monitor social media to uncover sentiment about its products, services, marketing campaigns, employees and partners. The questions that need to be asked at this stage include:
    - What are you company objectives? Are you looking to:
        - Attract customers?
        - Increase the value of existing customer relationships?
        - Retain customers?
    - How do customers interact with you today?
    - What are they interested in?
    - Where and when do they use social media?
    - Are there significant influencers who speak to your brand or products?
- Measure—proactive analytics can uncover hidden patterns that can reveal "unknown unknowns" in the data. Questions that businesses need to ask at this stage include:
    - Who are you targeting with your social media initiatives and why?
    - What will you be measuring:
        - Share of voice
        - Activation
        - Brand sentiment
        - Influencers

o   Sales over the life of the customer relationship?
- Integrate—social media can give businesses both a broad view of their operations as well as a detailed and intimate view of their individual customers. Questions to ask at this stage include:
  o   What is your vision for social media and its integration into the company's operational marketing systems?
  o   Do you have a profile of your customer advocates? Can you predict sentiment on products, services, campaigns?
  o   How do you measure the effects of social media on brand equity and reputation, pipeline, and sales orders and margins?
  o   How will you integrate social analytics into other customer analytics?

Regardless of the sophistication and scope of any social media initiative, the end goal, IBM argues, should be in alignment with corporate imperatives and goals as well as produce a measurable ROI.[340]

Table 13 lists the Social Media Tools and websites available to business users to track engagement and customer feedback.

Name	Comments
Addict-o-matic	Addictomatic searches the best live sites on the web for the latest news, blog posts, videos and images. It's a social media listening tool to keep up with the hottest topics, perform ego searches and get info on what's up, what's now or what other people are feeding on. You can personalize your results dashboard and keep coming back to your personalized results dashboard for that search. News pages provide the latest headlines on topics such as entertainment, politics, shopping, sports and more.
Board Reader	BoardReader allows users to search multiple message boards simultaneously, allowing users to share information in a truly global sense. Boardreader is focused on creating the largest repository of searchable information for our users. Users can find answers to their questions from others who share similar interests. Our goal is to allow our users to search the "human to human" discussions that exist on the Internet.
Buffer	Buffer makes your life easier with a smarter way to schedule the great content you find. Fill up your Buffer at one time in the day and Buffer automagically posts them for you through the day. Simply keep that Buffer topped up to have a consistent social media presence all day round, all week long. Get deeper analytics than if you just post to social networks directly.
Buzzsumo	Analyze what content performs best for any topic or competitor. Find the key influencers to promote your content: - Discover the most shared content across all social networks and run detailed analysis reports. - Find influencers in any topic area, review the content they share and amplify.

Name	Comments
	• Be the first to see content mentioning your keyword; or when an author or competitor publishes new content. • Track your competitor's content performance and do detailed comparisons.
Commun.it	Can help you organize, increase, and manage your followers, and can do so across multiple accounts and profiles. At a glance you can see different aspects of your community management, like the latest tweets from your stream and which new followers might appreciate a welcome message.
Crowdfire	Crowdfire is a powerful phone app and online website that helps you grow your Twitter and Instagram account reach. This tool has a variety of functions designed to understand your social analytics as well as manage your social publishing.
Cyfe	Cyfe is an all-in-one dashboard software that helps you monitor and analyze data scattered across all your online services like Google Analytics, Salesforce, AdSense, MailChimp, Facebook, WordPress and more from one single location in real-time.
Fanpage Karma	Shows a variety of valuable information related to your Facebook page, such as growth, engagement, service and response time, and of course Karma (a weighted engagement value). FanKarma also provides insight into Twitter and YouTube; the latter could be particularly valuable if you're creating a video marketing strategy.
Followerwonk	Followerwonk is a cool social media analytics tool thet lets you explore and grow your social graph. Dig deeper into Twitter analytics: followers, their locations, when do they tweet. Find and connect with influencers in your niche. Use visualizations to compare your social graph to competitors.
Google Alerts	Google Alerts are email updates of the latest relevant Google results (blogs, news, etc.) based on your searches. Enter the topic you wish to monitor, then click preview to see the type of results you'll receive. Some handy uses of Google Alerts include: monitoring a developing news story and keeping current on a competitor or industry.
Google Trends	Trends allows you to compare search terms and websites. With Google Trends you can get insights into the traffic and geographic visitation patterns of websites or keywords. You can compare data for up to five websites and view related sites and top searches for each one.
Hootsuite	Monitor and post to multiple social networks, including Facebook and Twitter. Create custom reports from over 30 individual report modules to share with clients and colleagues. Track brand sentiment, follower growth, plus incorporate Facebook Insights and Google analytics. Draft and schedule messages to send at a time your audience is most likely to be online. HootSuite has the dashboard for your iPhone, iPad, BlackBerry and Android.
HowSocialable	Monitor and post to multiple social networks, including Facebook and Twitter. Create custom reports from over 30 individual report modules to share with clients and colleagues. Track brand sentiment, follower growth, plus incorporate Facebook Insights and Google analytics. Draft and schedule messages to send at a time your audience is most likely to be online. HootSuite has the dashboard for your iPhone, iPad, BlackBerry and Android.

Name	Comments
Iconosquare	Key metrics about your Instagram account. Number of likes received, your most liked photos ever, your average number of likes and comments per photo, your follower growth charts and more advanced analytics. Track lead conversations, send private message as on Twitter, and improve communication with your followers.
Klear	Social media monitoring, analytics and reporting. Influencer marketing, find and create relationships with the top influencers in your sector and build your community. Competitive analysis tracks your social media landscape, see what's working for them and develop your strategy.
Klout	Klout's mission is to help every individual understand and leverage their influence. Klout measures influence in Twitter to find the people the world listens to. It analyzes content to identify the top influencers.
Kred	Kred is a social-media scoring system that seeks to measure a person's online influence. Kred, which was created by the San Francisco-based social analytics firm PeopleBrowsr, attempts to also measure a person or company's engagement, or as they call it, outreach. PeopleBrowsr hopes that that combination can offer a more informed metric for non-celebrities like entrepreneurs and those whom they follow and look to for advice.
LikeAlyzer	This Facebook analysis tool comes up with stats and insights into your page and begins every report with a list of recommendations. Keep track of where your Facebook page stands compared to other pages by following the comparison to average page rank, industry-specific page rank, and rank of similar brands.
Mention	Mention prides itself on "going beyond Google Alerts" to track absolutely anywhere your name or your company might be mentioned online. When you subscribe to Mention's daily email you get all these wayward hits right in your inbox, and the Web dashboard even flags certain mentions as high priority.
Mentionmap	Explore your Twitter network. Discover which people interact the most and what they're talking about. It's also a great way to find relevant people to follow. The visualization runs right in your browser and displays data from Twitter. Mentionmap loads user's tweets and finds the people and hashtags they talked about the most. In this data visualization, mentions become connections and discussions between multiple users emerge as clusters.
Must Be Present	Built by the team at Sprout Social, Must Be Present searches your Twitter account to find how quickly you respond to mentions. Their engagement reports place you in a percentile based on other accounts so you can see how you stack up to the speed of others.
NeedTagger	A super-powered Twitter search tool, NeedTagger runs language filters and keyword searches to determine which Twitter users might need your products or services. The tool shows you real-time search results and sends a daily email digest of new finds.
NutshellMail	Collects your activity on Facebook, LinkedIn, and Twitter (and even places like Yelp and Foursquare) to provide an email overview of your accounts. You set how often and when you want to receive the recap emails. Put it to use: If you have a weekly metrics plan you can have NutshellMail send a message once a week with an overview of your accounts. You can then

Name	Comments
	extract the data and insights straight into your weekly report.
Omgili	Omgili helps you find interesting and current discussions, news stories and blog posts. Direct access to live data from hundreds of thousands of forums, news and blogs. Very easy to use, no signup for web interface.
Pinterest Analytics	Find out how many people are pinning from your website, seeing your pins, and clicking your content. Pick a time-frame to see how your numbers trend over time. Get better at creating Pins and boards with metrics from your Pinterest profile. Learn how people use the Pin It button on your site to add Pins. See how people interact with your Pins from whatever device they use. Get a glance at your all-time highest-performing Pins.
Pluggio	Pluggio is a web-based social media tool to help marketers easily grow and manage their social media profiles (Facebook and Twitter). It includes a suite of tools to organize and keep track of multiple accounts, get more followers, and automate the finding and publishing of excellent targeted content.
Postific	The full set of social media tools. Post content to over 10 social networks with one single click of a button. Get real time click-through statistics with your domain name. Measure and analyze the best results from your social posts. Monitor the social media conversations that are important for your business.
Quintly	Quintly is the professional social media monitoring and analytics solution to track and compare the performance of your social media marketing activities. Whether you are using Facebook, Twitter or both, Quintly monitors and visualizes your social media marketing success. Benchmark your numbers against your competitors or best practice examples.
Sentiment	Sentiment was born in 2007 and now boasts a team of bright enthusiastic people dedicated to provide the best social customer service and engagement platform for business.
SocialMention	SocialMention tracks areas such as sentiment, passion, reach, and strength to not just tell you what's being said about your search but how those reactions feel. While you track your brand or yourself, you can also see how your sentiment changes over time.
Social Rank	Identifies your top 10 followers in three specific areas: Best Followers, Most Engaged, and Most Valuable. Your most engaged followers are those who interact with you most often (replies, retweets, and favorites); your most valuable followers are the influential accounts; and your best followers are a combination of the two. Social Rank will run the numbers for free and show you the results today, then follow-up each month with an email report.
Social Oomph	Schedule tweets, track keywords, extended Twitter profiles, save and reuse drafts, view @mentions and retweets, purge your DM inbox, personal status feed — your own tweet engine, unlimited accounts.
This tracking tool	Keeps track of your hashtag campaign or keyword on Twitter, Instagram, or Facebook with a full dashboard of analytics, demographics, and influencers.
Tip Top	TipTop Search is a Twitter-based search engine that helps you discover the best and most current advice, opinions, answers for any search, and also real people to directly engage and share experiences with. A search

Name	Comments
	on any topic reveals people's emotions and experiences about it, as well as other concepts that they are discussing in connection with the original search.
Topsy	A powerful search engine for Twitter content. Want to know how a certain term is being used on Twitter? You can search links, tweets, photos, videos, and influencers.
Twazzup	Offers real-time monitoring and analytics for Twitter on any name, keyword, or hashtag you choose. The Twazzup results page delivers interesting insights like the top influencers for your keyword and which top links are associated with your search.
Tweepi	Has a number of useful Twitter features, many of which fall into a couple categories: managing your followers and supercharging who you're following. For management, you can unfollow in batches those who don't follow you back, and you can bulk follow another account's complete list of followers or who they're following.
Tweetcaster	A Twitter management tool for iOS and Android devices and provides the basics of what you'd expect from a Twitter dashboard plus a few fun extras: enhanced search and lists, hiding unwanted tweets, and photo effects for your images.
Tweetdeck	Lets you track, organize, and engage with your followers through a customizable dashboard where you can see at a glance the activity from different lists, followers, hashtags, and more.
TweetReach	Shows you the reach and exposure of the tweets you send, collecting data on who retweets you and the influence of each. Identify which of your tweets has spread the furthest (and why) and then try to repeat the formula with future tweets.
TwitterCounter	Twitter Counter is the number one site to track your Twitter stats. Twitter Counter provides statistics of Twitter usage and tracks over 14 million users. Twitter Counter also offers a variety of widgets and buttons that people can add to their blogs, websites or social network profiles to show recent Twitter visitors and number of followers.
Twtrland	Provides a snapshot of your Twitter profile and can even track Facebook and Instagram as well. Two of Twtrland's most helpful tools are a live count of how many followers are currently online and advanced search functionality that includes keywords, locations, and companies. Local companies can perform a location search to see which area accounts are most popular and potentially worth following.
SumAll	SumAll is a powerful social media analytics tool that allows our customers to view all of their data in one simple, easy-to-use visualization. Social media, e-commerce, advertising, e-mail, and traffic data all come together to provide a complete view of your activity.
ViralWoot	Pin Alert feature lets you track what are people pinning from your website, who is pinning the most and what images from your website are trending on Pinterest. Thousands of social media marketers and agencies use Viralwoot for their clients. You can manage & grow multiple Pinterest accounts with a single Viralwoot account.

Name	Comments
WhosTalkin	WhosTalkin is a social media monitoring tool that lets you search for conversations surrounding the topics that you care about most. Whether it be your favorite sports team, food, celebrity, or brand name; Whostalkin will help you find the conversations that are important to you. WhosTalkin search and sorting algorithms combine data taken from over 60 of the most popular social media sites.
WhoUnfollowedMe	Who.unfollowed.me is a service that helps you track your unfollowers, in real time, without waiting for a DM, or email. It allows you to check your unfollowers on your schedule, every 15 minutes, without waiting for an email or a direct message.

Table 13: Social Media Tools
Source: Dreamglow.com[341]

Social Media Marketing

In their article *An Exploratory Study of Gambling Operators' Use of Social Media and the Latent Messages Conveyed[342]*, Gainsbury et al. argue that social media has become a powerful marketing channel because it "enables gambling operators to promote products and brands with fewer constraints than in traditional forms of media."[342] The study attempted to quantify features of social media presence among several popular Australia gambling operators, a majority of which did have some social media presence; Facebook was the most popular social media platform used.[342]

In the Gainsbury et al. study, "Information posted on Facebook and Twitter was inspected to examine content promoted or discussed via the respective social media channels. Many operators posted the same or similar content across various social media platforms, or linked between these. This was particularly the case for Facebook and Twitter linking to YouTube videos."[342]

According to Gainsbury et al., the types of content posted on social media sites included the following[342]:

- Information about the venue/operator, including information on gambling facilities as well as other non-gambling services available, contact details, and hours of operation.
- Promoting gambling products, offers, and specific events to encourage users to place bets. "Posts involved text and graphics that illustrate the types of gambling products available, how to use these, potential returns, and types of customers who use the products."[342] Land-based venues often posted information about in-venue events, such as bingo tournaments and upcoming jackpots."[342]
- Posts about competitions and promotions.
- Promoting gambling wins.

- Promoting features to assist with betting, including betting and payment options.
- Betting tips.
- Sports and racing news.
- Promoting in-venue events, which included drawing users' attention to special or regular weekly events, encouraging interaction with users.
- Promoting food and beverages.
- Encouraging customer engagement by encouraging users to follow, like, and share their own posted content.
- Links to sports teams.
- Promoting community engagement.

Many gambling operators also posted content unrelated to gambling, but this was "designed to be engaging, humorous, and encourage likes and sharing among user networks."[342] For example, "cartoons and images were often used to make jokes about the frenetic and mundane chaos as well as the drudgery of family life, with betting presented as a superior alternative option (e.g., a Facebook post by IASbet.com featuring a photo of a man surrounded by children thinking about being at the race with the caption "Where would you rather be?", May 16, 2013)."[342]

Conclusion

In this chapter, I have laid out the foundation for an understanding of the social media milieu sports books are faced with today. Few sports books will succeed in this new millennium without embracing social media. When first delving into social media, sports books should follow the four steps of social media—listen, join, participate and create—and these steps must be strictly followed in that order.[323]

Listening can be done on blogs, content communities, and social networks. By keeping an eye on any comments made on these blogs, or on the pages of Facebook, Instagram, Pinterest, Twitter, or a whole host of other social network pages, social media marketers can get a sense of what the community feels about its business and its products and services.

Social media is all about adding value to communities of customers and prospects by providing interesting content (blogs, podcasts, webinars, etc.). It allows immediate engagement with groups of customers and potential customers. Today, the traditional model of blasting messages to customers and potential customers is fading as trust in corporate America is at an all-time low. In today's difficult economic climate, peer referrals are becoming more and more important. Consumers are tuning out regular advertising and tapping into social media for advice. Listening and joining these conversations could prove highly lucrative to sports betting companies.

Social media is constrained only by the imagination of a sports book's marketers and it offers enormous potential, both creatively and financially, to any company willing to enter the arena. Social media can play an integral part in customer understanding.

The Thomas et al. study found that promotional messaging on social media, particularly on Twitter, was quite prevalent, with one company averaging over 50 tweets per day. Many of these tweets also used game-related hashtags, thus directly linking tweets with sporting matches."[322] The researchers hypothesized that "these tweets also target sports fans that may be watching the game and also engaging in commentary about the game via social media platforms."[322] "These real time promotions via Twitter also offer the opportunity to attract the attention of potential gamblers at times when they might not otherwise be considering betting."[322] This is something that should intrigue every sports book.

The study also found that there is a wide range of strategies used by the wagering industry on social media platforms.[322] The study revealed some variation in the content depending on the social media platform used. According to Thomas et al., "Facebook used a combination of videos, advertisements, pictures, text and links to other websites, and Twitter used similar strategies other than advertisements. YouTube is a video based platform and clips include various types of videos such as advertisements, funny videos, stunts, wagering promotions, sports commentary and clips relating to Corporate Social Responsibility activities."[322]

As for creative strategies, "all three platforms used humour, nostalgia, games statistics and cartoons. In addition to these, tributes and themes associated with fan engagement appeared on YouTube and Facebook, news articles and players/celebrities featured on YouTube and wagering information appeared on Twitter."[322]

All three platforms unsurprisingly featured promotions focused on the themes of sports and wagering.[322] "Sporting promotions included national and international sporting codes and horse racing. Wagering-related promotions included a wide range of wagering products, with all three platforms promoting refunds, tipping, betting promotions, odds, prompts to bet, winning and responsible gambling messages."[322]

The researchers "identified a number of promotional strategies that may not be clearly recognised by consumers as marketing promotions or advertisements." "Most commonly these included humorous videos which, on the surface, appeared unrelated to the wagering brand, however subtle branding was displayed throughout the clip, for example in the background or on products which appear in the video."[322]

This strategy, known as product placement, "is commonly used to build positive brand associations amongst consumers without overtly calling for product consumption."[322] Thomas et al. note that "This is perhaps even more commonly seen with brands associated with dangerous consumption products which in themselves can have negative associations amongst the public."[322] This approach helps "to elicit a positive response in the viewer, for example laughter and amusement, which in turn builds positive associations with the brand and encourages product consumption at a later time," explain Thomas et al.

Promotions like this help the brand communicate to an "audience who may not apply the usual cognitive defences that they would do when viewing advertisements which they know are trying to persuade them. While this type of strategy was found across all three social media platforms, the most viewed and shared promotions of this nature were on YouTube,' add Thomas et al.[322]

"A range of marketing strategies were identified that may reduce the perception of risk associated with gambling,"[322] which isn't really that surprising. The study found that these "strategies included the promotion of bonus bets which give punters extra bets when they place the required number of bets, cash out promotions which give individuals the chance to cancel their bets up until a certain point in the game, and refunds which commit to giving punters their money back under certain circumstances."[322] Each of these products may build upon "the perception that individuals are unlikely to lose and that they are receiving greater value for money from their original outlay." This effectively counters concerns punters may have about losing their money," conclude Thomas et al.[322]

China is an important player in social media. As Chiu et al. state in their paper *Understanding Social Media in China*[343], "The sheer number of the more than 300 million social-media users in China creates unique challenges for effective consumer engagement," but I believe the potential market is too massive to ignore. But it is a tricky market; in China, "People expect responses to each and every post, for example, so companies must develop new models and processes for effectively engaging individuals in a way that communicates brand identity and values, satisfies consumer concerns, and doesn't lead to a negative viral spiral."[343] Other problems include the "difficulty of developing and tracking reliable metrics to gauge a social-media strategy's performance, given the size of the user base, a lack of analytical tools (such as those offered by Facebook and Google in other markets), and limited transparency into leading platforms,"[343]

China is, unquestionably, making great strides, but they still have a long way to go before their social media analytics technology can rival the US's. However, as Chiu et al. make clear, this is not a barrier that should stand in the way of companies as "The similarity between the ingredients of success in China and in other markets makes it easier—and well worth the trouble—to cope with the country's many peculiarities."[343]

China might not allow marketing of sports betting products inside China, but, like the US, they might, one day, take a more enlightened approach. There are also huge Chinese communities outside of China that are highly interested in wagering on betting markets of all kinds.

---

308 Drury, G. (2008). Opinion piece: Social media: Should marketers engage and how can it be done effectively? Journal of Direct, Data and Digital Marketing Practice, Volume 9, pages 274-277.

309 As identified in Claude E. Shannon and Warren Weaver's *The Mathematical Theory of Communication*, the Source-Message-Channel-Receiver model is a basic model of communication; Source is the person who encodes the message and transmits it to the receiver; the Message is the intended meaning the source hopes the receiver will understand; the Channel is the medium through which the message is conveyed and it must tap into the receiver's sensory system; the Receiver is the person at the end of the communication, someone who will decode the message and create their own meaning.

310 Lefebvre, R. C. (2007). The New Technology: The Consumer as Participant Rather Than Target Audience. *Social Marketing Quarterly*, 31-42.

311 Outing, S. (2007, September). Enabling the Social Company. Enthusiast Group. Retrieved from Steveouting.com: http://www.steveouting.com/files/social_company.pdf

312 Business.com. (2010, November 8). Top Tools to measure your social media success. Retrieved from Business.com: http://www.business.com/info/social-media-monitoring-tools

313 Juniper Research. (2008). *Mobile User Generated Content: Dating, Social Networking & Personal Content Deliver*. Juniper Research.

314 Juniper Research. (2008). *Mobile User Generated Content: Dating, Social Networking & Personal Content Deliver*. Juniper Research.

315 OECD. (2007). Participative web and user-created content: Web 2.0, wikis, and social networking. Organisation for Economic Co-operation and Development. Paris.

316 Short, J. W. (1976). *The Social Psychology of telecommunication*. Hoboken, NJ: John Wiley & Sons, Ltd.

317 Daft, R. &. (1986). Organization information requirements, media richness, and structural design. *Management Science*, 32(5), 554-571.

318 Goffman, E. (1959). The Presentation of Self In Everyday Life. New York: Doubleday.

319 Sparkes, M. (2014, February 24). Betfair to offer 'self-destructing odds' via Snapchat. The Telegraph.

320 Benson, L. (2009, October 26). *Casinos saving face online*. Retrieved from Las Vegas Sun: www.lasvegassun.com/news/2009/oct/26/saving-face-online/

321 Thomas, Samantha, Bestman, Amy, Pitt, Hannah, Deans, Emily, Randle, Melanie, Stoneham, Melissa, and Daube, Mike. (2015). The marketing of wagering on social media: An analysis of promotional content on YouTube, Twitter and Facebook. Victorian

Responsible Gambling Association. October 2015. http://ro.uow.edu.au/cgi/viewcontent.cgi?article=1694&context=ahsri (Accessed 24 January 2018).

322 Elo, S & Kyngas, H (2008), The qualitative content analysis process, Journal of Advanced Nursing, 62 (1), 107-115.

323 Eley, B & Tilley S. *Online Marketing Inside Out: Reach New Buyers Using Modern Marketing Techniques*. May 28, 2009. Sitepoint

324 Nelson, A. (2013, November 21). *50 ways to drive traffic to your website with social media*. Retrieved from Exact Target Cloud Blog: http://www.exacttarget.com/blog/50-ways-to-drive-traffic-to-your-website-with-social-media/

325 Stampler, L. (2013, February 19). *How Maker's Mark turned its watered down whiskey debacle into a social media win*. Retrieved from Business Insider: http://www.businessinsider.com/makers-mark-turns-whiskey-fail-into-win-2013-2

326 Hierarchy of Social Marketing. John Jantsch. Duct Tape Marketing. https://www.ducttapemarketing.com/the-hierarchy-of-social-marketing (Accessed 23 August 2019).

327 http://www.simplypsychology.org/maslow.html

328 Li, C. a. (2008). Groundswell: Winning in a World Transformed by Social Technologie. Harvard Business Press.

329 Ramirez, A. (2009). The Effect of Interactivity on Initial Interactions: The Influence of Information Seeking Role on Computer-Mediated Interaction. Western Journal of Communication, 300-325.

330 Bates, P. (2011). Social Media Theory—the 1:9:90 rule. Retrieved from Yell: http://marketing.yell.com/web-design/social-media-theory-the-1-9-90-rule/

331 Davenport, T. (2006). Competing on Analytics. Harvard Business Review.

332 Lemon, K. (2007, May). How Can These Companies Leverage the Customer Data Responsibly. Retrieved from http://blog.hansacequity.com: http://blog.hansacequity.com/Portals/11224/docs/article%20on%20Analytics.pdf

333 Melville, P. &. (2009). Social Media Analytics : Channeling the Power of the Blogosphere for Marketing Insight. Retrieved from citeseerx.ist.psu.edu: http://citeseerx.ist.psu.edu/viewdoc/download?doi=10.1.1.157.3485&rep=rep1&type=pdf

334 Rouse, M. (n.d.). Social Media Analytics. Retrieved from techtarget.com: http://searchbusinessanalytics.techtarget.com/definition/social-media-analytics

335 Levine, Rick, Locke, Christopher, Searls, Doc, Weinverger, David. (1999). The Cluetrain Manifesto. https://www.cluetrain.com/book/ (Accessed 8/8/2019).

336 https://klear.com/

337 Hamill, J. and Stevenson, A. 2010. Step 3: *Key Performance Indicators (Post 1)*. Available at: www.energise2-0.com/2010/06/27/step-3-key-performance- indicators-post-1/ [accessed: 12 February 2011].

338 Salesforce.com. (2013). 10 Examples of Social Media Command Centers. Retrieved from Salesforce Marketing Cloud: http://www.salesforcemarketingcloud.com/resources/ebooks/10-examples-of-social-media-command-centers/

339 Gulbransen, Scott. January 22, 2014. Taking Back The Social-Media Command Center, Scott Gulbransen. Forbes. http://www.forbes.com/sites/onmarketing/2014/01/22/taking-back-the-social-media-command-center/#3c283a5d6513

340 IBM. (2013, February). Social Media Analytics: Making Customer Insights Actionable. Retrieved from IBM.com: http://www-01.ibm.com/common/ssi/cgi-bin/ssialias?infotype=SA&subtype=WH&htmlfid=YTW03168USEN

341 https://www.dreamgrow.com/69-free-social-media-monitoring-tools/ (Accessed 22 August 2019).

342 Gainsbury, Sally M., Delfabbro, Paul, King, Daniel L., and Hing, Nerilee. March 2016. An Exploratory Study of Gambling Operators' Use of Social Media and the Latent Messages Conveyed.

343 Chiu, C. I. (2012, April). Understanding social media in China. Retrieved from www.mckinsey.com:

http://www.mckinsey.com/insights/marketing_sales/understanding_social_media_in_china

CHAPTER FIVE

The A.I. Sports Book

"You can't win in the digital era with industrial-age technology."
~ Adobe

Overview

One of the first things that the *A.I. Sports Books* must do is build a master marketing record for each of its customer. The *A.I. Sports Book* should use Master Data Management (MDM) techniques to communicate important customer preference information to staff that sit at the company's customer interaction points, wherever and whenever this information is needed. MDM is the processes, governance, policies, standards and tools that consistently define and manage the critical data of an organization to provide a single point of reference.

One of the benefits of using MDM is that when that single point of reference is a customer profile, the master data can ensure that the treatment of a customer is consistent, and that preference information reaches all customer points of contact. As previously mentioned, this allows the sports book to test scenarios and options for the website, as well as develop personalized responses for individuals for a multitude of scenarios.

The system should include a combination of social listening, analytics, content publication and distribution, and tracking, as well as a workflow and rules engine that is geared around strong governance. All these applications are built to ultimately feed a master marketing profile—a centralized customer record that pulls in all data based on digital activity that can be identified through a single customer ID. Utilizing clickstream analysis and real-time streaming, a marketer can help build a Master Marketing Record for each customer in real-time. This allows the brand to test scenarios and options for the website, as well as develop personalized responses for individuals.

Once a master marketing record has been created, brands can build cognitive styles dimensions on their customers. As previously mentioned, a person's cognitive style is a "preferred way of gathering, processing, and evaluating information."[76] These styles "might include impulsive (makes decisions quickly) versus deliberative (explores options in depth before making a decision), visual (prefers images) versus verbal (prefers text and numbers), or analytic (wants all details) versus holistic (just the bottom line)."[75] The brand should quantify all of its website content and click actions to build functional displays for each customer morph type.

Heller says that one of the keys to personalization at scale is internal structure.[68] He expects companies in 2019 to work on building agile marketing execution models in which cross-functional teams can experiment, leveraging the data and technology stack to capture value."[68]

All of a sports book's information can be fed into a data lake and/or a company's EDW, where it can be utilized by a multitude of operational departments, including security, call center/customer service, HR, marketing, social media marketing, customer management, all the way up to the top executive branch, including individuals in the C-level suite.

One of the main goals of this book is to show brands how to bring more work in-house. If companies can utilize AI to automate many of their current processes, employees can be retrained to work in areas that are more creative and, hopefully, more interesting to them. The workforce of 2025 will be far different from the workforce of today and brands need to prepare themselves for these radical changes today.

In their article *Data-Driven Transformation: Accelerate at Scale Now*[344], Gourévitch et al. argue that, "Data-driven transformation is becoming a question of life or death in most industries." "Most CEOs recognize the power of data-driven transformation. They certainly would like the 20% to 30% EBITDA gains that their peers are racking up by using fresh, granular data in sales, marketing, supply chain, manufacturing, and R&D," claim Gourévitch et al.[394] What's not lost on these CEOs is the fact that today the top five companies with the highest market capitalization worldwide are all data-driven, tech companies—Apple, Alphabet (Google), Microsoft, Amazon, and Facebook.[394] Five years ago, only one of these tech companies was in the top five (Apple), whereas ten years ago only one was in the top ten (Microsoft).[394]

CEOs are correct in worrying about how their organizations are going to handle a tenfold increase in company data when their managers are already complaining about a lack of data skills and overburdened IT systems today.[394] "Transformations should start with pilots that pay off in weeks or months, followed by a plan for tackling high-priority use cases, and finishing with a program for building long-term capabilities," recommend Gourévitch et al.[394]

"It starts with small-scale, rapid digitization efforts that lay the foundation for the broader transformation and generate returns to help fund later phases of the effort," advocate Gourévitch et al.[394] "In the second and third phases, companies draw on knowledge from their early wins to create a roadmap for companywide transformation, 'industrialize' data and analytics, and build systems and capabilities to execute new data-driven strategies and processes."[394]

In terms of infrastructure and data transformation, Gourévitch et al. state that companies need to ask the following questions[394]:

> "Can our current infrastructure support our future data value map? Should we make or buy? Should we go to the cloud? Do we need a data lake? What role should our legacy IT systems play in our data transformation? The company should design a data platform (or data lake) that can accommodate its product map and should use that platform to progressively transform its legacy systems."

"To progressively transform its legacy system," is an important concept here because it is imperative that companies don't bite off more than they can chew when they decide to embrace a data-driven culture.

While the company architects the transformation roadmap, it needs to begin industrializing its data and analytics.[394] As Gourévitch et al. explain, "This means setting up a way to standardize the creation and management of data-based systems and processes so that the output is replicable, efficient, and reliable."[394] Digital systems need to have all the attributes of industrial machinery, including reliability and consistency.[394]

For analytics, a flexible open architecture that can be updated continuously and enhanced with emerging technologies works best.[394] "Rather than embracing an end-to-end data architecture, companies should adopt a use-case-driven approach, in which the architecture evolves to meet the requirements of each new initiative," advise Gourévitch et al.[394] "The data governance and analytics functions should collaborate to create a simplified data environment; this will involve defining authorized sources of data and aggressively rationalizing redundant repositories and data flows," recommend Gourévitch at al.[394]

To prepare an organization for a digitized future, a company "needs to move on four fronts: creating new roles and governance processes, instilling a data-centric culture, adopting new ways of working, and cultivating the necessary talent and skills."[394]

Change starts at the top and senior leaders need to both buy into and adopt data-driven objectives, as well as instill a data-driven culture in every department throughout the organization.[394] Gourévitch et al. recommend that top management "set up data councils to extend the work to all sectors of the organization and to carry it out more effectively."[394] "The company should promote data awareness by using data champions to disseminate data-driven practices," state Gourévitch et al.[394]

"Not everyone needs to become steeped in data analytics or learn to code in order for digital transformation to work. However, everyone does need to adopt a less risk-averse attitude," recommend Gourévitch et al.[394] The writers believe brands should embrace the software company model that utilizes a test-and-learn philosophy that accepts failure and is constantly changing–and learning.[394] The Japanese have a concept known as *Kaizen*—continuous incremental improvement—and it is an idea that should be kept in mind when a company steps into the data-driven world.

Businesses can also foster the desired cultural change through organizational moves, "such as creating internal startup units where employees can focus on experimentation or co-locating data labs within operating units."[394] "The company can also promote the new culture by using cross-functional teams that share data across silos, thereby encouraging openness and collaboration throughout the organization," advise Gourévitch et al.[394]

For any data-based transformation to succeed, a company needs talent with the right skills to execute data-driven strategies and manage data-based operations.[394]

Brands should be inspired by the idea of using data to make better decisions, to create stronger customer bonds, and to digitize all sorts of processes to improve performance. They should also be motivated "by fear that they won't be able to keep up with competitors who are ahead of them in data-driven digital transformation."[394]

Some caution is due here; sweeping, company-wide change to go digital can easily lead to counterproductive overreaching.[394] In this case, the contest will not necessarily be won by making huge bets.[394] As Gourévitch et al. conclude, "The winners will be agile, pragmatic, and disciplined. They will move fast and capture quick wins, but they will also carefully plan a transformation roadmap to optimize performance in the functions and operations that create the most value, while building the technical capabilities and resources to sustain the transformation."[394]

AI is a problem solver. One of the examples I give at my talks on AI is the idea of giving AI a goal to solve and then setting it off on its own to get an answer. For example, when it comes to marketing, the question for AI to solve might be, "How can I send an offer to a customer to give it the best opportunity to have it opened and be utilized?" Now, the variables to include here would be, what would be the best offer to send, what would be the best time to send, what would be the best channel to send it on, and perhaps there is a way to add social activity to increase the odds of offer use? Perhaps the customer has a potential for tweeting and the system notices he tweets in the early evening and the system discovers a strong correlation to tweets and the opening of email offers in the past. The natural conclusion could be that the customer arrives home, sits down at his computer, goes through his email and jumps on his social channels. The system then learns to watch for a tweet and then it sends out the offer.

Figure 26 lists out a few business questions, the AI or deep learning task needed to solve these questions, as well as particular example outputs, which are specifically for the retail industry but could also be useful for sports book.

WHAT PROBLEM ARE YOU SOLVING?

Defining the AI/DL task

INPUTS	BUSINESS QUESTIONS	AI / DL TASK	RETAIL EXAMPLE OUTPUTS
Text data **Images** **Video** **Audio**	Is "it" present or not?	Detection	Targeted Ads
	What type of thing is "it"?	Classification	Basket Analysis
	To what extent is "it" present?	Segmentation	Build 360 degree customer view
	What is the likely outcome?	Prediction	Sentiment & Behavior Recognition
	What will likely satisfy the objective?	Recommendations	Recommendation Engine

Figure 26: Defining the AI/Deep Learning task

At the beginning of the book, I broke down the general use cases for AI into five sections—text, image, video, audio, sound, and time series—and, in the next few sections, I will break down the first four of these as well as explain how the *A.I. Sports Book* would use them, but first a section on data governance, the base that is needed for any analytics or AI.

Data Governance

To begin with, some words of warning: according to its *Conquer the AI Dilemma by Unifying Data Science and Engineering*[345], Databricks believes that data-related challenges are hindering 96% of organizations from achieving AI. Nearly all of the respondents (96%) cited multiple data-related challenges when moving projects to production.[345] "According to the survey, 90% of the respondents believe that unified analytics—the approach of unifying data processing with ML frameworks and facilitating data science and engineering collaboration across the ML lifecycle, will conquer the AI dilemma."[345]

Databricks argues that, "Unified Analytics is a new category of solutions that unify data science and engineering, making AI much more achievable for organizations."[345] "Unified Analytics makes it easier for data engineers to build data pipelines across siloed systems and prepare labeled datasets for model building while enabling data scientists to explore and visualize data and build models collaboratively."[345] A unified analytics platform can "unify data science and engineering across the ML lifecycle from data preparation to experimentation and deployment of ML applications—enabling companies to accelerate innovation with AI," Databricks concludes.[345]

The rest of this chapter will focus on how to build the backbone of an IT system that will incorporate a structure that can help a marketer become predictive. General sections on data governance, Hadoop, IoT, Chips, deep learning frameworks, amongst other, will lay out the most common questions that a marketer should ask about an EDW, a data lake and an AI world. The rest of the chapter will detail specific business areas that can be improved with these technologies.

Today, Talend believes that, "Data governance is not only about control and data protection; it is also about enablement and crowdsourcing insights. Data governance is a requirement in today's fast-moving and highly competitive enterprise environment."[346] Ultimately, "Now that organizations have the opportunity to capture massive amounts of diverse internal and external data, they need the discipline to maximize that data's value, manage its risks, and reduce the cost of its management," claims Talend.[346]

Data governance is not optional in today's highly complex and fast-moving IT environment.[346] An effective data governance strategy provides so many crucial benefits to an organization including[346]:

- A common understanding of data: "Data governance offers a consistent view of, and common terminology for, data, while individual business units retain appropriate flexibility."
- Improved data quality of data.
- A data map.
- A 360-degree view of each customer and other business entities.
- Consistent compliance with government regulations.
- Improved data management because a human dimension is brought into a highly automated, data-driven world.
- Easy accessibility

To find the right data governance approach for your organization, Talend recommends brands look for "open source, scalable tools that are easy to integrate with the organization's existing environment."[346] Additionally, a cloud-based platform lets brands "quickly plug into robust capabilities that are cost-efficient and easy to use."[346] "Cloud-based solutions also avoid the overhead required for on-premises servers," argues Talend.[346] When comparing and selecting data governance tools, brands needs to focus on choosing ones that will help them realize the business benefits laid out in their data governance strategy.[346] Any chosen tool should help in the following ways:

- Capture and understand data through discovery, profiling, benchmarking and capabilities.[346] For example, the right tools can automatically detect a piece of personal data, like a national ID or social security number, in a new data set and then trigger an alert.[346]

- Improve the quality of a brand's data with validation, data cleansing, and data enrichment.[346]
- Manage a brand's data with metadata-driven ETL and ELT, and data integration applications so data pipelines can be tracked and traced with end-to-end, forward-looking and backward-looking data lineage.[346]
- Control a brand's data with tools that actively review and monitor it.[346]
- Empower the people who know the data best, so they can contribute to the data stewardship tasks with self-service tools.[346]

Modern data governance is about both minimizing data risks and maximizing data usage.[346] There is a need for a more agile, bottom-up approach, which "starts with the raw data, links it to its business context so that it becomes meaningful, takes control of its data quality and security, and thoroughly organizes it for massive consumption."[346] In addition, due to headline-grabbing data scandals and data leaks, government are enacting a proliferation of new regulations and laws that put higher stakes on data protection.[346]

Talend believes that, "New data platforms empower this new discipline, which leverage smart technologies like pattern recognition, data cataloging, data lineage, and machine learning to organize data at scale and turn data governance into a team sport by enabling organization-wide collaboration on data ownership, curation, remediation, and reuse."[346]

With data storage prices plummeting, data is becoming less commoditized.[346] large data repositories such as data lakes are creating vast reservoirs of known and unknown datasets.[346] Although it might take seconds to ingest data into a modern EDW or data lake, it could take weeks for this data to be made available to a business user.[346] At the same time, business users might not even be aware that the data they need is even available for use.[346] Humans are inventive creatures and they often employ data work-arounds, which can create additional governance headaches.[346] When business users add their own rules atop newly created data sources, multiple versions of "the truth" result, which can lead to data governance nightmares.[346]

The challenge "is to overcome these obstacles by bringing clarity, transparency, and accessibility to your data assets."[346] Wherever this data resides, proper data screening must be established so businesses have a holistic view of the data sources and data streams coming into and out of their organization.[346]

In the past, data experts might have manually processed the data using traditional data profiling tools.[346] However, this approach no longer works.[346] "The digital era's data sprawl requires a more automatic and systematic approach," says Talend.[346] Modern data cataloging tools can help schedule the data discovery processes that crawls an EDW or a data lake and intelligently inspect the underlying data, so that it can be understood, documented, and actioned, if necessary.[346] Today's data catalogs "can automatically draw the links between datasets and connect them to a business glossary."[346] Talend argues that, "this allows an organization to automate the data inventory and leverage smart semantics for auto-profiling, relationships discovery and classification thanks to an integrated semantic flow."[346] The benefits are twofold; data owners and providers get an overview of their data and can take actions; data consumers get visibility into the data before consuming it.[346]

Data profiling is the process of discovering in-depth and granular details about a dataset. It helps in accurately assess a company's multiple data sources based on the six dimensions of data quality—accuracy, completeness, consistency, timeliness, uniqueness, and validity.[346] It will help a brand to identify if and how its data could be inaccurate, inconsistent, and, possibly, incomplete.[346]

Oftentimes, the people who know the data best are not the data experts.[346] Sales admins, sales representatives, customer service reps, and field marketing managers know the data quality issues probably better than their company's central IT team.[346] Not only do they know the data best, but they are also the ones who most keenly feel the pain of data quality issues because it directly impacts upon their day-to-day job.[346]

Of course, these people can't become data quality experts so they must be provided with smart tools that can hide the technical complexity of data profiling. Many vendors provide data preparation tools that have "powerful yet simple built-in profiling capabilities to explore data sets and assess their quality with the help of indicators, trends, and patterns."[346] "While automatic data profiling through both a data catalog and self-service profiling addresses the case for bottom-up data governance, a top-down approach might require a deeper look into the data," says Talend.[346]

With products like Talend Data Quality, users "would start by connecting to data sources to analyze their structure (catalogs, schemas, and tables), and store the description of their metadata in its metadata repository."[346] Users would then "define available data quality analyses including database, content analysis, column analysis, table analysis, redundancy analysis, and correlation analysis," says Talend.[346] "These analyses will carry out data profiling processes that will define the content, structure, and quality of highly complex data structures," adds Talend.[346]

A "trust index" can be created out of all this data discovery and it can be calculated, reported, and tracked on a regular and automated basis.[346] Trigger alerts can be set when index moves beyond a certain comfortable threshold.[346]

According to Talend, "Data quality is the process of conditioning data to meet the specific needs of business users."[346] However, data quality is not a standalone operation or problem.[346] "To make it successful and deliver trusted data, you need to operate data quality operations upfront and natively from the data sources, along with the data lifecycle to ensure that any data operator or user or app could consume trusted data at the end," argues Talend.[346]

"Successful data governance frameworks require setting accountabilities and then delegating that authority appropriately," argues Talend[346] For example, Talend says, "a data protection officer in a central organization might want to delegate tasks to data stewards or business users in the operations: a sales engineer might be best positioned to ensure that contact data for his or her accounts are accurate and kept up-to-date. A campaign manager is the one that should ensure that a consent mechanism has been put in place and captured within its marketing database."[346] To support this kind of delegation, organizations need to provide workflow based, self-served apps to different departments, recommends Talend.[346] This provides additional autonomy without putting the data at risk.[346]

"The cloud drastically extends the boundaries of data. Lines of business use their own applications, and products, people, and assets create their own data pipelines through the web and the Internet of Things. Data can also be exchanged seamlessly between business partners and data providers," says Talend.[346]

"Data preparation is not just a separate discipline to make lines of business more autonomous with data; it's a core element for data quality and integration," says Talend.[346] Not only does it unlock people's data productivity, but it also captures the actions taken on that data, which can help make the data more trustable.[346] In addition to improving personal productivity, the true value of these collaborative and self-service applications is to drive collaboration between business and IT, not always an easy thing to do.[346]

Once the incoming data assets are identified, documented and trusted, it is time to organize them for massive consumption by an extended network of data users within an organization.[346] "This starts by establishing a single point of trust; that is to say, collecting all the data sets together in a single control point that will be the cornerstone of your data governance framework," explains Talend.[346] Datasets then need to be identified; roles and responsibilities have to be assigned directly into a single point of control.[346]

"It is one of the advantages of data cataloging: regrouping all the trusted data in one place and giving access to members so that everybody can immediately use it, protect it, curate it and allow a wide range of people and apps to take advantage of it," notes Talend.[346] "The benefit of centralizing trusted data into a shareable environment is that it will save time and resources of your organization once operationalized," they add.[346]

"Within a data catalog, a business glossary is used to define collections of terms and to link them to categories and sub-categories. Building a business glossary can be as simple as dragging in an existing well-documented data model, importing the terms and definitions from other sources (e.g., CSV, Microsoft Excel)," says Talend.[346] Once published, the glossary can be accessed company-wide anyone who has proper authorizations.[346]

Talend believes that, "As you are about to deliver access to your catalog to others, your dataset will become a living artifact, as you will enable authorized people to edit, validate, or enrich the data directly into data sets."[346] "Doing it automatically through a data catalog will allow you to save lots of time and resources," they contend.[346]

Talend claims that data lineage functionality gives users the ability to track and trace their data flows from source to final destination.[346] Data lineage can dramatically accelerate the speed to resolution of problematic data by helping users spot the specific problem at the right place and ensure that the data is always accurate.[346] Moreover, if new datasets come into an EDW and/or a data lake, data lineage rapidly helps identify these new sources.[346] Errors can quickly be uncovered and accountability understood. A data chain is both forward and backward-looking, upstream or downstream impact is easily seen and acted upon.

Once the data categories have been defined, a more accurate picture of the data environment sources can be created.[346] "It will also enable you to define better data owners: who is responsible for this particular data domain? Who is responsible for viewing, accessing, editing and curating the data sets?" explains Talend.[346]

At this step, using a RACI Model—a model derived from the four key responsibilities most typically used: Responsible, Accountable, Consulted, and Informed—will help users save time defining and assigning roles and responsibilities between stakeholders.[104]

"The next step is to define data owners who are ultimately accountable for one or more data categories and subcategories," says Talend.[346] "These data owners will be responsible for day-to-day operations regarding the data or appoint data stewards those operational data-centric tasks. They will identify critical datasets and critical data elements (CDEs) as well as establish standards for data collection, data use, and data masking."[346] "A data catalog may also catalog owners and stewards for data categories and sub-categories and assign their related roles and workflows," adds Talend.[346]

For example, a data cataloger "may catalog the data owners for 'customer' as well as 'customer identity', 'customer billing', 'customer contact' and 'customer ship-to information'."[346]

The RACI Model is a good example of a responsibility assignment matrix that is both easy to understand and use.[104] "It's particularly useful if your data governance will involve different departments and divisions in your organization," says Talend.[346]

According to Wikipedia, data curation "is the organization and integration of data collected from various sources. It includes annotation, publication, and presentation of data to make sure it's valid over time."[347] This will be enabled once you put in place an explicit RACI Model that clearly describes who can define, edit, validate, and enrich data in the systems.[346]

"A data governance project is not just intended to let trusted data be accessible to all," claims Talend.[346] "It's also about promoting data custodians' accountability to the rest of the organization so that they can enrich and curate trusted data and produce valuable, accurate insights out of the data pipelines," they add.[346] "In many cases, data owners realize that they should not manage everything in their data domain, and thus need act as orchestrators rather than doers," notes Talend.[346]

"The data governance team may also delegate responsibilities for data protection," adds Talend.[346] Data masking is a prime example for delegation.[346] "In a data lake, for example, IT specialists might not be the ones responsible for data masking and might even not have the authorization privileges to process the data before it has been masked," claims Talend.[346] Data protection tasks can be delegated to people who might not be technical experts with deep expertise in the data masking discipline.[346]

"This is why it is important to empower a large audience to mask the data on their own so that once they identify specific scenarios where sensitive data may be exposed, they can proactively act on it automatically with a user-friendly tool," says Talend.[346] For example, Talend offers the case of a campaign manager who prepares an event with a business partner that doesn't have explicit consent to see the personal data of customer because of a lack of third party privacy consent.[346] Thankfully, the campaign manager can utilize data prep tools that can mask the data directly on the data so that the data can be easily shared without violating data privacy rules.[346]

Once the data is accessible in a single point of access and reconciled properly, "it is time to extract all its value by delivering at scale to a wide audience of authorized humans and machines," says Talend.[346] Technologies like automation, data integration and machine learning can help enormously.[346]

"Advanced analytics and machine learning help democratize data governance and data management because they make things much simpler," argues Talend.[346] "They improve developers' productivity and empower non-data experts to work with data as well by suggesting next best actions, guiding users through their data journey," say Talend.[346]

"Machine learning also allows the capture of knowledge from business users and data professionals," says Talend.[346] One typical use case is data error resolution and matching.[346] Self-service tools can be used to deduplicate records on a data sample and then machine learning can be applied to a whole data set in a fully automated process, which turns low value and time-consuming tasks into an automated process that can be scaled up to handle millions of records.[346]

Data masking allows a company to selectively share production quality data across their organization for development, analysis and more, without ever disclosing any Personally Identifiable Information (PII) to people not authorized to see it.[346]

Failing to establish strict data privacy controls can leave a company exposed to financial risk, negative reputation, and stiff data privacy regulatory penalties.[346] To deal with this growing threat, businesses need to find ways to automatically spot sensitive datasets.[346] Data cataloging technologies can help with this.[346]

"A data catalog is the typical starting point for automating the personal data identification process," says Talend.[346] Once data elements have been defined with a PII, data sets that relate to them can automatically be spotted and masked, if necessary.[346] If personal data is not necessary for testing or analytics, why risk exposing it?[346]

In the past, disciplines like data masking were sparingly used, but with the explosion of data privacy scandals and the proliferation of regulations, a much more aggressive approach to data masking is needed.[346] Only then can businesses share production-quality data across their organizations for analysis and business intelligence, without exposing personally identifiable information.[346]

"Many data governance approaches fail because they cannot be applied in a systematic way," claims Talend.[346] Modern data governance controls "need to be embedded into the data chain, so that it can be operationalized and cannot be bypassed."[346] It needs to become part of the process. Data governance can help data engineers orchestrate and automate all of a company's data pipelines, whether they are physical EDWs or cloud-based ones, or even data that surfaces through a company app.[346] "It will act as an orchestrator to operationalize and automate any jobs or flows so that you keep on structuring and cleaning your data along the data lifecycle, all the while putting stewards at work for validation, users for curations or business users for data preparation," says Talend.[346]

A data catalog makes "data more meaningful for data consumers, because of its ability to profile, sample and categorize the data, document the data relationships, and crowdsource comments, tags, likes and annotations."[346] "All this metadata is then easy to consume through full text or faceted search, or through visualization of data flows," explains Talend.[346] Data catalogs make it "possible to locate, use, and access trusted data faster by searching and verifying data's validity before sharing with peers."[346]

Augmented and Virtual Reality

Not just the stuff of science fiction anymore, Augmented Reality (AR) is now a part of our everyday lives. In his article *CrowdOptic and L'Oreal to make history by demonstrating how augmented reality can be a shared experience*[348], Tarun Wadhwa states that augmented reality works by "displaying layers of computer-generated information on top of a view of the physical world." It is "a technology that alters the perception of reality by distorting it, allowing escape from it, and enhancing it—all at the same time."[348]

Webopedia.com adds that augmented reality or AR is[349]:

> *"A type of virtual reality that aims to duplicate the world's environment in a computer. An augmented reality system generates a composite view for the user that is the combination of the real scene viewed by the user and a virtual scene generated by the computer that augments the scene with additional information. The virtual scene generated by the computer is designed to enhance the user's sensory perception of the virtual world they are seeing or interacting with. The goal of Augmented Reality is to create a system in which the user cannot tell the difference between the real world and the virtual augmentation of it. Today Augmented Reality is used in entertainment, military training, engineering design, robotics, manufacturing and other industries."*

According to *Gartner's Top 10 Strategic Technology Trends 2017*[350], Augmented reality (AR) and virtual reality (VR) will "transform the way individuals interact with each other and with software systems creating an immersive environment. For example, VR can be used for training scenarios and remote experiences."

AR enables a blending of the real and virtual worlds, which "means businesses can overlay graphics onto real-world objects."[350] Immersive experiences with AR and VR are reaching tipping points in terms of price and capability but will not replace other interface models."[350] In the future, AR and VR are expected to expand beyond visual immersion and they might include all of the human senses[350], although this is a very complicated thing to pull off as smell-o-vision tried and failed to do in the entertainment business many decades ago.

According to its press release *Gartner Says Augmented Reality Will Become an Important Workplace Tool*[351], "Augmented reality is the real-time use of information in the form of text, graphics, audio and other virtual enhancements integrated with real-world objects."

Tuong Huy Nguyen, principal research analyst at *Gartner*, states that "AR leverages and optimizes the use of other technologies such as mobility, location, 3D content management and imaging and recognition. It is especially useful in the mobile environment because it enhances the user's senses via digital instruments to allow faster responses or decision-making."[351]

Gartner believes "AR technology has matured to a point where organizations can use it as an internal tool to complement and enhance business processes, workflows and employee training."[351] *Gartner* also believes that "AR facilitates business innovation by enabling real-time decision-making through virtual prototyping and visualization of content."[351]

According to Deloitte, Wearable AR devices can "allow users to access standardized sets of instructions for a particular task in real time, triggered by environmental factors and overlaid on the user's field of vision."[352] Research has shown that overlaying 3D instructions over a real-life process can reduce the error rate for an assembly task by 82 percent, with a particularly strong impact on cumulative errors due to previous assembly mistakes.[352]

"AR allows for improved senses and memory through the capture and enhancement of the user's perspective. By recording video/audio, capturing images and removing elements that obscure the senses, AR technology allows users' eyes to act as cameras, and can enhance the senses in ways not available naturally, such as night vision or the ability to zoom in on far-away objects," notes Deloitte.[352]

AR uses location-based data for navigation, overlaying digital maps and directions on real-world environments.[351] Through the lens of an AR device, a user can receive visual guidance based on GPS technology.[351] AR services generally fall into one of two categories—"location-based or computer vision. Location-based offerings use a device's motion sensors to provide information based on a user's location. Computer-vision-based services use facial, object and motion tracking algorithms to identify images and objects."[352]

Mr. Nguyen claims AR's benefits include the "potential to improve productivity, provide hands-on experience, simplify current processes, increase available information, provide real-time access to data, offer new ways to visualize problems and solutions, and enhance collaboration."[352]

Augmented reality has many potential applications in the gaming industry as well and the following ideas might seem a little like science fiction, but they are certainly within the realm of technical possibilities, and today there is no question that they would take the concept of personalization to a whole new level.

For a sports betting website, augmented reality could be used to offer live odds on players during a soccer match, a basketball game, or on a horse being paraded before a race. A punter could point his phone at a player on a soccer pitch or on a basketball court and see live odds of that player being the next scorer or being the *Man of the Match*. Bets could be done in one easy click and odds would be updated live throughout the games, or even, potentially, during a horse or dog race.

"Another usage is seeing the social media hashtag and discussion of an event as it is occurring."[348] Bettors could literally hold up their phones at a live sporting events and see the hashtags related to those events on their screens.

So where is AR going? In his article *Augmented reality: expanding the user experience*[353], John Moore claims that "app creators have begun to engage more of a mobile device's sensors—accelerometers and gyroscopes, for example. Augmented reality apps that use detailed animations are also in the works. The objective: inject augmented reality technology in a wider range of apps to boost the user experience."[348]

Pokémon Go was the first location based augmented reality game that hit it big. Despite mixed reviews, the mobile app quickly became a global phenomenon and it was one of the most used and profitable mobile apps of 2016, having been downloaded more than 500 million times worldwide.[354] It certainly revealed the enormous potential of AR and it proved, without a doubt, that the barriers to AR technology were limited and easily scaled by humans, at least to those seeking out little dueling pocket monsters.

Gartner believes "AR technology has matured to a point where organizations can use it as an internal tool to complement and enhance business processes, workflows and employee training."[351] *Gartner* also believes that "AR facilitates business innovation by enabling real-time decision-making through virtual prototyping and visualization of content."[351]

AR has a great future and many online gaming companies are already developing software to tap into it. In 2016, Infinity Augmented Reality teamed up with Google to reinvent online casino games.[355] In her article *Augmented Reality Is The future Of Real Money Gaming Industry*, Bidisha Gupta explains that "By using augmented eyewear and a 360-degree camera that can capture the whole set up, it plans to take players right in the middle of the action. It will be a never before experience for people interested in online card games and the like." [355]

Text

Text use cases break down into several different areas, including chatbots, NLP, sentiment analysis, augmented search, and language translation.

Clothing retailer the North Face has implemented a recommendation engine for their customer who want to buy jackets which is based on IBM's Watson. This solution, called XPS, uses a chatbot interface to ask a series of questions so that it can match the customers' requirements with the product line. According to North Face, 60% of the users clicks through to the recommended product."

According to Amazon, "Lex is a service for building conversational interfaces into any application using voice and text. Amazon Lex provides the advanced deep learning functionalities of automatic speech recognition (ASR) for converting speech to text, and natural language understanding (NLU) to recognize the intent of the text, to enable you to build applications with highly engaging user experiences and lifelike conversational interactions."[356] Amazon Lex contains the same deep learning technologies that power Amazon Alexa are they are now available to any developer. They will enable users to quickly and easily build sophisticated, natural language, conversational chatbots.[357]

Amazon Transcribe "is an automatic speech recognition (ASR) service that makes it easy for developers to add speech-to-text capability to their applications."[358] Using the Amazon Transcribe API, brands can analyze audio files stored in Amazon S3 and have the service return a text file of the transcribed speech. Brands can also send a live audio stream to Amazon Transcribe and receive a stream of transcripts in real time.

Amazon Transcribe can transcribe customer service calls and generate subtitles on audio and video content. The service can transcribe audio files stored in common formats, like WAV and MP3, with time stamps for every word so that you can easily locate the audio in the original source by searching for the text. Amazon Transcribe is continually learning and improving to keep pace with the evolution of language.

Amazon Comprehend is "a natural language processing (NLP) service that uses machine learning to find insights and relationships in text. No machine learning experience required."[359]

"There is often a treasure trove of potential sitting in a company's unstructured data. Customer emails, support tickets, product reviews, social media, even advertising copy represents insights into customer sentiment that can be put to work for a business," says Amazon.[359] Machine learning is "particularly good at accurately identifying specific items of interest inside vast swathes of text (such as finding company names in analyst reports)."[359] "Amazon Comprehend can learn the sentiment hidden inside language (identifying negative reviews, or positive customer interactions with customer service agents), at almost limitless scale."[359]

Amazon Comprehend "identifies the language of the text; extracts key phrases, places, people, brands, or events; understands how positive or negative the text is; analyzes text using tokenization and parts of speech; and automatically organizes a collection of text files by topic."[359]

In his article *Turning Up Your Brand's Voice to Reach the Most Advanced Customers*[360], Pini Yakuel explains why digital assistants are unique to every other channel when it comes to personalization—they cut through the noise. "Yes, emails can be personalized, just like paid search and social ads, but they share their real estate with thousands of other pieces of content. When there are 20 personalized messages asking for your attention, which one will consumers go for?" ask Yakuel.[360]

"Like any other marketing channel, the key to winning with digital assistants lies in the deep knowledge of the purchase lifecycle customers go through. Delving into the desire to know, go, do and buy that consumers have will deliver success," says Yakuel.[360]

"Micro-moments are defined as intent-rich moments when a person turns to their device to act on a need through the conversational nature of queries to digital assistants. Analyzing these intent-rich moments and acting upon them might be the gate to showing up as the preferred answer," says Yakuel.[360]

Brands should always keep in mind "that retention through digital assistants works so well because consumers want to make life easier for themselves every chance they get."[360] "For example, smart fridges that know when we're running out of food and talk to digital assistants are already out there. Digital assistants will likely broaden their reach across the broad spectrum of consumer needs to anticipate upcoming purchases," says Yakuel.[360]

"Whether by diving into data or by directly speaking with existing and past customers, marketers should always learn what questions and online behavior drives folks toward their brands. Analyze their pain points, and focus on creating content that uses their phrases and makes their lives easier quickly," advises Yakuel.[360] "The better you get at this, the more likely you are to be the digital assistant's chosen option," he concludes.[360]

Chatbots

In its *14 Powerful Chatbot Platforms*[361], Maruti Tech lists some of the best chatbot publishing platform and development platform for brands to use. According to Maruti Tech, a "chatbot publishing platform is a medium through which the chatbot can be accessed and used by the users."[361] "A chat bot development platform, on the other hand is a tool/ application through which one can create a chatbot," says Maruti Tech.[361] These chatbot platforms let users add more functionality to a bot by creating a flow, machine learning capabilities, API integration, etc.[361] These chatbot platforms are simple to use, and users don't need to have deep technical knowledge or programming skills as many come with drag-and-drop functionality.[361] {Please note, there aren't 14 platforms as several have been discontinued or acquired, which is a testament to how quickly this space can change.)

Chatfuel

Calling itself "the leading bot platform for creating AI chatbots for Facebook,"[362] Chatfuel (chatfuel.com) claims that 46% of Messenger bots run on its platform.[362] No coding is required with Chatfuel, which "provides features like adding content cards and sharing it to your followers automatically, gathering information inside Messenger chats with forms."[362] Chatfuel also uses AI to script interactive conversations.[362]

The platform is completely free for anyone to build a bot, but after the bot reaches 100K conversations/month users have to subscribe as a premium customer.[362] Chatfuel's client list includes multinational companies like Adidas, MTV, British Airways, and Volkswagen.

Botsify

"Let your bot chat like a human" is Botsify's (botsify.com) tagline[363] and it is another popular Facebook Messenger chatbot platform that uses a drag and drop template to create bots.[362] Botsify offers features like easy integrations via plugins, Smart AI, Machine learning and analytics integration.[361] Botsify's platform does allow seamless transition from a bot to a human.[361] First bot is free, but any others are charged for thereafter.[361]

Flow XO

According to its website (flowxo.com)[364], "Flow XO is a powerful automation product that allows you to quickly and simply build incredible chatbots that help you to communicate and engage with your customers across a wide range of different sites, applications and social media platforms." It is the only chatbot platform to provide over 100 integrations.[361] It boasts an easy to use and visual editor.[361] Flow XO's platform allows users to build one bot and implement it across multiple platforms.[361] In terms of pricing, users are limited to a certain number of conversations, surpassing that requires a subscription.[361]

Motion.ai

Recently purchased by Hubspot, Motion.ai was a chatbot platform that helps users to visually build, train, and deploy chatbots on FB Messenger, Slack, Smooch or your website.[361] Motion.ai lets users diagram a conversation flow like a flowchart to get a visual overview of the outcomes of a bot query.[361] The bot can be connected to a messaging service like Slack, Facebook Messenger, and go. Motion.ai allows Node.js deployment directly from its interface along with several other integrations.[361]

Chatty People

This platform has predefined chatbots with templates for e-commerce, customer support, and F&B businesses.[361] When users select the e-commerce chatbot, he or she can simply add products, Q&A information as well as some general settings.[361] The platform even includes PayPal and Stripe API integration.[361]

According to Maruti Tech, "The chatbot platform's simplicity makes it ideal for entrepreneurs and marketers in smaller companies."[361] While its technology makes it suitable for enterprise customers, users can make a simple bot answering customer service questions or integrating it with Shopify to potentially monetize one's Facebook fan pages. Chatty People was acquired by MobileMonkey in 2018 and can now be found at mobilemonkey.com.

QnA bot

Microsoft has created QnA (qnamaker.ai) bot for the same reason as its name suggests, i.e., for answering a series of user questions.[361] The URL FAQ page must be shared with the service and the bot will be created in a few minutes using the information on the FAQ page and the structured data.[361]

Furthermore, the bot can be integrated with Microsoft Cognitive Services to enable the bot to see, hear, interpret and interact in more human ways.[361] QnA Maker also seamlessly integrates with other APIs and can scale to be a know-it-all part of a bigger bot.[361]

Recast.ai

In January 2019, Recast.ai was integrated into the SAP portfolio and renamed SAP Conversational AI.[365] This bot building platform enables users to train, build and run their bots.[361] By creating and managing the conversation logic with Bot Builder, SAP Conversational AI's visual flow management interface and API lets users build bots that understand predefined queries as well as quickly set up responses.[361] Messaging metrics and bot analytics tools are also included.[361]

BotKit

Their rather alliterate tagline is "Building Blocks for Building Bots" and it is a toolkit that gives users a helping hand to develop bots for FB Messenger, Slack, Twilio, and more.[361] "BotKit can be used to create clever, conversational applications which map out the way that real humans speak," says Maruti Tech.[361] "This essential detail differentiates from some of its other chatbot toolkit counterparts," they add.[361]

"BotKit includes a variety of useful tools, like Botkit Studio, boilerplate app starter kits, a core library, and plugins to extend your bot capabilities. Botkit is community-supported open-source software that is available on GitHub," says Maruti Tech.[361] Online, the company can be found at botkit.ai.

ChatterOn

On its website, ChatterOn (chatteron.io), claims it can help users build a chatbot in five minutes. ChatterOn is a bot development platform which gives users the required tools to build Facebook Messenger chatbots without any coding.[361] The platform helps users "build the bot flow (each interaction with a user has to have a goal that the user has to be taken to the next chat) and setup the AI by entering a few examples of the expected conversation between the user and bot."[361] India's first full stack chatbot development platform, ChatterOn is, according to the company, "far superior in ease of development and functionalities than its international counterparts."[361] "All the bots on ChatterOn's platform are powered by a proprietary self-learning contextual AI," claims Maruti Tech.[361]

Octane AI

According to its website (octaneai.com), Octane AI "enables Shopify merchants to increase revenue with a Facebook Messenger bot that customers love."[366]

Octane AI has pre-built features that make it easy for users to add content, messages, discussions, showcase merchandise, and much more to their bot.[361] According to Octane AI, convos are conversational stories that can be shared with an audience. It's as easy as writing a blog post and the best way to increase distribution of a company's bot, at least according to Octane AI.[361] The platform also integrates with all of the popular social media channels as well as provides real-time analytics.[361]

Converse AI

The Converse AI (converse.ai) platform has been built to handle a wide range of use cases and integrates seamlessly with Facebook Messenger and Workplace, Slack, Twilio, and Smooch. Some of its features include[361]:

- A complete UI that allows easy, code-free builds.
- Integration with multiple platforms, including complete user, request and conversation tracking.
- Inbuilt NLP parsing engine, that includes the ability to easily build conversation templates.
- Can converse while using both plain text and rich media.
- Inbuilt query and analytics engine allow for easy tracking and drill down that helps brands understand how users are engaging with the service.

GupShup

The leading smart messaging platform that handles over 4 billion messages per month, GupShup (gupshup.io) has processed over 150 billion messages in total.[361] "It offers APIs for developers to build interactive, programmable, Omni-channel messaging bots and services as well as SDKs to enable in-app and in web messaging," says Maruti Tech.[361] "Unlike plain-text messages, GupShup's innovative smart-messages contain structured data and intelligence, thus enabling advanced messaging workflows and automation," add Maruti Tech.[361]

In conclusion, chatbot platforms are essential for the development of chatbots.[361] With the availability of such platforms, Maruti Tech argues, anyone can create a chatbot, even if they don't know how to code. However, to make an intelligent chatbot that works seamlessly, AI, machine learning and NLP are required.[361] Chatbots will undoubtedly revolutionize the future of industries by their rich features.[361] They will reduce human errors, "provide round the clock availability, eliminate the need for multiple mobile applications and make it a very seamless experience for the customer.[361]

Sentiment Analysis

In its article *Sentiment Analysis: Types, Tools, and Use Cases*[367], Altexsoft states that the goal of sentiment analysis is "to know a user or audience opinion on a target object by analyzing a vast amount of text from various sources." "It's not only important to know social opinion about your organization, but also to define who is talking about you," says Altexsoft.[367] Measuring mention tone can also help define whether industry influencers are discussing a brand and, if so, in what context. The power of sentiment analysis software is it can do all of the above in real time and across all channels, thereby making it useful for both sentiment analysis and customer service.[367]

"You can analyze text on different levels of detail, and the detail level depends on your goals," says Altexsoft.[367] "For example, you may define an average emotional tone of a group of reviews to know what percentage of customers liked your new clothing collection," explains Altexsoft.[367] "If you need to know what visitors like or dislike about a specific garment and why, or whether they compare it with similar items by other brands, you'll need to analyze each review sentence with a focus on specific aspects and use or specific keywords," add Altexsoft.[367]

When a brand wants to analyze sentiment, it first needs to gather all relevant brand mentions into one document.[367] Selection criteria must be carefully considered—should mentions be time-limited, should only one language be used, should specific locations be locked in, etc., etc.[367] Data must then be prepared for analysis, read, cleansed, and any irrelevant content should be excluded from the analysis.[367] Once the data has been prepared, full analysis can begin sentiment extracted.[367] Of course, since hundreds of thousands or even millions of mentions may need analysis, the best practice is to automate this tedious work with software and many of the tools I have mentioned throughout this book can help.[367] I have also included a list of social media monitoring tools at the end of this section.

Altexsoft mentions various customer experience software, such as InMoment and Clarabridge that "collect feedback from numerous sources, alert on mentions in real-time, analyze text, and visualize results."[367] "Text analysis platforms (e.g. DiscoverText, IBM Watson Natural Language Understanding, Google Cloud Natural Language, or Microsoft Text Analytics API) have sentiment analysis in their feature set," adds Altexsoft.[367]

"InMoment provides five products that together make a customer experience optimization platform," explains Altexsoft.[367] "One of them, Voice of a Customer, allows businesses to collect and analyze customer feedback in a text, video, and voice forms. The number of data sources is sufficient and includes surveys, social media, CRM, etc.," says Altexsoft.[367]

Clarabridge is a CEM platform that "pulls and analyzes text from chats, survey platforms, blogs, forums, and review sites," notes Altexsoft.[367] "Users can also gain insights from emails, employee and agent notes, call recordings and Interactive Voice Response (IVR) surveys: The system can convert them into text."[367] Clarabridge provides social media listening as well.[367] According to Altexsoft, "The system considers industry and source, understanding the meaning and context of every comment. Sentiment analysis results display on an 11-point scale. Users can modify sentiment scores to be more business-specific if needed."[367]

Another useful platform is DiscoverText, "a cloud-based collaborative text analytics system for researchers, entrepreneurs, and governments."[367] "Capterra users note the solution is great for importing/retrieving, filtering, and analyzing data from various sources, including Twitter, SurveyMonkey, emails, and spreadsheets," says Altexsoft.[367]

IBM Watson Natural Language Understanding is a set of advanced text analytics systems that supports analysis in 13 languages.[367] "Analyzing text with this service, users can extract such metadata as concepts, entities, keywords, as well as categories and relationships," says Altexsoft.[367] "It also allows for defining industry and domain to which a text belongs, semantic roles of sentence parts, a writer's emotions and sentiment change along the document," says Altexsoft.[367] Tools for developers to build chatbots and other NLP solutions are provided using IBM Watson services.[367]

"Microsoft Text Analytics API users can extract key phrases, entities (e.g. people, companies, or locations), sentiment, as well as define in which among 120 supported languages their text is written," explains Altexsoft.[367] "The Sentiment Analysis API returns results using a sentiment score from 0 (negative) to 1 (positive)," says Altexsoft.[367] The software can detect sentiment in English, Spanish, German, and French texts.[367] Developers recommend "the analysis be done on the whole document and advise using documents consisting of one or two sentences to achieve a higher accuracy."[367]

Google Cloud Natural Language API can "extract sentiment from emails, text documents, news articles, social media, and blog posts."[367] It can also extract "insights from audio files, scanned documents, and documents in other languages when combined with other cloud services."[367] "The tool assigns a sentiment score and magnitude for every sentence, making it easy to see what a customer liked or disliked most, as well as distinguish sentiment sentences from non-sentiment sentences," notes Altexsoft.[367]

Competitive analysis that involves sentiment analysis can also help brands understand their strengths and weaknesses and maybe find ways to stand out from the crowd.[367] In times of crisis, sentiment analysis can be instrumental in helping douse the flames of corporate crises.

Altexsoft believes, "There is one thing for sure you and your competitors have in common—a target audience."[367] Brands can track and research how society evaluates competitors just as they analyze attitudes towards their business. "What do customers value most about other industry players? Is there anything competitors lack or do wrong? Which channels do clients use to engage with other companies?"—these are all important questions that sentiment analysis can help answer.[367] Sports books can use this knowledge to improve "communication and marketing strategies, overall service, and provide services and products customers would appreciate."[367]

Most brands grapple with the question of how to bring a desired product to market?[367] The only approach, claims Altexsoft, is to ask people what they want.[367] Successful companies build a minimum viable product (MVP), gather early feedback, and continuously try to improve a product, even after its release.[367] "Feedback data comes from surveys, social media, and forums, and interaction with customer support," argues Altexsoft.[367] Sentiment analysis can be extremely handy here.[367] It helps brands learn about product advantages and drawbacks.[367] Armed with strong sentiment analysis results, "a product development team will know exactly how to deliver a product that customers would buy and enjoy."[367]

Using sentiment analysis, marketers can study consumer behavior patterns in real time, which can help to predict future brand trends.[367] "Another benefit of sentiment analysis is that it doesn't require heavy investment and allows for gathering reliable and valid data since its user-generated," says Altexsoft.[367] Sentiment analysis lets businesses harness an enormous amount of free data to help them understand their customers' attitude towards their brand.[367] This analysis can take customer care to the next level.

Sentiment Analysis Tools

Table 14 lists the Social Media Tools and websites available to business users to track engagement and customer feedback.

Name	Comments
Board Reader	BoardReader allows users to search multiple message boards simultaneously, allowing users to share information in a truly global sense. Boardreader is focused on creating the largest repository of searchable information for our users. Users can find answers to their questions from others who share similar interests. Our goal is to allow our users to search the "human to human" discussions that exist on the Internet.
Buffer	Buffer makes your life easier with a smarter way to schedule the great content you find. Fill up your Buffer at one time in the day and Buffer automagically posts them for you through the day. Simply keep that Buffer topped up to have a consistent social media presence all day round, all week long. Get deeper analytics than if you just post to social networks directly.
Buzzsumo	Analyze what content performs best for any topic or competitor. Find the key influencers to promote your content: • Discover the most shared content across all social networks and run detailed analysis reports. • Find influencers in any topic area, review the content they share and amplify. • Be the first to see content mentioning your keyword; or when an author or competitor publishes new content. • Track your competitor's content performance and do detailed comparisons.
Commun.it	Can help you organize, increase, and manage your followers, and can do so across multiple accounts and profiles. At a glance you can see different aspects of your community management, like the latest tweets from your stream and which new followers might appreciate a welcome message.
Crowdfire	Crowdfire is a powerful phone app and online website that helps you grow your Twitter and Instagram account reach. This tool has a variety of functions designed to understand your social analytics as well as manage your social publishing.
Cyfe	Cyfe is an all-in-one dashboard software that helps you monitor and analyze data scattered across all your online services like Google Analytics, Salesforce, AdSense, MailChimp, Facebook, WordPress and more from one single location in real-time.
Fanpage Karma	Shows a variety of valuable information related to your Facebook page, such as growth, engagement, service and response time, and of course Karma (a weighted engagement value). FanKarma also provides insight into Twitter and YouTube; the latter could be particularly valuable if you're creating a video marketing strategy.
Followerwonk	Followerwonk is a cool social media analytics tool thet lets you explore and grow your social graph. Dig deeper into Twitter analytics: followers, their locations, when do they tweet. Find and connect with influencers in your niche. Use visualizations to compare your social graph to competitors.
Google Alerts	Google Alerts are email updates of the latest relevant Google results (blogs, news, etc.) based on your searches. Enter the topic you wish to monitor, then click preview to see the type of results you'll receive. Some

Name	Comments
	handy uses of Google Alerts include: monitoring a developing news story and keeping current on a competitor or industry.
Google Trends	Trends allows you to compare search terms and websites. With Google Trends you can get insights into the traffic and geographic visitation patterns of websites or keywords. You can compare data for up to five websites and view related sites and top searches for each one.
Hootsuite	Monitor and post to multiple social networks, including Facebook and Twitter. Create custom reports from over 30 individual report modules to share with clients and colleagues. Track brand sentiment, follower growth, plus incorporate Facebook Insights and Google analytics. Draft and schedule messages to send at a time your audience is most likely to be online. HootSuite has the dashboard for your iPhone, iPad, BlackBerry and Android.
HowSocialable	Monitor and post to multiple social networks, including Facebook and Twitter. Create custom reports from over 30 individual report modules to share with clients and colleagues. Track brand sentiment, follower growth, plus Incorporate Facebook Insights and Google analytics. Draft and schedule messages to send at a time your audience is most likely to be online. HootSuite has the dashboard for your iPhone, iPad, BlackBerry and Android.
Iconosquare	Key metrics about your Instagram account. Number of likes received, your most liked photos ever, your average number of likes and comments per photo, your follower growth charts and more advanced analytics. Track lead conversations, send private message as on Twitter, and improve communication with your followers.
Klear	Social media monitoring, analytics and reporting. Influencer marketing, find and create relationships with the top influencers in your sector and build your community. Competitive analysis tracks your social media landscape, see what's working for them and develop your strategy.
Klout	Klout's mission is to help every individual understand and leverage their influence. Klout measures influence in Twitter to find the people the world listens to. It analyzes content to identify the top influencers.
Kred	Kred is a social-media scoring system that seeks to measure a person's online influence. Kred, which was created by the San Francisco-based social analytics firm PeopleBrowsr, attempts to also measure a person or company's engagement, or as they call it, outreach. PeopleBrowsr hopes that that combination can offer a more informed metric for non-celebrities like entrepreneurs and those whom they follow and look to for advice.
LikeAlyzer	This Facebook analysis tool comes up with stats and insights into your page and begins every report with a list of recommendations. Keep track of where your Facebook page stands compared to other pages by following the comparison to average page rank, industry-specific page rank, and rank of similar brands.
Mention	Mention prides itself on "going beyond Google Alerts" to track absolutely anywhere your name or your company might be mentioned online. When you subscribe to Mention's daily email you get all these wayward hits right in your inbox, and the Web dashboard even flags certain mentions as high priority.
Mentionmap	Explore your Twitter network. Discover which people interact the most and what they're talking about. It's also a great way to find relevant

Name	Comments
	people to follow. The visualization runs right in your browser and displays data from Twitter. Mentionmap loads user's tweets and finds the people and hashtags they talked about the most. In this data visualization, mentions become connections and discussions between multiple users emerge as clusters.
Must Be Present	Built by the team at Sprout Social, Must Be Present searches your Twitter account to find how quickly you respond to mentions. Their engagement reports place you in a percentile based on other accounts so you can see how you stack up to the speed of others.
NeedTagger	A super-powered Twitter search tool, NeedTagger runs language filters and keyword searches to determine which Twitter users might need your products or services. The tool shows you real-time search results and sends a daily email digest of new finds.
NutshellMail	Collects your activity on Facebook, LinkedIn, and Twitter (and even places like Yelp and Foursquare) to provide an email overview of your accounts. You set how often and when you want to receive the recap emails. Put it to use: If you have a weekly metrics plan you can have NutshellMail send a message once a week with an overview of your accounts. You can then extract the data and insights straight into your weekly report.
Omgili	Omgili helps you find interesting and current discussions, news stories and blog posts. Direct access to live data from hundreds of thousands of forums, news and blogs. Very easy to use, no signup for web interface.
Pinterest Analytics	Find out how many people are pinning from your website, seeing your pins, and clicking your content. Pick a time-frame to see how your numbers trend over time. Get better at creating Pins and boards with metrics from your Pinterest profile. Learn how people use the Pin It button on your site to add Pins. See how people interact with your Pins from whatever device they use. Get a glance at your all-time highest-performing Pins.
Pluggio	Pluggio is a web-based social media tool to help marketers easily grow and manage their social media profiles (Facebook and Twitter). It includes a suite of tools to organize and keep track of multiple accounts, get more followers, and automate the finding and publishing of excellent targeted content.
Postific	The full set of social media tools. Post content to over 10 social networks with one single click of a button. Get real time click-through statistics with your domain name. Measure and analyze the best results from your social posts. Monitor the social media conversations that are important for your business.
Quintly	Quintly is the professional social media monitoring and analytics solution to track and compare the performance of your social media marketing activities. Whether you are using Facebook, Twitter or both, Quintly monitors and visualizes your social media marketing success. Benchmark your numbers against your competitors or best practice examples.
Sentiment	Sentiment was born in 2007 and now boasts a team of bright enthusiastic people dedicated to provide the best social customer service and engagement platform for business.
SocialMention	SocialMention tracks areas such as sentiment, passion, reach, and strength to not just tell you what's being said about your search but how those reactions feel. While you track your brand or yourself, you can also

Name	Comments
	see how your sentiment changes over time.
Social Rank	Identifies your top 10 followers in three specific areas: Best Followers, Most Engaged, and Most Valuable. Your most engaged followers are those who interact with you most often (replies, retweets, and favorites); your most valuable followers are the influential accounts; and your best followers are a combination of the two. Social Rank will run the numbers for free and show you the results today, then follow-up each month with an email report.
Social Oomph	Schedule tweets, track keywords, extended Twitter profiles, save and reuse drafts, view @mentions and retweets, purge your DM inbox, personal status feed — your own tweet engine, unlimited accounts.
This tracking tool	Keeps track of your hashtag campaign or keyword on Twitter, Instagram, or Facebook with a full dashboard of analytics, demographics, and influencers.
Tip Top	TipTop Search is a Twitterbased search engine that helps you discover the best and most current advice, opinions, answers for any search, and also real people to directly engage and share experiences with. A search on any topic reveals people's emotions and experiences about it, as well as other concepts that they are discussing in connection with the original search.
Topsy	A powerful search engine for Twitter content. Want to know how a certain term is being used on Twitter? You can search links, tweets, photos, videos, and influencers.
Twazzup	Offers real-time monitoring and analytics for Twitter on any name, keyword, or hashtag you choose. The Twazzup results page delivers interesting insights like the top influencers for your keyword and which top links are associated with your search.
Tweepi	Has a number of useful Twitter features, many of which fall into a couple categories: managing your followers and supercharging who you're following. For management, you can unfollow in batches those who don't follow you back, and you can bulk follow another account's complete list of followers or who they're following.
Tweetcaster	A Twitter management tool for iOS and Android devices and provides the basics of what you'd expect from a Twitter dashboard plus a few fun extras: enhanced search and lists, hiding unwanted tweets, and photo effects for your images.
Tweetdeck	Lets you track, organize, and engage with your followers through a customizable dashboard where you can see at a glance the activity from different lists, followers, hashtags, and more.
TweetReach	Shows you the reach and exposure of the tweets you send, collecting data on who retweets you and the influence of each. Identify which of your tweets has spread the furthest (and why) and then try to repeat the formula with future tweets.
TwitterCounter	Twitter Counter is the number one site to track your Twitter stats. Twitter Counter provides statistics of Twitter usage and tracks over 14 million users. Twitter Counter also offers a variety of widgets and buttons that

Name	Comments
	people can add to their blogs, websites or social network profiles to show recent Twitter visitors and number of followers.
Twtrland	Provides a snapshot of your Twitter profile and can even track Facebook and Instagram as well. Two of Twtrland's most helpful tools are a live count of how many followers are currently online and advanced search functionality that includes keywords, locations, and companies. Local companies can perform a location search to see which area accounts are most popular and potentially worth following.
SumAll	SumAll is a powerful social media analytics tool that allows our customers to view all of their data in one simple, easy-to-use visualization. Social media, e-commerce, advertising, e-mail, and traffic data all come together to provide a complete view of your activity.
ViralWoot	Pin Alert feature lets you track what are people pinning from your website, who is pinning the most and what images from your website are trending on Pinterest. Thousands of social media marketers and agencies use Viralwoot for their clients. You can manage & grow multiple Pinterest accounts with a single Viralwoot account.
WhosTalkin	WhosTalkin is a social media monitoring tool that lets you search for conversations surrounding the topics that you care about most. Whether it be your favorite sports team, food, celebrity, or brand name; Whostalkin will help you find the conversations that are important to you. WhosTalkin search and sorting algorithms combine data taken from over 60 of the most popular social media sites.

Table 14: Social Media Tools
Source: Dreamgrow.com[368]

Augmented Search

In his article *How to use AI for link building and improve your search rankings[369]*, Kevin Rowe states that "AI's applications in the search engine optimization (SEO) world are continuing to expand to new horizons." Besides the Y Combinator-backed RankScience, which uses thousands of A/B tests to determine how best to positively influence search engine rankings, it is unlikely that a complete handling of SEO by AI will catch on any time soon.[369] While no software exists that leverages AI to build links, brands can still use multiple types of software for various stages of the link building process.[369] These include[369]:

- Data collection. NLP tools can be used to determine if the sites are contextually relevant and keyword relevant.
- Site analysis. AI can determine if a particular site will predictably have an impact on rankings.

This means that AI can be used to augment, automate or automatize processes, claims Rowe.[369] Link building can't specifically be a fully autonomous process, but AI can be leveraged to augment human processes, which can help find bloggers and influencers, as well as improve the quality of sites that are approached for links, says Rowe.[369]

Rowe believes to leverage existing AI in a link-building campaign, brands must first look at websites as a whole, including the multiple contributors or people on staff at these websites.[369] "These can be good link-building opportunities through sponsored or contributed content," says Rowe.[369] Sports books should find industry publications or other informative sites that appeal to the brand's target audience.[369] Rowe recommends searching by industry keywords.[369]

Brands should look for the following items[369]:

- Frequent publication: is new content often being published on the site?
- Last publish date: Has there been any new content in the last month?
- User experience and design: Is the design up-to-date and easy to use?

Secondly, brands should identify important industry blogs and influencers.[369] These usually have less people on staff than standard publications, however, they just might have a wider reach.[369]

Rowe believes that, "Text processing analytics like Watson Analytics can be used to find influencers and blog content that hits a brand's target market."[369] "For instance, someone might not always say, 'I am interested in polymer manufacturing,' online, but using AI tools that can predict related text patterns and speech, you might be able to find more influencers who haven't directly used the terms you're looking for," says Rowe.[369]

Things to look for include[369]:

- Comments and social shares on posts: Do the influencer's posts get a lot of engagement?
- Last publish time and frequency: Is content published actively consistently?
- User experience and design: Is it up-to-date and easy to use?
- Social platform: Does the influencer have a large social media following on the platforms that are preferred by the brand's industry players?
- Reputation: Sometimes, individual influencers or blogs might have a strong opinion about hot topics that you might not want to be associated with for either political or religious reasons.

Once a list of publications, influencers and blogs have been compiled, it's time for the hard part, determining if they will have an impact on your target keyword rankings.[369] Rowe calls this "the powerful part of AI—the part that can improve the impact of the links."[369] "AI can process data from multiple sources to identify likely variables or variable clusters that correlate with ranking in Google," claims Rowe.[369]

Image

Gartner predicts that image search will be a lucrative technology in the coming years.[370] Even with visual search still in its infancy, *Gartner* says early adopters will experience a 30 percent increase in e-commerce revenue by 2021.[370] The potential market is huge and brands that sell any type of physical items should utilize AI image technology to simplify the buying process.

To get started with Image search, brands should focus on solving customer problems and getting their own visual assets in order.[370] They shouldn't try to make their visual search workflows all about advertising.[370] Instead, brands should "aim to have solid metadata on products so that searching is easier and more natural."[370] From there, brands should work towards "visual search processes that are real time and increasingly intuitive, creating a positive customer experience that keeps people coming back," argues Butterfield argues.[217]

Facial Recognition

Facial recognition technology is the capability of identifying or verifying a person from a digital image or a video frame from a video source by comparing the actual facial features of someone on camera against a database of facial images, or faceprints, as they are also known.

Rapid advancements in facial recognition technology have reached the point where a single face can be compared against 36 million others in about one second.[371] A system made by Hitachi Kokusai Electric and reported by DigInfo TV shown at a security trade show recently was able to achieve this blazing speed by not wasting time on image processing.[108]

Using edge analytics, the technology takes visual data directly from the camera to compare the face in real time.[108] The software also groups faces with similar features, so it can narrow down the field of choice very quickly. The usefulness to the company's security enforcement is pretty obvious, but it can be used by multiple departments; facial recognition technology can be set up to send alerts to clerks, managers, or just about anyone who needs to identify customers.

As the *Consumer Reports* article *Facial Recognition: Who's Tracking Who in Public*[164] explains, as people enter an area, "security cameras feed video to computers that pick out every face in the crowd and rapidly take many measurements of each one's features, using algorithms to encode the data in strings of numbers."[372] The faceprints are compared against a database, and when there's a match, the system alerts the VIP department or sales people. Faceprints could also be used to allow people to purchase tickets or be part of a boarding recognition system.

Currently, facial recognition technology can be more useful for security departments than customer service departments, but that is changning.[164] At the 2014 Golden Globe Awards, facial recognition technology was used to scan for known celebrity stalkers.[164] The technology has also been used to bar known criminals from soccer matches in Europe and Latin America.[164] "Police forces and national security agencies in the U.S., the United Kingdom, Singapore, South Korea, and elsewhere are experimenting with facial recognition to combat violent crime and tighten border security."[164]

In some sense, facial recognition technology is becoming second nature to consumers, especially in Asia. Worldwide, consumers are used to tagging themselves in photos on Facebook, Snapchat, Picasa, and/or WeChat. In 2015, Google launched a photo app that helped users organize their pictures by automatically identifying family members and friends.[164] Google, however, suffered a public relations disaster when its system labeled a photo of two black people as gorillas.[164] The search giant quickly apologized profusely and promised to fix its algorithms[164], but this does show that the technology isn't foolproof and sensitivity is important.

Currently, MasterCard is "experimenting with a system that lets users validate purchases by snapping a selfie. Like fingerprint scanners and other biometric technologies, facial recognition has the potential to offer alternatives to passwords and PINs."[164]

This technology is moving so fast that privacy advocates are having trouble keeping up. In this regard, today's facial recognition technology is reminiscent of the World Wide Web of the mid-1990s.[164] Back then, few people would have anticipated that every detail about what we read, watched, and bought online would become a commodity traded and used by big business and sometimes, more sinisterly, hacked and used by nefarious individuals for criminal purposes.[164]

Facial recognition technology "has the potential to move Web-style tracking into the real world, and can erode that sense of control."[164] Experts such as Alvaro Bedoya, the executive director of Georgetown Law's Center on Privacy & Technology, and the former chief counsel to the Senate's subcommittee on privacy, technology, and the law finds this attack on privacy alarming.[164] "People would be outraged if they knew how facial recognition" is being developed and promoted, Bedoya states.[164] "Not only because they weren't told about it, but because there's nothing they can do about it. When you're online, everyone has the idea that they're being tracked. And they also know that there are steps they can take to counter that, like clearing their cookies or installing an ad blocker. But with facial recognition, the tracker is your face. There's no way to easily block the technology," Bedoya warns.[164]

Right now, facial recognition is largely unregulated, and few consumers seem to even be aware of its use. "Companies aren't barred from using the technology to track individuals the moment we set foot outside. No laws prevent marketers from using faceprints to target consumers with ads. And no regulations require faceprint data to be encrypted to prevent hackers from selling it to stalkers or other criminals," Bedoya warns.[164]

Users might be happy to tag their face and the faces of their friends and acquaintances on a Facebook wall, but they might shudder if every mall worker was jacked into a system that used security-cam footage to access their family's shopping habits.[164]

This could, however, be the future of retail, according to Kelly Gates, associate professor in communication and science studies at the University of California, San Diego.[373] In her article *Our Biometric Future: Facial Recognition Technology and the Culture of Surveillance*[165], Gates argues that "Regardless of whether you want to be recognized, you can be sure that you have no right of refusal in public, nor in the myriad private spaces that you enter on a daily basis that are owned by someone other than yourself." Gates concluded that by entering an establishment filled with facial recognition technology, you are tacitly giving your consent to the brands to use it, even if you are unaware of its use.[165]

Facial recognition technology in the offline world is now becoming more and more prevalent, particularly in the hospitality industry. "On Disney's four cruise ships, photographers roam the decks and dining rooms taking pictures of passengers. The images are sorted using facial recognition software so that photos of people registered to the same set of staterooms are grouped together. Passengers can later swipe their Disney ID at an onboard kiosk to easily call up every shot taken of their families throughout the trip."[164]

"In a recent study of 1,085 U.S. consumers by research firm First Insight, 75 percent of respondents said they would not shop in a store that used the technology for marketing purposes. Notably, the number dropped to 55 percent if it was used to offer good discounts."[164] Sports books should take this into account if they choose to implement facial recognition technology. However, it could be useful to recognize high rollers as well as problem gamblers.

Consumers may warm to facial recognition technology once it becomes more widespread, especially if brands offer enough incentives to make it worth their customer's time. In some cases, full facial recognition isn't needed, some marketers just want to determine the age, sex, and race of shoppers, although many vendors are now rolling out technology that not only recognizes the face but also the emotion.

In Germany, the Astra beer brand recently created an automated billboard directed solely at women, even to the point of shooing men away.[164] The billboard approximated the women's age, then played one of 80 pre-recorded ads to match.[164] For a marketer, this could help if they want to direct specific advertising towards women, or to men, or to a certain age group.

In 2014, Facebook announced a project it called DeepFace, "a system said to be 97.35 percent accurate in comparing two photos and deciding whether they depicted the same person—even in varied lighting conditions and from different camera angles. In fact, the company's algorithms are now almost as adept as a human being at recognizing people based just on their silhouette and stance."[164]

"Entities like Facebook hold vast collections of facial images," says Gates, the UC, San Diego professor.[164] "People have voluntarily uploaded millions of images, but for their own personal photo-sharing activities, not for Facebook to develop its facial recognition algorithms on a mass scale."[164] Unfortunately for privacy advocates, there is no difference between the two.

Potentially Facebook, Instagram, WeChat, Pinterest, Snapchat, Google, and a whole host of other social media platforms could use their vast databases of faceprints to power real-world facial recognition.[164] "Hypothetically, a tech giant wouldn't need to share the faceprints themselves. It could simply ingest video feeds from a store and let salespeople know when any well-heeled consumer walked through the door."[164] It could also, potentially, do this for a marketer as well, to prevent money laundering.

According to his article *Qantas have seen their Future. It's Facial Recognition*[374], Chris Riddell explains how Qantas is taking facial recognition technology to a whole new level. According to Riddell[374]:

> "Qantas have just started a brand-new programme of trialing facial recognition to enable them to monitor passengers from the very moment they check in, all the way through to the gate when they board the plane. They're also going to be monitoring everything in between, including what café you're getting your coffee at, and where you are shopping for that last minute pair of jeans. They'll also know what electrical gadgets you were playing with at the tech shop, and whether you were too busy trying free shots of cognac to buy that gift for your other half that you promised, but then 'forgot'"

Riddell sees this as "a big retail play by the red kangaroo and it is pushing the national airline into very new and unchartered territory. Qantas are exceptionally interested in the movement of people through the terminals, and how they spend their time."[374]

Riddell adds that, "Qantas will want to know what people are doing, how long they are doing it, which shops they are spending the most time, and which shops they spend the least time in. By combining that with the incredible amount of data from frequent flyer programme and passenger information they collect, they'll be catapulting themselves into the world of hyper intelligent retail."[374]

Of course, Qantas are not alone in wanting to capture all this customer data, explains Riddell, every major airline is doing it.[374] "The truth is though, few are using the data they hoard with any level of real sophistication for the customer," claims Riddell.[374]

"All airlines know who you work for, who you book travel through, where you go on holiday, where you travel for work and for how long you are away for," says Riddell.[374] "They also know what food you like, what food you are allergic to, and who you bank with. They also know where you live, and who lives there with you, whether you've got children, and how old they are. The list goes on…. If you've linked other loyalty programmes to your frequent flyer account, they also know a whole lot about your shopping habits," adds Riddell.[374]

All of this data helps a business understand its customer down to a macro level, which is more critical than ever.[374] For a business like Qantas this data helps them deliver services and experiences that are relevant, personal and predictive.[374]

Next up, Riddell believes "will be the delivery of experiences in real-time as you are in an airport retail store. Facial Recognition technology will be able to deliver you services based on *how you feel* at the exact moment it matters. *This is the future*, and it's called emotional analytics."[374] It is a step beyond facial recognition technology, but the natural next step.

As CB Insights reports in its *What's Next in AI? Artificial Intelligence Trends*[69], "Academic institutions like Carnegie Mellon University are also working on technology to help enhance video surveillance." "The university was granted a patent around 'hallucinating facial features'—a method to help law enforcement agencies identify masked suspects by reconstructing a full face when only periocular region of the face is captured. Facial recognition may then be used to compare 'hallucinated face' to images of actual faces to find ones with a strong correlation."[69]

However, CB Insights warns that the tech is not without glitches. The report that, "Amazon was in the news for reportedly misidentifying some Congressmen as criminals"[69]—although perhaps there's a predictive element in the technology that we're unaware of?

"'Smile to unlock' and other such 'liveness detection' methods offer an added layer of authentication," states CB Insight.[69] For example, "Amazon was granted a patent that explores additional layers of security, including asking users to perform certain actions like 'smile, blink, or tilt his or her head.'"[69] These actions can then be combined with 'infrared image information, thermal imaging data, or other such information' for more robust authentication."[69]

In his article *Machine Learning and AI: If Only My Computer Had a Brain Wired for Business*, Michael Klein states that, fifty-nine percent of fashion retailers in the U.K. are using facial recognition to identify V.I.P clients and provide them with special service.[56] "The technology also enables retailers to track customer sentiment and gauge how customers respond to in-store displays, how long they spend in the store and traffic flow in each of their retail locations," says Klein.[56]

"But that's not the only way retailers are taking advantage of facial recognition and its AI technology. They're using the technology, which is typically employed in airports, for added security," notes Klein.[56] For example, Saks "has leveraged facial recognition technology to match the faces of shoppers caught on security cameras with that of past shoplifters. From this perspective, AI can serve the dual purpose of preventing losses while improving the customer experience—and that ultimately helps retailers boost sales."[56] And, once again, what's good for retailers is good for sports books.

Image Search

"If a picture is worth a thousand words, visual search—the ability to use an image to search for other identical or related visual asset—Is worth thousands of spot-on searches—and thousands of minutes saved on dead-end queries," says Brett Butterfield in his Adobe blog *See It, Search It, Shop It: How AI is Powering Visual Search*.[217] In the article, Butterfield explains how visual search could become a big part of a buyer's shopping future. With visual search, you don't need to try and guess the brand, style, and/or retail outlet something was purchased on, you can simply snap a picture of the item you like, upload the image, and immediately find exactly the same sneakers or ones like them, and purchase them, all rather seamlessly.[217]

"That spot-it/want-it scene is common, and good for business. It could be a shirt on someone walking down the street, an image on Instagram, or a piece of furniture in a magazine—somewhere, your customer saw something that made them want to buy one, and now they're on a mission to find it," explains Butterfield.[217]

"While it's a seemingly simple task, in many cases the path from seeing to buying is a circuitous and friction-filled route that leads to a subpar purchase—or no purchase at all. Just one in three Google searches, for example, leads to a click—and these people come to the table with at least a sense of what they're searching for," notes Butterfield.[217]

"Visual search is all about focusing your attention toward a target," says Gina Casagrande, senior Adobe Experience Cloud evangelist, "and helping you find what you're looking for that much faster. You also get the added benefit of finding things you didn't even know you were looking for."[217]

"Like text-based search, visual search interprets and understands a user's input—images, in this case—and delivers the most relevant search results possible. However, instead of forcing people to think like computers, which is how the typical text search works, visual search flips the script," adds Butterfield.[217]

"Powered by AI, the machine sees, interprets, and takes the visual cues it learns from people. After applying metadata to the image, AI-powered visual search systems can dig through and retrieve relevant results based on visual similarities, such as color and composition," explains Butterfield.[217] Visual search is another technology that can facilitate better, more frictionless retail experiences that can help buyers find what they want faster.[217]

"One early adopter of visual search is Synthetic, Organic's cognitive technology division, an Omnicom subsidiary," explains Butterfield.[217] "Synthetic's Style Intelligence Agent (SIA)—powered by Adobe Sensei—uses AI to help customers not just find specific clothing items, but also find the right accessories to complete their new look."[217]

To use SIA, customers simply upload an image, either from a website, from real life or even from an ad in a magazine and from there, "Adobe Sensei's Auto Tag service extracts attributes from the image based on everything from color, to style, to cut, to patterns."[217] SIA's custom machine-learning model then kicks in, correlating those tags with a massive catalog of products.[217] "SIA then displays visually similar search results as well as relevant recommendations—items with similar styles, cuts, colors, or patterns, for example."[217] Just as importantly, SIA then "uses these visual searches to build a rich profile for that customer's preferences and tastes—a much deeper profile than what could be built from text-based searches alone."[217] Here you are getting customer preferences on steroids, an enormous of amount of personalized data that can then be used in customer marketing.

"This is where visual search goes beyond just search and becomes a true shopping consultant," says Casagrande, "and a superior, more sophisticated way to search for what you want and what you didn't know you wanted."[217]

"In delivering such a simple, seamless experience, AI-powered visual search removes the friction from traditional search-and-shop experiences," says Butterfield.[217] "No longer do customers have to visit multiple retailers or sites and strike out. They can now find virtually anything, anywhere, even without knowing exactly where to find it," he adds.[217]

Several retailers currently "use visual search to make the distance between seeing and buying virtually nonexistent—within their own brand experience."[370] "Macy's, for example, offers visual search capabilities on its mobile app, which allows customers to snap a photo, and find similar products on Macys.com. It's 'taking impulse buying to new heights,' one source says."[217] Sports books could use image search to offer bets on football players snapped in an image in a book or on the internet.

Frictionless image search is just the beginning.[217] "The value of visual search technology grows as the customer returns to the site," says Casagrande.[217] "On that next visit, it's a more personalized, powerful targeted search. Just being able to pick up where I left off and get to that product that much faster helps reduce friction, and has been shown to increase conversions and order rate."[217]

"Visenze, which builds shopping experiences using AI, is already seeing these benefits," says Butterfield.[217] For example, "the company saw a 50 percent increase in conversion among clients such as Nike and Pinterest that implemented visual search technology."[217]

"In the United States, Amazon and Macy's have been offering this feature for some time," says Visenze CEO Oliver Tan. "Consumers are crying out for a simpler search process," claims Tan.[217] If brands don't have that, their customers will move on to other companies that do.[217]

Though the benefits of visual search are clear, there's still a gap in between customer expectations and delivery.[217] "Our current Iteration of visual search gets us maybe 70 percent of the way there," says Casagrande.[217]

"Keep in mind, as more data and content become available the algorithms will get smarter, and the visual search experience will only continue to get better," says Casagrande.[217]

Video

In his article *The Future of Video Advertising is Artificial Intelligence*[375], Matt Cimaglia sees a video advertising world that is completely different to the current one. He describes it as such: "Meanwhile, somewhere in another office, in that same year, a different team is creating a different digital video. Except they're not shooting a single video: They're shooting multiple iterations of it. In one, the actor changes shirts. In another, the actor is an actress. In another, the actress is African-American. After finishing the shoot, this agency doesn't pass the footage off to a video editor. They pass it off to an algorithm."[375]

Cimaglia states that, "The algorithm can cut a different video ad in milliseconds. Instead of taking one day to edit one video, it could compile hundreds of videos, each slightly different and tailored to specific viewers based on their user data."[375] "As the video analytics flows in, the algorithm can edit the video in real-time, too—instead of waiting a week to analyze and act on viewer behavior, the algorithm can perform instantaneous A/B tests, optimizing the company's investment in a day," claims Cimaglia.[375]

Cimaglia believes this is what is happening right now.[375] Cimaglia contends, "We are witnessing a moment in video marketing history, like moments experienced across other industries disrupted by the digital revolution, where human editors are becoming obsolete."[375] This is the evolution of advertising—personalized advertising, i.e., tailoring content to individuals rather than the masses[375]; surgically striking relevant offers to a market of one, rather than blasting a shotgun of offerings to the uninterested many.

"Savvy agencies are turning to artificial intelligence for help making those new, specialized creative decisions," says Cimaglia.[375] "It's the same logic that's long overtaken programmatic banner and search advertising, machine learning and chatbots: There are some things computers can do faster, cheaper and more accurately than humans," contends Cimaglia.

"In this future of data-driven dynamic content, viewers' information is siphoned to AI that determines aspects of the video based on their data," explains Cimaglia.[375]

Cimaglia sees advertising being tailored towards individuals.[375] "The options for customization extend beyond user data, too. If it's raining outside, it could be raining in the video," easily done by the agency plugging in a geolocating weather script.[375] Similarly, if a user is watching the video at night, the video could mirror reality and be a night scene filled with cricket sounds.[375] For Cimaglia, "This is a logical progression for a society already accustomed to exchanging their privacy for free services."[375] The video could also be in multiple languages thanks to tools like Amazon Polly.

Cimaglia believes that "this customization model of video production is more effective than the current model of creating a single video for the masses."[375] He rightfully questions the current preoccupation in investing tremendous resources in single, groundbreaking commercials.[375] Currently, "It's all about producing a multimillion-dollar, 30-second mini-film that screens during the Super Bowl, gets viewed on YouTube 10 million times and wins a Cannes Lion," claims Cimaglia, but what really does that gain you? It's less about the viewer and more about stroking the already inflated egos of a select creative set, who are doing nothing more than delivering a one-size-fits-all product to millions of prospects.[375]

Cimaglia believes there is a place for this in a one-size-fits-all advertising product, but making them "the centerpiece of a multimillion-dollar campaign is foolhardy in an era when companies are sitting on more customer information than ever before—and when AI is even taking over in that arena."[375] "Personalization is the way of the future, but, unfortunately, most companies simply don't know what to do with their stores of customer data," laments Cimaglia.[375] However, the companies that do will surely reap large financial rewards.

Audio

In his article *AI's role in next-generation voice recognition*[376], Brian Fuller notes that "speech is a fundamental form of human connection that allows us to communicate, articulate, vocalize, recognize, understand, and interpret. But here's where the complexity comes in: There are thousands of languages and even more dialects." "While English speakers might use upwards of 30,000 words, most embedded speech-recognition systems use a vocabulary of fewer than 10,000 words. Accents and dialects increase the vocabulary size needed for a recognition system to be able to correctly capture and process a wide range of speakers within a single language," states Fuller.[376]

Today, the state of speech-recognition and AI still has a long way to go to match human capability.[376] Fuller claims that, "With the continually improving computing power and compact size of mobile processors, large vocabulary engines that promote the use of natural speech are now available as an embedded option for OEMs."[376]

"The other key to improved voice recognition technology is distributed computing," says Fuller.[376] We've gotten to this amazing point in voice-recognition because of cloud computing, but there are limitations to cloud technology when real-time elements are needed.[376] Things are improving radically but this is a very tricky world to operate in because user privacy, security, and reliable connectivity are difficult to get to work in concert.[376] "The world is moving quickly to a new model of collaborative embedded-cloud operation—called an embedded glue layer—that promotes uninterrupted connectivity and directly addresses emerging cloud challenges for the enterprise," says Fuller.[376]

As Fuller explains it[376]:

> "With an embedded glue layer, capturing and processing user voice or visual data can be performed locally and without complete dependence on the cloud. In its simplest form, the glue layer acts as an embedded service and collaborates with the cloud-based service to provide native on-device processing. The glue layer allows for mission-critical voice tasks—where user or enterprise security, privacy and protection are required—to be processed natively on the device as well as ensuring continuous availability. Non-mission-critical tasks, such as natural language processing, can be processed in the cloud using low-bandwidth, textual data as the mode of bilateral transmission. The embedded recognition glue layer provides nearly the same level of scope as a cloud-based service, albeit as a native process."

Fuller believes that, "This approach to voice recognition technology will not only revolutionize applications but devices as well."[376]

Voice Activated Internet

In his article *2019 Predictions from 35 voice industry leaders[377]*, Bret Kinsella quotes Jason Fields, Chief Strategy Officer of Voicify, who claims that "2019 is going to be the year voice and IVA's are integrated into brands overall CX strategy."

In her article *Voice search isn't the next big disrupter, conversational AI Is[378]*, Christi Olson explains the importance of being what she calls 'position zero' in the search rankings. She says[378]:

> "When you type a query into a search engine, hundreds of options pop up. It's different with voice. When people engage in a voice search using a digital assistant, roughly 40 percent of the spoken responses today (and some say as many as 80%) are derived from 'featured snippet' within the search results. In search speak, that's position zero. When you are that featured snippet in an organic search, that's what the assistant is going to default to as the spoken response. Siri, Google, Cortana and Alexa don't respond with the other ten things that are a possibility on that search page. Just the one."

Understanding this, it's clear why position zero is so important; "while you might be number two in the text-based searches, you're getting little to no traffic if people are engaging with intelligent agents and listening to the spoken response."[378]

The opportunity here is for companies to reverse-engineer the process to ensure they get position zero, so they can win the search race and therefore gain the traffic. But how? "It goes back to the best practices of organic search, basic SEO, and having a solid strategy," argues Olson.[378] "It's embracing schema markup and structured data within your website, so you are providing search engines with signals and insights to be included in the knowledge graph. It's claiming your business listings so that the data is up-to-date and correct. It's understanding the questions people are asking and incorporating that question and conversational tone into your content," says Olson.[378] "Simply put: It's understanding the language your customers are using so that you can provide value and answers in their own words and phrases," adds Olson.[378]

"Conversational AI for voice-assisted search is different from text-based search. If you look at the top 80 percent of queries, text-based searches typically range between one to three words. When we (at Microsoft, my employer) look at our Cortana voice data, the voice searches coming in range from four to six words. That's substantially longer than a text-based search," says Olson.[378]

It means that people are engaging with the digital assistant conversationally, asking questions and engaging in almost full sentences.[378] "Given this insight, there's an opportunity to think about the questions your customers are now asking. Think about what their need is in the way that your customers naturally talk, not in marketer speak or marketing terms. Then, provide value back to them in that manner," recommends Olson.[378]

"With conversational AI, we're going back to being able to create an emotional connection through more meaningful conversations with our customers to build relationships," says Olson.[378] "Brands will be able to differentiate themselves by adding emotional intelligence to IQ through these conversations," concludes Olson.[378]

Another service that could be useful to sports book is Amazon Polly, a service that turns text into lifelike speech, allowing users "to create applications that talk, and build entirely new categories of speech-enabled products.[379] Amazon Polly is a text-to-speech service that uses advanced deep learning technologies to synthesize speech that sounds like a human voice."[380]

Amazon Polly contains dozens of lifelike voices across a wide range of languages, allowing users to select the ideal voice and build speech-enabled applications that work in many different countries.[380] At Intelligencia, we use Polly to quickly create videos in multiple languages. Some of the Polly voices sound a little stilted and machine-like, but there is usually one in the series of specific languages who does a passable job.

Voice Search

In its article *The Next Generation of Search: Voice*[381], seoClarity argues that brands should take voice search very seriously because it is becoming a zero-sum game. seoClarity states that[381]:

> "Because of the rise in voice search, Google has recognized the increasing need to improve the experience for consumers conducting these searches. Instead of simply displaying a list of 10 blue links, Google increasingly provides a single direct answer to queries. This makes sense since voice searches are often conducted when our hands and eyes are otherwise occupied (for instance, while driving). A standard SERP result would not be helpful in such situations. Rather, having the answer (which Google believes to be the best answer for the query) read out aloud provides immediate gratification and a much better use experience. Therefore, Google's response of creating the Answer Box is no accident."

"Now, and for the foreseeable future, Google's Answer Box is the golden ticket in the organic search rankings sweepstakes," says seoClarity.[381] "In addition to it being the only answer to voice search queries, it is the result that appears above all other results on the SERP, 'ranking zero', seoClarity notes.[381] "Capturing the

Google's Answer Box can mean a dramatic increase in traffic to your website, credibility and overall brand awareness," they add.[381]

Google's Answer Box, or "featured snippet block," is the summary of an answer.[381] "Not only is the Google Answer box at the very first spot, above standard organic results, but also has a unique presentation format that immediately sets it apart from the remainder of the page. This instantly increases the credibility and authority of the brand providing the answer to the user's query. Consequently, Google's Answer Box may be the only search result viewed by the user," says seoClarity.[381] Perhaps more importantly, it is the only answer read in response to a voice search.[381] "Not only does Google's Answer Box dominate the SERP, it also boosts organic traffic, leverages mid- to long-range keywords, and focuses on the searcher's intent," notes seoClarity.[381] "Given the great importance of the Answer Box, brands should be focused on delivering the best search experience rather than worrying about any specific tactic to trick the algorithms," argues seoClarity.[381]

"It's valuable to think about the shopper's journey. Shoppers at different stages of their journey are searching for different things. So, it is crucial that brands provide content that meet shoppers' needs wherever they are in their journey. When you are able to capture Google's top result for searches along the shopper's journey, you will maximize your brand's credibility and authority," argues seoClarity.[381]

"Voice search users tend to use specific, long-tail search phrases. Instead of inquiring about a term or phrase, voice searchers typically ask proper questions," says seoClarity.[381] "For example, when looking for places to dine out, desktop users might type 'Italian restaurant.' However, when using voice search, they're more likely to ask, 'where's the nearest Italian restaurant?'"[381]

Voice searchers tend to use language that's relevant to them.[381] "When speaking to their device, queries are more conversational, leaving it to the search engine to decipher the actual intent," says seoClarity.[381]

Voice searches are more targeted in the awareness and consideration phase.[381] Many voice searches have local intent—"as much as 22 percent of voice queries inquire about local information such as directions, restaurants, shopping, local services, weather, local events, traffic, etc.," says seoClarity.[381] "The remainder of queries is distributed between non-commercial queries like personal assistant tasks, entertainment, and general searches," note seoClarity.[381] "This makes local the biggest commercial intent among voice searches. As a result, you should incorporate new strategies to position your business in local voice search," argues seoClarity.[381]

Voice search is still messy and complex.[381] "Google's RankBrain algorithm leverages artificial intelligence to discover contextual connections between searches," says seoClarity.[381] Google "tries to understand 'intent' based on context of the search (such as location, time of day, device used, previous searches, connected data from email and other assistant sources) instead of just plainly matching words from on a page."[381] However, the machine is learning and training, so, "instead of trying to keep up with Google's algorithms, it is essential to understand what your audience needs and focus your optimization to your end user, not on chasing the latest algorithm shifts."[381]

seoClarity recommends brands "build a more effective content marketing strategy to win the Answer Box by optimizing for topics that reflect the intent of your audience instead of just optimizing for keywords."[381] When brands focus their content strategies on the intent of the audience, it better addresses the real needs of the customer.[381] Additionally, the created content can solve challenges and answer most commonly asked brand questions.[381] By targeting the awareness and consideration phases of the customer journey, brands can capture their audience early in the customer journey.[381]

Sports books should optimize to short attention spans.[381] It is essential to connect with customers at the right moment.[381] seoClarity says that, "Google outlines the following moments that every marketer should know: I-want-to-know moment; I-want-to-go moment; I-want-to do moment; I want-to-buy moment."[381]

Always create a FAQ page as it can provide answers to common questions that users may have.[381] "By figuring out what questions your customers are asking, you can create the type of content that they are most likely to find useful," says seoClarity.[381]

"Answer the five W's & H—Be sure to answer the essential questions that everyone asks when collecting information or solving a problem: Who, What, Where, When, Why. And don't forget the all-important How," says seoClarity.[381] "The data also showed some other important trigger words including Best, Can, Is, and Top," says seoClarity.[381] Brands should also "Explain steps to complete tasks—Focus on content that details steps and how to complete tasks that relate to your product or service and also other explanations specifically for your product or service. "How to" and "What Is" contain significant lead over other trigger words."[381]

Other things seoClarity recommends are, "Highlight the best options for customers. Create buying guides that help aid the decision making process in list and bullet point type of format to demonstrate the best options for customers."[381]

"Focus on structuring content in a way that matches consumer intent—Use formats that work for your customers and structure the content to intent," recommends seoClarity.[381] "Consider using tables, ordered lists, bullet points, and video. Use schema markup—Always use the best SEO practices by placing your keywords and key phrases in your header, metadata, URL structures, and alt tags," says seoClarity.[381]

One of the most important recommendations seoClarity offers is for brands to produce in-depth content.[381] "In your SEO efforts, you must never forget that content is the most important thing. Be sure to create relevant content that provides in-depth answers to the questions your target audience asks," says seoClarity.[381]

According to seoClarity[382], nearly 20% of all voice search queries are triggered by only 25 keywords (see Table 15), which include "how", "why", or "what", as well as adjectives like "best" or "easy". The top ten are listed below, others included "Why", "Who", "New", "Recipe", "Good", "Homes", "Make", "Does", "Define", "Free", "I", "List", "Home", "Types", and "Do."

Trigger Words	Count	% of Total
How	658,976	8.64%
What	382,224	5.01%
Best	200,206	2.63%
The	75,025	0.98%
Is	53,496	0.70%
Where	43,178	0.57%
Can	42,757	0.56%
Top	42,277	0.55%
Easy	31,178	0.41%
When	27,571	0.36%

Table 15: Voice search words
Search: Dialogtech.com[382]

Programmatic Advertising

When it comes to advertising, the Adobe Sensei Team believes that, "the promise of AI is that customers will receive the most relevant ads, while allowing brands to drive awareness, engagement, conversions, and loyalty."[17] This should result in happier customers and less wasted ad spend.[17] "With AI, advertisers can budget, plan, and more effectively spend limited ad dollars," claim the Adobe Sensei Team.[17]

The Sensei team provides the following example: "Cynthia is a travel and hospitality media buyer trying to determine the best mix of search advertising for her global hotel brand."[17] "She knows that with millions of keywords, multiple search engines, and different audience segments to consider, coming up with the right bid amount for each combination, as well as determining how to allocate her budget across her campaigns to most efficiently meet her goals is simply too much for her to handle alone."[17] Cynthia "turns to her media buying platform to help her make sense of the data."[17] The Adobe Sensei Team sees the process working as follows for Cynthia[17]:

> *"With AI leading the way, she reviews a forecast simulation to see how an increase or decrease in budget will impact her clicks, revenue, conversions, and other metrics. Once she selects her budget, she reviews AI-powered ad spend recommendations to see how to best allocate her advertising budget. She clicks on her preferred allocation. Later, as her ad campaigns are running, she accesses model accuracy performance reports so she can see how actual performance numbers compare with AI-generated forecasts, allowing her to make any necessary adjustments along the way. Once her campaigns have run, she's thrilled to see that they delivered 99 percent of the clicks that were forecast, and actual revenue was five percent higher than forecasted. Now that Cynthia has a clear picture of what worked during her search ad campaigns, she checks the performance of her display and video campaigns. Again, she calls on AI to report on awareness and performance while letting her demand-side platform (DSP) guide automated budget allocation so she can stay focused on strategic media planning and buying.*

The Adobe Sensei Team believes that with the help of AI, brands "can keep up with changing customer preferences, navigate mountains of data, and make adjustments multiple times per day if needed to make sure"[17] budgets are allocated "most effectively across channels like search, display, and video, or even within a specific channel."[17]

In her article *Experts Weigh in On the Future of Advertising*, Giselle Abramovich believes that AI can help build a media-buying platform that allows a marketer to input goals "and a transparent algorithm does the rest, executing buys and optimizing every millisecond."[272] The ad could dynamically change the tone of the voiceover based on the preferences of the viewer.[272] Abramovich believes that, "The convergence of AI with human creativity and insight will transform advertising, and we're just beginning to see what's possible."[272]

One of the companies delving into AI head-first is Citi, which recently launched its "Welcome What's Next" campaign.[272] "[AI] is allowing us to create custom ads that meet people where they are. For example, if you're looking at the weather, it's serving up the ad in a customized way so it's relevant to what you're looking at," says Jennifer Breithaupt, global consumer CMO at Citi.[272] "It integrates with a consumer's path online and provides a more seamless way to experience the ad."[272]

AI is already helping Citi surpass its advertising benchmarks, Breithaupt adds.[272] "For example, the financial giant has realized a 10%+ lift in video completion rates versus standard, non-customized ads as a result of AI."[272]

"But what's going to be crucial to the success of AI is structuring it in a transparent manner that involves a partnership between parties," says Breithaupt.[272] "In other words, above all as advertisers, it's crucial we're clearly defining the value exchange and providing consumers with the opportunity to make an informed choice about their participation."[272]

In his article *How AI is Driving a New Era of TV Advertising*[383], Varun Batra states that in November 2017, eMarketer reported that 70% of U.S. adults "second screen" while watching TV. Although that sounds pretty discouraging for brands that spend millions on their TV spots, one should consider that this is reported behavior, not observed behavior.[383] "No doubt we all second screen, but we don't do so all the time. That begs the question: how does a brand know consumers paid attention to its $5 million Super Bowl ad rather than their mobiles?" asks Batra.[383]

"Using AI, data scientists have been able to map multiple devices to the same individual and household, as well as to connect online behavior with offline behavior, such as watching the Super Bowl via a connected TV and engaging with a smartphone during commercials," explains Batra.[383] Brands "can determine when consumers second screen during the commercials by counting the number of bid requests from their devices," says Batra.[383]

"Of course, AI can't tell us if an inactive device meant the consumer watched the ad or went to the kitchen for another beer, but if we track ad requests across millions of household, we can get a lot of insight into a creative's ability to captivate consumers," says Batra.[383]

"AI can also help determine the impact of an ad on consumer behavior, thanks to that same ability to link online and offline behavior. For example, if we know that a particular household was presented with a TV ad for a 'one-day-only sale' on GM pickup trucks, and a mobile device associated that household shows up at the local dealer on sale day, then we can assume the ad had an impact," explains Batra.[383] "The connection becomes more compelling when the behavior is seen across all households that see the ad," he adds.[383]

"Marketers will continue to see new opportunities to improve their campaigns as TV becomes more digitized," argues Batra.[383] He adds that, "As of 2017, there are nearly 133 million connected TV users in the US and will grow to at least 181 million in" 2018.[383] That means the online and offline behavior of 55% of the population can now be tied to ad-views, which is obviously a huge number.[383]

"Many programmatic companies allow marketers to incorporate TV inventory into their multi-channel programmatic campaigns. These connected TVs are targeted using first- and third-party data sets, just as if they were laptops and tablets," says Batra.[383] "Marketers can create surround-sound marketing, hitting consumers with messages on their laptops, mobile devices, and TVs," he adds.[383]

"AI is more precisely transforming the very segments we use to pinpoint consumers who are in the market for a particular product," says Batra. "Machine learning excels at sifting through massive amounts of observed online and offline user behavior to discover distinct signals that indicate purchase intent," explains Batra.[383] AI can also make sub-millisecond decisions to remove a consumer from a targeting segment as soon as he or she stops sending in-market signals.[383] Humans just don't have the capacity to do this, so the models do it completely autonomously and at a scale far beyond human capability.[383]

"Through numerous applications of machine learning, we've learned that there is a host of common—and often non-intuitive—behaviors that people engage in before they exhibit the signals of being in the market," says Batra.[383] For example, "in the classic digital marketing use case, airlines will retarget consumers who search for flights to Las Vegas. In a machine-learning use case, airline marketers would target consumers who look at wedding chapels, an early signal that they'll soon look for a flight to the city."[383] "In other words, the machine predicts who an airline's future customer will be, giving the airline the opportunity to get a jump on its competition," notes Batra.[383] For sports books, consumers who look at champions league or FIFA World Cup websites would obviously be more interested in having a bet on the action of those tournaments than browsers who are looking at the latest cashmere sweaters on Pinterest.

Batra believes that, "Television has always been a powerful awareness tool, enabling brands to reach millions of consumers quickly and effectively."[383] He concludes that, AI can only enhance "that power by predicting the right people to receive a TV ad, gauging its effectiveness, and assessing its impact on online and offline consumer behavior."[383]

Customer Journey

As I wrote in chapter one, successful marketing is all about reaching a consumer with an interesting offer when he or she is primed to accept it. Knowing what might interest the consumer is half the battle to making the sale and this is where customer analytics and AI come in. Customer analytics have evolved from simply reporting customer behavior to segmenting customers based on their profitability, to predicting that profitability, to improving those predictions (because of the inclusion of new data), to *actually manipulating customer behavior* with target-specific promotional offers and marketing campaigns. AI is central to this process.

A sports book needs to create a single view of the customer so that its marketers can deliver a personalized experience that wows the customer. Data can come from transactional systems, CRM systems, app impressions, operational data, facial recognition software, wearables, iBeacons, and clickstreams. Dan Woods explains this in his amusing comparison of the different environments that today's marketers face in comparison to what their 1980's counterparts saw.[36] Today, stealthy marketers are forced to use "email campaigns, events, blogging, tweeting, PR, ebooks, white papers, apps, banner ads, Google Ad Words, social media outreach, search engine optimization."[36] Woods didn't include SMS or OTT, but these are important channels to use as well.

In practice, all these channels should work together in concert; an email campaign can promote a sale at an event, which can be blogged and tweeted about through social media. PR can also promote the event through a sports book's typical news channels. Coupons for the event can be disseminated through the brand's mobile app and SMS messaging channel. Banner ads will appear on the brand's website, while Google ads and SEO will drive buyers and potential buyers to the brand's website or its social channels. Hopefully, viral marketing then kicks in, with customers and potential customers sharing on Facebook, Instagram, Pinterest, Weibo, WeChat, etc., etc. Of course, influencer marketing can also help the viral marketing process at some point.

Seen through the lens of the *Engagement and Loyalty Platform*, all these activities can increase personalization to the point where it will be recognized and coveted by the customer. Lovelock and Wirtz's "Wheel of Loyalty"[89] concept and its three sequential steps—building a foundation for loyalty, creating loyalty bonds, and identifying and reducing factors that result in churn should be kept in mind when building up the foundation of *The A.I. Sports Book's* CRM system. The most important part of the second step is the cross-selling and bundling of products and a real-time stream processing recommendation engine will certainly help with that.

Listening

In her article *Engage Customers and Gain Advocates Through Social Media and Social Networking*[384], Wendy Neuberger argues that: "Social commerce is about making a retailer's brand a destination. Retailers really need to listen to what their customers are saying. Customers can provide valuable input and feedback that can be used to make more informed assortment decisions, changes to website features and enhancements to the shopping experience."

"When customers feel their voice is being heard, they gain a stronger connection to the retailer and are more likely to become advocates."[384] Neuberger claims it is important for brands to identify and engage with the key influencers for several reasons, the two most important being: "to empower their advocacy or capabilities, which helps build and foster a sense of community among brand loyalists, and empowers those loyalists to better advocate on behalf of a brand, product and/or service."[384]

In Bain & Company's *Management Tools 2015 An Executive's Guide*[95], Darrell K. Rigby claims, CRM requires managers to defining strategic 'pain points' in the customer relationship cycle. Pain points can be things like hard-to-navigate customer service channels, providing inaccurate information to customers, poorly designed websites, complicated fee structures, high shipping costs, etc., etc. Pain points can even be problems with data quality that is negatively affecting a sports book's CRM system.

Sports books should evaluate whether—and what kind of—CRM data can fix those pain points, as well as calculate the value that such information would bring the company. As Dan Shewan explains in his article *Pain Points: A Guide to Finding & Solving Your Customers' Problems*[385], "One of the best ways to learn your customers' biggest problems is by *really* listening to them." The best way to do this is by conducting qualitative research.[385]

"The reason you need to conduct *qualitative* research (which focuses on detailed, individualized responses to open-ended questions) as opposed to *quantitative* research (which favors standardized questions and representative, statistically significant sample sizes) is because your customers' pain points are highly subjective," says Shewan.[385] "Even if two customers have exactly the same problem, the underlying causes of that problem could differ greatly from one customer to another," he adds.[385]

Qualitative research is, of course, a lot harder to quantify, especially without AI and machine learning. With them, it is still difficult because customer complaints can be so subjective—and often wrong. NLP can help with this, as I explained earlier.

"There are two primary sources of the information you need to identify your customers' pain points—your customers themselves, and your sales and support teams," states Shewan.[385] I have listed several ways to listen to your customer throughout this book, as well as include more ideas in the customer journey section in this chapter, but they are just one part of the equation, a brand's sale staff is the other. A brand's sales reps work on the frontlines of the battle for the hearts and minds of the company's prospective customers every single day, which makes them an invaluable source of feedback on your customers' and/or prospects' pain points.[385]

"However," Shewan warns that, "as valuable as your sales team's feedback can be, it's important to distinguish your sales reps' pain points from your prospects' pain points; your sales reps' problems may be very real, but you're not building a product or providing a service to make your sales reps' lives easier."[385]

Select the appropriate technology platform and calculate the cost of implementing it and training employees to use it.

1. Assess whether the benefits of the CRM information outweigh the expense involved.
2. Design incentive programs to ensure that personnel are encouraged to participate in the CRM program. Many companies have discovered that realigning the organization away from product groups and toward a customer-centered structure improves the success of CRM.
3. Measure CRM progress and impact. Aggressively monitor participation of key personnel in the CRM program. In addition, put measurement systems in place to track the improvement in customer profitability with the use of CRM. Once the data is collected, share the information widely with employees to encourage further participation in the program."[95]

In his article *Taking Back The Social-Media Command Center*[386], Scott Gulbransen argues that, "To do the command-center model right, a setup has to envision a real-time workflow empowered to take action on all of the relevant content being analyzed, whether it be insights derived from real-time monitoring, opportunities to respond, or great discovered content to feature that elevates you and your fans." Gulbransen recommends breaking down a command center into the following critical functions[339]:

5. Identify trends and insights—track not only the key themes, but also how they evolve over time.
6. Review the content—monitor a wide variety of terms that are meaningful to the brand and assign employees to sort through the responses, deciding which one warrants a response, and what might interest the community at large.
7. Curate the best stuff—leverage the great content that is being said about the company, as well as champion those great content providers.
8. Listen and Respond—this is a two-way conversation, listen and respond quickly and accordingly.

In the *Listening* part, brands should define and look out for triggers, such as photos, hashtags, keywords, likes, video views, etc. Hootsuite's *14 of the Best Social Media Monitoring Tools for Business*[387] lists some of the best tools for brands to use for this step, including Reddit, Streamview, Reputology, and Synthesio, Crowd Analyzer, amongst others (see Table 16).

SERVICE	DESCRIPTION
Streamview for Instagram	With a community of over 700 million users it makes sense to monitor what people are posting on Instagram, especially if your

SERVICE	DESCRIPTION
	audience falls in the 18 to 29 age range. With the Streamview for Instagram app you can monitor posts by location, hashtag, or username. The app within Hootsuite allows you to monitor and engage with users that are posting in your area, or an area you choose to follow. For example, you can use this tool during events to see what is being posted and to engage with attended.
Hootsuite Syndicator Pro	Manage and monitor all your favorite blogs and websites with Hootsuite Syndicator Pro. This tool provides a quick and easy way to view RSS feeds and quickly share them to your social media channels, as well as rich filtering, monitoring, and tracking tools. You can also track which stories you've shared.
Reputology	Online (and offline) reputation management is extremely important and surprisingly easy. The Reputology app lets you monitor and check major review sites, such as Yelp, Google, Facebook reviews, so that you can engage with reviewers and resolve any issues in a timely manner. You can track activity across multiple storefronts and locations and respond quickly via quick links.
Hootsuite Insights	Hootsuite Insights combines social media listening, analytics, and powerful social media monitoring capabilities. It allows you to gain powerful real-time insights about your brand, track influencers, stories, and trends, and visualize the metrics—all in one place. You can filter and tailor results by sentiment, platform, location, and language, and engage directly from your stream to take action on previously hidden results.
Brandwatch	The name says it all; the Brandwatch app in Hootsuite lets you keep watch over your brand through deep listening. You can identify key insights from more than 70 million traffic sources across the web, including major social channels, blogs, forums, news and review sites, and much more. This tool lets you make real-time, informed decisions and take action on them.
ReviewInc	Whether it's a positive or negative online review, your response should be in the same place as that review. The ReviewInc app for Hootsuite lets you view over 200 popular review sites across over 100 countries. Organize positive reviews for sharing on social media sites and resolve negative issues instantly.
Synthesio	Synthesio is a comprehensive social monitoring tool for finding the information you need to gain deeper insights and better informed business decisions. The tool lets you monitor multiple mention streams at once, so you can listen to the social media conversations most important to you. You can then analyze these conversations and join them.
Crowd	If you or your customers are based in the Middle East, Crowd Analyzer is an invaluable analytics and social media monitoring tool.

SERVICE	DESCRIPTION
Analyzer	As the first Arabic-focused social media monitoring platform, Crowd Analyzer analyzes "Arabic content in terms of relevancy, dialect and sentiment." It not only monitors major social networks, but also blogs, forums, and news sites.
76Insights	If content marketing is an important aspect of your Facebook marketing strategy, consider 76Insights. This social media monitoring tool measures the resonance of your social media content and breaks down your resonance score, which measures how much social media engagement someone receives after publishing something.
Keyhole	Keyhole lets you see what's being said about you on Twitter and Instagram in real-time. You can monitor keywords, hashtags, URLs, and usernames, and see historical as well as real-time data. One cool feature is the heat maps that show you activity levels around the world.
Digimind	Digimind lets you track keywords in news outlets and social media platforms for mentions of your company in real-time. It also measures sentiment, so you can gauge whether what is being said about you is good, bad, or "meh." You can also compare how your company is perceived online against your competitors.
Google Alerts	Google Alerts lets you monitor the web for mentions of your company, your competitors, or other relevant topics. Just go to the Google Alerts page, type a keyword or phrase in the search box, and provide your email address to receive a notification every time Google finds results relevant to your alert criteria. You can set alerts for specific regions and languages.
Hootsuite	On top of all the social media monitoring tools mentioned above, Hootsuite Pro provides social listening capabilities right in the dashboard. Monitor specific keywords, hashtags, regions, and more. Stay on top of what people are saying about your brand and listen to your customers and competitors to gain competitive advantage.

Table 16: Hootsuite's Social Media Monitoring Tools
Source: 14 of the Best Social Media Monitoring Tools for Business[387]

Sports books should also be listening to comment boards or short-term blogging sites like Tumblr or social news aggregation sites like Reddit for comments about their company and their services. Customers are often happy to post wonderful reviews about their purchases, and this is gold for word-of-mouth marketing, so brands should do their best to motivate customers to write up reviews on these sites. AI can be utilized to cull these websites for content so brands can be made aware of positive and negative comments that require responses.

Check-ins and geo-posts from sites like Foursquare, WeChat, Instagram, Facebook,

WhatsApp, YouTube, as well as a whole host of other social networks can help brands connect with nearby audiences. Underlying these check-ins is a treasure-trove of collected data. As Aaron Gell explains in his *New Yorker* article *The Not-so-Surprising Survival of Foursquare*[388], "Foursquare's stockpile of location-data breadcrumbs has allowed the company to steadily augment its map of the world, and to test the fuzzy signals it receives from users' phones (the service gleans from G.P.S., Wi-Fi, and Bluetooth, and from other markers) against the eleven billion definitive check-ins provided by its users over the past seven years."

"According to Mike Boland, a chief analyst at the market-research firm BIA/Kelsey, Foursquare can now pinpoint a phone's location with an accuracy that matches, and may in some cases surpass, that of much larger rivals," notes Gell.[388] "Facebook has a much larger sample of data points," Boland says, but "Foursquare has more accurate and reliable data."[388] Foursquare claims its map now "includes more than a hundred million locations, many of them in tightly crowded areas, like office buildings and malls, that other services still struggle to identify."[388] "The accuracy of Foursquare's Places database has led more than a hundred thousand other apps and developers—including Snapchat, Twitter, Pinterest, Uber, and Microsoft—to use its application programming interface (A.P.I.) to power their own features," notes Gell.[388]

As the Adobe Sensei Team explains in its article *AI: Your behind-the-scenes marketing companion*, "Analysts spend thousands of hours slicing and dicing data to find insights about what encourages people to purchase, what pushes them away, and which actions they can take to increase conversions. But with the time it takes humans to manually sift through massive amounts of data to find the hidden gems or red flags, you can easily miss opportunities."[17] "This is where AI can act as your personal data analyst to get a holistic view of customers—recognizing patterns, alerting you to unusual activity, and making recommendations," says the Adobe Sensei Team.[17]

The Adobe Sensei Team provides the following example[17]:

> "Daniel is an analyst for a software company that develops project management apps for various industries. After a year of strong sales, his analytics platform alerts him that sales have slowly stalled, and he needs to find out why. Daniel knows that sifting through potentially millions of data points and conducting hours upon hours of flow analysis to find out why people aren't buying is impossible without help, so he turns to his virtual assistant, AI, to run the analysis for him.

> "Using his AI-powered analytics platform, in three clicks he's quickly presented with a segment analysis that displays the top 10 indicators that lead people to purchase their software. Surprisingly, more important than a particular feature or low

price point, he sees that one of the biggest reasons why people buy their software is access to their online community, which makes it easy for customers to share ideas about how they've successfully used the app. This tells him that the post-sales support his company provides is not only valuable for onboarding and customer retention, but for acquiring new customers, as well."

Knowledge in hand, Daniel can then explain this unexpected development to his boss, as well as provide his fellow marketers with ideas on how they can better promote their online community to address customer needs and increase sales.[17] By relying on predictive analytics tools that use AI, brands can uncover unexpected correlations in the data that might help increase customer satisfaction and have more time to make strategic decisions that could, potentially, make a huge difference to the company's bottom line.[17]

Rules Engine

The Rules Engine step is a straightforward concept, brands are already creating business rules for their establishments and these rules should be extended to each company's defined rewards program, their reward's economy, and the marketing of the program.

Rewards can be as simple as a reward for a store visit, a points threshold reached, a birthday or anniversary, loyalty card utilization, or reaching a spending tier. Reward rules engine must contain the conditions of the loyalty program, i.e., if the activity of a member fulfills the conditions, the loyalty engine executes the assigned rule actions, which could be giving the member a unique offer based on his or her spend.

Automation

If AI was made for anything it was automation. One of the big benefits of automating campaigns is that offers based on either stated or inferred preferences of customers can be developed. Analysis can identify which customers may be more responsive to a particular offer. The result: more individualized offers are sent out to the brand's customers and, because these offers tap into a customer's wants, desires, needs *and* expectations, they are more likely to be used; more offers used means more successful campaigns; more successful campaigns means a higher ROI.

By understanding what type of customer is using its products and services, sports books can individualize marketing campaigns so that they can be more effective, thereby increasing the company's ROI.

Once a customer leaves the sports books' website, the marketing cycle begins anew. RFM models can project the time at which a customer is likely to return and social media should be checked for any comments, likes or uploads, left by a customer. All captured customer information can now become part of the master marketing profile that will be the basis for future marketing efforts. Combining the daily, weekly and monthly master marketing profiles will also allow the sports book to develop insightful macro views of its customer data, views that could help with labor management, and other brand needs as well.

Moderation

Moderating boards and UGC posts create a double whammy for brands because, as Rachel Perlmutter explains in her article *Why You Need Social Proof on Your Website*[389], "People need to see that others also enjoy that product. It's what we call social proof: the idea that buyers are influenced by the decisions and actions of others around them." Perlmutter offers the following reasons why it is so important to have UGC reviews on your site[389]:

- Testimonials add credibility for the products and services offered.
- People tend to trust online reviews when making purchases.
- Social proof earns better SEO because it adds more favorable language surrounding a brand online.
- When sourcing customers opinions, brands show that they care about the customer experience, thus strengthening the client bond.[389]

Perlmutter states that brands can gather testimonials in a variety of ways, including sending surveys to new clients.[389] Perlmutter also advises brands to encourage buyers to post on social media.[389] Brands should use hashtags to track customers' responses to the company's products and services so they can be easily found and responded to.[389] Instagram should be a big part of a marketer's strategy because testimonials with images usually trump text testimonials alone.[389] Testmonials are powerful examples of social proof as well.[389]

Messaging

The goal here is to surgically strike relevant offers to a market of one, rather than blast a shotgun of offerings to the uninterested many. The proliferation of marketing channels has made it easier to reach customers and potential customers, but the messaging is still of paramount important. Send the right offer to the right person on the right channel at the right time of day In the wrong context might mean the customer passes on the offer. Everything has to work in concert to give the brand the best possible chance for success, which usually means sales.

In her *Digiday* article *How Facebook is wooing luxury brands*[390], Bethany Biron writes that "Facebook is advocating for 'digitally influenced sales,' that assist consumers with the discovery process while still driving them to e-commerce sites and physical stores. This concept has helped major retailers like

Barneys break out of the traditional retail rut and embrace e-commerce."

Neuberger recommends that brands use the following social media platforms for messaging[384]:

- Blogs: brands can provide additional product or category information here as well as post how-to information in the form of text, photos and/or videos. Brands should also provide space for customers to add feedback and/or comments about their brand experience.
- Micro-blogging: coupons, sales and promotions can be offered through these channels. Brands can "'tweet press releases, provide exclusive tips and tricks to customers, and ask for customer feedback, suggestions or ideas for improvements. Some forward-thinking brands even use Twitter as a customer service channel."[384]
- Co-Shopping: this is a form of social shopping and it enables two people—a customer and sales associate or two shoppers in different locations—to share a joint shopping experience using live instant messaging such as Skype, WeChat, or any number of other OTT services.
- Widgets: these are tiny applications that can be embedded into a website, blog or social network that are portable and relatively inexpensive to create and use.
- Social Bridging: anyone who has signed into a website using their Facebook, Pinterest or Twitter account knows what social bridging is. "This level of authentication provides enough credentials to participate in the social elements of the site. Additional authentication is required to complete a shopping transaction due to the sensitivity of the content included in a shopper's account. Social bridging can be used to drive traffic and engage existing and new customers. It can access a user's identity, their social graph, and stream activities such as purchases and other social participation on the retailer's site" says Neuberger.[384]
- In-Store Kiosks and Flat Panels can enable customers to use social networking tools from within a store.[384]

In her article *Whatsapp For Business–What Does It Mean?*[391], Holly Turner explains that in August 2017, "WhatsApp announced it was experimenting with verified business accounts on the platform, which would offer brands the opportunity to communicate with its users; a platform the average user checks 23 times a day and which boasts 1.2 billion monthly active users."

"Businesses can gain a verified green checkmark icon to indicate the authenticity of the account, assuring users its legitimacy, alongside opening the door to the platform's previously walled off garden," explains Turner.[391]

"The platform could be following in the footsteps of other messaging apps such as Facebook Messenger and Kik, implementing a chatbot function to enable WhatsApp users to ask businesses questions, make purchases and receive

THE A.I. SPORTS BOOK

instant bot responses."[391]

The opportunity is considerable. WhatsApp business accounts offer up one more channel for brands to send out simple automated messaging to users who opt into their messages.[391] "Whether it be discount codes, new products or brand news, users could stay up to date with businesses they invest in and brands would be presented with the opportunity to reach people on a platform that, sees 6 out of 10 users accessing the app on a daily basis," argues Turner.[391]

WhatsApp's history will work in its favor. Having never allowed any form of advertising previously, WhatsApp currently feels like a very intimate and private environment for its users.[391] Turner believes that "content delivered to users would, therefore, benefit from having an 'organic' feel; providing useful and totally personalised content."[391]

"Whether WhatsApp intends to follow the crowd by implementing a chatbot strategy or go against the grain to offer users something truly useful and personalised will soon become clear," adds Turner. "What is already very clear, however, is the opportunity WhatsApp business accounts presents, regardless of what strategy they choose, to reach inside the walled gardens of messaging apps," concludes Turner.

Sports books can use social media to manage their brand, enhance brand loyalty, as well as engage both their current customers and their potential customers. The social media world is also the perfect place to harvest customer feedback, provide real-time customer service, build fanbases, and drive traffic to a company's website.

Blogs and micro-blogging sites are also important mobile and social media channels and Twitter feeds for both their satisfied and dissatisfied customers.

Sports books should also feel compelled to reward their customers through Facebook, Twitter, WeChat, and Weibo, or any number of blogging and micro-blogging services. The beauty of using these channels is the ability of customers to share these awards or stories of these awards with friends and acquaintances. It wouldn't be that hard to do, either, as a marketer can ask customers for their social media accounts upon sign up, like many already do.

Jones and Sasser warn that, "Extremely dissatisfied customers can turn into 'terrorists,' providing an abundance of negative feedback about the service provider."[93] Through social media channels, negative feedback can reverberate around the world within seconds. Today, more than ever, brands must spot dissatisfied customers and approach them before they do irreparable harm to the company's image and reputation and social media is one of the best channels in which to engage them.

In the *zone of indifference*, customers willingly switch if they can find a better alternative, while in the *zone of affection*, satisfaction levels are high and "customers may have such high attitudinal loyalty that they don't look for alternative services."[93] It is within this group that "Apostles"—members who willingly praise the firm in public—reside and this is the group that is responsible for improved future business performance.[94] Sports books should empower their customers to post on Facebook or WeChat or Twitter or comment about their experiences and, hopefully, turn their customers into apostles.

Facebook should be a part of every brand's social and mobile media marketing plan, but simply putting up a Facebook page won't cut it these days; creativity and uniqueness are needed to get noticed in today's highly competitive social media world. Gamification is also a good way to stand out from the crowd. Facebook bots can also add a customer service channel that can answer common customer service questions quickly, efficiently and inexpensively.

The best part of being on Twitter or Weibo or any of the other instant messaging services is the ability to interact with a customer in real time. A direct, two-way dialogue can be created, which helps with engagement and, probably, sales.

In its article *The 5 Different Types of Influencer Marketing Campaigns*[392], Mediakix claims that there are probably a limitless amount of ways for brands to create effective influencer marketing campaigns, but, in general, these campaigns fall within one of the following five subcategories:

1. Product Placement—this involves incorporating a company's product, services, or logo into a digital influencer's content just as it has been done in the film industry for decades. Just like actors in films, social media stars have earned the trust of their followers, so product placements are an excellent opportunity for brands to gain valuable exposure to millions of engaged consumers through the influencer's YouTube, yy.com, Instagram, or Snapchat account.[392]

2. Contests, Giveaways, Sweepstakes—Hosting social media contests like giveaways, sweepstakes, or best-of contests, such as best photograph, video, or blog competitions can generate buzz about a marketer, as well as foster goodwill among consumers. These contests compel social media users to take a specific action (like following the brand's channel or increasing company exposure by using branded hashtags). Aligning with a social media influencer, a sports book can promote a contest that will leverage the social media star's large follower base and ensure that consumers participate in the campaign.[392]

3. Theme/Hashtag Campaign—Hashtags are great ways to build a theme around a campaign. Focusing each influencer marketing campaign around a central theme or hashtag that is leveraged throughout all of the social channels helps build cohesion and encourages consumers to get involved by using the brand's hashtag in their own content. As Mediakix recommends, "Developing and implementing an influencer marketing campaign around a memorable branded hashtag is one of

the best ways brands can facilitate a genuine social conversation and increase brand exposure, especially if the hashtag happens to go viral."[392]

4. Creative Influencer Campaign—These give the social media star much more freedom to create content and these campaigns usually center around a specific concept or idea. Done right, these campaigns allow the digital influencer to interpret themes to create unique brand-sponsored content, leading to increased levels of engagement from the social media influencer's followers and/or subscribers.[392]

5. Campaign to Build Social Followers—brands can invite social media influencers to expose new audiences to their brand's social media accounts. Snapchat Takeovers—having a social media influencer "take over" a brand's Snapchat account for a set period of time—is one of the most effective ways for businesses to reach thousands or millions of new followers, as well as organically grow their own Snapchat follower fanbase.[392]

Data & Analytics

In this final section of the customer journey, brands should acquire social identity tied to customer records. Neuberger argues that it is very important to monitor the market conversation to understand what the marketplace is (or isn't) saying about a brand (their products, services, etc.).[384] Companies "need to understand the tone and impact of the conversation and begin to identify areas of opportunity for helping shape that conversation and gather valuable market intelligence," says Neuberger.[384]

As previously mentioned, ROI is not that difficult to measure with social media, quite the contrary. Today, the endless search for Facebook fans should be replaced by short-term campaign ROI as the main measure for individual campaigns. Brands should look at correlation analysis between activities, engagement and sales, which might be unsettling for some traditional marketers, but the reward should be worth the time and the effort.

As Josh Constine reports in his *Techcrunch* article *How Uber Will Become an Ad Company, Starting with Eats Pool*,[393] Uber plans to help users choose between restaurants that it is promoting through paid ads. Uber could "become the marketing platform through which the physical world vies for your attention," says Costine.[393]

In their article *10 Principles of Modern Marketing*[16], Lewnes and Keller contend that, "The amount of data available today mandates that every brand knows its customers and caters to them at every possible touch point, but at the same time, it is still important to actually meet with customers!" "No dashboard alone can provide the same rich insights as an in-depth conversation with an engaged customer," say Lewnes and Keller.[16] Along with traditional qualitative methods like focus groups and research, Adobe holds live events worldwide because it sees an unprecedented level of engagement from them, something far different to an online connection.[16] "Nothing beats the power of companies and their customers coming together in person to learn, get inspired, and have a little fun," Lewnes and Keller conclude.[16]

Sports books should look to assign a percentage value to social media so that a true attribution measurement can be created. Values should be ascribed to social media for being the site of new customer contact or for numbers of positive reviews by current customers. These are all important metrics to know and track because a highly followed influencer might not be spending that much time with the brand, but their followers might be.

For Neuberger, "Social media metrics include sentiment, activity, share-of-voice, and thematic content of online conversations. Trends and key influencers ('mavens') and the most active sites/blogs are identified and tracked. By understanding the impact, retailers will have a way of identifying measurable progress, quantifying the return on social media investment, and enabling benchmarking against future efforts."[384]

"To be a great technology marketer in today's digital world, it is important to build a culture of testing," argue Lewnes and Keller.[16] The writers work for Adobe and, from "a *product* perspective, Adobe does active beta testing with its customers, releasing versions of its software into the market and actively engaging with customers during the beta period to solicit feedback, add new functionality, and shape product road maps."[16]

"From a *marketing mix* perspective, Adobe applies state-of-the-art econometric modeling, as well as real-time attribution modeling, to test, predict, and ultimately validate the right levels and mix of media investments," explain Lewnes and Keller.[16]

"From a *marketing* perspective, Adobe uses data to build more precise segmentation models based on factors such as the type of content customers create and engage most with and their stage in the customer journey to offer more personalized, relevant experiences—a valuable asset in today's digital world," claim Lewnes and Keller.[16]

Of course, Adobe is not unique in using data analytics to drive marketing experimentation.[16] "Amazon, Capital One, Netflix, and Pandora famously run thousands of tests to optimize their marketing efforts"[16] Facebook can certainly be added to the mix of companies with standout data analytics capabilities.

"To successfully activate these different insights to improve the customer experience, it is imperative to also work across the organization to integrate data and build real-time data models and decision-driving dashboards," say Lewnes and Keller.[16] "That requires blending marketing inputs like behavioral data (for example, social, PR, web data, and media performance) with inputs from other areas (for example, sales, CRM, in-product, and finance). In today's world, marketing simply can't operate in a silo," conclude Lewnes and Keller.[16]

In their article *Data-Driven Transformation: Accelerate at Scale Now*[394], Gourévitch et al. argue that "Data-driven transformation is becoming a question of life or death in most industries." It is more so for the sports betting industry than many others because of its highly competitive nature. "Most CEOs recognize the power of data-driven transformation. They certainly would like the 20% to 30% EBITDA gains that their peers are racking up by using fresh, granular data in sales, marketing, supply chain, manufacturing, and R&D," claim Gourévitch et al.[394]

A flexible open architecture that can be updated continuously and enhanced with emerging technologies works best for analytics.[394] "Rather than embracing an end-to-end data architecture, companies should adopt a use-case-driven approach, in which the architecture evolves to meet the requirements of each new initiative," advise Gourévitch et al.[394] "The data governance and analytics functions should collaborate to create a simplified data environment; this will involve defining authorized sources of data and aggressively rationalizing redundant repositories and data flows," Gourévitch et al. recommend.[394]

Problem Gambling

Problem gambling is the inability to resist recurrent urges to gamble excessively despite harmful consequences to the gambler or others. The American Psychiatric Association's Diagnostic and Statistical Manual of Mental Disorders classifies pathological gambling (PG) as an Impulse Control Disorder that is defined by the presence of at least five symptoms that cause significant distress or impairment in social, family or occupational areas of life and that are not otherwise explained.[395] Some of the symptoms are similar to phenomena seen in substance use disorders (i.e., mood alteration, tolerance, withdrawal, loss of control and preoccupation with gambling), and some are more specific to gambling behavior and consequent financial difficulties (i.e., chasing losses, lying about losses, harm to relationships or occupation, seeking a financial bailout, and committing illegal acts to obtain money).[395]

In their article *Problem gambling and harm: Towards a national definition*[396], Neal, Delfabbro, & O'Neil state that "Problem Gambling is characterized by difficulties in limiting money and/or time spent on gambling which leads to adverse consequences for the gambler, others, or for the community."[396] This definition captures a general conceptual framework for problem gambling, but it should be understood that there are varying degrees of problem gambling, ranging from mild to moderate, up to severe, or what's known as "pathological" gambling.

On a scale of issues, the effects of problem gambling can run from minor to problematic to tragic, including bankruptcy[397] [398], suicide and, in even some cases, murder.[399] Problem gamblers suffer from serious mental health issues, such as feelings of guilt, depression, and anxiety. Even physical problems can be associated with those ailments; high blood pressure and gastric disorders are found in problem gamblers at higher rates than in control subjects.[400] Problem gamblers also have higher rates of suicide and attempted suicide.[401]

Sometimes the problem turns deadly, including the shocking and tragic story of Jessie Javier Carlos, a problem gambler who tried to steal millions in chips from Manila's Resorts World Casino because he owed $80,000 in gambling debts.[399] As Stradrooke explains in his article, *Resorts World Manila gunman a problem gambler, not a terrorist*[399]: "While Carlos never shot anyone during his attack, dozens of individuals—a mix of hotel guests and casino staffers—lost their lives during the ensuing chaos. Carlos set fire to multiple casino gaming tables and the resulting smoke and fumes caused most of the victims to suffocate in the cramped hallway in which they'd taken refuge."

Although the Philippine Amusement and Gaming Corporation (PAGCOR) had banned him from entering any Philippine casino, Carlos had a long history of problem gambling that included betting up to US$20,000 a night on cock fighting.[399] In an ironic case of you're-damned-if-you-do-and-damned-if-you-don't, police have suggested it was "PAGCOR's ban that may have 'triggered' Carlos to embark on his robbery attempt."[399]

This episode is perhaps the clearest case of how complex the problem of gambling addiction really is. It also shows how situations can spin out of control when desperate people don't receive the help that they need when they need it. "News of Carlos' gambling problems has led local politicians to call on PAGCOR to offer more assistance to gambling addicts."[399] It is a worldwide problem that sports books need to start taking very seriously.

Problem gambling can start at a young age and negatively affect a person's school or work life, sometimes resulting in job loss.[402] A small number of gamblers use criminal activity, such as fraud or embezzlement, to fund their gambling activities[402] [403], while upwards of 33% of prison inmates have a history of problem gambling.[404] This indicator, in particular, could be useful to sports books as this is, in some cases, public information.

Problem gamblers often have difficult home lives as well, with relationship problems that often lead to divorce, domestic violence and/or child abuse.[405] Many of these problems can feed upon themselves, making the problem gambler a mentally fragile person. Sadly, there is an intergenerational aspect to this afflication as well; children who have a parent who suffers from problem gambling often turn out to be problem gamblers themselves.[406] [407]

According to Williams, West, & Simpson there are "a large number of biological, psychological, experiential, and social factors which interact in complex ways to both contribute to and protect individuals from developing addictive behaviour."[405] These include[405]:

- Indirect biological risk factors—genetic inheritance creates biological propensities that increase or decrease a person's likelihood of engaging in gambling and/or developing gambling problems.
- Indirect environmental risk factors—"having an abusive or neglectful upbringing, parental involvement or modeling of gambling, peer group involvement in gambling, lower income, less education, societal acceptance of gambling, gambling opportunities being readily available, the presence of significant ongoing stressors and/or poor support systems, and gambling being commercially provided in an unsafe manner."[405]
- Direct risk factors—heightened risk factors, including the failure to understand the risks associated with gambling, whether or not gambling serves a psychological need, what was the reward magnitude and frequency of the person's early gambling activity, as well as whether the gambler was engaging in risky gambling practices.

As Williams, West, & Simpson state, "Within this constellation of problems, each reinforces each other's existence, hampering recovery from any. Even with recovery, most problem gamblers will have an ongoing propensity for re-engaging in the behavior, and a significant portion will experience at least a few relapses in their lifetime."[405] This makes clear that any problem gambler who is added to an exclusion list has a high probability of relapsing and every gambling company should recognize that inclusion on a gambling exclusion list is only the start of monitoring problem gambling activity, rather than the end of it.

Modeling a problem gambler's behavior can reveal gambling traits to create a unique "gambling personality" that could be logged and, going forward, potentially tracked to uncover problem gamblers working under confederate accounts.

Williams, West, & Simpson conclude that: "In light of the negative consequences that begin to occur for the gambler, the number and strength of the direct and indirect risk factors determines whether gambling continues or abates. Gamblers who have developed impaired control are persistently unable to stay within time and financial limits, often chase their losses, and find themselves unable to cut back or quit gambling."[405]

Signs of Problem Gamblers

Studies have shown that there are predictors that reveal the potential for individuals to become gambling addicts. Table 17 lists several of the predictors that a sportsbook should be looking out for in its customers, as well as ways to verify the problem within their datasets.

Signs	Study findings	How to verify
Genealogy	Half of all children whose parents were problem gamblers will become addicts.	Search internal exclusion list
Gambling history	Customer constantly Increases the betting amount to attain the same high.	Search customer history for every increasing bet amounts
Impulsivity	In contrast to alcoholics and cocaine users, gamblers scored significantly higher on impulsivity and inability to resist cravings; however, gamblers were not significantly higher than either alcoholics or cocaine users on sensation seeking.	Facebook or Twitter OCEAN test
Age	The age groups 18-29 and 40-49 were more likely to report gambling problems, with 30 to 39-year-olds less involved, and those 50 and over reporting the fewest gambling problems.	Search customer records
Gender	Males were overwhelmingly represented among the problem gamblers, being 72% of those with three to four problems or likely people affected by problem gambling, and 79% of those with five or more problems as likely pathological gamblers.	Search customer records
Marital status	People with gambling problems were most likely to report being single, i.e., either never married or divorced/separated. Other studies have shown widows have a propensity to be problem gamblers.	Search customer records
Preferred forms of gambling	People affected by problem gambling often play a variety of games. Nonetheless, many see one or more games as their principal problem. Rupcich found, with 207 gamblers in treatment, casino gambling accounted for 64% of their principal problem, and lotteries were problematic 43% of the time. Automated "electronic gambling machines (EGMs)" (i.e., slot machines, video lottery terminals (North America); fixed odds betting terminals, fruit machines (U.K.); pokies (Australia); pachinko (Japan); electronic bingo machines, etc.) epitomize continuous play and are the form of gambling most often identified by problem gamblers, treatment agencies, and gambling researchers in Western countries as creating the most problems. Two other forms of continuous gambling with a greater theoretical propensity for addiction are casino table games and 'continuous' lotteries. EGMs are essentially lottery machines that initiate a new draw with every play or spin. 'Continuous lotteries' have a draw every few minutes throughout the day (e.g., 'electronic keno', 'Rapido') are slower	Search customer records

Signs	Study findings	How to verify
	variants on this and theoretically have correspondingly similar addictive potential. Casino table games and sports betting are stronger correlates of problem gambling in Asian jurisdictions.	
Level of debt accumulate through gambling	Nick Rupcich was quoted in a Globe and Mail article as stating that 207 gamblers in treatment had an average debt of UK $16,000, on an average income of $31,000.[408]	Services like Experian can provide some of this data, but this is not easily attained by means other than self-admission
Alcohol use	Heavy drinking and drinking problems are associated with higher levels of spending on gambling and reports of gambling problems.	Self-assessment might be the best way to acquire this information
Drug use	Smart's 1994 population survey found no real relationship between drug use and gambling problems, but other studies have shown there may be a correlation.	Criminal records
Comorbid psychiatric problems	They found that 40% had a lifetime anxiety disorder, 60% had a lifetime mood disorder, and 87% had a personality disorder, "...the most common being obsessive-compulsive, avoidant, schizotypal, and paranoid personality disorders"	Facebook and Twitter OCEAN assessments
	Increased impulsivity was associated with more severe gambling and behavioural problems in two samples of pathological gamblers.[409 410]	Facebook and Twitter OCEAN assessments
	A "small but significant subset" of pathological gamblers may have antisocial personality disorder, but the rest of the minority of pathological gamblers who may show such symptoms do so as a result of their gambling activities, not as part of psychiatric comorbidity.[411]	Facebook and Twitter OCEAN assessments
	The addicted gamers scored significantly higher on boredom, loneliness, depression, and anxiety, compared with nonproblem gamers and nongamers.	Facebook and Twitter OCEAN assessments

Table 17: Signs that a customer might have the propensity to be a problem gambling

A Problem Gambling Solution

A problem gambler solution attempts to understand a bettor's gambling habits so that a profile of each bettor can be devised and the problem gamblers can be grouped into segments of like gamblers. Utilizing analytical models like K-means clustering can help segment a sport book's customer base, revealing such things as winning and losing segments, bet preferences, time between bets, and activity that could reveal signs of problem gambling, like constantly doubling down after losing bets.

Because most problem gamblers are losing gamblers, a subset of losing gamblers and the losing segment they are in can be culled through for potential problematic behavior. Things like genealogy (half of all children whose parents were problem gamblers will become addicts) to age (those between 18 and 29 and 40 and 49 are more likely to report gambling problems) to psychological problems (increased impulsivity is associated with more severe gambling).

Rest APIs can connect to Facebook, Twitter, and other social media platforms to retrieve data on the sports book's social media accounts. These can be correlated with customer accounts to get a fuller psychological profile of each potential problem gambler.

As there are over 15 verifiable predictors of problem gambling behavior, analytics models can search a sports book's internal database of people who have been added to the gambler exclusion list in the past to build a unique addicted gambler profile for the sports book. This will be the basis or starting point for any future problem gambler search.

Once the segmentation clusters have been built, the losing segment cluster could be tested for the psychological behavioral signs that might predict problem gambling. Table 18 contains the signs that might reveal a problem gambler, as well as the model or service that can be used to uncover or segment them.

Interacting with Facebook, Twitter, Instagram, or other social media systems is made possible because they often provide an API. The API can leverage a 3GL such as Java or JavaScript or even something simpler, like, for instance, a RESTful service. At times, software developers/vendors will write connectors in the native API that can be distributed and used in many software applications. These connectors can offer a quicker and easier approach than writing code alone. Both Facebook and Twitter provide a number of APIs, one worth mentioning is the Facebook Graph API.

The Graph API is a RESTful service that returns a JSON response. Simply stated an HTTP request can initiate a connection with the FB systems and publish / return data that can then be parsed with a programming language or even better yet—without programing using a multitude of data integration tools via their JSON input step.

Signs	Question	Model / Service
Genealogy	Is the customer's parents on the government exclusion list?	Decision tree
Impulsivity	Does customer display impulsive behavior?	Facebook or Twitter OCEAN assessment

Signs	Question	Model / Service
Age	Customer between the ages of 18 and 29 or 40 to 49?	Decision tree
Gender	Male of female?	Decision tree
Marital status	Customer single?	Decision tree
Preferred forms of gambling	Does customer play one or more game types?	Decision tree
Level of debt accumulate through gambling	Does customer have gambling debt? If so, how much? Average debt greater than UK $16,000? What is customer's average yearly income?	Experian
Alcohol use	Does the customer consume alcohol heavily?	Decision tree
Drug use	Does customer have a criminal drug record?	Criminal records, then Decision tree
Psychiatric problems	Does customer have a history of anxiety disorder, mood disorder, a personality disorder, including obsessive-compulsive, avoidant, schizotypal, and paranoid personality disorders?	Facebook and Twitter OCEAN assessments
	Does customer display impulsive behavior?	Facebook and Twitter OCEAN assessments
	Does customer display antisocial personality disorder?	Facebook and Twitter OCEAN assessments
	Does customer display signs of boredom, loneliness, depression, and/or anxiety?	Facebook and Twitter OCEAN assessments

Table 18: Problem gambling and predictive signs

Match Fixing

Ever since human beings engaged in sports, they've probably been engaged in fixing the outcome of that sport; it is just too lucrative for greedy and nefarious individuals to try to fix—and game—the system. The human emotion of greed and the get-rich-quick mindset are just too powerful for many people to control and the fact that few people get prosecuted for match fixing doesn't help. Even those who do get caught, in many cases, get a slap-on-the-wrist punishment, which does little to de-incentivize the problem. This all means that matchfixing will probably continue to flourish and there will be an ongoing fight to try to uncover this nefarious behavior wherever it rears its ugly head.

Match fixing is nothing new and there will, undoubtedly, be another match fixing scandal on the level of the Italian match fixing scandal of 2011 or the Pakistan cricket spot-fixing scandal in the not too distant future.[412] Interpol "estimates the volume of illegal betting and match fixing to be worth $500bn (£311bn) on the Asian market. The focus of its investigations has been China, Malaysia, Vietnam, Singapore and Thailand."[413] Worldwide match fixing volume is, unquestionably, substantially higher.

In their paper *Match Fixing and Sports Betting in Football: Empirical Evidence from the German Bundesliga[414]*, Deutscher, Dimant and Humphreys argue that by analyzing variation in bet volume on Betfair they uncovered evidence of abnormal patterns associated with specific officiating match referees. "An analysis of 1,251 Bundesliga 1 football matches from 2010/11 to 2014/15 reveals evidence that bet volume in the Betfair markets in these matches was systematically higher for four referees relative to matches officiated by other referees," Deutscher et al. ascertain.[414]

According to Deutscher et al. [414]:

> "Economic models of match fixing predict that referees are prime candidates for corruption, since they can exert a strong influence on match outcomes and receive relatively low levels of compensation. Betting exchange markets provide convenient, highly liquid markets where match fixers can profit from influence on outcomes in sporting events. Previous match fixing scandals contain evidence that referees are sometimes involved in match fixing scandals."

Matches can be fixed in a multitude of ways, with the involvement of either team managers, training staff, players, and match officials.[414] Match fixing by referees is common in many different sports, even in international matches, with bets being laid on numerous margins, including outcome (home win, draw, away win), goals scored, and other outcomes colloquially known as "proposition bets" or "prop bets".[415]

The Deutscher et al. research focused "on the role played by referees in conjunction with specific wagers on the total number of goals scored in football matches that can be linked to match fixing."[414] "This type of match fixing requires a small number of initiators, increasing the individual benefit for all parties involved."[414] With his or her career potentially at stake, a referee takes on a huge risk when fixing a match, so the financial rewards are usually commensurate to that risks.[414]

The source of the exchange betting market data, Betfair, "bills itself as the 'world's largest betting exchange' and reported 1.7 million active customers in 2015 and a turnover of 475.6 million British pounds (approximately $694 million)."[414] Deutscher et al. capitalized "on a unique dataset to analyze variation in the volume of Betfair wagers on the total number of goals scored in German Bundesliga 1 games in the 2010/11 – 2014/15 seasons."[414] The researchers posited that, "match fixing in terms of total goals scored is more likely to occur than match fixing in terms of win/loss/draw outcomes as it has a lower detection rate and hence is less risky to the parties involved in the fixing process. In addition, unbiased referees should not affect the expected number of goals scored in a match."[414]

For Deutscher et al, regression models included "control variables capturing specific match characteristics, including the identity of the referee for each match and unobservable home team-, away team-, matchday-, and season-level heterogeneity." Regression results showed that "Betfair betting volume on the proposition that games end with over or under 2.5 total goals scored was higher in games refereed by four specific Bundesliga referees over this period, even when controlling for team and match level observable and unobservable factors that might affect goal scoring."[414] These results, researchers concluded, were "consistent with the hypothesis that corruption might have influenced some Bundesliga 1 match outcomes over this period."[414]

Obviously "match fixing occurs because some individual or organization wants to profit from sporting event outcomes by influencing the outcome of these events in predictable ways."[414] Deutscher et al. assumed "that matches with an unusually large bet volume, or with unusual patterns in said bet volume, could potentially be fixed in some way, reflecting bets made by the match fixers."[414]

Match fixing, and profits from match fixing, can take many forms, including prizes for winners, payoffs to participants who guarantee specific outcomes.[414] However, the simplest "way to profit from match fixing is to bet on some match outcome that has been determined in advance, or that some participant in the match has been paid or coerced to influence in a specific way."[414]

Deutscher et al. speculate that, "An individual or organization attempting to profit from match fixing by betting on Betfair would need to place bets on an outcome that would be relatively straightforward to influence and relatively difficult to detect."[414] Betfair's largest "football betting markets, in terms of bet volume, are the match odds markets (home win, draw, away win) and the over/under 2.5 goals markets."[414] "To profit on match odds betting, the match fixer would have to influence the outcome of the match," argue Deutscher et al. This is not only a difficult thing to do, but it is also an easily detected form of corruption.[414] "Exact match score markets have low volume and this outcome would be relatively difficult to fix. The over/under 0.5 and 1.5 goal markets also have low volume, so individual high volume bets would likely be identified as suspicious by market monitoring systems," argue Deutscher et al.[414]

"Based on these considerations, the over/under 2.5 goal market appears to be a likely candidate for match fixers to exploit to earn profits on fixed matches," conclude Deutscher et al.[414] The researchers found that, "In the 1,530 Bundesliga 1 matches played in the 2010/11 through 2014/15 seasons, the average number of goals scored in a match was 2.92."[414] "Two or fewer goals were scored in 44% of the matches and three or more goals were scored in 56% of the matches."[414] "A player or referee would not need to influence scoring in a glaringly obvious way to drive scoring over/under 2.5 goals," speculate Deutscher et al.[414]

In their research, Deutscher et al. performed an "ex post analysis of betting volume in Betfair markets for over/under 2.5 goals scored in Bundesliga 1 football matches to determine if variation in this bet volume is consistent with the idea that some referees might have been engaged in match fixing."[414] The conclusion: "a small number of referees that were associated with larger than average volume in both the Over 2.5 and Under 2.5 markets."[414]

Although the findings were compelling, the researchers did "not claim to have identified match fixing in these Bundesliga 1 matches per se."[414] Rather, they concluded that they had spotted anomalous patterns in Betfair exchange betting data that was consistent with the story of match fixing.[414]

"Since match fixing can be difficult to detect, especially match fixing by referees or team officials, it is important to develop methods for detecting match fixing based on observed data in betting markets," advise Deutscher et al.[414] "In general, only data on odds set by bookmakers on specific sporting events are publicly available; data on bet volume on specific sporting events at individual bookmakers are not easily available," warn Deutscher et al.[414] This makes Betfair's data analysis of notable interest and Betfair does make its data available through an API for its developers.

Badminton and Racket Sport Match fixing

In their article *Preliminary Study to Detect Match-Fixing: Benford's Law in Badminton Rally Data*[416], Park et al. argue that "match fixing has emerged as a social problem that threatens the presence of modern sports itself." "Match fixing is a universal phenomenon and a serious issue that affects the development of sports," add Park et al.[416] This article is about badminton, but match fixing has been found in a multitude of sports, including soccer[417], figure skating[418], cricket[419], basketball[420], and motor racing[421], esports[432], nor is it confined to specific nations.[416]

In his *The Olympic fight against match fixing*[422], J. Chappelet explains that the former president of the International Olympic Committee (IOC) Jacques Rogge defined match fixing as a "cancer," adding, "Doping affects one individual athlete, but the impact of match fixing affects the whole competition. It is much bigger."

Vodde[423] reports that 80% of the world's match fixing scandals occur in soccer and basketball, two sports that offer an enormous amount of data, not only on individual players, but also on the teams where they ply their trade. Tennis is the second most popular betting sport, however, so any system that can help a sports book keep tennis clean should be warmly received.

The Park et al. study was an attempt to use a statistical approach to uncover potential match fixing.[416] Park et al. acknowledge that, "As match fixing is done secretively by players, coaches, and executives, detecting anomalies of players involved in match manipulation is considered a difficult job."[416] However, they believed their method could help prove whether players were making mistakes intentionally and, therefore, throwing the game.[416] "The fact that the games in which players deliberately underperform do not conform to Benford's law while other games do can be a theoretical basis of identifying the anomalies that players make during the games," argue Park et al.[416]

Park et al. report on a study that was done to investigate the possibility of detecting match fixing in badminton and, potentially, other racket sports, like tennis.[416] The study aimed "to verify whether the number of rallies in universal and anomalous badminton matches follows Benford's law."[416] According to the authors, "The study counted the number of rallies in 685 international badminton tournaments selected through purposive sampling and analyzed the first significant digits of the rally data through the x^2 test and intra class correlation coefficient."[416] The results were quite conclusive because "two well-known fixed badminton matches were found to be anomalous, and hence, the finding is that the number of badminton rallies in universal matches follows Benford's law while the anomalous matches do not."[416]

So what is Benford's law? As Park et al. explain, "It may appear that the frequency of individual numbers between 1 and 9 appearing as the first digits of the infinite natural numbers used in real life, such as various economic indicators, geo-statistical data, and crime rates, is the same for each of these digits, at 11.1%."[416] However, this is not the case, as the rate actually forms a distribution with a strict rule.[416] According to Newcomb[424], that is, "the rate of using 1 as the first digit of a number is disproportionate to the rate of using the rest of the numbers, and the lower the digit, the higher its frequency."[416]

Benford's Law[425] "refers to the phenomenon in which as the first digit of a number increases from 1 to 9, the occurrence rate of this number reduces, as the rate of the first digit being 1 is about 30.10%, that of 2 is 17.61%, and that of 9 is about 4.58%[426]." According to Park et al., "Benford proved the fact that the numbers starting with 1 are more specifically distributed among the numbers that are used in every day such as the area of the lake, demographics, mortality statistics, and numbers appearing in newspapers, and these numbers follow a unique rule, called Benford's law."[416] The law is illustrated below:

$$PD = \log 10 \, (1+1/D)^{416}$$

"P_D represents the occurrence probability of the first significant digit (FSD), D

(D=1, 2, ..., 9) of a number," explain Park et al.[416]

For 50 years, Benford's law was considered nothing more than a mathematical oddity, and few scientist tried to apply it to real-world problems.[416] "However, as vast amounts of data are applied to Benford's law accordingly with the development of computer processing technology, interesting research results that followed this law arose," marvel Park et al.[416] The fact that artificially produced data does not follow Benford's law can be used to uncover instances of fraud.[416] Benford's law has been used to detect corporate fraud[427] [426] as well as for verifying the veracity of survey data, amongst other things.[428]

Varian argues that although conformity with Benford's law does not necessarily ensure the veracity of data, data veracity may be questioned in case of nonconformity.[429] The Park et al. study aimed "to investigate whether the data on sports tournaments such as badminton rallies would conform to Benford's law."[416] The writers speculated that, "Given that the accounting data generated, which involves corporate competition, conforms to Benford's law, there is no reason that sports tournament data that are generated as a result of competition between players would not follow Benford's law."[416]

Park et al. argue that, "Sports data generated as a result of competitive matches are natural numbers like the real-life sets of numbers that follow Benford's law such as the height of mountains and buildings and the width of rivers."[416] If this were so, then "determining whether particular sports data conforms to Benford's law can be applied to detect unnaturally performed anomalous matches (e.g., match fixing)."[416] "For instance, if data on length of badminton rallies that is collected in a particular badminton match does not follow Benford's law despite the fact that data on length of badminton rallies conforms to this law, it may imply that the competition has not been carried out as per naturally occurring perfect competition."[416] That's the theory, at least.

Several studies[430] [431] have "shown that numbers with less than 4 digits, numbers with fixed ranges, such as adult height and IQ, artificially determined numbers such as $1.99, and rounded numbers are known to not follow Benford's law."[416] "Although the number of badminton rallies generally has two digits, it can be infinite starting from 1 since the range is not determined theoretically," argue Park et al.[416] Furthermore, the authors state that, "the number of rallies can be considered as a variable for application of Benford's law among the various badminton records since it cannot be determined by players artificially as well as the integer numbers are used."[416] The study's objective was to verify whether badminton rally data in universal matches followed Benford's law.[416] In addition, this study investigated whether Benford's law could detect match fixing by looking at past matches that were known to have been fixed.[416]

In the study, data from 685 international badminton tournament matches of the Korean national badminton team between 2012 and 2016 were analyzed.[416] This comprised 64 international badminton tournaments.[416] The 685 games were played by athletes who ranked in the world's top 20.[416] The rally data of two well-known fixed badminton matches as anomalous cases were also collected.[416]

Chappelet explains that, in one case the South Korean and Chinese pairs competing in the women's doubles preliminary round at the 2012 London Olympic Games intentionally lost their match in order to obtain higher seeds because they wanted to avoid playing against the number one ranked team in the tournament.[422] The Badminton World Federation (BWF) determined this match was fixed and immediately disqualified the players.[416] "The other case was one of the matches in 2008 All England Championship in which the then globally 1st ranked Chinese player who had already been qualified for the Olympics intentionally lost against another Chinese player who was in need of being qualified for the Olympics."[416] "A total of 157 valid cases of rallies were collected from those two anomalous matches," report Park et al.[416]

Park et al. argue that, "if the difference in the rate of the numbers that occur in the real world is significant compared to Benford's law, the veracity of the number may be questioned."[416] Park et al. believe that the badminton rally data conform to Bedford's strict law conditions because they "are recorded in numbers and collected for the actions of players with the intention of competing; the size of the number of rallies is not limited theoretically; and the number of rallies cannot be adjusted artificially."[416]

The main question here is whether the number of badminton rallies were manipulated rather than being spontaneous and if the two anomalous matches selected actually conform to Benford's law or not.[416] As Table 19 reveals, the "study examined the conformity to Benford's law by comparing this law's reference values with the expected value of Benford's law. This was done by classifying two anomalous badminton matches, a well-known case of match fixing or intentionally defeated games, by set."[416]

Table 19: Expected Value of Benford's law

	First digit								
	1	2	3	4	5	6	7	8	9
Expected value	30.10	17.61	12.49	9.69	7.92	6.69	5.80	5.12	4.58

According to Park et al., "Only the FSD was analyzed in this study, since Benford's law focuses on verifying the distribution of FSD and the number of badminton rallies is typically of two or fewer digits."[416] The Park et al. study "calculated the observed rate of badminton rally data from 1 to 9, which was collected from 685 matches and compared with Benford's expected rate."[416] Beyond that, the fixed match from the 2012 London Olympics was analyzed to detect match fixing."[416]

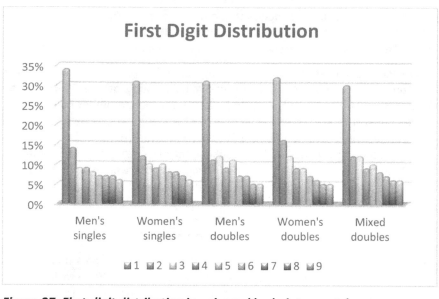

Figure 27: First-digit distribution in universal badminton matches
Source: *Preliminary Study to Detect Match-Fixing: Benford's Law in Badminton Rally Data*[416]

Figure 27 illustrates Benford's expected distribution as well as the distribution of the first digits of numbers of badminton event-specific rallies.[416] "The distribution of the first digit of numbers that targeted 57,404 badminton rallies shows that the number 1 has a ratio of 30% in all events including men's singles, women's singles, men's doubles, women's doubles, and mixed doubles, and is in line with Benford's law," conclude Park et al.[416] The graph clearly shows that, "the observed rates in badminton rally data are perfectly identical to Benford's law except for the fact that the observed value of the number 2 is slightly low compared to Benford's distribution in the distribution of the first digit of badminton rallies number."[416]

Park et al.'s study then looked at results from the 2012 London Olympics fixed matches.[416] They conducted "an analysis of whether the distribution of the first digit of rallies number follows Benford's law."[416] They didn't. For the first and second sets, the distribution of the number of rallies deviated considerably from the expected Benford distribution.[416] Apparently, the game was so farcical that the referee warned the players to improve their performance after the first set and they did, but, even for the second set, the numbers remained far off from a normal Benford distribution.[416] A similar situation was found for the 2008 All England Championship men's singles.[416] The distribution of the number of rallies in the first and second sets were also not in compliance with Benford's law.[416]

The study found that "the fixed matches between the Korean and Chinese players (intentional defeat) during the 2012 London Olympics, and between the Chinese players during the 2008 All England Championship were far off from Benford's law."[416] "Some badminton players attempted to lose intentionally and did not play hard," notes Chappelet.[422] "The finding that the fixed match does not conform to Benford's law implies that the badminton rally data may not be generated randomly when artificial behavior is present in sports competition," conclude Park et al.[416] Although two findings don't fully make a case and more empirical evidence is needed, Park et al. believe they have uncovered a process of identifying sports match fixing in data[416]; a pretty inexpensive one at that.

Park et al. speculate that Bedford's law could be useful for other sports.[416] "Whether the records such as the distance covered or time taken for soccer players to sprint during the game, the number of touches to the ball while dribbling, and the number of passes of the ball during basketball games follow Benford's law would be an interesting topic for future studies," they add.[416] The methodology could easily be ported over to tennis and other racket sports, even table tennis.

Park et al. conclude that, "Benford's law is a useful means to identify abnormal numbers In various areas, and the present study found that the number of badminton rallies also follow the law."[416] A sports book could easily implement a system that took live tennis, or badminton, or table tennis feeds, run it through a real-time processing engine and track the first digit distribution as it was occurring. Alerts could be set for FSD anomalies that fall outside Benford's law and that would allow the sports book to cancel all questionable bets before the end of a match, as well as alert authorities that match fixing was occurring.

Esports

Even esports is not immune to gambling and match fixing. According to its article *Match-fixing goes digital*[432], *The Economist* states that, "The first eSports-fixing scandal was in 2010, when South Korean players threw professional matches for financial gain. In 2016, Lee 'Life' Seung-hyun, one of the biggest names in eSports, was convicted for his part in a series of fixes in Starcraft 2, a science-fiction strategy game." Lee received a lifetime banned from eSports in South Korea.[432] According to the article, "The case was uncovered by a police investigation into illegal gambling that stumbled across eSports-fixing, rather than eSports organisers attempting to ensure clean play."[432]

"Fixing in eSports is a mix of old and new. Players can be paid to underperform in time-honoured fashion. Or they can be paid in "skins"—decorative frills that have no bearing on gameplay."[432] These digital goods can be cashed out on many unregulated sites, which makes it much easier for fixers to avoid detection.[432] In 2014 several *CS: GO* players used skins to bet against themselves and deliberately lost, making more than the prize money of the tournament they were playing in.[432] "There are new ways to tilt the outcome, too, says David

Forrest of the University of Liverpool, such as strategically timed internet glitches," explains *The Economist*.[432]

Currently esports has no overarching governing body, but organizations like South Korea's International eSports Federation (IeSF) is working hard to help build one, as well as to work tirelessly to get esports accepted as an Olympic sport. In 2015 the biggest esports game publishers "formed the eSports Integrity Coalition to crack down on fixing."[432] "Gambling firms have started to certify hardware and software before competitions, in the hope of rooting out technological malfeasance." Raising awareness among players is imperative, argues Ian Smith, the coalition's head.[432] They can "go from playing in their parents' basement to playing in a $5m tournament in six months."[432]

Right now, traditional sports offers higher returns to fixers[432], but that might not be true for much longer as the total bet on eSports is expected to exceed $150bn a year by 2020.[432] "ESports betting is increasingly attractive to the kind of people that eSports does not want attracted to it," says Smith.[432] The fact that many of the esports players will be familiar with the world of cryptocurrencies, which allow completely anonymous and untraceable payments, is another factor to keep in mind when accepting bets on these sports.

The Future

To keep consumers interested in paying for their products and services, sports books must continue to innovate and explore new marketing and messaging avenues. Mobile marketing's ability to do one-on-one advertising, anytime-anywhere to any individual with a mobile device is vastly superior to any other marketing channel currently available. In the future, it is likely that all marketing will become interactive and the consumer will become a participant rather than a "target audience". As Shar VanBoskirk states in his article *US Interactive Marketing Forecast, 2007 To 2012*[433], "Instead of planning for a set 'search budget' or an 'online video campaign', marketers will instead organize around 'persona planning'—that is, they will plan around generating a desired response from a customer type. In response to changing customer behavior, channel optimization will take place on the fly, shifting between channels dynamically."

Sports betting companies can also use social media to manage their brand, enhance brand loyalty, as well as engage both their current customers and their potential customers. The social media world is also the perfect place to harvest customer feedback, provide real-time customer service, build fanbases and drive traffic to a sports book's website.

Jones and Sasser warn that, "Extremely dissatisfied customers can turn into 'terrorists,' providing an abundance of negative feedback about the service provider."[93] Through social media channels, negative feedback can reverberate around the world within seconds. Today, more than ever, sports books must spot dissatisfied customers and approach them before they do irreparable harm to the company's image and reputation and social media is one of the best channels in which to engage these potentially problematic customers.

Sports books need to empower their patrons to post on Facebook or Instagram or Twitter or comment about their experience and, hopefully, turn them into apostles. In Jones and Sasser's *zone of affection*, satisfaction levels are high and "customers may have such high attitudinal loyalty that they don't look for alternative service."[93] It is within this group that "Apostles"—members who praise the firm in public—reside and this is the group that is responsible for improved future business performance.[94] A simple search of the Twitter feed on the multiple services I mentioned in the previous chapter will probably reveal a list of patrons who could be courted for marketing purposes.

Real time technology gives sports books the ability to see—and know—what is going on in real time around them, and this allows them to instantly counter negative perceptions. To maintain credibility with customers, sports books shouldn't remove negative comments or constructive criticism from these social media sites unless the person posting the comment uses foul language or says something offensive to others.

Facebook should be a part of every sports book's social and mobile media marketing plan, but simply putting up a Facebook page won't cut it anymore; creativity and uniqueness are needed to get noticed in today's highly competitive social media market. Gamification is also a good way to stand out from the crowd. Facebook bots can also add a customer service channel that can answer common customer questions.

As Kahle states, eventually we're going to set a time frame on the sales funnel that never expires.[97] From the moment of first contact, when the sports book's systems capture an IP Address, through capturing the social ID, to understanding the social activity, all the way through to the patron card sign up process so that the sports book can understand the customer's gaming and commerce behavior. The only thing remaining is to capture post-transaction information, if and when it comes in.

Once all of this data is captured, geofencing, location-based services, and location-based advertising offer some unique ways to reach consumers when they are in the all-important "decision mode." A sports book that is able to offer highly specific advertisements to customers who might just need a little extra nudge to make that purchase should find an investment in geofencing applications very profitable.

With *The A.I. Sports Book*, a patron can sign into the sports book's company app and he or she will be able to pull up his or her player card points balance as well as use them to place bets. The patron will be able to receive and use coupons at onsite or nearby restaurants and/or bars, as well as to sign up for sports betting tournaments.

DATA	DETAILS
Structured data	• Behavioral targeting with cross-device data; mobile, location-based, and social analytics. • Fusing data generated within the firm with data generated outside the firm; integrating "small stats". • Combining machine learning approaches with econometric and theory-based methods for big data applications; computational solutions to marketing models for big data.
Unstructured data	• Development of diagnostic, predictive, and prescriptive approaches for analysis of large-scale unstructured data. • Approaches to analyze unstructured social, geo-spatial, mobile data and combining them with structured data in big data contexts. • Using, evaluating, and extending deep learning methods and cognitive computing to analyze unstructured marketing data.
Marketing-mix modeling	• Aligning analysis of disaggregate data with that of aggregate data and including unstructured data in the analysis of the marketing mix. • New techniques and methods to accurately measure the impact of marketing instruments and their carryover and spillover across media and devices using integrated path-to-purchase data. • Dynamic, multi–time period and cross-category optimization of the marketing mix. • Approaches to incorporate different planning cycles for different marketing instruments in media-mix models.
Personalization	• Automated closed-loop marketing solutions for digital environments; fully automated marketing solutions. • Personalization and customization techniques using cognitive systems, general artificial intelligence, and automated attention analysis; personalization of content. • Mobile, location-based personalization of the marketing mix.
Security and privacy	• Methods to produce and handle data minimization and data anonymization in assessing marketing-mix effectiveness and personalization. • Distributed data solutions to enhance data security and privacy while maximizing personalized marketing opportunities.

Table 20: Area of Focus Promising and Important Issues for Research

In their paper *Marketing Analytics for Data-Rich Environments*[113], Wedel and Kannan, argue that there are many promising areas of research that businesses should keep on their radar. The technological developments of tomorrow might just be some of the ones discussed in Table 20.

With their *Cluetrain Manifesto*[335], Rick Levine et al. warned that not only are markets conversations, but the Internet is revolutionizing the way businesses communicate with their customers and if businesses don't adapt and treat their customers with respect, their customers will desert them.[335] What better way to treat them with respect than to listen to them and respond accordingly, which mobile and social media channels do better than any other form of advertising.

"It's not just customers who expect more from the brands and providers they patronize these days," warns the *MIT Technology Review* in its article *Transform Customer Experiences by Harnessing the Power of AI in CRM*.[98] "The forces of digital disruption set the bar high for intuitive experiences that anticipate what someone likes—or doesn't like—and serves up what they need or desire at any moment. That includes improving employees' digital experiences on the job," *MIT Technology Review* adds.[98]

"As people acclimate to higher levels of engagement in their personal lives, they come to expect comparable flexibility, interactivity, and productivity with the tools and business processes they use to do their work," argues the *MIT Technology Review*.[98] After all, in many cases, employees are customers, too.

"To stay ahead, companies need to use personalized platforms with advanced capabilities such as AI and ML. These platforms are powered by the terabytes of data companies now collect to create personalized customer experiences that evolve with consumer preferences and needs," adds the *MIT Technology Review*.[98] Emphasizing a customer-centric focus throughout every experience, and every step of every business process, can provide organizations with serious competitive advantage. An intelligent customer platform provides the ideal springboard for this next phase of business and digital transformation," concludes the *MIT Technology Review*.[98]

In Greek mythology, once Pandora opened the box and let out all of the evils of the world, the one thing that remained inside was hope. Now, hope is unquestionably what the sports betting industry is selling, the hope of getting rich, and the hope of leaving one's financial troubles behind and living a life of luxury from them on. Of course, this only happens to a small minority, but most of the others at least get entertained and entertainment of the mind isn't usually free; that's the deal one makes with a sports book when one places his or her bet on an event.

I wrote this book hoping that it would help clients and, possibly, potential clients, discover the treasure that is hidden within their data, so that they shouldn't feared the incredible technology that is out there; technology that can make every sports book customer's instore or online visit a personalized adventure that will make them want to return again and again.

FIN

---

344 Gourévitch, Antoine, Faeste, Lars, Baltasis, Elias, and Marx, Julien. May 23, 2017. Data-Driven Transformation: Accelerate at Scale Now. Boston Consulting Group. https://www.bcg.com/en-in/publications/2017/digital-transformation-transformation-data-driven-transformation.aspx (Accessed 8 September 2017).

345 Databricks. Conquer the AI Dilemma by Unifying Data Science and Engineering. https://databricks.com/company/newsroom/press-releases/databricks-conquers-ai-dilemma-with-unified-analytics (Accessed 8 October 2018).

346 Talend. Definitive Guide to Data Governance. Talend.com. https://www.talend.com/resources/definitive-guide-data-governance/ (Accessed 18 August 2019).

347 https://en.wikipedia.org/wiki/Data_curation (Accessed 10 April 2019).

348 Wadhwa, T. (2013, June 3). CrowdOptic and L'Oreal to make history by demonstrating how augmented reality can be a shared experience. Retrieved from Forbes.com: http://www.forbes.com/sites/tarunwadhwa/2013/06/03/crowdoptic-and-loreal-are-about-to-make-history-by-demonstrating-how-augmented-reality-can-be-a-shared-experience/

349 http://www.webopedia.com/TERM/A/Augmented_Reality.html

350 Gartner. October 18, 2016. Gartner's Top 10 Strategic Technology Trends for 2017. http://www.gartner.com/smarterwithgartner/gartners-top-10-technology-trends-2017/

351 Gartner. 2014, January 14). Gartner believes augmented reality will become an important workplace tool. Retrieved from Gartner.com: http://www.gartner.com/newsroom/id/2649315

352 Deloitte. (2013). *Augmented Government, Transforming Government Services Through Augmented Reality.* Retrieved from Deloitte Development LLC: http://www.deloitte.com/assets/Dcom-UnitedStates/Local%20Assets/Documents/Federal/us_fed_augmented_government_06 0613.pdf

353 Moore, J. (2012). *Augmented reality: expanding the user experience.* Retrieved from Digital Innovation Gazette: http://www.digitalinnovationgazette.com/uiux/augmented_reality_app_development/ #axzz2z8tFKN00

354 https://en.wikipedia.org/wiki/Pokémon_Go

355 Gupta, Bisdisha. July 22, 2016. Augmented Reality Is The Future Of Real Money Gaming Industry. Socialblog.com. http://www.sociableblog.com/2016/07/22/augmented-reality-future-of-real-money-gaming/

356 https://aws.amazon.com/lex/ (Accessed 11 March 2019).

357 https://aws.amazon.com/lex/ (Accessed 11 March 2019).

358 https://aws.amazon.com/transcribe/ (Accessed 11 March 2019).

359 https://aws.amazon.com/comprehend/ (Accessed 11 March 2019).

360 Yakuel, Pini. Optimove. Turning Up Your Brand's Voice to Reach the Most Advanced Customers. October 25, 2018. https://www.optimove.com/blog/using-digital-assistant-to-help-market-your-brand (Accessed 14 April 2019).

361 Maruti Tech. 14 Powerful Chatbot Platforms. https://www.marutitech.com/14-powerful-chatbot-platforms/ (Accessed 8 April 2019).

362 https://chatfuel.com (Accessed 8 April 2019).

363 https://botsify.com (Accessed 8 April 2019).

364 https://flowxo.com/ (Accessed 8 April 2019).

365 Baron, Justine. SAP.com. Recast.AI will be renamed SAP Conversational AI early 2019! November 15, 2018. https://cai.tools.sap/blog/recast-ai-renaming/ (Accessed 14 April 2019).

366 https://www.octaneai.com/ (Accessed 14 April 2019).

367 Altexsoft. (2018). Sentiment Analysis: Types, Tools, and Use Cases. September 21, 2018. https://www.altexsoft.com/blog/business/sentiment-analysis-types-tools-and-use-cases/ (Accessed 15 April 2019).

368 Dreamgrow.com. https://www.dreamgrow.com/69-free-social media monitoring-tools/ (Accessed 22 November 2017).

369 Rowe, Kevin. (2017). Search Engine Land. How to use AI for link building and improve your search rankings. September 26, 2017. https://searchengineland.com/use-ai-link-building-improve-search-rankings-283150 (Accessed 14 April 2019).

370 Butterfield, Brett. (2018). Adobe. See It, Search It, Shop It: How AI is Powering Visual Search. 12 December 2018. https://theblog.adobe.com/see-it-search-it-shop-it-how-ai-is-powering-visual-search/ (Accessed 20 January 2019).

371 Bea, Francis. March 25, 2012. Goodbye, anonymity: latest surveillance tech can search up to 36 million faces per second. www.digitaltrends.com http://www.digitaltrends.com/cool-tech/goodbye-anonymity-latest-surveillance-tech-can-search-up-to-36-million-faces-per-second/ (Accessed 25 November 2017).

372 Facial recognition: Who's Tracking You In Public. (December 30, 2015) Consumer Reports. Online: http://www.consumerreports.org/privacy/facial-recognition-who-is-tracking-you-in-public1/ (Accessed 25 November 2017).

373 Gates, Kelly A. January 23, 2011. Our Biometric Future: Facial Recognition Technology and the Culture of Surveillance. NYU Press.

374 Riddell, Chris. Qantas have seen their Future. It's Facial Recognition. 1 August 2017. Chrisriddell.com. http://chrisriddell.com/qantas-future-facial-recognition/ (Accessed 9 October 2018).

375 Matt Cimaglia, Matt. (2019). Entrepreneur. The Future of Video Advertising is Artificial Intelligence. December 12, 2018. https://www.entrepreneur.com/article/323756 (Accessed 4 January 2019).

376 Fuller, Brian. 2018. Arm Community. AI's role in next-generation voice recognition. IoT Blog. https://community.arm.com/iot/b/blog/posts/artificial-intelligence-is-changing-voice-recognition-technology (Accessed 12 January 2019).

377 Kinsella, Bret. 2019 Predictions from 35 voice industry leaders. January 1, 2019. Voicebot.ai. https://voicebot.ai/2019/01/01/2019-predictions-from-35-voice-industry-leaders/ (Accessed 21 January 2019).

378 Olson, Christi. (2018). Marchtech Today. Voice search isn't the next big disrupter, conversational AI Is. October 11, 2018. https://martechtoday.com/voice-search-isnt-the-next-big-disrupter-conversational-ai-is-226537 (Accessed 3 March 2019).

379 https://aws.amazon.com/polly/ (Accessed 11 March 2019).

380 https://aws.amazon.com/polly/ (Accessed 11 March 2019).

381   SeoClarity.   The   Next   Generation   of   Search: Voice. https://go.seoClarity.net/hubfs/docs/research/seoClarity_whitepaper_next-generation-search-voice.pdf (Accessed 16 April 2019).

382 https://www.dialogtech.com/blog/search-marketing/voice-search-statistics

383 Batra, Varun. Marchtechseries. How AI is Driving a New Era of TV Advertising. March 29, 2018. https://martechseries.com/mts-insights/guest-authors/how-ai-is-driving-a-new-era-of-tv-advertising/ (Accessed 12 April 2019).

384 Neuberger, W. (n.d.). Engage Customers and gain advocates through social media and social   networking.   January   24,   2013. ftp://public.dhe.ibm.com/software/solutions/soa/newsletter/2010/newsletter-mar10-article_social_media.pdf (Accessed 13 November 2017).

385 Shewan, Dan. (2018). Wordstream. Pain Points: A Guide to Finding & Solving Your Customers'   Problems.   November   28,   2019. https://www.wordstream.com/blog/ws/2018/02/28/pain-points (Accessed 7 April 2019).

386 Gulbransen, Scott. January 22, 2014. Taking Back the Social-Media Command Center, Scott   Gulbransen.   Forbes. http://www.forbes.com/sites/onmarketing/2014/01/22/taking-back-the-social-media-command-center/#3c283a5d6513 (Accessed 22 November 2017).

387 Mathison, Rob. Hootsuite. (2017). 14 of the Best Social Media Monitoring Tools for Business. August 14, 2017. https://blog.hootsuite.com/social-media-monitoring-tools/ (Accessed 23 November 2017).

388 Gell, Aaron. (2017) The Not-so-Surprising Survival of Foursquare. The New Yorker. March 1, 2017. https://www.newyorker.com/business/currency/the-not-so-surprising-survival-of-foursquare (Accessed 23 November 2017).

389 Perlmutter, Rachel. (2016) Why You Need Social Proof on Your Website. Entrepreneur.com. July 6, 2016. https://www.entrepreneur.com/article/296644 (Accessed 23 November 2017).

390 Biron, Bethany. (2017). How Facebook is wooing luxury brands. Digiday. https://digiday.com/media/bringing-retail-speed-feed-facebooks-quest-court-luxury-brands/ (Accessed 24 November 2017).

391 Turner, Holly. 2017. Whatsapp For Business—What Does it Mean? M&C Satchi Mobile. http://www.mcsaatchimobile.com/whatsapp-business-mean/ (Accessed 23 November 2017).

392 The 5 Different Types of Influencer Marketing Campaigns. March 30, 2016. Mediakix.com.   http://mediakix.com/2016/03/influencer-marketing-campaigns-5-examples/#gs.Lz0k6B4 (Accessed 13 November 2017).

393 Constine, Josh. (2018). Techcrunch. How Uber Will Become an Ad Company, Starting with Eats Pool. 12 December 2018. https://techcrunch.com/2018/12/10/uber-ads/ (Accessed 1 January 2019).

394 Gourévitch, Antoine, Faeste, Lars, Baltasis, Elias, and Marx, Julien. May 23, 2017. Data-Driven Transformation: Accelerate at Scale Now. Boston Consulting Group. https://www.bcg.com/en-in/publications/2017/digital-transformation-transformation-data-driven-transformation.aspx (Accessed 8 September 2017).

395 https://www.ncbi.nlm.nih.gov/books/NBK230632/

396 Neal, Penelope & Delfabbro, Paul H. (Paul Howard) & O'Neil, Michael & Victoria. Dept. of Justice. Office of Gaming and Racing & Australia. Ministerial Council on Gambling et al. (2005). Problem gambling and harm : towards a national definition. Office of Gaming and Racing, Dept. of Justice, Melbourne, Vic

397 Petry, N.M. (2005). Pathological Gambling: Etiology, Comorbidity, and Treatment. Washington, DC: American Psychological Association.

398 Williams, R.J., Rehm, J., & Stevens, R. (2011). The Social and Economic Impacts of Gambling. Final Report for the Canadian Consortium for Gambling Research. March 11, 2011. http://hdl.handle.net/10133/1286. (Accessed 10 July 2017)

399 Stradbrooke, Steven. (2017). Resorts World Manila gunman a problem gambler, not a terrorist. June 04, 2017. CalvinAyre.com. https://calvinayre.com/2017/06/04/casino/resorts-world-manila-gunman-problem-gambler/. (Accessed 10 July 2017)

400 Williams, R.J., West, B.L., & Simpson, R.I. (2012). Prevention of Problem Gambling: A Comprehensive Review of the Evidence, and Identified Best Practices. Report prepared for the Ontario Problem Gambling Research Centre and the Ontario Ministry of Health and Long Term Care. October 1, 2012. http://hdl.handle.net/10133/3121. (Accessed 10 July 2017)

401 Williams, R.J., Rehm, J., & Stevens, R. (2011). The Social and Economic Impacts of Gambling. Final Report for the Canadian Consortium for Gambling Research. March 11, 2011. http://hdl.handle.net/10133/1286. (Accessed 10 July 2017)

402 National Research Council. (1999). Pathological Gambling: A Critical Review. Washington, DC: National Academy Press.

403 Williams, R.J., Rehm, J., & Stevens, R. (2011). The Social and Economic Impacts of Gambling. Final Report for the Canadian Consortium for Gambling Research. March 11, 2011. http://hdl.handle.net/10133/1286. (Accessed 10 July 2017)

404 Williams, R.J., Royston, J., & Hagen, B. (2005). Gambling and problem gambling within forensic populations: A review of the literature. Criminal Justice & Behavior: An International Journal 32(6), 665-689.

405 Williams, R.J., West, B.L., & Simpson, R.I. (2012). Prevention of Problem Gambling: A Comprehensive Review of the Evidence, and Identified Best Practices. Report prepared for the Ontario Problem Gambling Research Centre and the Ontario Ministry of Health and Long Term Care. October 1, 2012. http://hdl.handle.net/10133/3121. (Accessed 10 July 2017).

406 Kalischuk, R.G., Nowatzki, N., Cardwell, K., Klein, K., Solowoniuk, J. (2006). Problem gambling and its impact on families: A literature review. International Gambling Studies, 6 (1), 31- 60.

407 Shaw, M.C., Forbush, K.T., Schlinder, J., Rosenman, E., & Black, D.W. (2007). The effect of pathological gambling on families, marriages, and children. CNS Spectrums, 12(8), 615-622.

408 Downey, D. (February 27, 1995). Ontario dealing with addiction. The Globe and Mail.

409 Blaszczynski, A, Steel, Z, McConaghy, N. 1997. Impulsivity in pathological gambling: the antisocial impulsivist. Blackwell Publishing Ltd

410 Steel, Z, Blaszczynski, A. 1998. Impulsivity, personality disorders and pathological gambling severity. Carfax Publishing Limited

411 Crockford DN, el-Guebaly N. Psychiatric comorbidity in pathological gambling: a critical review. Canadian Journal of Psychiatry - Revue Canadienne de Psychiatrie. 1998.

412 https://en.wikipedia.org/wiki/Pakistan_cricket_spot-fixing_scandal (Accessed 10 August 2019).

413 Scott-Elliot, Robin. (2011). The Independent. Fifa aware of match fixing fears. 11 March 2011. http://www.independent.co.uk/sport/football/news-and-comment/fifa-aware-of-match fixing-fears-2238456.html (Accessed 16 January 2018).

414 Deutscher, Christian, Dimant, Eugen and Humphreys, Brad R. Match Fixing and Sports Betting in Football: Empirical Evidence from the German Bundesliga. papers.ssrn.com. http://www.sas.upenn.edu/ppe-repec/ppc/wpaper/0008.pdf (Accessed 27 January, 2018).

415 LaBrie, R. A., LaPlante, D. A., Nelson, S. E., Schumann, A., & Shaffer, H. J. (2007). Assessing the playing field: A prospective longitudinal study of internet sports gambling behavior. Journal of Gambling Studies, 23(3), 347-362.

416 Park, Jae-Hyeon, Choi, Chang-Hwan, Cho, Eunhye. (2016). Preliminary Study to Detect Match-Fixing: Benford's Law in Badminton Rally Data. The Journal of Physical Education and Sports Management. June 2016, Vol. 3, No. 1, pp. 64-77. http://jpesm.com/journals/jpesm/Vol_3_No_1_June_2016/5.pdf (Accessed 15 January 2018).

417 Abbott, J., & Sheehan, D. (2014). The INTERPOL approach to tackling match fixing in football. In M.R. Haberfeld & D. Sheehan (Eds.), Match-fixing in international sports (pp. 263-287). Berlin: Springer International Publishing.

418 Clarey, C. (2002). (2002, May 1). Figure skating; 2 French officials suspended 3 years in skating scandal. The New York Times. Retrieved from http://www.nytimes.com/2002/05/01/sports/figure-skating-2-french-officialssuspended-3-years-in-skating-scandal.html

419 Carpenter, K. (2012). Match-fixing: The biggest threat to sport in the 21st century? International Sports in Law Review, 2, 13-24.

420 Cohen, S. (2008, March 1). Ref pals bet on 'not guilty'. New York Post. Retrieved from http://nypost.com/2008/03/01/ref-pals-bet-on-not-guilty/

421 Cary, T. Renault F1 to pay Nelson Piquet huge compensation for libel after 'Crashgate' scandal. (2010, December 7). The Telegraph. Retrieved from http://www.telegraph.co.uk/sport/motorsport/formulaone/lotus/8186825/Renault -F1-to-pay-Nelson-Piquet-huge-compensation-for-libel-after-Crashgate-scandal.html

422 Chappelet, J. (2015). The Olympic fight against match fixing. Sport in Society, 18(10), 12601272.

423 Vodde, R. F. (2013). The role of the academe in match fixing. In M.R. Haberfeld & D. Sheehan (Eds.), Match-fixing in international sports (pp. 303-329). Berlin: Springer International Publishing.

424 Newcomb, S. (1881). Note on the frequency of use of the different digits in natural numbers. American Journal of Mathematics, 4, 39-40.

425 Benford, F. (1938). The law of anomalous numbers. Proceedings of the American Philosophical Society, 78(4), 551-572.

426 Miller, S.J., Berger, A., & Hill, T. (2010). Theory and applications of Benford's law. New Jersey: Princeton University Press. Portney.

427 Hill, T. P. (1998). The first digit phenomenon. American Science, 86(4), 358-363.

428 Judge, G., & Schechter, L. (2009). Detecting problems in survey data using Benford's Law. Journal of Human Resources, 44(1), 1-24.

429 Varian, H.R. (1972). Benford's law. The American Statistician, 26(3), 65-66.

430 Diekmann, A., & Jann, B. (2010). Benford's law and fraud detection: facts and legends. German Economic Review, 11(3), 397-401.

431 Günnel, S., & Tödter, K. H. (2009). Does Benford's law hold in economic research and forecasting? Empirica, 36(3), 273-292.

432 Economist, The. (2017). Match-fixing goes digital. 21 September 2017. https://www.economist.com/news/international/21729428-esports-are-likely-see-much-more-corruption-coming-years-match-fixing-goes (Accessed 27 January 2018).

433 VanBoskirk, S. (2007). US Interactive Marketing Forecast, 2007 To 2012 for Interactive Marketing Professionals. Forrester Research.

ABOUT THE AUTHOR

ANDREW PEARSON was born in Pakistan, grew up in Singapore and was educated in England and America. With a degree in psychology from UCLA, Pearson has had a varied career in IT, software consulting, marketing, mobile technology, social media and entertainment.

In 2016, Pearson founded Intelligencia Limited. Pearson is currently the managing director of the company, which is a leading analytics, AI, BI, CX, digital marketing and social media provider based in Hong Kong and Macau. Pearson has overseen implementations of complex analytics and marketing projects for clients throughout the world, including The Venetian Macau, Galaxy Macau, Genting HK, The Logrand Group, Tatts Lottery, Tabcorp, Junglee Games, Resorts World Casino New York, TAL Apparel, and Macau Slot.

In 2010, Pearson wrote *The Mobile Revolution*, and, in 2013, Pearson was invited to write a chapter in *Global Mobile: Applications and Innovations for the Worldwide Mobile Ecosystem*, a book on mobile technology written by some of leading voices in the field. *The A.I. Sports Book* is the second in the *A.I.* series, a series that will soon tackle the social gaming, banking, retailing and ecommerce industries.

Pearson is also a noted columnist, writing on such topics as mobile, social, analytics, real-time stream processing, and cloud technology. Pearson has written for such publications as *ComputerWorld HK*, *The Mobile Marketer*, *The Journal of Mobile and Social Media Marketing*, where he is also a contributing editor. Pearson is the president of the *Advanced Analytics Association of Macau* and one of the founders of *Grow uP eSports*, a Macau association that promotes esports teams and events throughout the world.

An avid traveler, Pearson is a sought-after speaker on such disparate topics as AI, analytics, social media, gaming, customer experience, personalization, psychometrics, and marketing attribution. If he's not pounding the pavements of Hollywood, he's probably wandering the labyrinthine streets of Hong Kong's Lang Kwai Fong, or tearing up useless betting slips at Happy Valley (perhaps the most perfectly named racecourse in the world (for some)), or dining at a hawker center in Singapore, or navigating the wondrous madness of Manila and the beauty of the Philippines, or doubling down at the gaming tables in Macau. Basically, Pearson's trying to find the next great story that the world doesn't yet know that it desperately wants to see.

Social Media
LinkedIn: andrew-pearson-96513a3
Twitter: intelligenciaMD
Academia: PearsonAndrew
Blog: medium.com/@intelligentsiaf

ANDREW W. PEARSON

INDEX

CPSIA information can be obtained
at www.ICGtesting.com
Printed in the USA
LVHW111506220721
693425LV00004B/654

9 781688 116146